Modern Diplomacy

Modern Diplomacy

Second Edition
R.P. Barston

LONGMAN
London and New York

Addison Wesley Longman Limited
Edinburgh Gate,
Harlow, Essex CM20 2JE,
United Kingdom
and Associated Companies throughout the world

Published in the United States of America
by Addison Wesley Longman Inc., New York

First published 1988
Second edition 1997
Second impression 1998

ISBN 0 582-09953 6 (PPR)

British Library Cataloguing in Publication Data

A catalogue record for this book is
available from the British Library

Library of Congress Cataloging-in-Publication Data

Set by 8 in Times 10/11pt
Printed in Malaysia, PP

To my mother and father

CONTENTS

LIST OF FIGURES AND TABLES

PREFACE

The concern of this book is to analyse some of the main elements which make up contemporary diplomacy. Since the completion of the first edition, a number of important changes have occurred within the international system, which have affected players, procedures and the content of diplomacy. These and other developments have as far as possible been taken into account in revising this edition. In addition, new chapters have been included on multilateral diplomacy, together with case examples; mediation; and the process of normalisation. The opportunity to revise the book has also enabled further thought to be given to a number of concepts used within the book for example on the negotiating process, issue learning and conference typology, and develop others such as the process of normalisation. The book has been organised around four main parts, after the first chapter, which examines the changing nature of diplomacy since the early 1960s. These sections of the book deal with organisation, representation, diplomatic correspondence and assessments. The second section examines negotiation and diplomatic methods. This is followed by the third part which examines diplomacy through international financial relations; trade; environment; security; mediation and normalisation. The final section of the book is concerned with the use and development of international treaties and agreements.

Professor R.P. Barston
University of Cardiff
1996

ACKNOWLEDGEMENTS

In the preparation of this and earlier editions I have benefited from the comments of Professor Alan James of Keele. In addition, discussion with colleagues in the Department of International Relations at the London School of Economics, including Professors Michael Leifer, Fred Halliday, Christopher Hill, as well as Michael Yahuda, Michael Donelan, Paul Taylor and Nicholas Sims, helped greatly to clarify ideas. A research grant from the ESRC on law of the sea helped considerably to sustain work not only in that area but also, more generally, on developing ideas with regard to multilateral conference diplomacy. Specific debts are owed to Foreign Ministries and officials from a number of countries. Particular thanks are owed to the United Kingdom Foreign and Commonwealth Office; Department of State, Legal and Treaty and Ocean Affairs Divisions, Ambassador Richard Jackson, Dean of the Foreign Service Institute, and John Kneale (Canadian Foreign Service Institution). Dr Robert Smith (Department of State), David Anderson (Foreign and Commonwealth Office) and Maxwell Watson (IMF) provided invaluable help. The Institute of Public Administration (INTAN), Kuala Lumpur, Malaysia, provided a valuable setting for the exchange of ideas. Assistance of the Malaysian High Commission library staff is gratefully acknowledged. Susan Halls and Nigel Montieth (Librarians, Foreign and Commonwealth Office) has provided friendly help over a number of years. Long-standing thanks are due to I.G. John, Robert Purnell, John Garnett and Professor P.A. Reynolds. The department of international relations at LSE provided invaluable secretarial support, including that of Elizabeth Leslie and Judy Aitkens. Secretarial assistance at Cardiff was ably provided by Heather Sedgebeer and Melanie Bonnar, and library assistance by Dr Terry Wall and his staff. I should also wish to thank Professor John King at Cardiff for his continued support in many ways.

The author gratefully acknowledges HMSO for the use of a number of command papers and other correspondence, as well as the United States for use of quotations from the US Treaty Series and State Department Bulletin.

Finally a debt remains once more to my wife Pamela and sons Robert and Neill for this particular edition.

We are grateful to the following for permission to reproduce copyright material:

Office for Official Publications of the European Committee/The Controller of Her Majesty's Stationery Office for an extract from *CMND 9896 – EC 'MADEGASCAR ON FISHING OFF THE COAST OF MADEGASCAR'* 28.01.96, *'Official Journal of the European Communities'* (*OJ*) No 38 (1986) Cmnd 9896; The Controller of Her Majesty's Stationery Office for extracts from *CM 2769 TREATY ON PRINCIPLES . . . UK NI AND UKRAINE,* 10.02.93, *CM 2954 UK . . . KAZAKHSTAN AGREEMENT* 21.03.94, *CM 9247 UK . . . CHINA AGREEMENT, CM 2298 UK . . . SULTAN OF OMAN COMPOUND MUSCAT, CM 591 PROTOCOL ESTABLISHING THE FISHING RIGHTS OFF ANGOLA, CMD 8501 TEXT OF NOTE CORRESPONDENCE ABOUT THE FUTURE OF GERMANY* and *TEXT OF NOTE TO HM GOVT IN THE UK FROM USSR* 10.03.52, all Crown Copyright; Royal Institute for International Affairs for an extract from *NOTE TO INDIA FROM CHINA 30.12.60 from DOCUMENTS ON INTERNATIONAL AFFAIRS 1960* published by Oxford University Press for the Royal Institute of International Affairs, London (1964, p. 192).

LIST OF ABBREVIATIONS

ABM	anti-ballistic missile
ACP	African, Caribbean and Pacific countries
ADB	Asian Development Bank
ANZUS	Australia, New Zealand, United States (Pact)
ASEAN	Association of South-East Asian Nations
BIS	Bank for International Settlements
CAP	Common Agricultural Policy
CARICOM	Caribbean Community
CCD	Conference of the Committee on Disarmament
CFF	Compensatory financing facility (IMF)
CFR	*Code of Federal Regulations*
CMEA	Council for Mutual Economic Assistance
COCOM	Co-ordinating Committee (NATO)
COREPER	Committee of Permanent Representatives (European Community)
CPA	Caracas Programme of Action
CSCE	Conference on Security and Cooperation in Europe
DAC	Development Assistance Committee (OECD)
DTAs	double taxation agreements
EBRD	European Bank for Construction and Development
ECDC	economic cooperation among developing countries
ECOSOC	United Nations Economic and Social Council
EDC	European Defence Community
EDF	European Development Fund
EEC	European Economic Community (EC)
EEZ	Exclusive Economic Zone
EFF	extended fund facility (IMF)
EIB	European Investment Bank
ENDC	Eighteen Nation Disarmament Committee
ESA	European Space Agency
ESCAP	Economic and Social Commission for Asia and the Pacific (UN)
ETS	*European Treaty Series*
FAO	Food and Agriculture Organisation
FRG	Federal German Republic
G-5	Group of 5
G-10	Group of 10
G-24	Group of 24
G-77	Group of 77

GAB	General Arrangements to Borrow (IMF)
GATT	General Agreement on Tariffs and Trade
GCC	Gulf Cooperation Council
GSA	General Services Administration
GSTP	global system of trade preferences
HCP	*House of Commons Papers*
IBRD	International Bank for Reconstruction and Development (World Bank)
ICAO	International Civil Aviation Organisation
ICJ	International Court of Justice
IDA	International Development Association
ILM	*International Legal Materials*
IMF	International Monetary Fund
IMO	International Maritime Organisation
IPAs	investment protection agreements
IPC	Integrated Programme for Commodities
ITO	International Trade Organisation
JCC	Joint Coordinating Committee
JETRO	Japan External Trade Organisation
Libor	London interbank offered rate
LNTS	*League of Nations Treaty Series*
MFA	Multifibre Arrangement
MBFR	Mutual Balanced Force Reduction
MFN	most favoured nation
MITI	Ministry of International Trade and Industry (Japan)
MYRAs	multi-year re-scheduling agreements
NATO	North Atlantic Treaty Organisation
NGOs	non-governmental organisations
NIEO	New International Economic Order
NLF	National Liberation Front
NPT	Non Proliferation Treaty
OAU	Organisation of African Unity
OECD	Organisation for Economic Cooperation and Development
OMAs	orderly marketing arrangements
ONUC	Opération des Nations Unies (Congo)
OPEC	Organisation of Petroleum Exporting Countries
PLO	Palestine Liberation Organisation
SALT	Strategic Arms Limitation Treaty
SAMA	Saudi Arabian Monetary Agency
SCOR	*Security Council Official Records*
SDI	Strategic Defence Initiative
SDR	special drawing rights
SFF	supplementary financing facility (IMF)
TIAS	*Treaties and Other International Acts Series*
TRIMS	Trade Related Investment Measures
UN	United Nations
UNDP	United Nations Development Programme

UKTS	*United Kingdom Treaty Series*
UNCLOS	United Nations Conference on the Law of the Sea
UNCTAD	United Nations Conference on Trade and Development
UNEF	United Nations Emergency Force
UNEP	United Nations Environment Programme
UNESCO	United Nations Educational, Scientific and Cultural Organisation
UNFICYP	United Nations Force in Cyprus
UNIDO	United Nations Industrial Development Organisation
UNIFIL	United Nations Interim Force in Lebanon
UNOGIL	United Nations Observation Group in Lebanon
UNTS	*UN Treaty Series*
UST	*United States Treaties and Other International Agreements*
VERs	voluntary export restraints
WIPO	World Intellectual Property Organisation
WTO	World Trade Organisation
ZOPFAN	zone of peace, freedom and neutrality

CHAPTER 1

The changing nature of diplomacy

Diplomacy is concerned with the management of relations between states and between states and other actors. From a state perspective diplomacy is concerned with advising, shaping and implementing foreign policy. As such it is the means by which states through their formal and other representatives, as well as other actors, articulate, co-ordinate and secure particular or wider interests, using correspondence, private talks, exchanges of view, lobbying, visits, threats and other related activities.

Diplomacy is often thought of as being concerned with peaceful activity, although it may occur for example within war or armed conflict or be used in the orchestration of particular acts of violence, such as seeking overflight clearance for an air strike. The blurring of the line, in fact, between diplomatic activity and violence is one of the developments of note distinguishing modern diplomacy. The point can be made more generally too, in terms of the widening content of diplomacy. At one level the changes in the substantive form of diplomacy are reflected in terms such as 'dollar diplomacy', 'oil diplomacy', 'resource diplomacy', 'atomic diplomacy' and 'global governance' diplomacy. Certainly what constitutes diplomacy today goes beyond the sometimes rather narrow politico-strategic conception given to the term. Nor is it appropriate to view diplomacy in a restrictive or formal sense as being the preserve of foreign ministries and diplomatic service personnel. Rather, diplomacy is undertaken by officials from a wide range of 'domestic' ministries or agencies with their foreign counterparts, reflecting its technical content; between officials from different international organisations such as the International Monetary Fund (IMF) and the United Nations (UN) Secretariat, or involve foreign corporations and a host government transnationally; and with or through NGOs and 'private' individuals.

In this chapter we are concerned with discussing some of the main changes which have taken place in diplomacy since the 1960s – the starting-point for the overall study. Before looking at the changes, some discussion of the task of diplomacy is necessary.

Tasks of diplomacy

The work of diplomacy can be broken down into six broad areas, within which there are a number of subdivisions. The first and most important of these is representation. This consists of formal representation, including presentation of credentials, protocol and participation in the diplomatic circuit of the national capital or institution. Arguably the most important aspect is substantive representation. This includes the explanation and defence of national policy through embassies and other outlets; negotiations and interpreting the foreign and domestic policies of the receiving government. Second, and related to this, is the function of acting as a listening post. Next to substantive representation, an embassy, if it is functioning correctly, should identify key issues and domestic or external patterns which are emerging, together with their implications, in order to advise or warn the sending government. As Humphrey Trevelyan notes, '... apart from negotiating, the ambassador's basic task is to report on the political, economic and social conditions in the country in which he is living, on the policy of its government and on his conversations with political leaders, officials and anyone else who has illuminated the local scene for him'.[1] Above all, timely warning of adverse developments is one of the major functions of an embassy, requiring considerable expertise, judgement and political courage. A third function of diplomacy is laying the groundwork or preparing the basis for a policy or new initiatives. Fourth, in the event of actual or potential bilateral or wider conflict, diplomacy is concerned with reducing friction or oiling the wheels of bilateral or multilateral relations. Fifth, an extension of this, is contributing to order and orderly change. As Adam Watson suggests: 'the central task of diplomacy is not just the management of order, but the management of change, and the maintenance by continued persuasion of order in the midst of change'.[2] The converse of this can also of course be put in that diplomacy may be a vehicle for the continuation of a dispute or conflict. In other words differing state and non-state interests and the absence of generally accepted norms concerning local, regional or international order produce quite substantial differences between parties, in which diplomacy through direct initiatives, informal, secret contacts or third parties simply cannot provide bridging solutions. Finally, at a more general level, an important function of diplomacy is the creation, drafting and amendment of a wide body of international rules of a normative and regulatory kind that provide structure in the international system.

Development of diplomacy

In discussing the development of diplomacy an overview of the period will help initially to give some perspective in which to consider certain of the major changes which have taken place. Harold Nicolson's analysis, written in 1961 in *Foreign Affairs* on the theme 'Diplomacy then and now',[3] is coloured especially by the impact of the Cold War, the intrusion of ideological conflict into diplomacy and its effect on explanation, and the transformation from the small international élite in old-style diplomacy to a new or 'democratic' conception of international relations requiring public explanation and 'open' diplomacy, despite its growing complexity.[4] A further striking change for Nicolson was in values, especially in the loss of relations based on the 'creation of confidence, [and] the acquisition of credit'.[5] Writing shortly after Nicolson, Livingston Merchant noted the decline in the decision-making power of the ambassador but the widening of his area of competence through economic and commercial diplomacy; the greater use of personal diplomacy and the burden created by multilateral diplomacy, with its accompanying growth in the use of specialists.[6] In reviewing the period up to the late 1970s, Plishke[7] endorsed many of these points, but noted as far as the diplomatic environment was concerned the proliferation of the international community, including the trend towards fragmentation and smallness,[8] and the shift in the locus of decision-making power to national capitals.[9] Writing at the same time, Pranger additionally drew attention to methods, commenting on the growing volume of visits and increases in the number of treaties.[10] Adam Watson in reviewing diplomacy and the nature of diplomatic dialogue noted the wide range of ministries involved in diplomacy; the corresponding decline in the influence of the foreign minister; the increase in the direct involvement of heads of government in the details of foreign policy and diplomacy; and the growth in importance of the news media.[11]

Diplomatic setting

The continued expansion of the international community after 1945 has been one of the major factors shaping a number of features of modern diplomacy. The diplomatic community of some forty-odd states which fashioned the new post-war international institutions (UN, International Monetary Fund/IBRD and the General Agreement on Tariffs and Trade) had tripled less than a quarter of a century later.[12] A third phase of expansion occurred after 1989 with the break-up of the former Soviet Union and Yugoslavia.[13] The expansion in membership has affected diplomatic styles and altered the balance of voting power within the UN General Assembly. The growth in the number of states, and hence interests and perspectives, has continuously fashioned the agenda of issues addressed by the Assembly, and led to the emergence of UN conference management styles; lobbying and corridor diplomacy. Other features such as the institutionalisation within the UN of the G-77, have also had a significant influence on the development of the way in which diplomacy is conducted within the UN.[14]

Another important effect of expanded membership has been on the entry into force of conventions. For example, the entry into force of the 1982 law of the sea convention was triggered by smaller members of the UN, such as Honduras, St Vincent, and, eventually Guyana in November 1993,[15] without ratification or accession at that time by the major powers. Although the possibility of conventions entering into force without the participation of major players remains, in some instances e.g. The Montreal Protocol on Ozone Depleting Substances,[16] thresholds or specific barriers to entry into force have been created in some agreements.

A second structural feature of the post-1945 diplomatic setting is the development of the bloc groupings from 1947 to 1990. These included the East–West diplomatic system; the establishment of an initially charismatic-led non-aligned movement after the Bandung conference; and the extension of Third World diplomatic agenda-setting and interactions after 1964 with UNCTAD, and NIEO at the 1973 Algiers conference. In addition, other specialist developing country diplomatic groupings have been set up, loosely linked to the G-77, for example, within the IMF (G-24),[17] reflecting the financial and economic pressure which developing countries exerted in order to internationalise a range of development-related objectives. These aims too were channelled unsuccessfully through the large-scale periodic North–South conferences.[18]

Apart from the above global structures, the continued development of regional multilateral diplomacy further distinguishes diplomacy from the 1960s onwards. Most regional groupings are economically based. An exception in the security field was the establishment of the Gulf Co-operation Council (GCC). As an illustration of economically based institutions, the Association of South-East Asian Nations (ASEAN) is an interesting example of a regional institution which has remained essentially concerned in its diplomacy with economic issues rather than expand into defence during the Cold War period. ASEAN's links with its dialogue partners (e.g. Australia, New Zealand, United Kingdom, EU) too is an interesting illustration of the phenomenon of functional *associative* diplomacy. The end of the Cold War by 1990–91 created opportunities for the extension of ASEAN's regional diplomacy *vis-à-vis* other South-East Asian states.

Economic regionalism has become a marked feature of the international system since 1990. Within Europe, enlargement brought in Austria, Finland, Sweden and closer ties to Baltic, Eastern European and Mediterranean states. The EU's relations with Eastern Europe and the Russian Federation were important factors in the decision to extend political membership to the Russian Federation to the G-7 and hence transform the functioning of the Western G-7 economic summits, set up originally in 1975. Other examples of the growth of economic regionalism post Cold War include the North American Free Trade Agreement (NAFTA) and Asia-Pacific Economic Council (APEC).

Players in diplomacy

In the first instance a marked feature of modern diplomacy is the enhanced role of *personal* diplomacy by the head of state or government.

Frequently such initiatives are at the expense of the local ambassador, who might have only a limited *formal* involvement for example in a special summit. However, it can be argued that whilst the importance of political reporting, part of traditional diplomacy, has been eroded by developments in communications, the decline of the role of ambassador is overstated. The role remains important in terms of explanation of policy at crucial moments; political assessments; involvement in economic and trade work; and participation from time to time in international conferences.

Second, the growth of post-war multilateral diplomacy has seen periodic involvement of a wider range of ministries with some involvement in external relations, such as industry, aviation, environment, shipping, customs, health, education and sport. The task for the foreign ministry is to establish in effect a lead position or otherwise co-ordinate both the formulation *and* implementation of international agreements. This is particularly important in technical agreements, where choice of presentation, drafting of instructions and follow-up post-conference are especially important.

Third, non-state actors have proliferated in number and type, ranging from traditional economic interest groups through to resource, environmental, humanitarian, criminal and global governance interests. In some instances NGOs are closely linked to official administrations, while others are transnationally linked. Above all, the institutionalisation of NGOs in the diplomatic process, especially in multilateral conferences, has become an important distinguishing feature of recent diplomacy.

Content of diplomacy

One of the most striking aspects of post-war diplomacy is the rapid growth in volume of diplomatic activity since the end of the 1960s. To a large extent this has come about because of the expansion of multilateral and regional diplomacy, much of it economic or resource related. At a national level, the changes in volume can be seen, for example, in United States diplomatic practice, which annually now concludes over 160 treaties, and 3,500 executive agreements. The broadening of the international agenda especially since the 1970s into issues concerning trade, technology transfer, aviation, human rights, transnational environmental and sustainable development questions has continued with the increasing addition of novel or revived threats. Examples of the latter include global sea-level rise; stratospheric ozone depletion; environmental sabotage; money laundering; refugee dumping;transnational stock exchange fraud and 'black market' nuclear materials trade. Underlying the expanded diplomatic agenda are a range of issues concerning the relationship between domestic and external policy, sovereignty and the adequacy of agreements and arrangements at a bilateral, regional, international or global level.

Diplomatic methods

Diplomatic methods have undergone more profound changes in the past decade than in any other period of diplomatic relations since 1945. The decline of East–West type summit diplomacy during the 1990s, though not absolute since the format could be revived, was a direct function of the internal weakness of the Russian Federation. Second, the loss of significance of global North–South negotiating structures, particularly the demise of UNCTAD, has shifted the arena of North–South conflict into the WTO. In terms of international security, diplomatic methods have been above all distinguished by multiple and competing security agencies, including OSCE, UN, NATO, WEU and the EU. Fourth, international agreements have become increasingly informal, accompanied correspondingly by unilateral actions. Finally, an important new strand in modern diplomacy is so-called 'governance' diplomacy, involving four elements. These include *ad hoc* global conferences (e.g. Habitat II); Rio (Agenda 21) follow-up environment conferences; UN 'domestic' security operations, and global co-ordinating institutions such as the Commission on Sustainable Development. The development of 'governance' diplomacy has been accompanied by increasing conflict between international institutions over responsibility and budgetary control of this form of diplomacy.

Diplomatic process

The use of consensus decision-making in international conferences rather than unanimity or majority voting is a marked feature of multilateral conference diplomacy. The consensus rule has significantly influenced both the processes and type of outcomes of multilateral negotiations. Consensus decision-making tends to produce frenetic, final phase negotiations; framework type agreements and excessively qualified obligations.

Changes in the processes of multilateral conferences since 1990 have been influenced by several other factors. The break-up of the Soviet Union has meant the end of special voting and other provision for the socialist 'bloc' in multilateral conferences, and led to new disputes over 'categories of countries'. The G-77 have opposed any additional provision for so-called ex-socialist 'countries in transition', arguing G-77 members are also developing economies in transition. A second notable factor is the difficulty the G-77 has experienced in developing new economic ideologies in a highly fractionalised and unstable international system, which has lost one of its key defining structural features – the East–West division. That division acted as a kind of reference point for not only the Non-Aligned but also the G-77 itself. Third, multilateral conferences have been distinguished by fewer group-sponsored resolutions, and, changes in implementation procedures. The trend of informality in conferences is directly linked to the decline of blocs or large groupings; growing 'individuality' of states, especially in technical negotiations, and, *ad hoc* or shifting coalitions of interests. A noted exception to the decline of blocs is the EU. One of the important effects of EU enlargement is to largely take out of play Sweden, Austria and Finland, who as non-EU members performed active roles in multilateral conferences, as conference officers, chairing working groups, drafting and broker roles.

A further exception is the continued use within the UN system of politico-geographical groupings for the election of conference officers and heads of organisations. The election of particularly the latter has become a source of enhanced dispute (e.g. WTO, WHO) as states seek access and control of strategic multilateral institutions.

International agreements have been influenced by two other important factors – the decline in the role of the International Law Commission in preparing treaties and the growing use at a global level of 'soft' law instruments such as Action Plans and framework agreements, influenced by the international and regional practice of UN specialised agencies such as UNEP, UNCTAD and FAO.

Implications of the changes in diplomacy

The expansion of the international community – by the early 1960s there were still fewer than 100 independent states, although this rose from 159 by 1985 to 190 by 1996 – has affected style, procedures and substance. It has necessarily brought with it divergent regimes and ideologies. Rather than diminishing, the ideological element has, if anything, increased. It necessarily raises the question, can diplomacy in a broad sense 'cope'? Apart from the East–West dimension, numerous national as well as wider ideologies have been introduced, such as those of an economic kind associated with North–South relations, which demand economic redistribution and the transfer of technology. Although these demands were partly diverted in the 1980s into the promotion of South–South relations between developing countries, they nevertheless remained as a marked feature of the diplomatic setting of economic confrontation. The great expansion of multilateral diplomacy, a lot of it economically based, forms one of the themes examined in this book (see Chs 7 and 8). Apart from this, the growth of state and other actors in the international community is reflected in the policies of sub-national actors which are projected, often violently, on to the international arena.

The procedures of diplomacy have undergone several important changes, particularly in terms of the effects of the demise or decline of traditional blocs; the emergence of shifting or temporary conditions in multilateral diplomacy and the extensive use of informal, interim and short-term arrangements. Finally the agenda of diplomacy in terms of the volume of bilateral and multilateral meetings, and the range of issue areas continue to undergo considerable expansion during a period of

8 *Modern diplomacy*

uncertainty over the role and functions of established international institutions, alliances and other arrangements.

References and notes

1. See Humphrey Trevelyan, *Diplomatic Channels* (Macmillan, London, 1973) p. 85.
2. Adam Watson, *Diplomacy: The Dialogue Between States* (Methuen, London, 1984) p. 223.
3. Reprinted with revisions in Harold Nicolson, *Diplomacy*, 3rd edn (Oxford University Press, London, 1963) pp. 244–62.
4. Ibid., p. 245.
5. Ibid., pp. 245–6.
6. Livingston Merchant, 'New Techniques in Diplomacy', in E.A.J. Johnson (ed.), *The Dimensions of Diplomacy* (John Hopkins Press, Baltimore, 1964) pp. 117–35.
7. Elmer Plishke (ed.), *Modern Diplomacy: The Art and the Artisans* (American Enterprise Institute, Washington, DC, 1979).
8. Ibid., pp. 92–8.
9. Ibid., p. 58.
10. Robert J. Pranger, 'Contemporary Diplomacy at Work', in Plishke, op. cit., p. 76. Pranger notes that in 1977 the United States signed approximately 20 new treaties and nearly 500 new agreements with other states and international organisations.
11. Watson, op. cit., p. 126.
12. Fiji became the 127th member of the United Nations in 1970.
13. During 1992 13 states were admitted to the UN including 9 former Soviet Republics, 3 former Yugoslav Republics and San Marino. These were Armenia, Kirghizia, Tajikistan, Uzbekistan, Moldova, Turkmenistan, Azerbaijan and Georgia. See GA Resolutions 46/241 31 July 1992; and Croatia, Slovenia, Bosnia and Herzegovina, GA Resolutions 46/238 22 May 1992; 46/236, and 46/237 22 May 1992.
14. In the first five years of its existence the Security Council passed some 89 resolutions. By 1990 the number had risen to 683, and the Council held over 2,900 meetings. Index to Resolutions of the Security Council 1946–91, ST/LIB/SER. H/5, United Nations, New York, 1992.
15. United Nations Convention on the Law of the Sea (1982). Under the terms of Article 308(1) the Convention entered into force one year after the 60th ratification. A number of smaller states including Malta, Honduras, St Vincent and the Grenadines, Barbados and Guyana (60th) brought the convention into force in November 1994. See *Ocean Policy News*, Vol. x, No. 7, November 1994.
16. Montreal Protocol on Substances that Deplete the Ozone Layer, 26 ILM, 1541, 1550 (1987).
17. See *Modern Diplomacy* (Longman, London, 1991) pp. 137–8, 169.
18. Bahgat Korany 'North-South Conflict', in R.P. Barston, *International Politics since 1945* (Eduard Elgar, Aldershot, 1991) pp. 92–112.

CHAPTER 2

Foreign policy organisation

Central organisation of foreign policy

In general the differences which exist in the central arrangements for conducting foreign policy in various states have been influenced by the expansion in the content of foreign policy, the loosening of central control and the increasingly technical nature of much of external policy. In advanced industrial states especially, the development of an increasingly complex foreign policy agenda including such varied issues as energy, resources, telecommunications, trans-frontier land pollution, as well as the more conventional or traditional political issues, has had several implications for central foreign policy organisation.

The extension of the agenda finds its expression in the international role of ministries which have traditionally been considered as essentially 'domestic'. In other words external policy is no longer necessarily the preserve of the ministry of foreign affairs. The increasing complexity of foreign policy too has also been accompanied, especially in larger states, not only by a proliferation of ministries but also a tendency for fragmentation of responsibility. Ministries or agencies acquire foreign policy interests, stakes and perspectives, which are promoted and defended. Departments are not necessarily monolithic, although patterns of thinking can nevertheless be found within various government departments and their subdivisions as well as alliances between departments. During, for example, the later part of the Kennedy administration, elements of the US Defense Department, armed forces and the European Bureau of the Department of State were joined in opposition to an overemphasis on African regional concerns. These groups stressed the importance of maintaining close ties with America's North Atlantic Treaty Organisation (NATO) allies, such as Portugal even if this meant riding roughshod over Black African interests.[1]

The tendency for fragmentation or independent action, especially in advanced industrial states, necessarily places constraints on the central political control of foreign policy. Lack of co-ordination was well illustrated by the continuation of routine submarine operations by the former Soviet Union off the Swedish coast, highlighted by the grounding of a Soviet Whiskey-class submarine in November 1981, at a time when another strand of Soviet external policy involved diplomatic moves to promote a regional nuclear-free zone.[2] Independence of ministries is a particular feature of the German foreign policy process and is well illustrated by the differing policies of the Defence Ministry and Foreign Ministry over the sale of military equipment to Turkey. Continued military sales led the then German Foreign Minister, Herr Genscher to resign eventually in 1993, on the grounds of the inappropriateness of the sales in view of Turkey's poor human rights record. It is not always clear what the foreign policy of a state actually in fact is. Objectives may in fact be the subject of drawn-out bureaucratic dispute, aggravated by divisions within an executive,[3] while novel or unexpected international events may cause fragmented or poorly co-ordinated ministerial responses.

For smaller advanced industrial states, especially in Western Europe, a distinctive feature of the political system is the impact of the open, pluralistic process on the central direction of foreign policy. The problems caused by the expansion in the agenda of foreign policy tend however to be less acute because of higher degrees of selection of issues and, at an organisational level, greater decentralisation along with wider delegation to specialist ministries as in the Netherlands, Sweden and Denmark.

Developing country political systems

Although Third World systems are often thought of in single leader terms, in practice a variety of systems of central foreign policy organisation can be distinguished, shaped by complex domestic and socio-economic considerations.[4] Korany and Dessouki, for example, in examining the foreign policies of selected Arab states use a presidential, collegiate and oligarchical typology.[5] Korany and Dessouki's study, furthermore, underlines the point that for newer states the type of central organisation should not be considered as being static. Countries may in fact move from one type of central organisation to another, from, for example, bureaucratic to presidential, e.g. Algeria post-Boumedienne, or to a more bureaucratic system as with Egypt post-Sadat.

From the prevalence of centralised head of state systems (i.e. strong central executive, relatively weak bureaucracy and narrow basis of policy formulation) in developing countries a number of effects on foreign policy can be seen. Perhaps the most important impact is on the style of conducting policy, with a preference for relying on direct negotiation by the head of state and the use of personal diplomacy.[6] Presidential emissaries (not necessarily career diplomats) are also frequently used on assignments. In those centralised head of state type systems in developing countries which have frequent political instability, the bureaucracy, especially the foreign ministry, tends to be weakened even further by being cut off from interactive decision-making.[7]

Efforts to improve the co-ordination and direction of foreign policy in the Third World and other states have in the main involved building up agencies under the direct control of or attached institutionally to the office of the head of government or state. Of the developed countries, this type of system has been particularly used by Japan. Not dissimilar systems have been adopted by a number of newly industrialised countries, e.g. Malaysia, whose foreign policy and external diplomacy are heavily economically orientated. In South Korea, there is considerable departmental autonomy for rapid decision-making, although a clear feature of the organisational style is the central co-ordinating role performed by the Economic Planning Board, generally headed by the Deputy Prime Minister. In these cases, the foreign ministries are generally relatively weak.

While the agency system described above provides some measure of greater central political control, it almost inevitably leads to or enhances personalisation and the tendency to concentrate foreign policy decision-making and diplomacy at the political centre. This feature is accentuated by the fact that if at all possible foreign companies and organisations prefer to deal directly with the head of state or government of smaller powers, for organisational and other reasons. The effect often is to slow decision-making and create decision bottlenecks, for example over the participants in major projects or the terms of loan agreements.

The foreign ministry

Foreign ministries as part of the overall machinery for conducting external policy, along with diplomatic posts overseas, differ in structure and importance. In looking at these differences, three areas are of interest. These are the internal organisational structure, the relations between foreign ministries and other ministries and, for newer states, the appropriate organisational structure for the formulation and implementation of development strategies.

At first sight, foreign ministries tend to have certain common organisational characteristics in so far as they generally contain geographic, protocol, legal and administrative divisions. Apart from the question of size, which tends to have a telescopic effect, with divisions or departments covering greater geographic areas the smaller the actor, differences in organisational structure occur partly because of particular foreign policy interests, e.g. the Cyprus Foreign Ministry devotes a separate department to the Cyprus problem. Functional rather than geographic departments may be set up within foreign ministries for several reasons including: the importance attached to a particular international grouping, for example the Organisation of the Islamic Conference (IOC) bringing together Islamic states; the importance of bilateral trade relations, e.g. Finnish–Russian Federation trade (see Fig. 2.1); special emphasis placed on cultural diplomacy (e.g. in Austria, Canada, France, Mexico); or as a response to new policy issues, such as international energy questions

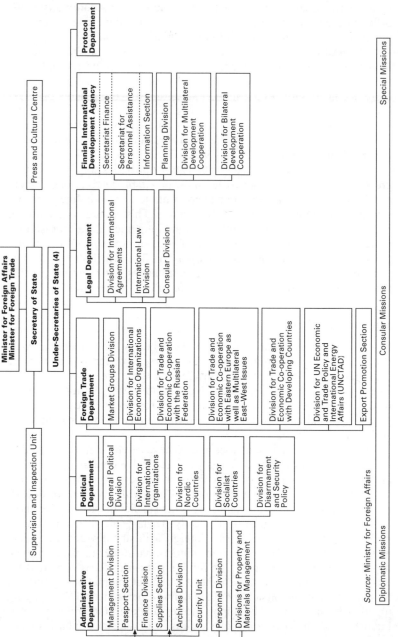

Figure 2.1   Ministry for Foreign Affairs: Finland

Source: Ministry for Foreign Affairs

which span several departments. Among the functional departments, for example in the United States Department of State, are those of energy, human rights, international narcotics matters, economic and business affairs, oceans and international environmental and scientific affairs (see Fig. 2.2). Such departments enable a foreign ministry to monitor and follow the work of other agencies and if necessary take the lead.[8] The main potential benefits are the possibility of greater co-ordination and a broader perspective. The staffing of the more specialist functional departments, e.g. civil aviation, however, generally poses difficulties in view of the traditional training and preferences of diplomatic service personnel. To some extent the problem has been lessened by the secondment of officials from the relevant 'domestic' ministry to functional departments in the foreign ministry.

Another noticeable difficulty encountered by the foreign ministries in newer as well as some established states, is the handling of the international economic aspects of foreign policy. As international economic issues moved up the international agenda, many foreign ministries simply found themselves ill-equipped for managing this aspect of international relations in view of their traditional political emphasis or lack of resources. An Economic Division of the Indian Ministry of External Affairs was set up in 1947, but three years later the post was left unfilled as part of an economy drive. The division went out of existence for over a decade until it was revived in 1961 as the Economic and Co-ordination Division.[9] In contrast, Japan has laid particular emphasis (see Fig. 2.5) on the regional and economic related divisions of its foreign ministry. Similar strong regional divisions dealing with Asia, America and Europe are a noticeable feature of the foreign ministry of, for example, Korea (see Fig. 2.3).

In general, pay and conditions of service have been important constraints on recruitment into the economic divisions of foreign ministries. The same, too, in many respects could be said about the overall recruitment problems of the foreign ministries of new states as well as some established West European States.[10] In order to ensure the paramountcy of the foreign ministry in international financial diplomacy, some countries which play active international financial and commodity roles, such as France, Brazil[11] and Mexico have developed cadres in the foreign ministry through training, secondment and other measures. By the late 1980s most states had established some form of economic division within their foreign ministries.[12]

A number of new states, especially former members of the Soviet Union, have addressed recruitment issues by putting the balance of effort not so much in the central machinery of the foreign ministry, but in an as wide 'on the ground' presence as possible. For example, the Lithuanian foreign ministry is staffed by some 170 personnel, while 23 embassies are maintained, plus permanent Missions to the UN, EU, UN (Geneva) Council of Europe and UNESCO, and six Consulates General (see Fig. 2.4).[13]

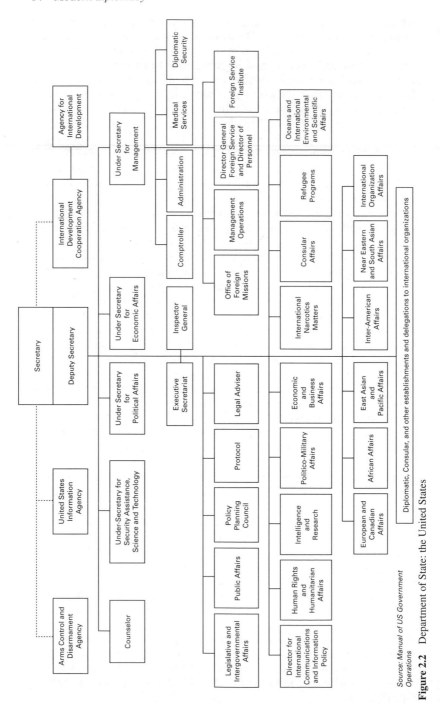

Source: Manual of US Government Operations

Figure 2.2   Department of State: the United States

Trade

The arrangements for managing trade at a central and representational level have often fitted uneasily into the running of other parts of foreign policy. The uneasy relationship partly derives from problems such as duplication and poor liaison, stemming from dual trade and diplomatic representation overseas and from rivalry about who should be responsible for directing and co-ordinating overseas trade policy. The primacy of the trade or commerce ministry is justified in terms of expertise, continuity and administrative links with export-financing agencies. In contrast, the arguments in favour of overall responsibility resting with the foreign ministry rely on the capacity of the foreign ministry to provide an overview, co-ordinate initiatives and its traditional skills of political analysis and persuasion. In practice, while most states retain separate foreign and trade ministries, arrangements for overseas representation vary. Some states have, however, attempted to unify trade promotion in the foreign ministry. In the case of Canada, the External Affairs Ministry was reorganised in 1982, and the department became directly responsible for the promotion of Canadian trade overseas, as the primary federal government contact with foreign governments and international organisations which influence trade.[14] There is also some indication that those states which have previously relied largely on chambers of commerce or other bodies for trade promotion have sought greater involvement by the foreign ministry, in view of the enhanced direct role of governments in trade promotion.[15]

Development

Development issues are generally at the forefront of the foreign policies of many newer states. Diplomacy is likely to be directed to securing international finance, problems arising from the scheduling of loans, restrictions on key exports, the promotion of regional co-operation and relations with major foreign corporations. While the conduct of foreign policy is often thought of as involving external action, this may well be an inappropriate model for a number of states.[16] Rather, an important part of a country's foreign relations in the main may be conducted *domestically* with a foreign oil corporation, bank or UN local or regional representatives.[17] The economic aspects of development necessarily involve several ministries in this form of internal diplomacy as well as external action. Establishing the boundaries of responsibility and more co-ordinated rather than *ad hoc* initiatives do present newer states with difficulties due to manpower constraints and the volume of business.[18] In an attempt to overcome some of these difficulties Zimbabwe, in an unusual experiment, merged the Ministry of Finance with the Economic Planning and Development Ministry in 1982.[19] In donor states the difficulty is one of the proliferation of ministries and agencies with some interest or stake in aid, the more especially as aid

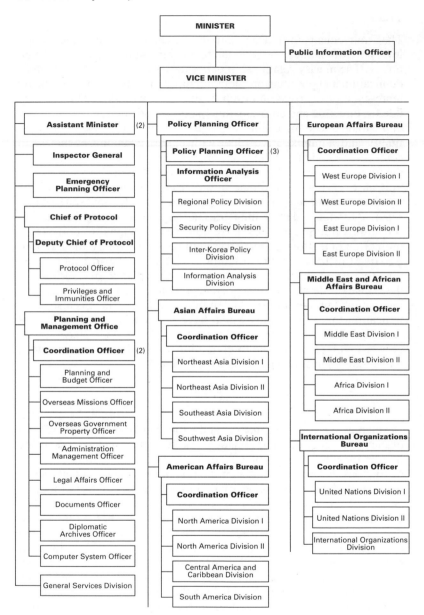

Figure 2.3   Ministry of Foreign Affairs: Republic of Korea

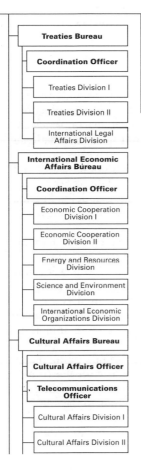

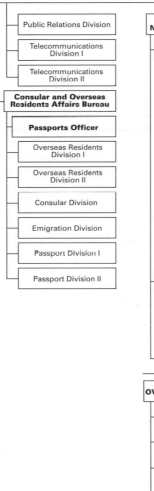

Treaties Bureau

Coordination Officer

Treaties Division I

Treaties Division II

International Legal Affairs Division

International Economic Affairs Bureau

Coordination Officer

Economic Cooperation Division I

Economic Cooperation Division II

Energy and Resources Division

Science and Environment Division

International Economic Organizations Division

Cultural Affairs Bureau

Cultural Affairs Officer

Telecommunications Officer

Cultural Affairs Division I

Cultural Affairs Division II

Public Relations Division

Telecommunications Division I

Telecommunications Division II

Consular and Overseas Residents Affairs Bureau

Passports Officer

Overseas Residents Division I

Overseas Residents Division II

Consular Division

Emigration Division

Passport Division I

Passport Division II

Foreign Affairs and National Security Institute

Research Office

Planning and Research Division

Library Division

National Security and Unification Studies Department

China Studies Department

Russian Federation

Asia and Pacific Studies Department

Western Europe, Africa and Middle East Studies Department

International Economy Studies Department

Education and Training Office

Education and Training Division

Foreign Language Training Division

General Affairs Division

OVERSEAS MISSIONS : 142

Embassy : 101

Permanent Mission : 5

Consulate-General : 35

Consulate : 1

has become blurred with trade and finance.[20] The other common problem for newer states is the composition of delegations to international conferences. In the context of development diplomacy, ministry of finance, trade or other appropriate officials cannot always be spared. As a result the separation of representation from policy-making tends to have the effect of emphasising the rhetorical aspects of policy, and producing brittle international agreements or arrangements which are subject to frequent reinterpretation.[21]

Representation

In general, states establish and maintain overseas representation for four main reasons. Representation is part of the process of either achieving statehood and identity in international relations, or, for established states, essential to being considered a power in the international system. Second, embassies are an important but by no means exclusive means of communication and source of contact with other states and entities, enabling a state to participate in international discourse. Third, embassies are the agencies for promoting, explaining or defending the interests and policies of a country. Fourth, embassies are a means of acquiring continuous information.

Most states have a core group of countries within their overall diplomatic representation. Those states within that group will be included for historical, alliance, ideological and economic reasons. For newer states the grouping generally will include the former colonial power, and staff would be assigned as a matter of priority to the United Nations, a regional organisation, European capitals, selected neighbouring states and representation set up in the capital of one or more important regional powers. For most states the membership of the core group is likely to remain relatively stable unless the state is undergoing major reorientation of its foreign policy, or is in dispute with the former colonial power. Adjustments in the ranking of countries in the core group, nevertheless, take place through modifications to the staffing, budgetary allocation and tasks of posts, in the light of such factors as changes in the volume of political work, trade opportunities, defence relations and tourism.

Beyond the core group the spread of representation may be influenced by such principles as balance, reciprocity and universality, and, above all, the availability of finance. The principle of universality is generally of importance only for primary powers and neutral states. Neutral states, because of their perceived status, have seen it important to have as wide a representation as is practicable. High international representation is common to all vulnerable states. Austria is represented, for example, in 170 countries through 77 embassies. The idea of balance has been considered important, especially by non-aligned countries to avoid the distribution of embassies becoming excessively weighted in favour of one bloc or region. Pressures to reciprocate representation necessarily reduce freedom of action. States, nevertheless, often do not comply with the principle on political and above all economic grounds.

Apart from the general principles noted above, several other factors can come into play. The opening of further embassies may be part of a policy of prestige. In this sense, diplomatic real estate is seen as part of the accoutrements of power. Conflict between two or more states may lead to the extension of representation. For example, following the outbreak of the Iran–Iraq war both countries competitively extended their representation as part of the battle for political and diplomatic support. The effect of the Iran–Iraq war on petroleum revenues has influenced the enhanced role of the respective embassies of both countries in facilitating intergovernmental oil sales agreements and other barter trade agreements.[22] Economic factors are among the more important leading to increases or reductions in representation. Diplomatic relations may be opened up with another state because it has become important in trade, investment or financial terms. The opening of diplomatic relations between Malaysia and Kuwait, for example, reflected, apart from religious factors, the growing oil relationship between the two countries as well as the Malaysian aim of attracting inward Arab financial investment.[23] Other reasons such as the need for economic intelligence may sometimes influence the decision to establish an embassy. For example, Brazil maintains a significant representation in Kenya, an important coffee producer.[24]

Embassies are not necessarily the sole means of handling the economic aspects of diplomacy. Apart from a separate trade commissioner service used by some states, consular arrangements are used to varying degrees by most states. For example, the Netherlands provides a striking illustration of a small but active economic power, with very high consular coverage, reflecting the widespread range of commercial, technical assistance and maritime operations of its companies and nationals.[25]

Much depends both on the scale of resources and perception of interests in international relations. These might be relatively limited or localised. Jamaica maintains, for example, 11 embassies and high commissions, 4 missions to international organisations and 6 consulates general. These are supported by some 19 honorary consulates in Europe, Latin America and the United States.[26] Jamaica has no significant diplomatic presence in the Far East, Southeast Asia, much of Africa or the Middle East. The main focus of representation is US, UK, EU and UN. In contrast, Zimbabwe, in line with its active foreign policy and geostrategic location, has rapidly expanded its foreign ministry and diplomatic service which at independence was limited to one official mission in Pretoria. By 1985 25 embassies or high commissions, 2 consulates and 1 trade mission had been established, with a total staff of 700, of which 200 are in the Foreign Ministry. This subsequently remained largely unchanged, however, with additions limited (e.g. Kuwait and Malaysia).[27]

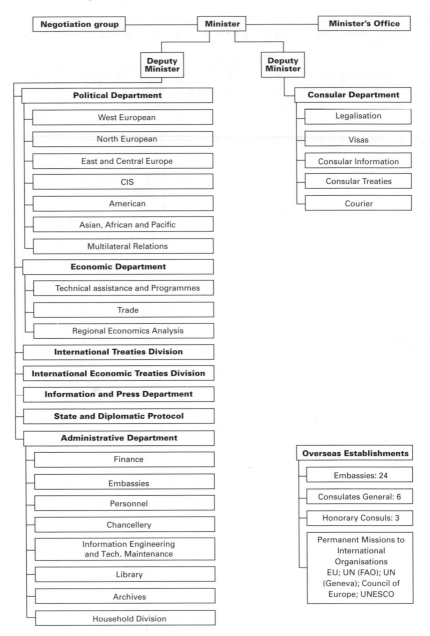

Figure 2.4   Organisational Structure Ministry of Foreign Affairs of Republic of Lithuania

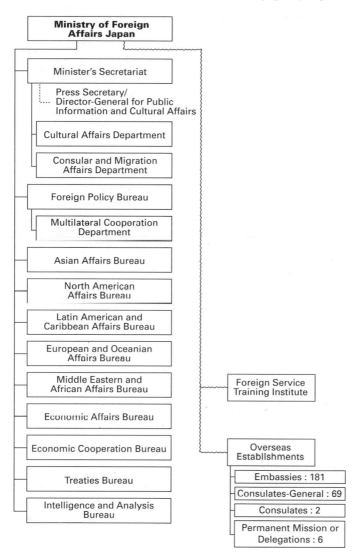

Figure 2.5 Ministry of Foreign Affairs: Japan

Other forms of representation

The growing international involvement of internal ministries has resulted in the proliferation of representative offices overseas. These include development corporations, investment agencies, trade and tourist offices and student liaison bureaux. To these must be added state and para-statal agencies such as banks, airlines and large corporations. In modern diplomacy, the blue neon sign of Toshiba has come to symbolise one aspect of the changing form of representation; the regional office of a major corporation is likely to be as important as or sometimes more important than its diplomatic counterpart. The growth of representative offices overseas and specialists from home departments in diplomatic posts has contributed to increased bureaucratic rivalry. One aspect of this is the development of multiple information channels for receiving, gathering and evaluating information. In Japan, for example, the information-gathering monopoly of the Foreign Ministry (see Fig. 2.5) is rivalled by the Ministry of International Trade and Industry (MITI) (using the overseas branches of the Japan External Trade Organisation (JETRO)) and links with corporations, the Defence Agency through its attachés and the Ministry of Finance through its personnel attached to Japanese embassies.[28] Another noticeable effect is on the traditional embassy functions of reporting and assessments which can become downgraded through overloading from routine protocol associated with inward visits by, for example, representatives of domestic ministries or parliamentarians and other political leaders. Third, and most important, are the enhanced problems of co-ordination and control brought about by the splintering of policy. The independent action by para-statal agencies, a particular feature of the international debt crisis, is discussed in Chapter 7.

Representation and public relations

Information is one of the several specialist posts which have been added to many embassies in recent years.[29] Putting across the correct image of a country, its people and life-style, gathering the support of foreign media and public are major preoccupations. In this way modern diplomacy has changed to being concerned with information, not in a crude propaganda sense of the Cold War or the high-tempo marketing style of 'Expo', but in a more limited and fragmentary way. The concern now is with creating confidence in a country and its products; gaining a paragraph in a major newspaper; correcting a press story. In other words information work is short-term and incremental, more akin to diplomatic journalism than propaganda.

The importance of this aspect of diplomacy can be further seen in that states have frequently augmented their official diplomatic channel by hiring the services of public relations agencies. During the Anglo-Icelandic 'Cod War', Iceland used a London-based public relations firm, Whittaker Hunt, to put across its case.[30] Lobbying by legal and other professional agencies is also a significant aspect of the public relations of states. The area covered by lobbying is wide, including such efforts as the attempts by the Bahamas to counteract their drug-trafficking image,[31] or Thai efforts to amend US tariff legislation during Thai–US trade disputes (see Ch. 8). Formal and informal developments in information work have to some extent taken the conduct of foreign policy outside its traditional diplomatic framework, by introducing new participants and widening, in certain instances, the arena of debate by bringing, for a short period, greater public attention to the issue.

Abnormal relations and non-recognition

The transformation of disputes and conflicts into higher levels of tension, leading eventually to breaks in diplomatic relations or other states of abnormal relations is generally signalled by one or more factors relating to, for example, negotiation or border provision. These include abrogation of treaties or agreements dealing with security or non intervention;[32] the reintroduction of fundamental demands at a critical stage of negotiation;[33] the cancellation and non-continuation of key talks;[34] economic sanctions and border closure.[35]

The transition to armed conflict has several important implications for the conduct of diplomacy. The Vienna Convention on Diplomatic Relations (1961) treats this question broadly in three areas: the implications for diplomatic agents, assets and protection of interests.[36] The first two of these will only be briefly noted here. Under Article 44 of the Vienna Convention the receiving state is under an obligation to grant those with privileges and immunities the right to leave at the earliest possible moment.[37] Article 45 deals *inter alia* with assets, which in the event of a break or recall (either permanent or temporary) the receiving state has a duty to protect, including premises of the mission, its property and archives (Article 45(a)). The custody of these and the protection of interests, including materials, may be undertaken by a third state with the consent of the receiving state (Article 45(b) and (c)).[38]

The conduct of relations under conditions of armed conflict or other serious conflict becomes extremely difficult in the absence of diplomatic relations. Three kinds of difficulties can be distinguished: over lines of contact, the official competence to negotiate, and the scope of negotiations. Lines of contact may be opened directly, through a friendly power either in a third state or at the United Nations, or other intermediaries. It is not always the case that lines of contact can be easily established. In the Russo-Finnish war for example, Finland having gone through the suite of possibilities, used in an act of unconventional diplomacy an informal envoy, Hella Wuolijoki, a left-wing Finnish playwright, to establish contact with the Soviet ambassador to Sweden.[39] In cases where there is a lengthy absence of formal diplomatic relations, efforts to establish lines of communication can often be fragile and inconclusive.[40]

At a formal level more certainty may be achieved through the use of a third party as a protecting power,[41] as provided for under the Law of Armed Conflict and the Vienna Convention.[42] Third parties are quite widely used as protecting powers as in the 1982 Falklands conflict in which the United Kingdom and Argentina were represented through interest sections respectively by Switzerland and Brazil.[43] Agreements for the protection of interests in foreign states cover a range of matters extending to administrative, humanitarian and commercial questions, and the protection of nationals. The protecting power can also be involved in the process of normalising relations to varying degrees ranging from the onward transmission of notes through to the 'grey' area of informal discussions and draft proposals.[44]

It should be noted that the resumption of diplomatic relations may also be achieved through other means including direct contact, friendly powers and intermediaries. The ending of diplomatic relations also does not mean necessarily the termination of consular relations. Consular officials have been used in those instances in which either there are no diplomatic relations, or diplomatic relations have been broken, for diplomatic and political functions.[45] In these cases involving non-recognition, de-recognition or exiled entities, several different mechanisms have evolved for transacting official and other business. These include honorary representative;[46] liaison office; representative office and trade mission. The use of a permanent trade mission is probably the most common of these devices, especially in instances of long-standing formal absence of relations. In some cases the style 'representative office' is preferred to liaison office, presumably since it more closely connotes recognition and statehood. For example, the Turkish Federated State of Northern Cyprus maintains representative offices in Belgium, UK, US and the UN. Indeed, US proposals to Vietnam following the Paris Peace Accords of 1973, for a liaison office, along the lines of the US–PRC liaison office prior to recognition, were rejected by Vietnam.[47] The US offer was subsequently withdrawn until 1991, when, as a result of progress on the Cambodian question, business pressure, and a desire to resolve the outstanding US missing prisoners of war issue (POW/MIA), the policy was revised. The US subsequently opened POW/MIA liaison offices in Vietnam, Cambodia and Laos, staffed by non-permanent Defense Department personnel, with no diplomatic or political responsibility. The Hanoi office was upgraded in 1993 by diplomatic personnel, prior to full diplomatic relations.

Taiwan's relations with China and the US are interesting for the contrasting light they throw on issues of the pace of informality, and on the other hand the need to conduct international trade and implement international conventions in a stable, legal framework. Following recognition of the PRC, the US established through the Taiwan Relations Act (1979)[48] a framework to enable trade and multilateral shipping and other technical agreements to be implemented through the American Institute in Taiwan (AIT) and Co-ordination Council for North American Affairs (CCNAA).[49] In contrast, Taiwan allowed its officials to participate formally in the semi-official liaison body, the Straits Exchange Foundation with China, only in 1995, in view of the sensitivity of contacts with the PRC and constant military tension.[50]

Reform

States have traditionally reviewed from time to time the operation and effectiveness of their foreign ministries and diplomatic services.[51] More often than not such inquiries have been occasioned by wider economy moves in the public sector or institutional rivalry. Although the expenditure costs of the foreign ministry and diplomatic service are often low in comparison with other ministries, many items on the foreign ministry budget come under criticism since they are not easy to evaluate in cost-effective terms. Certain regular expenditure components have risen significantly in recent years. In particular, increases in the cost of general budget and voluntary contributions to international organisations have added significantly to the foreign affairs budgets of smaller powers. The acquisition of diplomatic property has now become a further major budgetary item. The opening of five posts by New Zealand between 1983 and 1986 added some $NZ4.6 million to the cost of the overseas service, which rose to $NZ110.2 million.[52] Attempting to offset these types of increases is difficult in some instances in that further reductions in embassy staffing would reduce the staff level below the minimum operational level of three to four personnel.

Reviews have in the main examined six areas; (i) interdepartmental co-ordination; (ii) the direction given by the foreign ministry to its embassies and the conduct of diplomacy; (iii) the number, location and function of embassies and other missions; (iv) expenditure; (v) training; (vi) recruitment. Relatively few reviews have made major recommendations aimed at altering the central machinery of government, with the exceptions of those such as the Canadian reorganisation of trade within the Ministry of External Affairs discussed above. Rather, most reviews have recommended improvements in existing arrangements, particularly co-ordination between the foreign ministry and trade and finance. The Swedish reorganisation, for example, sought to improve the links between the Ministry for Foreign Affairs, the Swedish Trade Council and private sector business in order to enlarge the role of the former in directing export promotion.[53] The co-ordination of information policy has been another recurrent issue. In a wide-ranging report on the Indian Foreign Service the Pillai Committee noted that less than half of India's embassies had information officers and proposed closer links between the Ministries of External Affairs and Information.[54]

The review of the Australian Department of Foreign Affairs and Trade in 1993–94 introduced the new concept of 'portfolio' management, comprising 'core' responsibilities and separate programmes of services provided by the Department to others. The portfolio comprises the following programmes:

1. International relations, trade and business liaison (core);
2. Passport and consular services;
3. Services for other agencies;
4. Secure government communications and security services;
5. Executive and DFAT corporate services;
6. Development corporation;
7. Austrade;
8. Australian Secret Intelligence Service (ASIS).

The first five programmes, plus ASIS, are administered by the Department of Foreign Affairs and Trade. The underlying purpose behind the reforms was to increase ministerial direction and attention to Australian overseas trade interests, development co-operation and relations with the South Pacific. The review introduced corporate plan concepts, assessments of costs and performance indicators.[55]

The other general areas in which recommendations for reform have been put forward have been in the number, size and work of embassies and the training of diplomatic personnel. In a major review of British representational effort overseas in 1969 the Duncan Committee, some twelve months after the merger of the Commonwealth Relations Office with the Foreign Office, looked at expenditure, manpower, diplomatic reporting and the grading of overseas missions.[56] In an attempt to establish some general guidelines for distinguishing between regions of importance for the location of embassies, the Duncan Report identified an inner area of concentration (essentially the Atlantic and developed world) and an outer area. The proposal was rejected in a later review[57] on the grounds that the division was too broad and that an unjustifiably high volume of resources was already devoted to representation in inner area countries. The Duncan Report did, however, have a major influence on altering the emphasis of British posts to greater economic work, including export promotion. By 1985 over 30 per cent of British diplomatic staff abroad were involved in economic work, while only half that number were engaged in political work.[58]

Expenditure reviews

Expenditure reviews in a number of foreign ministries now take the form of annual economic planning based on a corporate plan for the ministry. For example, the New Zealand Ministry of Foreign Affairs and Trade has within the annual estimates introduced the concept of contracted outputs.[59] The outputs are subject to six-monthly review and quality assurance targets. The reviews have helped not only to focus on policy objectives and their performance costs, but also to provide a strategic perspective on the functions of the ministry. For example the

Acts which the Ministry of Foreign Affairs and Trade administers are[60] now clearly collated and numbered. However, one difficulty with this type of quality assurance system is that too much organisational effort may be increasingly devoted to the administrative or mechanical aspects of audits at the expense of the conduct of diplomacy.

Technical personnel

The growing requirement in diplomatic services for the foreign ministry to have or use cadres of technical personnel has posed difficult problems of training and recruitment. Large and established services have now developed multiple levels of phased career training, with an emphasis on international relations, international economics, international institutions, negotiation and management skills. In the course of developing appropriate training, established services have encountered, mainly as a result of economic constraints, two major policy issues: the nature and extent of language training for diplomatic services officers, and the value or continued utility of regional areas of specialisation.[61]

New states coming into the diplomatic community since the late 1980s, along with some small established services, such as Singapore and Jamaica, have responded by using a variety of non-permanent (and sometimes non-national) personnel. For example, the ambassador to Washington of one small state, in reviewing his embassy staff complained: 'I need someone who can negotiate a bilateral telecommunications agreement.' Non-permanent personnel used to augment the diplomatic services of small states include senior businessmen as ambassadors; technical personnel on short-term non-career contracts and, in some instances, unconventional citizen diplomacy. The latter involves, for example, indirect foreign ministry support for transnational cultural and educational contacts involving individuals and groups.

Implications for diplomatic culture

The above developments have had a number of effects on the traditional international diplomatic corps. Changes in the membership of the corps, including career and non-career officers, means that universal norms, attitudes and diplomatic procedures are less widely shared in national capitals, or at international institutions by those who make up what is an increasingly heterogeneous diplomatic corps. Second, diplomatic culture – the norms associated with the conduct of negotiations, the forms of diplomatic communication and types of agreements – is becoming less universal, with greater varieties of national and regional level approaches. Third, from a national point of view, training has to deal with issues such as an ambassador's links with the foreign business community in the capital to which he or she is accredited; the adequacy of traditional reporting methods, and what *interests* an ambassador should be representing. Taken together these functions underline the differing and, above all, increasingly conflicting tasks the modern ambassador has to undertake.

Summary

The differing arrangements states have for managing foreign policy have been influenced particularly by the growth in the volume of international business. As more departments and agencies have become increasingly involved so this has created problems of national co-ordination and institutional rivalry over the responsibility for the direction of non-traditional areas of policy which are now considered as foreign policy. Trade, international economic policy and technology have been difficult to accommodate and co-ordinate as foreign ministries, which have generally lacked expertise in these areas, have adapted to the new international agendas. In many respects the issue is more complex for newer states, since development policy is to a large extent foreign and national security policy. The strands of development policy almost automatically, by design or otherwise, have an international dimension. There are, on the other hand, those countries which have only very limited resources which place considerable constraints on conducting any significant external policy. Others simply hope to get by. In some instances, the tradition of a foreign ministry and diplomatic service has remained weak since independence because of recurrent internal instability.[62] Yet for those with a stake in the international system having a foreign policy is something which is increasingly expensive, the product very intangible with few clearly identifiable benefits, but which is nevertheless considered an essential part of continued statehood.

References and notes

1. David A. Dickson provides a valuable discussion of bureaucratic influences on US African policy in *United States Foreign Policy Towards Sub-Saharan Africa* (University of America Press, New York, 1985) p. 31 *passim*.
2. *The Times*, 20 Oct. 1981. On the Soviet attitude to a Nordic nuclear-free zone, comprising Finland, Sweden, Norway and Denmark, see *The Times*, 27 June 1981.
3. For an illustration of this point in the context of the differing agency interests in the US involved in arms control, see Jonathan Dean 'East–West Arms Control Negotiations', in Leon Sloss and M. Scott Davis, *A Game for High Stakes* (Ballinger, Cambridge, Mass., 1986) pp. 102–3.
4. For a discussion of socio-economic influences see Olatunde Ojo, D.K. Orwa and C.M.B. Utete, *African International Relations* (Longman, London, 1985) pp. 18–27.
5. Bahgat Korany and Ali E. Hillal Dessouki, *The Foreign Policies of Arab States* (Westview Press, Boulder, Colo., 1984) p. 327.
6. See Peter Calvert, *The Foreign Policy of New States* (Wheatsheaf Books, Sussex, 1986) pp. 95–8.
7. For example, the Nigerian Foreign Ministry was not informed of the decision to expel illegal aliens by the Shagari Government in late 1983. See Olojide Aluko, 'The Expulsion of Illegal Aliens from Nigeria: A Study in Nigerian Decision Making', *African Affairs*, Vol. 84, No. 337 (Oct. 1985) p. 559.
8. By 1997, there were 70 departments in the Foreign and Commonwealth Office. Of these 48 were now functional (e.g. Energy, European Integration Department,

Financial Relations, Trade Relations and Exports. Maritime Aviation and Environment) and 22 were geographical. The other departments were specialist departments such as the Overseas Labour Adviser, Inspectorate and Legal Advisers.

9. *Report of the Committee on the Indian Foreign Service* (Ministry of External Affairs, New Delhi, 1966) p. 3.

10. The Italian Foreign Ministry has been operating at nearly 20 per cent of its diplomatic service establishment level owing to the competitive pay and conditions offered by the commercial sector. In 1984 the Foreign Ministry was established for 938 diplomats but had 777 on strength. See *Financial Times*, 7 Sept. 1984.

11. Ronald M. Schneider, *Brazil Foreign Policy of a Future World Power* (Westview Press, Boulder, Colo., 1976).

12. See, for example, *Economic and Technical Cooperation among Developing Countries*, Vol. 1 (Office of the Chairman of the Group of 77, New York, 1984) Annex III, pp. 291–5, and *A Guide to ECDC* (Office of the Chairman of the Group of 77, New York) 27 April 1983, Annexes III, IV, pp. 22–8.

13. Correspondence Lithuanian Foreign Ministry, March 1995.

14. *Annual Report 1983–4* (Department of External Affairs, Ottawa, 1984) p. 2255.

15. *The Swedish Budget 1986–7* (Ministry of Finance, Stockholm, 1986) pp. 64–5.

16. Susan Strange, 'Protectionism and World Politics', *International Organisation*, Vol. 39, No. 2 (Spring 1985) pp. 253–4 on the new government-corporation diplomacy.

17. For a discussion of government relations with foreign economic groups, including, for example, Ghana and the US-based Volta Aluminium Co. (Valco), see R.I. Onuka and A. Sesay, *The Future of Regionalism in Africa* (Macmillan, Hong Kong, 1985) p. 158 *passim*.

18. The same kind of point is made in the context of the lack of integrated technology policies in many African countries. See Onuka and Sesay, op. cit., p. 166.

19. *Public Service Bulletin* (Harare) Vol. 1, No. 3 (1984) p. 1.

20. For example, the need for a review of the administration of the Danish technical cooperation programme in view of its considerable growth was noted in *The Foreign Service of Denmark 1770–1970* (Foreign Ministry, Copenhagen, 1970) pp. 36–8. On the dispute over competence over foreign aid in Japan, see J.W.M. Chapman, R. Drifte and I.T.M. Gow, *Japan's Quest for Comprehensive Security* (Frances Pinter, London, 1983) p. 85.

21. Calvert, op. cit., p. 95.

22. GATT, L/5915, 18 Oct. 1985, pp. 43–4.

23. A Malaysian diplomatic mission was established in Kuwait on 25 May 1974. See *Foreign Affairs*, Malaysia, Vol. 7, No. 2 (June 1974).

24. Wayne A. Selcher, *Brazil's Multilateral Relations* (Westview Press, Boulder, Colo., 1978) p. 221.

25. *Vertegenwoordigingen van het Koninkrijk der Nederlanden in het buitenland* (Staatsuitgeverijs–Gravenhage, Sept. 1984) pp. 97–9.

26. Correspondence Jamaican High Commissioner, London, March 1995.

27. *Public Service Bulletin* (Harare), Vol. 2, No. 2 (July 1985), Supplement, pp. 3–4.

28. Drifte illustrates the institutional rivalry by citing the example of the difficulties caused by the proposal by the US Special Trade Representative for trilateral trade talks being put through the MITI in Sept. 1981. The displeasure and opposition of the Japanese Foreign Ministry delayed the talks until Jan. 1982. See R. Drifte, 'The Foreign Policy System', in Chapman, Drifte and Gow, op. cit., p. 87.

29. Lord Gore Booth (ed.), *Satow's Guide to Diplomatic Practice* (Longman, London, 1979) Appendix VI, p. 487. Of the 2,000 or so officials on the diplomatic lists of 130 countries in London in the mid-1970s, 380 were non-career diplomats working in specialist fields such as commercial, economic and financial, press and cultural relations. Diplomatic service officers also occupied positions in these areas.

30. *Sunday Times*, 20 Aug. 1972. Iceland established a secretary for information at the outset of the fisheries dispute with Britain in 1971. See R.P. Barston and Hjalmar W. Hannesson, 'The Anglo-Icelandic Fisheries Dispute', *International Relations* (David Davies Memorial Institute, London) Vol. IV, No. 6 (Nov. 1974) p. 575.

31. *Financial Times*, 25 June 1985.
32. See Arie E. David, *The Strategy of Treaty Termination* (Yale University Press, London, 1975).
33. For example, in the November 1941 US–Japanese negotiations prior to the Pearl Harbour attack, Ambassador Nomura presented so-called Proposal B, involving the stationing of a significant number of Japanese troops in Asia, on 20 Nov. 1941, knowing at that stage that the US would find the proposals unacceptable. At that point the State Department, having broken Japanese ciphers, were aware that Japan had decided to terminate the negotiations on 29 Nov. 1941. See Paul Hyer, 'Hu Shih, the diplomacy of gentle persuasion', in Richard Dean Burns and Edward M. Bennett, *Diplomats in Crisis* (ABC-Clio, Santa Barbara, California, 1974) pp. 164–5 on Ambassador Nomura's role in the 20–4 Nov. 1941 negotiations.
34. Iraqi demands, for example, prior to the occupation of Kuwait in 1990 were set out in a letter of 16 July 1990 to the Arab League, including those related to the disputed Rumailan oil-field. Subsequently only one meeting was held on 1 Aug. 1990 between an Iraqi delegation led by Izzat Ibrahim and the Kuwaiti Prime Minister, Prince Saad. See John Bulloch and Harvey Morris, *Saddam's War* (Faber and Faber, London, 1991) p. 105.
35. Border closure is indicative of a serious deterioration in relations, rather than the next step to war or armed conflict. It is therefore generally combined with one of the other five measures outlined. For example, following the breakdown of the Iraq–Kuwait talks on 1 Aug., Iraq, having moved troops to the Kuwait border, closed the land border between the two countries. The Iraqi invasion began 12 hours later. See Bulloch and Morris, op. cit., pp. 105–6.
36. 55 *AJIL* 1961 pp. 1062–82, Articles 44 and 45. The notion of armed conflict is implicit in Article 40 which deals with diplomatic agents in or passing through the territory of third states.
37. Under Article 44, the receiving state is to facilitate departure for those with diplomatic privileges and immunities without discrimination as to nationality, and, where necessary, provide transport.
38. The duties of third states *vis-à-vis* diplomatic agents, administrative staff and diplomatic bags which are in or pass through their territory are set out in Article 40(1)–(3) of the Vienna Convention. The duty to accord inviolability, administrative and other assistance is extended in Article 40(3) to situations of *force majeure*.
39. See Max Jakobson, *The Diplomacy of the Russo-Finnish War 1939–40* (Harvard University Press, Cambridge, Mass., 1961) p. 155.
40. See, for example, Harold H. Saunders, 'The Beginning of the End', in Warren Christopher (ed.), *American Hostages in Iran* (Yale University Press, 1985) p. 289.
41. See Vaughn Lowe, 'Diplomatic War: Protecting Powers', *International and Comparative Law Quarterly*, Vol. 39 (1990) pp. 472–3.
42. Geneva Convention for the Amelioration of the Condition of Wounded and Sick Armed Forces in the Field 1949, 75 *UNTS*, 31, Arts 8–10; Geneva Protocol I, Cmnd 6927, Art. 5.
43. *Financial Times*, 3 April 1982; *Hansard* (House of Commons) Vol. 59, col. 235 (1984). Diplomatic relations between the United Kingdom and Argentina were resumed in July 1990. See *The Times*, 19 July 1990. Up until then the interests sections had been limited to four staff, plus secretaries, on each side. See *The Times*, 19 Aug. 1989.
44. States other than the protecting powers may be used to promote the resumption of relations. In the UK/Argentina conflict over the Falklands, apart from Switzerland, the US brokered informal proposals on a settlement during 1987. See *The Times*, 3 April 1987 on both initiatives.
45. For example, following the Suez Crisis in 1956, Australia and the UK retained officials in a consular capacity in the Canadian embassy in Cairo, see *Satow's Guide to Diplomatic Practice*, 5th edn (Longman, London, 1959) p. 213. See also the US–PRC and Congo Civil War examples. In the Congo conflict, the Belgian consul in Elisabethville was used for discussions with the sessionist president Moise

Tshombe. See Luke T. Lee, *Vienna Convention in Consular Relations* (A.W. Sijthoff, Leyden, 1966) p. 180.

46. Lithuania, for example, maintained honorary representatives in London, Paris, Washington, prior to independence in 1991. Interview Washington, DC.

47. See G.R. Berridge, *Talking to the Enemy* (Macmillan, London, 1993) pp. 56–7.

48. *Taiwan Relations Act* (1979), as Stat 14, 17, 22 USC 3305(a), in *American Digest of International Law 1981–8* (Department of State, 1994) p. 1209.

49. The Act provides for the bilateral implementation of certain multilateral conventions, e.g. in a shipping field where both countries have strong mutual shipping interests, the Exchange of Letters, 17 Aug. 1982, Arlington, Virginia, provides for the application of the Safety of Life at Sea, Marine Pollution 73/74 (MARPOL) Convention and Load Lines.

50. *Financial Times*, 23 Feb. 1995.

51. Prior to the Foreign Service Act of 1961, the Danish Foreign Service and Organisation was reviewed by commissions in 1906, 1919 and 1957. In 1905 Denmark had only 18 career officers in the Foreign Ministry, which rose to 58 by 1919. The great expansion of 1921 was followed by cut-backs in 1927 which reduced the number of career officers from 146 in 1922 to 113 in 1927. The number of diplomatic missions was reduced to 16, covering 35 countries. The 1961 Act, which reaffirmed the principle of a unified home and foreign service, provided for further expansion. At the beginning of 1970, the Foreign Service comprised 280 career officers, and 76 diplomatic missions. See Klaus Kjolsen, *The Foreign Service of Denmark 1770–1970* (Foreign Ministry, 1970) pp. 23–5.

52. *Commentary on the Estimates of the Expenditure of the Government of New Zealand* for year ending 31 March 1986 (Wellington, Government Printer, 1985) pp. 52–3.

53. *The Swedish Budget 1986–7*, p. 66. Co-ordinators from the Swedish Trade Council were attached to the Foreign Ministry.

54. *Report of the Committee on the Indian Foreign Service*, pp. 56–72.

55. See *Annual Report 1993–4* (Foreign Affairs and Trade, Canberra, 1994) pp. 9–10. Cf. *Annual Report* (1993) for details of the Australian Senate's inquiry, pp. 16–18. Cf. New Zealand review of the same period Annual Report (1994) pp. 12–17.

56. *Report*, Review Committee on Overseas Representation 1968–69, Cmnd 4107, July 1969.

57. *Review of Overseas Representation* (Report by the Central Policy Review Staff) (HMSO, London, 1977) pp. xiii–xiv.

58. *Minutes of Evidence* by Sir Antony Acland, 3 July 1985, Trade and Industry Committee, House of Commons Papers, no. 335, pt vi, Session 1984–85, p. 87. The Diplomatic Service was given special responsibility for export promotion in the Plowden Report (Cmnd 2276, Feb. 1964) and the Trade Commission Service merged with it. See also *Financial Times*, 4 July 1985.

59. See *Annual Report* Ministry of Foreign Affairs and Trade, New Zealand (Wellington, 1995) pp. 10–11.

60. Ibid., p. 72. The Acts include Antarctica Act 1960; Antarctic Marine Living Resources Act 1981.

61. I am grateful for discussions on this point with Ambassador Richard Jackson, United States Foreign Service Institute.

62. P.J. Boyce, *Foreign Affairs for New States* (University of Queensland Press, St Lucia, 1977) pp. 86–98.

CHAPTER 3

Foreign policy orientations

Foreign policy assessments

Foreign policy assessments are central to the work of the foreign ministry official or diplomat. The role of the diplomat in this process has been aptly summed up in the following way: '... of judging accurately what other people are likely to do in given circumstances, of appreciating accurately the views of others, of representing accurately his own'.[1] Foreign policy itself can be thought of as being made up of three segments. In the first of these are generalised statements containing the broad aims and the overall interests of the state, as articulated in statements, communiques and other public pronouncements. There may, of course, be entirely different, and secret, general and particular interests that are pursued in a 'covert' foreign policy through secret or private diplomacy. In the second place, foreign policy can be thought of as the range of issue areas and preoccupations of a state. These might be European Community questions to do with the Community budget; harmonisation of Organisation for African Unity (OAU) policies on a development programme; bilateral issues in Anglo-American defence co-operation; international currency stability for the major Western powers, or fisheries questions for Iceland. In other words, these and similar types of issue areas constitute the foreign policy 'agenda'. Individual items on the agenda will normally be given some sort of order of importance or priority, which can and will frequently change over time. In the third sector are the specific daily operational problems which make up the routine of the 'external' ministries, such as visits, instructions to a delegation, lobbying on a vote in the UN, overflight clearance, consular problems and so on. This threefold distinction helps to put operational problems, especially of a short-term kind, into the broader context of issue areas and objectives. The threefold categorisation also enables questions to be asked about changes in the types of issue area a country is dealing with and any reordering of its priorities.

Assessment normally takes one of three forms. First there are analyses of short-run events, for example, the stability of a coalition, the effect of ministerial change, the current state of the economy after a devaluation or the significance of a visit or speech. Second are the longer-range reviews of the national political scene of a country and its foreign policy over a period of, for example, twelve months. The latter are likely to note departures in policy and highlights in bilateral relations. Third are estimates which attempt to give an indication of future patterns, trends of events or likely developments. Assessments of this kind normally ask 'what if' questions, such as what can be expected in terms of defence policy, political relations, investment legislation, taxation if there is a change of government in, for example, four years.

Another common set of questions is of a comparative kind on anticipated levels of trade or the likelihood of continued political support on an issue. Apart from these main types, other forms of assessment include the 'devil's advocate' or reversal type and very long-range estimates. This chapter is mainly concerned with the second or review type of assessment and looks at orientation and change in foreign policy. The first part of the chapter provides an overview of the factors influencing the setting and process of foreign policy.

The foreign policy setting

The influences on the foreign policy of a country can be initially grouped into domestic and international. These include location, historical background, culture, organisation, the extent of non-governmental interests, degree of domestic stability, economic and leadership influences. External influences include the structural systemic features of the international system, such as the level of violence; the nature and state of local and regional relations; international currency movements; the policies of a powerful extra-regional neighbour or proceedings of an international institution. To these broad categorisations must, of course, be added 'boundary cutting' or transnational influences. These are defined to include the autonomous or semi-autonomous actions of individuals and entities over which a government may have limited knowledge or control. Often transnational influences are thought of in terms of multinational corporations or terrorism, though in practice the range is far greater than this. It includes, for example, radio propaganda, refugees, trans-border smuggling, narcotics, the commercial operations of international companies, repatriated earnings, migrant labour and tourism.[2] Many of these transnational influences are not necessarily new. Some have in fact become instruments of national policy such as the 'boat people' in Southeast Asia.[3] Other transnational developments are new including rapid developments in high-resolution, satellite-gathered intelligence and data transmission, which have not only altered transnationalism but helped to create further technological stratifications in the international system.[4] Another major development of note is the growth of international capital centres in Europe, the Middle East, Southeast Asia and the Far East. The growth of capital markets and related technology has facilitated the rapid movement of both private and officially sourced capital. These developments are something with which sovereign states have to coexist uneasily. For some states, particularly those weaker ones on the immediate periphery of capital centres, new problems of economic security have been created through financial and trade services competition.[5] In other instances, sovereign states have continued to remain highly vulnerable to large, short-term capital outflows and runs on currencies. States and NGOs have also become increasingly vulnerable to large scale financial fraud from unauthorised or poorly regulated trading activities on stock and futures markets.[6]

The influences outlined above combine in different configurations to shape the overall foreign policy profile of a state by setting the constraints and opportunities for particular decisions and courses of action. Configurations of course vary considerably. A state may be influenced by relatively few transnational influences because of internal economic weakness but nevertheless have an important strategic location. What is therefore important is to determine the relevant mix of factors in each case. Some may be more or less permanent features of a state's environment, such as location, effective economic territory, climate, resources, land and sea routes and level of development. These might be termed 'intrinsic' factors. Another relatively fixed component of a state's foreign policy environment is the set of treaties, agreements and other formal legal instruments a regime inherits on coming to power. Acceptance of agreements provides continuity and is with some exceptions part of the practice of most established states. Regimes in new states are likely to exercise greater selectivity over inherited agreements. Selectivity is one of the distinguishing features of the conduct of their external policy, though the degree of volatility has been overstated.[7]

Other factors are less pervasive and can be termed 'contingent'. These include personality factors, the effectiveness of the foreign policy machinery, the extent of bureaucratic or public opposition and the type of issue being dealt with.

Characteristics of foreign policy

In assessing the foreign policy of another country it is normally possible to construct a profile based on the core and secondary interests. That is there is likely to be a pattern of central interests involving selected states and issues, the range of which will vary according to the capability, location and perceived role of the country in question. Secondary interests are distinguished by the intermittent time and organisational attention devoted to them, along with their 'sectoral' or limited nature. Some, however, may be long-standing, especially territorial disputes and take considerable time to resolve, as in the case of the Beagle Channel dispute between Argentina and Chile.[8]

Second, a major paradox of foreign policy is the contrast between the smooth inter-connectedness of declared objectives and the disjointedness of routine problem-solving. Foreign policy in practice often appears rather brittle – the product of brief diplomatic visits, hasty cables and rapid exchanges of views – as it continually moves from item to item, rather like a scanner on a radar screen. Third, unlike other areas of public policy, foreign policy is made under extreme time constraints.[9] This tends to accentuate the tendency to deal with issues in a short-term manner.

Longer-range assessments need to disentangle the short-term pre-occupations and actions and impose some kind of framework of explanation without becoming unnecessarily distracted by the short-term or immediate actions. Decisions, which are the component parts of policy, have a context. It is essential therefore to analyse whether a similar move or decision has been made by that country before or whether it is an apparent departure in policy. Again, an assessment of the importance of a high-level visit must not only take into account the level at which it was conducted, the extent to which the visit was perhaps largely ceremonial and the scope of the agenda, but also measure it against what, if anything, was achieved in the last analogous visit. In journalistic assessments, preoccupation with the day-to-day aspects of foreign policy inevitably affects the metaphors of explanation. For example, the metaphor of the United States 'playing the China card' is often used in the context of Sino-American relations. Assessments of Russian Federation policy tend to focus excessively on leadership politics, attempting to see splits between 'conservatives' and 'reformers'. Metaphors of this type have the effect of obscuring other more probable or complex reasons for behaviour such as organisational, bureaucratic, historical and external influences. Foreign policy is often conducted at multiple levels. The audience can be internal or external, regional or international, public or private. Assessing why countries, organisations and other entities act is one of the major and fascinating tasks of diplomacy. Finally, more than any other area of policy, foreign policy is both more easily reversed and subject to change.

Orientation

In considering why states and other entities act in particular kinds of ways the concept of orientation offers a useful starting-point. Orientation can be defined as the pattern of governmental and politically significant private attitudes, actions and transactions, which go to make up the alignment of a country. The more important of these are élite views, political groupings, alliance membership and trade patterns. States, in other words, interact in varying degrees with other members of the international community on political, economic, military, cultural, social and many other levels. These interactions generally show certain patterns, which indicate, reinforce or suggest the foreign policy directions and preferences of a country.

Several different foreign policy profiles can be constructed.[10] These can be as varied as the profiles for a complex advanced Western European state, an Asian Islamic republic, micro-state, through to isolation. Some states in fact have very low international involvement, e.g.

Malagasy, Mongolia, Mauritania, Solomon Islands, Federated States of Micronesia. Other orientations might be essentially local, with interactions focusing on immediate neighbours, e.g. Thailand, Bolivia, Kenya, Mali. More complex orientations necessarily involve membership of regional and international political and economic groupings, defence and other arrangements. These may not always be 'uniform' in that there may be divergent political and trade orientations, e.g. Angola,[11] or defence and trade orientations may differ, e.g. Malaysia, during its 'Look East' economic policy phase directed towards Japan and South Korea and its mixed Western and non-aligned defence posture.[12]

Levels of interaction and aggregation

In any discussion of changes in orientation and the development of a country's foreign policy, it is necessary to look at the various levels of interaction which that state has with other actors. How far are the political and economic transactions largely autonomous of one another? Are there frequent disruptions in political relations or economic disputes? Do cultural questions spill over into political relations? The answers to these and similar questions give an indication whether an orientation is changing, taking on some new form, or whether disruptions are episodic and with no general effect on the overall orientation.

The process by which levels of interactions or transactions become linked or related can be termed 'aggregation'. Aggregation may consist of either internally directed domestic measures (e.g. the promotion of political relations by inward investment schemes, export subsidies, withdrawal of special privileges) or be externally directed or influenced. States which have pursued isolationist or withdrawal policies, e.g. Myanmar, Oman, will exhibit high degrees of aggregation in the process of attempting to control entry and limit political contacts. Examples of externally influenced aggregations are economic sanctions, such as the sanctions of the United States against the Soviet Union after the invasion of Afghanistan, or reprisals such as the People's Republic of China's threatened retaliation against American exports to China following the 'pirate goods' copyright dispute in 1995.[13]

The degree of aggregation can vary considerably. In the European Union (EU) the interlocking of budgetary, agricultural and social policies in periodic 'wine lake', fisheries and 'lamb war' disputes is a marked feature of Community politics and style. Also noticeable in EU methods is the very wide range of trade-offs between different subject areas which are found in negotiations. For example in negotiations in the agricultural sector, solutions might be found involving compromise packages on wine and farming. In contrast, the Association of South-East Asian Nations (ASEAN) is a regional organisation distinguished by quite distinct areas of interaction and low levels of aggregation. Although initially conceived of as an economic organisation at its founding in 1967, pulling together the economies of the five original members (Malaysia, Indonesia, Thailand, Philippines, Singapore) these early aspirations have been gradually replaced by foreign policy rather than development questions.[14] While ASEAN developed institutional machinery and a committee structure which resembled that of the European Community (although there is no provision for a commission) ASEAN institutions have tended to remain largely autonomous of one another. ASEAN's economic diplomacy, too, became increasingly replaced by political preoccupations as the member states considered how to deal with issues such as the opportunities (and problems) created by the defeat of South Vietnam, the impending withdrawal of the US, recognition of the People's Republic of China and the Vietnamese invasion of Kampuchea. Since the end of the Cold War further major political preoccupation has involved how to accept, limit or accommodate the territorial aspirations of the People's Republic of China which has hindered ASEAN aggregation.

Consistently high levels of aggregation over lengthy periods of time are relatively rare. High aggregation is likely to occur only where economic objectives are directly and closely connected to political interests and policy, as with Saudi Arabian bilateral relations with West European states after the 1973 Arab–Israeli War. Again, Kissinger's policy during the early 1970s of 'linkage' was based on the *realpolitik* concept of doing business with the Soviets on all possible fronts, in the hope of moderating Soviet behaviour and bringing about international and domestic change.[15] The Strategic Arms Limitation Treaty (SALT I) in 1972 was accompanied by a suite of co-operation agreements in trade, medicine and space. The first meeting of the Soviet-American trade commission took place six weeks after the signing of the SALT I agreement.[16]

Nevertheless, *détente* was never subsequently underpinned by extensive bilateral trade, in view of the asymmetrical economies and limited scope for such linkage. The differing foreign policy interests of the West and the Russian Federation since the end of the Cold War, coupled with the economic weakness and instability of the Russian Federation reform process, has limited the aggregation envisaged in *détente*. Russian Federation domestic weakness too has meant that the West has been reluctant to apply coercive economic measures to restrain Russian Federation policy on human rights or other military operations in its so-called 'near abroad'.

Low aggregation

Low aggregation in bilateral relations can occur for a number of reasons. It is especially seen in small or micro-state external relations, which are very often typified by the dominance of a single economic issue. In general, micro-states would have limited international political interactions.[17] An extreme example is Papua New Guinea, whose external relations were to a large extent taken up with the mining and retailing of copper (the country's major export, prior to the discovery of oil) from Bougainville, a substantial part of which went to Japan. Another reason for low aggregation is minimal political attention or 'pick-up'. This itself may be a facet of limited foreign policy control.[18] Central decision-makers may be switching rapidly from domestic to international issues, machinery may be limited or there may be a high degree of individual departmental autonomy. Apart from these reasons, low aggregation can occur because of the dominance of one sector of a state's external relations, e.g. the Sabah territorial dispute in Malaysian–Philippine relations.[19]

Some implications of differing aggregation

For most states aggregation in their external policy is normally relatively low since most governments tend to handle issues in a separate manner. When aggregation occurs it is likely to be between the political and economic levels of interaction. However, in general, the tendency for organisational autonomy limits the extent to which issues are related to one another. A further important aspect of the nature of the interactions between states is differential evaluation. An issue area may not only be perceived differently by another state but be given quite different degrees of importance. What may be high or central on one state's agenda in its bilateral relations, may be quite low for the other state. Thus, for example, in Malaysian–United States relations, an important bilateral issue, on the Malaysian side (Malaysia is a major tin producer) is the release of tin by the United States from the General Services Administration (GSA) stockpile, depressing tin prices. For the United States, however, the tin issue ranks low, and it is more likely to regard questions concerning Malaysia's security role in the South China Sea as more important.[20]

Finally, it is worth noting that by looking at disruptions or discontinuities in relations at various levels, questions can be raised about possible changes of direction. These might indicate that the state in question has acquired new political partners or is lessening its dependency either economically or politically, on one of the major powers. In addition, it is also possible to see whether a state's bilateral or multilateral relations recover quickly from a dispute or whether it has more lasting and widespread effects.

Change and reorientation

States as a matter of course make routine and continuous adjustments to their external relations in order to improve political relations with another country, deal with particular trade problems, open up new contacts and a host of other matters. These readjustments are for the most part likely to be marginal. Fundamental shifts involving major changes in the pattern and extent of most sectors of external policy are relatively rare. Such a reorientation can take the form of the rejection of a long-standing ally, for example, the break between the People's Republic of China and the Soviet Union from 1960; switching from one bloc or dependent relationship to another (e.g. Cuba, Ethiopia, Egypt, Baltic States, Eastern Europe) or diversification (e.g. Vietnam). Other fundamental reorientations can take the form of greater emphasis on self-reliance (e.g. Tanzania); privatisation of domestic state-run development agencies (e.g. Zambia); internal socio-religious revolution (e.g. Iran, Sudan); or changing economic or security groupings (e.g. Mexico, Baltic and Central Asian states). In rare instances some states deliberately limit their international involvement and adopt an orientation of isolation or withdrawal (e.g. Myanmar). Although a country may change its orientation in one of the ways outlined above, fundamental shifts are not always permanent. Dissatisfaction with a revised orientation often leads to protracted and sometimes contradictory attempts to readjust.

The primary indicators of reorientation are substantial changes in patterns of trade, inward and outward visits, and agreements with other countries. In addition, for a developing country further indicators of potential or actual reorientation would be developments in civil–military relations, the performance of the core export earners, expropriation of foreign assets, foreign exchange liquidity or the collapse of an economic programme. Secondary indicators include: alterations in diplomatic representation; joining or leaving international or regional organisations; voting behaviour; trends in inward investment and joint venture agreements.

It is unlikely that reorientation would occur simultaneously or to the same extent in all the primary sectors. In fact, it may be some time before changes in the economic sector, for example trade patterns, become aligned with the new political orientation. The initial public indicators of fundamental reorientation include official statements, major ministerial changes, foreign visits or preferences shown in contracts. Reorientation itself may take anything between two and five years to complete. It may, as noted above, be subsequently short-lived and reversed, as in the case of the Cultural Revolution in China, or the Norwegian referendum which eventually kept Norway out of the EU.[21]

Mixed orientation and reorientation

In general, states make adjustments to one or two sectors, or parts of those sectors, of their external relations, rather than try to carry out fundamental shifts. Such partial readjustments are likely sometimes to produce unusual configurations, as in the case of the 'mixed' profile of Mozambique, or Libya after 1969 which has highly antagonistic political relations with the United States, contrasting with continued oil and other economic links. These examples serve to underline the limited options, particularly at an economic level, but also in security terms, for many states. Examples of partial reorientation at a political level include the reduced international role of Yugoslavia after the death of Tito, Costa Rica's declaration of neutrality in 1983[22] and the several shifts in Malta's foreign policy orientation, including the development of political relations between Libya and Malta prior to the eventual declaration of neutrality in 1981.[23] Another indicator of partial readjustment of role is decline in participation in international conferences. For example, Indian involvement in international conferences has declined by two-thirds since the high point of non-alignment in 1970.[24] At a security level, for example, Indonesia, although keen to achieve the withdrawal of the United States from the Subic Bay base, nevertheless has retained defence purchase and other military links with Western countries.

Attempts to orientate at an economic level have become increasingly frequent, especially by the larger developing countries and some of the newly industrialised countries. For example, Brazil as a leading newly industrialised country has been particularly concerned to reduce its net imported oil account. As part of a policy of trade reorientation oil has been imported as far as possible from countries to which manufactured goods can be sold.[25] While oil links with Iraq (arms purchases) and Algeria (motor vehicles) have been retained, oil is no longer imported from Abu Dhabi, Libya or Kuwait. Of the other large developing countries, Thailand, for example, began a major petroleum reorientation on economic grounds after 1982 away from Saudi Arabia, which accounted for 15 per cent of Thai imports.[26] Thai foreign policy also placed importance on closer relations with the People's Republic of China, a new Asian petroleum exporter, as part of its policy of containing Vietnam after the Vietnamese invasion of Kampuchea. Trade redirection has also been used by other states such as Nigeria, following, for example, the military coup in 1983, which involved an attempt to shift to countertrade policy.[27]

Economic reorientation can involve changes in membership of international groupings, or regional institutions. For example, the Baltic and East European states, following the break-up of the Soviet Union have negotiated bilateral economic co-operation agreements with the EU as a step towards subsequent full membership of the Union. The Russian Federation itself had earlier joined the IMF and sought membership of the G-7. An unusual example of a switch in international grouping is provided by Mexico, which left the G-77 in 1994, no doubt concerned at continuing weakness of the Mexican economy, and joined the OECD.

Conclusion

Orientation and change are among the main areas of enquiry for longer-term assessments and reviews of a state's foreign policy. As such, assessments of this kind are concerned with the composition of the basic external policy profile of a country and any shifts which might indicate or suggest change in the fundamental pattern of relations with other members of the international community. The patterns of bilateral and multilateral relations may be conducted at different levels which may be 'aggregated' to a greater or lesser extent. As we have also argued, major shifts are relatively rare and in most cases tend to be reversed. Rather, longer-range assessments are likely to be concerned with identifying and explaining the significance of partial or limited reorientation which has to be distinguished from routine adjustment. In doing so, longer-range assessments need to strike a balance of interpretation between the short-run or operational problems and the more fundamental assumptions, whether public or secret, underlying policy.

References and notes

1. Attributed to Bismarck. Quoted by Livingston Merchant, 'New Techniques in Diplomacy', in E.A.J. Johnson (ed.), *The Dimensions of Diplomacy* (Johns Hopkins Press, Baltimore, 1964) p. 126.
2. Robert O. Keohane and Joseph S. Nye, *Transnational Relations and World Politics* (Harvard University Press, Cambridge, Mass., 1973) pp. x–xxv.
3. See H.S. Teitelbaum, 'Immigration, Refugees and Foreign Policy', *International Organisation* (Summer 1984) esp. pp. 437–43; Edwin F. McWilliams, 'Hanoi's Course in Southeast Asia', *Asian Survey*, Vol. XXIV, No. 8 (Aug. 1984) pp. 878–85.
4. On Brazil's attempts to control its domestic market in mini and micro computers for Brazilian companies, through the October 1984 Informatics Law, see Anne Piorkowski, 'Brazilian Computer Import Restrictions. Technological Interdependence and Commercial Reality', *Law and Policy in International Business*, Vol. 17, No. 3 (1985) pp. 619–45.
5. Maxwell Watson, Russell Kincaid, Caroline Atkinson, Eliot Kalter and David Folkerts-Landau, *International Capital Martets: Developments and Prospects* (IMF, Washington, DC, Dec. 1986).
6. For the international crisis negotiations involving the Bank of England, Brunei, Singapore and other states following the collapse of the merchant bank Barings, see *Financial Times*, 3 March 1995.
7. Peter Calvert overstates this in terms of the inadequacy of archives, in *The Foreign Policy of New States* (Wheatsheaf Books, Sussex, 1986) pp. 83–4, 95–6.
8. See Thomas Princen, 'Mediation by the Vatican', in Jacob Bercovitch and Jeffrey Z. Rubin, *Mediation in International Affairs* (St Martins, London, 1992), pp. 155–6.
9. Robert Wendzel, *International Relations: A Policymaker Focus* (John Wiley, New York, 1980).
10. See K.J. Holsti, *Why Nations Realign* (George Allen and Unwin, London, 1982) Ch. 1.
11. See Fola Soremekun, 'Angola', in Timothy M. Shaw and Olajide Aluko (eds), *The Political Economy of African Foreign Policy* (Gower, Aldershot, 1984) pp. 36–7; Garrick Utley, 'Globalism or Regionalism? United States Policy Towards Southern Africa', in Robert Jaster (ed.), *Southern Africa* (Gower, Aldershot, 1985) pp. 27–8.
12. Documents on the early post-independence period can be found in Peter Boyce, *Malaysia and Singapore in International Diplomacy* (Sydney University Press, 1968).
13. See *Far Eastern Economic Review*, 11 Aug. 1983, pp. 72–3.
14. See Alison Broinowski (ed.), *Understanding Asean* (Macmillan, London, 1982).
15. Henry Kissinger, *The White House Years* (Weidenfeld and Nicolson, London, 1979) pp. 127–30 for an explanation of the concept of linkage, and *Department of State Bulletin*, 14 Oct. 1974, p. 508.
16. The agreements included the Joint US–USSR Commercial Commission, 26 May 1972, TIAS, Vol. 26, Part 2 (1975) pp. 1335–9; commercial facilities agreement, 3

Oct. 1973, TIAS, Vol. 24, Part 2, 1973, p. 2223; long-term economic and industrial co-operation agreement, 29 June 1974, TIAS, Vol. 25, Part 2, 1974. The US–USSR commercial facilities agreement of 22 June 1973 lists the ten approved corporations allowed to operate in and with the USSR under the agreement, including Pullman, Occidental Petroleum, Chase Manhattan and the Caterpillar Tractor Company, and can be found in TIAS, Vol. 24, Part 2 (1973) p. 1503.

17. See J.A. Ballard, *Policymaking in a New State. Papua New Guinea 1972–77* (University of Queensland Press, London, 1978).

18. For a discussion of the concept of foreign policy control in the context of French diplomacy and reorientation, see Edward L. Morse, *Foreign Policy and Interdependence in Gaullist France* (Princeton University Press, NJ, 1973) pp. 24, 38–44.

19   See Lela Garner Noble, *Philippine Policy Toward Sabah* (University of Arizona Press, Tucson, 1977).

20. For the same kind of point illustrated over tariff barriers by Japan on Indonesian plywood exports, see *Far Eastern Economic Review*, 14 Feb. 1985, p. 92.

21. One of the few accounts in English of the Norwegian attempts to join the EEC and the referendum is Hilary Allen, *Norway and Europe in the 1970s* (Universitetsforlaget, Oslo, 1979).

22. See *Financial Times*, 28 Feb. 1985.

23. *Italian Yearbook of International Law* (Napoli, Editorial Scientifica, 1983) pp. 352–3, on the exchange of notes between Italy and Malta, 15 Sept. 1981, on Malta's neutralised status.

24. See *Annual Report* (Government of India, Ministry of External Affairs, 1970–84).

25. Wayne A. Selcher, *Brazil's Multilateral Relations* (Westview Press, Boulder, Colo., 1978) pp. 221–2.

26. See *Monthly Review*, Bank of Thailand, Vol. 26, No. 2 (Feb. 1985) pp. 77–80 on Thai–Saudi trade relations.

27. See *Financial Times*, 26 Feb. 1985; *Sunday Times*, 5 May 1985.

CHAPTER 4

Diplomatic correspondence

In modern diplomatic practice states generally use four methods for communicating directly with one another and other international actors. These are notes, letters, memoranda and *aides-mémoire*. In addition political leaders and other national personalities communicate with one another directly or indirectly through speeches, statements, communiqués and interviews with the press. Declarations, too, have become an important feature of modern international political life. We are, however, mainly concerned in this chapter with the four methods of diplomatic communication noted above. Examples are provided of some of the different usages of each of the forms of communication, although the variety of state practice makes it difficult to lay down hard-and-fast rules as to when one method should be used rather than another. The examples themselves have been chosen from a wide variety of international problems as a way also of introducing the reader to the documentation on some of the post-war issues. From this range of material it is hoped to convey some of the flavour and scope of post-war diplomacy and diplomatic exchanges.

Notes

Notes are the most widely used form of diplomatic correspondence. It is necessary to distinguish those notes which form a correspondence and may either be in the first or third person, from notes or letters which are used to bring an agreement into effect. The note is probably, despite the range of usage, the most formal of the four methods under discussion. When used in the third person the note generally commences with customary courtesies (the Embassy of — presents its compliments to) and concludes in a similar manner (avails itself of the opportunity, etc.). In certain circumstances, for example protest notes or in third-person correspondence sometimes with an international organisation, customary formalities may be partly or wholly dispensed with. Paragraphs in the note are not normally numbered and the note is initialled but not signed. In some state practice, for example Japan, the third-person note is styled a *note verbale*. In these instances, the title *note verbale* is put at the head of the note, but there are no other significant differences. The *note verbale* is used in diplomatic practice within the United Nations, as an alternative to a letter, for the circulation to members of statements, or reports.[1]

Note Verbale dated 2 December 1994 from the Secretary-General addressed to the President of the Security Council

The Secretary-General presents his compliments to the President of the Security Council and, in accordance with paragraph 8 of Security Council resolution 816 (1993) of 31 March 1993, has the honour to bring to his attention further information received by the United Nations Protection Force (UNPROFOR) regarding apparent violations of the ban on flights in the airspace of Bosnia and Herzegovina.

Between 29 November and 1 December 1994, there appear to have been 18 flights of fixed or rotary-wing aircraft in the airspace of Bosnia and Herzegovina other than those exempted in accordance with paragraph 1 of resolution 816 (1993) or approved by UNPROFOR in accordance with paragraph 2 of that resolution. Details as to the itinerary of flights in the reporting period are attached as an annex to the present note verbale.

The total number of flights assessed as apparent violations is now 3,317.

_____

(S/1994/5/Add.87, 5 December 1994)

Uses of diplomatic notes

Diplomatic notes are used for a variety of purposes ranging from routine matters of administration between an embassy and host foreign ministry, registration of treaties, granting or refusing overflight clearance, peace proposals through to official protests at the actions of other states. An interesting illustration of an exchange of notes on peace proposals followed from the so-called Soviet 'peace note' of 10 March 1952 on German reunification. The Soviet note, proposing a peace treaty and the formation of an all-German government, was put forward at a time when Cold War tension had heightened following the Berlin airlift crisis and the Bonn Basic Law establishing the Federal Republic. Negotiations were in progress between the Western powers to establish a European Defence Community (EDC) and ultimately incorporate a rearmed West Germany into NATO. The German problem was a central Cold War issue and the Soviet proposal foundered among other things on the question of free elections and the unwillingness of the Western powers to let a four-power conference in Germany slow up progress on EDC. The following are extracts from the exchanges:[2]

Text of a Note to Her Majesty's Government in the United Kingdom Handed to Her Majesty's Ambassador at Moscow by the Deputy Minister of Foreign Affairs of the Union of Soviet Socialist Republics on 10 March 1952.

The Soviet Government consider it necessary to call the attention of Her Majesty's Government in the United Kingdom to the fact that although seven years have passed since the war ended in Europe a peace treaty with Germany has still not been concluded. ...

... Analogous notes have been sent by the Soviet Government to the Governments of the United States and France.

APPENDIX

Soviet government's draft of a peace treaty with Germany
Political provisions

* Germany is restored as a united state. The partition of Germany is thereby ended and the united Germany obtains the possibility of developing as an independent, democratic peace-loving State.
* All armed forces of the occupying Powers must be withdrawn from Germany not later than one year from the day the peace treaty goes into force. Simultaneously with this all foreign military bases on the territory of Germany will be liquidated.
* Democratic rights must be guaranteed to the German people so that all persons under German jurisdiction, irrespective of race, sex, language or religion, may enjoy the rights of man and the fundamental freedoms including freedom of speech, press, religious cults, political convictions and assembly.
* The free activity of democratic parties and organisations must be made secure in Germany, they being granted the right freely to decide their internal affairs, hold congresses and assemblies and enjoy freedom of press and publication.
* The existence of organisations hostile to democracy and to the cause of maintaining peace must not be permitted on the territory of Germany.
* All former servicemen of the German Army, including officers and generals, all former Nazis, save for those who are serving terms on conviction for crimes which they committed, must be granted civil and political rights on a par with all other German citizens for taking part in the building of a peace-loving democratic Germany.
* Germany pledges not to take part in any coalitions or military alliances aimed against any Power which participated with its armed forces in the war against Germany.

Territory The territory of Germany is defined by the borders established by the decisions of the Potsdam Conference.

Economic provisions No restrictions are placed on Germany as to the development of her peaceful economy, which must serve the growth of the welfare of the German people. Nor will there be any restrictions on Germany in respect of trade with other countries, navigation and access to world markets.

Military provisions

* Germany will be permitted to have its national armed forces (land, air and naval) necessary for defence of the country.
* Germany is permitted to produce military materials and materiel, the quantity or types of which must not go beyond the confines of what is required for the armed forces established for Germany by the peace treaty.

Germany and the United Nations The States which have concluded the peace treaty with Germany will support Germany's application for admission to membership of the United Nations.

The British Government's reply was delivered to the Soviet Union by the Chargé d'Affaires in Moscow in a note of 25 March 1952. The note sets out the basic British position on the German question, including concern over the relationship between the formation of an all-German government and talks on a peace treaty, frontiers and German rearmament.[3]

Text of a Note to the Soviet Government Delivered by Her Majesty's Chargé d'Affaires at Moscow on 25 March 1952.

1. Her Majesty's Government in the United Kingdom in consultation with the Governments of France and the United States have given the most careful consideration of the Soviet Government's note of 10th March which proposed the conclusion of a peace treaty with Germany. They have also consulted the Government of the German Federal Republic and the representatives of Berlin.

2. The conclusion of a just and lasting peace treaty which would end the division of Germany has always been and remains an essential objective of Her Majesty's Government. As the Soviet Government themselves recognise, the conclusion of such a treaty requires the formation of an all-German Government, expressing the will of the German people. Such a Government can only be set up on the basis of free elections in the Federal Republic, the Soviet Zone of occupation and Berlin. ...

3. The Soviet Government's proposals do not indicate what the international position of an all-German Government would be before the conclusion of a peace treaty. Her Majesty's Government consider that the all-German Government should be free, both before and after the conclusion of a peace treaty, to enter into associations compatible with the principles and purposes of the United Nations.

4. In putting forward their proposals for a German peace treaty, the Soviet Government expressed their readiness also to discuss other

proposals. Her Majesty's Government have taken due note of this statement. In their view, it will not be possible to engage in detailed discussion of a peace treaty until conditions have been created for free elections and until a free all-German Government, which could participate in such discussion, has been formed. There are several fundamental questions which would also have to be resolved.

5. For example, Her Majesty's Government noted that the Soviet Government make the statement that the territory of Germany is determined by frontiers laid down by the decisions of the Potsdam Conference. Her Majesty's Government would recall that in fact no definitive German frontiers were laid down by the Potsdam decisions, which clearly provided that the final determination of territorial questions must await the peace settlement.

6. Her Majesty's Government also observe that the Soviet Government now consider that the peace treaty should provide for the formation of German national land, air and sea forces, while at the same time imposing limitations on Germany's freedom to enter into association with other countries. Her Majesty's Government consider that provisions of this kind would be a step backwards and might jeopardise the emergence in Europe of a new era in which international relations would be based on co-operation and not on rivalry and mistrust. ...

The exchanges on the Soviet note, which became known as the 'battle of the notes' continued until September 1952. A four-power conference was not convened until 1954 in Geneva. As Coral Bell comments:[4] 'Since the Soviet negotiating position of March 1952 was never really explored it is not of course possible to identify the note with certainty as a "bargaining bid", rather than a delaying bid.'

Protest notes

When states find it necessary to protest at certain actions this may be done verbally, by calling the ambassador or chargé to the foreign ministry. Alternatively, depending on the context and type of protest, a protest note may be issued. When put in the form of a note, the purpose is usually to place on record for political or legal purposes the state's position. This may form the basis for a claim or counter-claim at a subsequent date, or be a means of seeking political support in a wider forum.

A number of reasons for protests can be distinguished, such as seeking to stop a policy developing (e.g. to contest a state's offshore maritime legislation); secondly, to protect interests (e.g. to maintain or counter a boundary claim by another state, or the occupation of territory); thirdly, to affirm the right to do something (e.g. offshore exploration); or fourthly condemn an action (e.g. repeated or serious violation of air or sea space; arrest of vessels; breaches of cease fire) with a view to exerting pressure to get violations stopped.

Nuclear testing

The following examples illustrate these and other uses. The first illustration is taken from New Zealand's dispute with France over the French decision in 1963 to alter the location of its long-term nuclear test programme from the Sahara to the South Pacific. A number of protests and other diplomatic efforts were made by New Zealand to try and change the French decision. New Zealand subsequently took the case to the International Court of Justice (ICJ) on 9 May 1973.[5] The following are extracts from the second New Zealand note of protest, the French reply of 25 June 1963[6] and the New Zealand position on overflight.[7]

Note from New Zealand Embassy to French Ministry of Foreign Affairs, 22 May 1963

The French authorities have been aware for some time of the grave concern felt by the New Zealand Government at various reports concerning France's plans to conduct test explosions of nuclear devices in the South Pacific region. The New Zealand Government has sought clarification of the intentions of the French Government in this respect through the New Zealand Embassy both in interviews with officials of the Ministry of Foreign Affairs and in the Embassy's Note of March 1963. In that Note it was indicated that if reports concerning the French Government's intention to test in the South Pacific were confirmed, the New Zealand Government would wish to convey certain other views to the French authorities. In spite of recurrent and increasingly detailed reports, which have produced growing public anxiety in New Zealand, it has continued to await official confirmation, in response to the Embassy's Note, that a decision to proceed with the establishment of a nuclear testing centre in the area has been taken.

On and about 2 May, reports of a press conference given in Papeete by General Thiry, head of a French civil and military mission, appeared both in the French metropolitan press and in New Zealand. It appeared from the statements attributed to General Thiry that a decision to establish a nuclear test zone in the area of Mururoa Atoll had been taken. Oral confirmation that a nuclear test zone had been decided on in the area described was subsequently given by the Ministry in response to enquiries by the Embassy.

In these circumstances, and even though it is understood that a period of some years may elapse before the first test can be held, the New Zealand Government feels compelled without further delay to present its views to the French authorities . ...

The New Zealand Government must therefore protest strongly against the intention of the French Government to establish a nuclear testing centre in the South Pacific. It urges that the French Government reconsider, in the light of the views advanced in this Note, any decisions which may already have been taken.

Note from French Ministry of Foreign Affairs to New Zealand Embassy, 25 June 1963

Le Ministère des affaires étrangères présente ses compliments à l'Ambassade de Nouvelle-Zélande et a l'honneur de lui faire part de ce qui suit:

Le Ministère des affaires étrangères à pris connaissance avec attention de la note 1963/10 du 22 mai par laquelle l'Ambassade de Nouvelle-Zélande faisait connaître le point de vue de son gouvernement sur la création d'un polygone de tir français pour des essais nucléaires en Polynésie et au sujet de la cessation des essais nucléaires.

La position de la France à l'égard des expériences nucléaires est bien connue et n'a pas varié. A de nombreuses reprises ses représentants ont rappelé que l'immense pouvoir de destruction que représentent pour l'humanité les armes nucléaires demeurerait intact si la suspension des expériences n'était pas accompagnée de l'arrêt contrôlé des fabrications nouvelles et l'élimination progressive et vérifiée des stocks d'armes existants.

Le Gouvernement français demeure prêt à s'associer à tout moment à une politique de désarmement qui soit efficace et contrôlé. Mais en l'absence d'une telle politique et aussi longtemps que d'autres puissances posséderont les armes modernes il estime de son devoir de conserver sa liberté dans ce domaine.

C'est dans cette perspective qu'une décision tendant a l'établissement d'un polygone de tir pour des essais nucléaires en Polynésie française a été prise. Un delai assez long s'écoulera encore avant que ce champ de tire soit équipé et que des expériences nucléaires puissent y être effectuées.

Au demeurant le Gouvernement français croit devoir rappeler qu'il ne sera pas le premier à effectuer de telles expériences dans le Pacifique. D'autres Etats l'ont fait avant lui ainsi que le sait le Gouvernement de la Nouvelle-Zélande et il pourrait en être encore de même à l'avenir.

Le Ministère des affaires étrangères croit devoir également souligner que les services français chargés de la réalisation des essais nucléaires dans cette region veilleront tout particulièrement à assurer la protection des populations des pays riverains de l'océan Pacifique Sud. A cet égard le Gouvernement français se propose, ainsi qu'il en a déjà été fait part à l'Ambassade de Nouvelle-Zélande, de faire connaître aux autorités néozélandaises, au moment opportun, les conditions dans lesquelles se dérouleront ces expériences et les mesures prises pour éviter tout risque de retombées et éventuellement d'en discuter avec ces autorités.

Le Ministère des affaires étrangères saisit cette occasion pour renouveler à l'Ambassade de Nouvelle-Zélande les assurances de sa haute considération.

Note from New Zealand Ministry of External Affairs to French Embassy, 15 April 1966

The Ministry of External Affairs presents its compliments to the Embassy of France and has the honour to refer to the Embassy's Note No. 23 of 13 April 1966, which requested authorization for an aircraft of the French Air Force to overfly the islands of Niue and Aitutaki in the course of a flight from Noumea to Hao.

The Ministry desires to inform the Embassy that steps have been taken to advise the Ministry of Foreign Affairs in Paris that if the French Government proceeds with its intentions to conduct a series of nuclear weapons tests in the South Pacific Ocean, New Zealand, consistent with its obligation under the Partial Nuclear Test Ban Treaty of 1963, will be unable to grant authority for any visits to New Zealand territory by French military aircraft or ships or overflights of New Zealand by French military aircraft, unless assured that they are not carrying material intended for the test site, or for the monitoring of the tests, or for the support of forces and personnel engaged in the tests or in monitoring the tests, other than monitoring to detect possible health hazards. ...

Note from New Zealand Ministry of External Affairs to French Embassy, 19 April 1966

The Ministry of External Affairs presents its compliments to the Embassy of France and has the honour to refer to the Embassy's Note No. 23 of 13 April and the Ministry's Note No. PM 59/5/6 of 15 April 1966.

The Ministry has been in consultation with the Government of the Cook Islands concerning the Embassy's request for authorization of the DC8 of the French Air Force to overfly Aitutaki on 24 April in the course of a flight from Noumea to Hao. The Government of the Cook Islands has requested that the Embassy be informed that its position is precisely the same as that of the New Zealand Government and that it cannot grant permission for the overflight without a similar assurance to that requested by the New Zealand Government.

The Ministry of External Affairs avails itself of this opportunity to renew to the Embassy of France the assurances of its highest consideration.

Note from French Embassy to the New Zealand Ministry of External Affairs, 21 April 1966

L'Ambassade de France présente ses compliments au Ministère des affaires extérieures, et a l'honneur de lui accuser réception de ses notes en date des 15 et 18 avril derniers, qui contiennent la réponse du Gouvernement néozélandais à la demande d'autorisation de survol de l'île Niue et de l'archipel des Cook présentée au nom de son gouvernement.

Les modalités de la réponse néozélandaise ont été communiquées au Gouvernement français. Celui-ci a fait savoir a l'Ambassade qu'il souhaitait annuler sa demande. De ce fait, au cours de l'étape Nouméa–Hao, qui avait fait l'objet de cette demande, l'appareil militaire français se tiendra à l'écart de tout territoire et eaux territoriales néozélandais.

L'Ambassade de France saisit cette occasion pour renouveler au Ministère des affaires extérieures les assurances de sa très haute considération.

Protests at dumping wastes

The growing use of the coastal and ocean areas for land-based sourced discharges, toxic dumping and other activities such as the disposal of the military bi-products of the Cold War, has led to increases in the number of protests in this area. For example, Japan has protested on a number of occasions over Russian Federation nuclear dumping in the Sea of Japan, off the Maritime Provinces.[8]

Maps, boundaries and claims

States regard questions to do with boundaries and territory, such as the publication of maps by other states, claims and boundary adjustments, as highly sensitive matters. For example, India found it necessary to protest to the People's Republic of China about the map attached to the Burmese–Chinese Boundary Treaty. India contested the map which showed the western extremity of the Sino-Burmese boundary as ending at the Diphu L'Ka Pass, whereas on Indian and other maps the tri junction was five miles north of the pass.[9]

Note from India to China, 30 December 1960

- The Government of India present their compliments to the Government of the People's Republic of China, and with reference to the text and the maps attached to the Burmese–Chinese Boundary Treaty of 1 October 1960 which were recently presented to the Parliament of the Union of Burma, have the honour to bring to the attention of the Government of the People's Republic of China the following facts pertaining to the western extremity of the Burma–China boundary, where it meets the eastern extremity of the India–China boundary.

- Although Article 5 of the Treaty does not specify the exact location of the western extremity of the Sino-Burmese boundary, in the map attached to the Treaty the boundary is shown as ending at the Diphu L'Ka Pass. The traditional boundary of India west of the Sino-Burmese boundary follows the watershed between D-chu in India and Lat-te in the Tibet region of China; and the tri-junction of India, Burma and China is five miles north of the Diphu L'Ka Pass, and not at the Diphu L'Ka Pass itself. The coordinates of the tri-junction are approximately longitude 97° 23′ east and latitude 28° 13′ north. The fact that the traditional boundary running along the Himalayan watershed passes through this point has in the past been accepted by the Governments of Burma and China and it has for many years been shown correctly on official maps published in India.

• The Government of India recognise that the text of the Treaty has left the exact location of this point unspecified. The Government of India are however obliged to point out that the extremity of the boundary between the two countries has been shown on the maps attached to the Treaty in an erroneous manner. As the location of the tri-junction at the Diphu L'Ka Pass has an adverse implication on the territorial integrity of India, the Government of India wish to make clear to the Government of the People's Republic of China that they would be unable to recognise this map in so far as it prejudicially affects Indian territory.

The Government of India take this opportunity to renew to the Government of the People's Republic of China the assurances of their highest consideration.

In the case of land or maritime boundaries which have been left incomplete and undelimited due to political disputes, difficulties can arise if attempts are made to close gaps or enclaves in a boundary. For example, Argentina issued a protest note on 24 August 1994 after the United Kingdom closed a gap in the 200 mile fisheries boundary of the Falkland Islands.[10]

Letter dated 23 August 1994 from the Permanent Representative of Argentina to the United Nations addressed to the Secretary-General

I have the honour to transmit to you the text of the protest note, dated 22 August 1994, from the Government of the Argentine Republic, regarding the unilateral measure taken by the United Kingdom of Great Britain and Northern Ireland extending its alleged maritime jurisdiction in the waters adjacent to the Malvinas.

I request that this note and its annex be circulated as an official document of the General Assembly, under item 45 of the provisional agenda of the forty-ninth session of the General Assembly entitled 'Question of the Falkland Islands (Malvinas)', and of the Security Council, and drawn to the attention of the Special Committee on the Situation with regard to the Implementation of the Declaration of the Granting of Independence to Colonial Countries and Peoples.

(*Signed*) EMILIO J. CARDENAS
Ambassador
Permanent Representative

(A/49/150; A/49/334/S/1994/24 August 1994)

In territorial disputes, in which territory has been occupied by one of the disputants, issuing a protest note serves to show that a claim is not extant, and the right to recover the territory is reserved. In the South China Sea conflict between *inter alia*, China and Vietnam, China protested over Vietnam's occupation of some of the Nansha islands:[11]

Letter dated 20 April 1987 from the representative of China to the Secretary-General

I have the honour to enclose herewith the text of the statement issued on 15 April 1987 by the spokesman of the Ministry of Foreign Affairs of the People's Republic of China concerning the illegal occupation by the Vietnamese authorities of some of China's Nansha Islands.

I should be grateful if you would have this letter and the full text of its enclosure circulated as an official document of the General Assembly and of the Security Council.

(*Signed*) LI LUYE
Permanent Representative of the
People's Republic of China to the United Nations

ANNEX

Statement issued on 15 April 1987 by the spokesman of the Ministry of Foreign Affairs of China

Recently Vietnamese authorities have once again encroached upon China's territorial integrity and sovereignty by brazenly sending troops to Bojiao Island of China's Nansha Islands and illegally occupying it. The Chinese Government has stated on many occasions that Nansha Islands as well as Xisha Islands, Zhongsha Islands and Dongsha Islands have always been China's sacred territory and that China has the indisputable sovereign right over these islands and their adjacent waters, which brook no encroachment by any country under whatever excuse and in whatever form. The Chinese Government strongly condemns the Vietnamese authorities for their illegal invasion and occupation of some islands of China's Nansha Islands and firmly demands that the Vietnamese side withdraw its troops from all the illegally occupied islands of Nansha Islands. The Chinese Government reserves the right to recover these occupied islands at an appropriate time.

Affirmation of rights

The use of protest notes to affirm rights is illustrated by the Libyan–Tunisian dispute over the delimitation of the continental shelf. During the course of the dispute the two sides signed a special agreement on 10 June 1977[12] to put the case before the ICJ. Prior to this Libya had granted oil concessions in the disputed sector of the Gulf of Gabes and undertaken exploratory drilling. Tunisia protested at the Libyan actions, but Libya rejected the Tunisian protests in a *note verbale* of 2 May 1976 and affirmed its right to carry out drilling on the disputed continental shelf.[13]

Note Verbale 1/7/76 Du 2 Mai 1976

Le ministère des affaires étrangères de la République arabe libyenne adresse ses compliments à la haute représentation de la République tunisienne et a l'honneur de la prier de transmettre ce qui suit au Gouvernement de la République tunisienne.

Se référant à la note du ministère des affaires étrangères tunisien no 1630 du 15 avril 1976 relative aux activités du bateau français *Maersk Tracker* lié par un contrat avec le Gouvernement de la République arabe libyenne pour effectuer des opérations d'exploration et de forage dans ses eaux territoriales et sur son plateau continental, le ministère des affaires étrangères de la République arabe libyenne désire affirmer ce qui suit:

1. Le Gouvernement de la République arabe libyenne rejette entièrement le contenu de la note du ministère des affaires étrangères tunisien no 1630 du 15 avril 1976.

En conséquence, le Gouvernement de la République arabe libyenne attire l'attention du Gouvernement de la République tunisienne sur le fait qu'il va continuer à exercer ses droits légitimes sur son territoire et poursuivre l'exploration et l'exploitation de ses eaux territoriales et de son plateau continental.

Il prie donc le Gouvernement de la République tunisienne de reconsidérer sa note no 1630 du 15 avril 1976 et de ne pas faire obstacle aux opérations d'activité economique ou autres de la République arabe libyenne dans cette région.

A La Haute Représentation
De La République Tunisienne Soeur
Tripoli

Violation of airspace

The following illustration is taken from the famous U-2 incident of May 1960. On 1 May 1960, in a major incident on the eve of the Paris summit, the Soviet Union shot down a US U-2 intelligence aircraft over Sverdlovsk. The United States issued the following note on 6 May 1960:[14]

As already announced on 3 May, a United States National Aeronautical Space Agency unarmed weather research plane based at Adana, Turkey, and piloted by a civilian American has been missing since 1 May. The name of the American civilian pilot is Francis Gary Powers, born on 17 August 1929, at Jenkins, Kentucky.

In the light of the above the United States Government requests the Soviet Government to provide it with full facts of the Soviet investigation of this incident and to inform it of the fate of the pilot. ...

The Soviet Union issued a protest note on 10 May 1960.[15]

Soviet Note to the United States, 10 May 1960

The Government of the Union of Soviet Socialist Republics considers it necessary to communicate the following to the Government of the United States of America.

At 5.36 a.m. (Moscow time), on May 1, this year, a military plane violated the frontier of the USSR and invaded the air space of the Soviet Union to a distance of over 2,000 kilometres. The Government of the USSR, of course, could not leave unpunished such a gross violation of the Soviet state frontiers. When the deliberate nature of the flight of the intruding plane became obvious, it was brought down by Soviet rocket forces near Sverdlovsk. ...

These and other data cited in the speeches by the head of the Soviet Government have utterly refuted the invented and hastily concocted story of the US State Department, set forth in an official press release on 5 May and alleging that the plane was conducting meteorological observations in the upper layers of the atmosphere along the Turkish–Soviet frontier.

It goes without saying that the Soviet Government has been compelled by the present circumstances to give strict orders to its armed forces to take all the necessary measures against the violation of Soviet frontiers by foreign aircraft. ...

The Government of the Soviet Union strongly protests to the Government of the United States of America in connection with the aggressive acts by American aircraft and warns it that should such provocations be repeated, the Soviet Government will have to take retaliatory measures, the responsibility for whose consequences will rest with the governments of the states committing acts of aggression against other countries. ...

The United States replied on 12 May to the Soviet protest note as follows:[16]

The Embassy of the United States of America refers to the Soviet Government's Note of 10 May concerning the shooting down of an American unarmed civilian aircraft on 1 May, and under instruction from its Government, has the honour to state the following.

The United States Government, in the statement issued by the Department of State on 9 May, has fully stated its position with respect to this incident.

In its Note the Soviet Government has stated that the collection of intelligence about the Soviet Union by American aircraft is a 'calculated policy' of the United States. The United States Government does not deny that it has pursued such a policy for purely defensive purposes. What it emphatically does deny is that this policy has any aggressive intent, or that the unarmed U-2 flight of 1 May was undertaken in an effort to prejudice the success of the forthcoming meeting of the Heads of Government in Paris or to 'return the state of American–Soviet relations to the worst times of the cold war'. Indeed, it is the Soviet Government's treatment of this case which if anything, may raise questions about its intention in respect to these matters.

For its part, the United States Government will participate in the Paris meeting on 16 May prepared to cooperate to the fullest extent in seeking agreements designed to reduce tensions, including effective safeguards against surprise attack which would make unnecessary issues of this kind.

Disputes on the record and the search for support

In some circumstances states transmit protest notes through the United Nations in order to publicise their case by putting it on record, or have the matter discussed by the Security Council. Many aspects of the Cyprus problem have been disputed through the UN in this way, such as the lodging of a protest note by the Cyprus Government against Turkish incursions of its air space.[17] In the dispute between the United Kingdom and Guatemala over Belize, the Guatemalan Government lodged with the Secretary-General, on 17 September 1981, the text of a protest note sent to the United Kingdom, for circulation as a Security Council document:[18]

Letter dated 17 September 1981 from the representative of Guatemala to the Secretary-General

(Original: Spanish)
(17 September 1981)

I have the honour to reproduce below the text of a note of protest against the United Kingdom dated 16 September 1981 and delivered yesterday to the Embassy of Switzerland, which is handling that country's affairs in Guatemala. The note reads as follows:

'The Ministry of External Relations presents its compliments to the Honourable Embassy of Switzerland, as the Embassy handling the affairs of the United Kingdom of Great Britain and Northern Ireland, and wishes to inform it that on Thursday, 10 September 1981, at 2 p.m., a British reconnaissance aircraft entered Guatemalan airspace without proper authorization, flying over several departmental capitals as well as over the national capital, at an altitude of 35,000 feet.'

'This unusual act constitutes a flagrant violation of the most elementary rules of international law and an abuse of territorial inviolability.

Moreover, it demonstrates the aggressive attitude of the British Government in provoking a peaceful nation so insolently.'

'The Ministry of Foreign Affairs request the Honourable Embassy of Switzerland to convey to the Government of the United Kingdom the most energetic protest of the Government of Guatemala against this act.'

Please arrange for this communication to be circulated as a Security Council document, with reference to Guatemala's request drawing the Council's attention to the dispute with the United Kingdom concerning the Territory of Belize.

(Signed) EDUARDO CASTILLO ARRIOLA
Permanent Representative of Guatemala
to the United Nations

Again, the United States protest note to Libya following the clash in the Gulf of Sirte, was transmitted to the President of the Security Council as a means *inter alia* of putting on the record US policy on freedom of navigation in international waters and the right of self-defence:[19]

Letter dated 19 August 1981 from the representative of the United States of America to the President of the Security Council

(Original: English)
(19 August 1981)

In accordance with Article 51 of the Charter of the United Nations, I wish, on behalf of my Government, to report that United States aircraft participating in a routine peaceful naval exercise in international waters in the Mediterranean Sea were subject to an unprovoked attack by Libyan aircraft. The attack took place at 0520 hours GMT on 19 August 1981. Acting in self-defence, United States aircraft returned fire, and two Libyan aircraft were shot down.

The United States Government today transmitted the following protest to the Government of Libya:

'The United States Government protests to the Government of Libya the unprovoked attack against American naval aircraft operating in international airspace approximately 60 miles from the coast of Libya. The attack occurred at 0520 GMT on 19 August 1981. The American aircraft were participating in a routine naval exercise by United States Navy Forces in international waters. In accordance with standard international practice, this exercise had been announced on 12 and 14 August through notices to airmen and to mariners. Prior notification of air operations within the Tripoli FIR (flight information region) had also been given. In accordance with these notifications, the exercise which began on 18 August will conclude at 1700 GMT 19 August.'

'The Government of the United States views this unprovoked attack with grave concern. Any further attacks against United States Forces operating in international waters and airspace will also be resisted with force if necessary.'

In view of the gravity of Libya's action, and the threat it poses to the maintenance of international peace and security, I ask that you circulate the text of this letter as a document of the Security Council.

(Signed) CHARLES M. LICHENSTEIN
Acting Representative of the United States of America
to the United Nations

In the course of long-running disputes, reporting frontier, airspace or maritime violations to the United Nations becomes an important feature of the propaganda battle or 'phoney' war (e.g. Iraq–Kuwait/Saudi conflict) to gain international allies and diplomatic support within the UN.[20]

Letter dated 29 November 1994 from the Permanent Representative of Iraq to the United Nations addressed to the President of the Security Council

On instructions from my Government, I have the honour to inform you that at 1115 hours on 7 November 1994 a Kuwaiti military helicopter coming from Kuwaiti territory entered Iraqi airspace and overflew the town of Safwan at an altitude of 800 to 1,500 metres. It then returned to Kuwaiti territory.

My government wishes to lodge a protest against this violation by the Kuwaiti side of the provisions of the cease-fire and the instructions relating to the implementation of the demilitarized zone.

I should be grateful if you would have this letter circulated as a document of the Security Council.

(Signed) NIZAR HAMDOON
Ambassador
Permanent Representative

Other uses of notes

Collective notes

A number of other uses of notes need to be distinguished. First of all a collective note is one which is presented by several parties to a government or international institution on a matter upon which they wish to make joint representation. In the case of a regional organisation (e.g. ASEAN, Caribbean Community (CARICOM)), the text may be delivered by the current chairman, secretary-general or individual ambassadors as appropriate. In a similar way letters may take a collective form.[21] An interesting example is provided by the collective letter to the UN Secretary-General signed by Fiji, Ireland and Senegal, representing the participating members of United Nations Interim Force in

Lebanon (UNIFIL), on the serious difficulties encountered by UNIFIL in carrying out its mandate in the Lebanon. Another illustration can be seen in the collective letter of Argentina, Brazil, Chile and the United States to the President of the Security Council in their capacity as countries guaranteeing the 1942 Peruvian–Ecuadorian Protocol of Peace, Friendship and Frontiers.[22]

Similar or identical notes

Apart from collective notes or letters, other uses take the form of identical and similar notes. The FRG, for example, sent identical notes to France, the United Kingdom, the United States and the USSR on the implications of the 1970 German–Polish normalisation treaty for other relevant treaties involving those powers:[23]

Note from the Federal Government to the Three Western Powers, 19 November 1970

The German Federal Foreign Office presents its compliments to Her Britannic Majesty's Embassy and has the honour to communicate to the Embassy the following text of a note of today's date of the Government of the Federal Republic of Germany to the Government of the United Kingdom of Great Britain and Northern Ireland.

In the course of the negotiations which took place between the Government of the Federal Republic of Germany and the Government of the People's Republic of Poland concerning this Treaty, it was made clear by the Federal Republic that the Treaty between the Federal Republic of Germany and the People's Republic of Poland does not and cannot affect the rights and responsibilities of the French Republic, the United Kingdom of Great Britain and Northern Ireland, the Union of Soviet Socialist Republics, and the United States of America as reflected in the known treaties and agreements. The Federal Government further pointed out that it can only act in the name of the Federal Republic of Germany.

The Government of the French Republic and the Government of the United States of America have received identical notes.

In the case of similar notes, states may agree after consultation to draft broadly similar though not identical language. This may occur when a number of states consult each other concerning the effect of reservations made by another state when acceding to an international treaty. Again, groups of states may agree to use similar language when reserving their positions on an issue.

Speaking and other notes

A quite different usage of note is in the sense of 'speaking notes' or *bout de papier*, which may be left at the end of a call or a meeting to act as a form of *aide-mémoire* to reduce the likelihood of misunderstanding about the points made. An example of the use of speaking notes occurred during US–North Vietnamese talks:[24] 'The US delegation repeated its position at twelve different meetings and on at least one occasion US negotiator Cyrus Vance read from "talking points", which he left on the table for his counterpart Colonel Han Van Lau to pick up.' In United Nations practice, finally, documents are issued by the Secretary-General with the title 'note'. These are not third- or first-person notes as such, have no formalities of introduction or conclusion but resemble rather memoranda. As such they tend to contain formal statements recording details of conference meetings or intercessional consultations.

Letters

Along with notes, letters are extensively used for diplomatic correspondence. Letters of correspondence should be distinguished, like notes, from letters which bring agreements into effect, although the opening and closing formalities are generally the same. Of the several uses of letters a number are worth highlighting. In the first place, a personal letter from one head of government (or foreign minister) to another is often used after changes of government or if relations between the states have been 'frozen' for some time due to a dispute. The letter may be delivered by an ambassador, or, more often, by a special envoy. A personal letter from one head of state to another may be used to supplement a note,[25] as well as make a diplomatic initiative or appeal. For example, President Reagan in an attempt to break the deadlock in negotiations on the Cyprus problem, sent a personal letter of 22 November 1984 to the President of Turkey, General Kenan Evren, urging resumption of negotiations.[26]

In conflicts states warn enemies, and on occasion, friends. The initial phase of the Cyprus problem provides a famous illustration of the latter. Against the background of growing Greek–Turkish Cypriot intercommunal violence and the possibility of military intervention by Turkey, President Johnson sent an extremely tough warning to Turkey on 5 June 1964. The so-called 'Johnson letter' has been described as the 'bluntest document ever sent to an ally'. In warning against intervention the letter to President Inonu continued:[27] 'I hope you will understand that your NATO allies have not had a chance to consider whether they have an obligation to protect Turkey against Soviet intervention, without the full consent and understanding of its NATO allies.'

The letter was also a model of Secretary of State, Dean Rusk, and Department of State drafting, in that it was sensitive to likely Turkish feelings and reaction. The tone of the letter was softened to appeal to Turkish national pride:[28]

We have considered you as a great ally with fundamental common interests. Your security and prosperity have been the deep concern of the American people, and we have expressed that concern in the most practical terms. We and you fought together to resist the ambitions of the communist world revolution. This solidarity has meant a great deal to us, and I hope it means a great deal to your government and your people.

Questions, explanation and lines of action

Letters are most commonly used to raise questions and explain policy, as well as set out intended lines of action. An example of the latter, which had a major impact on post-war Japanese orientation, is the so-called 'Yoshida letter'. The letter of 25 December 1951, from Prime Minister Shigeru Yoshida to John Foster Dulles, was the product of considerable pressure by Dulles to persuade the Japanese Prime Minister to conclude a peace treaty with the Republic of China and not Beijing. Yoshida was ambivalent as he sought to keep Japanese options open. However, he finally conceded shortly after the second meeting with Dulles on 18 December 1951 and accepted Dulles's draft memorandum. The Yoshida letter helped the peace treaty with Japan through the US Senate in March 1952. Japan continued to recognise the Nationalist regime in Taiwan until 1972, after which it changed its recognition policy, in the wake of revised policy of the United States (the so-called 'Nixon shock') to the People's Republic of China. The relevant section of the Yoshida letter sets out Japan's recognition policy as follows:[29]

My government is prepared as soon as legally possible to conclude with the National Government of China, if that government so desires, a Treaty which will re-establish normal relations between our governments in conformity with the principles set out in the multilateral Treaty of Peace, the terms of such bilateral treaty to be applicable as regards the territories now or hereafter under the actual control of the Japanese and Chinese National Governments ... I can assure you that the Japanese Government has no intention to conclude a bilateral Treaty with the Communist regime of China.

Crisis

In crisis diplomacy, states find it necessary sometimes to duplicate or reinforce the channels of communication. This might be a safeguard to ensure that their policy is actually getting through, or, alternatively, an attempt to influence opinion in the other state by the use of a wide number of channels. The former was no doubt the reason why, in the Cuban missile crisis, the United States attempted to use the Secretary-General of the United Nations as one of the routes to communicate the US decision on a 500-mile quarantine around Cuba to the Soviet Union:[30]

Letter of 27 October 1962, from Adlai E. Stevenson Defining Interception Area Around Cuba

Excellency:

My Government has instructed me to inform you that the 'interception area' referred to in your letter of 25 October to the President of the United States and in his reply of 26 October, comprises:

(a) the area included within a circle with its centre at Havana and a radius of 500 nautical miles, and,

(b) the area included within a circle with its center at Cape Maysi (Maisi), located at the eastern tip of the island of Cuba, and a radius of 500 nautical miles.

You may wish to pass the above information to Chairman Khrushchev, so that he can proceed in accordance with his 26 October letter to you, in which he stated that he had ordered the masters of Soviet vessels bound for Cuba, but not yet within the interception area, to stay out of the area.

Accept, Excellency, the renewed assurances of my highest consideration.

ADLAI E. STEVENSON

In the lead up to the Gulf War, former President Bush, in circumstances of mounting tension, sent Secretary Baker on a final mission to deliver a letter to President Saddam Hussein, at a meeting with Iraqi Foreign Minister Tariq Aziz in Geneva, warning Iraq not to use chemical or biological weapons and to step back from war. Aziz refused to deliver the letter, leaving it on the table and the talks broke up.[31]

Disputes and letters

A further general category of correspondence worthy of comment is the many types of letters states address to the Secretary-General and other UN office-holders in the course of a dispute. These may serve one of a number of purposes such as putting a complaint, establishing a case, indicating that UN recommendations have been complied with, or, as in the following example, internationalising a dispute by seeking to put it before the Security Council:[32]

Letter dated 16 September 1981 from the representative of the Sudan to the President of the Security Council

(Original: English)
(16 September 1981)

Upon instructions from my Government, I have the honour to inform you that in another wanton act of aggression aimed at destabilising the security and tranquillity of the Sudanese people, the occupying Libyan armed forces in Chad have once again committed a series of hostile acts of aggression against the sovereignty and territorial integrity of the Democratic Republic of the Sudan.

In gross violation of the principles of respect for sovereignty, territorial integrity and non-interference in the internal affairs of other States, the Libyan forces have escalated their acts of aggression against the Democratic Republic of the Sudan as follows:

1. On 10 September 1981, a Libyan military plane violated Sudanese airspace and bombed a number of Sudanese villages in the vicinity of Eltina area in western Sudan. No casualties were reported.
2. On 15 September, at 0600 hours and 0930 hours a number of Libyan planes based in Chad have twice bombarded Kulbus area in western Sudan. Four persons, including two children, were seriously injured in the souk (market-place).
3. On the same day, 15 September, at 1100 hours, two Libyan aircraft overflew the Sudanese city of El Geneina in another provocative act.

The Democratic Republic of the Sudan strongly condemns these repeated acts of aggression by Libya against the sovereignty and territorial integrity of the Sudan in flagrant violation of the principles and objectives enshrined in the Charter of the United Nations.

The Democratic Republic of the Sudan would like to draw the attention of the Security Council to the dangerous situation arising from the repeated Libyan acts of aggression against the Democratic Republic of the Sudan which would undoubtedly lead to the destabilization of the region and threaten International peace and security. The Democratic Republic of the Sudan trusts that the Council will closely follow the situation and take all necessary and appropriate measures to ensure that such Libyan acts of aggression would immediately stop and not be repeated.

My Government reserves the right to seize the Security Council of the above-mentioned situation and requests that this letter be circulated as a document of the Council.

(*Signed*) ABDEL-RAHMAN ABDALLA
Permanent Representative of the Sudan
to the United Nations

Identical letters

In disputes, identical letters are issued by associated or allied states for a variety of purposes such as providing information, rebutting an opponent's claims and setting out policy. In some state practice an identical letter may actually take the form of a collective declaration.[33] Common to the declaration or joint letter is the intention of conveying solidarity and commonly defined purposes. During the continued dispute for example with Iraq following the Gulf war, Kuwait and Saudi Arabia have issued a number of identical letters rebutting Iraqi claims of provocative military action.[34]

Identical letters dated 16 August 1994 from the representatives of Kuwait and Saudi Arabia addressed respectively to the Secretary-General and the President of the Security Council

With reference to the letter dated 19 July from the Minister for Foreign Affairs of Iraq in document S/1994/843 and concerning allegations by Iraq of warplanes taking off from the territory of the Kingdom of Saudi Arabia and the State of Kuwait and perpetrating provocative acts, we wish to inform you that the Governments of the Kingdom of Saudi Arabia and the State of Kuwait officially deny these allegations, which are entirely unfounded.

We should be grateful if you would have this letter circulated as a document of the Security Council.

(*Signed*) NASSER AL-SABEEH	(*Signed*) GAAFAR ALLAGANY
Chargé d'affaires	Ambassador
Permanent Mission of the State	Permanent Mission of the
of Kuwait to the United Nations	Kingdom of Saudi Arabia
	to the United Nations

Setting out positions

Letters to the Secretary-General or President of the Security Council are most frequently used by states to set out their view on an issue before the Council or Assembly. Small states in particular have relied heavily upon transmitting rapidly to the Secretary-General information on military attacks by more powerful neighbours and seeking support through personal diplomacy by their resident representative to the UN. Laos for example has extensively used the technique reasonably successfully to put a 'brake' on Thailand, during the course of the ongoing Laos–Thai frontier disputes.[35]

Letter dated 28 December 1987 from the representative of the Lao People's Democratic Republic to the Secretary General

Upon instructions from my Government, and further to my earlier correspondence, in particular my letter dated 17 December, as well as the letter of the Permanent Representative of Thailand of 22 December [S/19378], I have the honour to transmit to you herewith the text of a statement issued on 27 December by the Ministry of Foreign Affairs of the Lao People's Democratic Republic on the Thai military attack against Lao territory.

I should be grateful if you would arrange to have the text circulated as an official document of the General Assembly and of the Security Council.

(*Signed*) KITHONG VONGSAY
Permanent Representative of the
Lao People's Democratic Republic
to the United Nations

ANNEX

Statement issued at Vientiane on 27 December 1987 by the Ministry of Foreign Affairs of the Lao People's Democratic Republic

The government of the Lao People's Democratic Republic, since its foundation on 2 December 1975, has consistently pursued a policy of peace, friendship and good-neighbourliness with the Kingdom of Thailand, for the two peoples share similarities as to race, language, traditions and customs, enabling them to create better relations on a political basis, as stipulated in the Lao–Thai and Thai–Lao joint communiqués signed by the two Governments in 1979.

But it is regrettable that this policy of the Lao side has always been obstructed by the very serious frontier incidents between the two countries, particularly those of the three Lao hamlets in 1984, which are still far from being solved. This year, the Thai side once again has created a new grave incident: the Thai third army region forces have dispatched their paramilitary units to assure the protection of Thai private merchants engaged in the illegal felling of fine wood in Lao territory on the west side of Na Bo Noi canton, Botene district, Sayaboury province. And between 14 and 18 August 1987, the Thai side sent several infantry battalions to occupy this area, repeatedly attacked the Lao local force strongholds which are defending that area and then proclaimed deliberately this area to be part of Thai territory by unilaterally claiming that Nam Huang Nga river constitutes a frontier between the two countries. This arrogant claim runs counter to the 1907 Franco-Siamese treaty, which stipulates the following on the side of Luang-Prabang: 'The frontier leaves the Mekong river, in the South, at the mouth of Nam Huang river and follows the thalweg of this river up to its source located at Phou Khoa Mieng mountain. From there the border follows the watershed between the Mekong river and the Menam river until it reaches the Mekong river at the point called Keng Pha Day.

Reports

Reports undertaken by UN envoys, representatives and other mediators are sometimes circulated to UN members as letters. For example the text of the Contact Ministerial Group (France, Germany, Russian Federation, United Kingdom, and the United States) statement on territorial and other solutions for Bosnia–Herzegovina was issued in this form.[36]

Cease-fire violations

Letters are the commonest form for expressing concern for circulation to the Security Council or as a more general document within the UN. Thus a state can attempt to focus the attention of the Security Council on specific aspects of a cease-fire violation, or other aspects of a mandate. In this form the letter can become close to a protest note. For example Bosnia–Herzogovina drew attention to continual attacks against Bihac by Croatian and Bosnian Serb forces, despite the cease-fire.[37]

Letter dated 27 December 1994 from the Permanent Representative of Bosnia and Herzegovina to the United Nations addressed to the President of the Security Council

While there is supposed to be a cease-fire throughout the Republic of Bosnia and Herzegovina, the Bihac region continues to be under the coordinated attack of the so-called Croatian and Bosnian Serb forces. It appears that some United Nations spokespersons have adopted the view that this does not constitute a violation of the cease-fire because, as they claim, the attacks are coming solely from elements directed by the so-called Croatian Serbs. (These assertions are being made by the same authorities who, at the height of the onslaught against the Bihac safe area, when it was politically convenient, maintained that there was no evidence of involvement on the part of the so-called Croatian Serbs.) In our view, this endeavour of ignoring the coordinated forces seriously undermines the credibility of the cease-fire and those who are empowered to enforce it.

May I ask for your kind assistance in circulating this letter as a document of the Security Council.

(Signed) MUHAMED SACIRBEY
Ambassador and Permanent Representative˙

Secretary-General

Finally we should note the use of correspondence by the UN Secretary-General for two important purposes: to initiate or recommend action, and defend action taken. The first of these functions is illustrated in the Secretary-General's letter to the President of the Security Council on the United Nations Angola verification Mission (UNAVEM II). In a letter of 7 December 1994 the Secretary-General indicated that, despite uncertainties on the cease-fire, he intended to proceed on the basis of Resolution 952 (1994) to restore the strength of UNAVEM to its previous level.[38]

Letter dated 7 December 1994 from the Secretary-General addressed to the President of the Security Council

As members of the Security Council will recall, paragraph 4 of Council resolution 952 (1994) of 27 October 1994, with the aim of consolidating the implementation of the peace agreement on Angola in its initial and most crucial stages, authorized the restoration of the strength of the United Nations Angola Verification Mission (UNAVEM II) to its previous level of 350 military observers and 126 police observers, with an appropriate number of international and local staff. The deployment of such additional personnel would take place upon receipt of my report to the Security Council that the Government of Angola and the Uniao Nacional para a Independencia Total de Angola (UNITA) had initialled a peace agreement and that an effective cease-fire was in place.

Council members are aware that the representatives of the Government and UNITA initialled the Lusaka Protocol on 31 October 1994 and signed it on 20 November.

Having assessed the situation, and in accordance with the provisions of resolution 952 (1994), I intend to proceed with the restoration of the strength of UNAVEM to its previous level, with an appropriate number of international and local staff, and the deployment of the mission throughout the country. I should like to stress that the actual enlargement of the mission would be dependent on the strict observance by the parties of an effective cease-fire, and on the provision by them of satisfactory guarantees regarding the safety and security of the United Nations personnel concerned.

In addition to existing tasks, the mission would monitor and verify all major elements of the Lusaka Protocol and provide good offices to the parties, including at the local level. If need be, it would conduct inspections/investigations of alleged violations independently, or jointly with the parties. In the meantime, my Special Representative would chair the Joint Commission in charge of implementation of the provisions of the Protocol.

I would be grateful if you would bring these matters to the attention of the members of the Security Council.

(*Signed*) BOUTROS BOUTROS-GHALI

Letters have also been used by the Secretary-General to provide detailed explanations of the legal and administrative basis for actions taken. A clear example of this usage was the extended rebuttal by the Secretary-General of Iraqi criticism of the procedures he proposed to use to establish a Boundary Commission to demarcate the Kuwait–Iraq boundary under Security Council Resolution 687 (1991). The Secretary-General argued *inter alia*:[39]

Letter dated 30 April 1991 from the Secretary-General addressed to the Minister for Foreign Affairs of Iraq

I have the honour to refer to your letter dated 23 April 1991, which was transmitted to me by a letter of the same date from the Permanent Representative of Iraq to the United Nations and which contained comments on the proposals made with regard to the implementation of paragraph 3 of Security Council resolution 687 (1991) and on which I must report to the Security Council no later than 2 May 1991. ...

The first comment of your Government is that, in international law, a boundary demarcation between two States can be carried out only by agreement between the parties and that the Security Council has no competence to impose such a demarcation. In this connection, I would like to recall that, in paragraph 2 of Resolution 687 (1991) the Security Council, acting under Chapter VII of the Charter of the United Nations demanded that Iraq and Kuwait respect the inviolability of their international boundary and the allocation of islands 'set out in the "Agreed Minutes between the State of Kuwait and the Republic of Iraq regarding the Restoration of Friendly Relations, Recognition and Related Matters", signed by them in the exercise of their sovereignty at Baghdad on 4 October 1963'. In paragraph 3 of that resolution the Council called upon me to lend my 'assistance to make arrangements with Iraq and Kuwait to demarcate the boundary between Iraq and Kuwait'. In an identical letter dated 6 April 1991 addressed to me and to the President of the Security Council (S/22456), your Government formally notified its acceptance of the provisions of that resolution. You further reconfirmed your Government's acceptance of paragraph 3 of resolution 687 (1991) at the end of your letter of 23 April 1991 (see annex II, enclosure). ...

Secondly, your Government states that the proposed demarcation would be prejudged by a specific reference to a map made available by the United Kingdom and which, according to the letter, the Legal Counsel described as 'a factual point'. I wish to state that the Legal Counsel of the United Nations did not describe the map as having been mentioned in the 1963 agreed minutes. In response to a question as to which map was referred to in document S/22412, your Permanent Representative was informed that the map in question was a 'United Kingdom map'. On a substantive level, however, I am obliged to point out that the resolution provides that the demarcation of the boundary should be based on 'appropriate material, *including* the map transmitted by Security Council document S/22412' [emphasis added]. In the light of this wording, I have proposed that the Commission will have to make 'necessary arrangements for the identification and examination of appropriate material relevant to the demarcation of the boundary'.

Thirdly, your Government queries the independence of experts to be appointed by me to serve on the Boundary Commission and comments on the proposed decision making by majority. I would like to assure you that, in appointing the independent experts of the Commission, I shall, as always, base my decisions on the need to ensure independence, competence and integrity. Furthermore, to ensure an equitable approach and the effective functioning of the Commission, I have proposed that neither Government should be able to frustrate the work of the Commission. ...

(*Signed*) JAVIER PÉREZ DE CUELLAR
Secretary-General

Draft letters

Draft letters should be distinguished from speaking notes. The draft letter is in effect a form of an advanced copy of a text. Its purpose is to alert another state as to the likely contents and use it as a vehicle for conveying reassurance or clearing up misunderstandings. For example President Clinton's European special envoy presented clarifications of United States policy towards the Russian Federation over the NATO 'partnership for peace proposals' in the form of a draft letter to President Yeltsin in February 1995.[40]

Negotiation by correspondence

The last usage of letters discussed in this section is that of the conduct of negotiations by correspondence. In exchanges of this type states might seek to obtain agreement about interpretations of a treaty or draft article, establish general principles or question certain interpretations. A clear example of this type of 'positional' negotiation can be found in the diplomatic correspondence of the opening sessions of the Preparatory Commission for the International Sea-bed Authority. The Preparatory Commission, or 'Prep. Comm.' as it became known, had been set up as part of the machinery envisaged under the Law of the Sea Convention, which was opened for signature on 10 December 1982. The purpose of the Commission was to establish rules and regulations for the international management of deep sea-bed resources in line with the provisions of the Convention. Several states, including the Soviet Union and India, were anxious to register as so-called 'pioneer' investors, within the timetable laid down by the Convention, and have their proposed areas of exploration registered with the Commission. Difficulties arose in that the Convention envisaged exchanges of co-ordinates taking place, although at that point generally accepted procedures for this and other matters connected with the working of the Commission had not been agreed upon.

Some states, including France, generally sought to protect their position, while others criticised the Soviet and Indian interpretations. The exchange opens with the Soviet letter to the chairman of the Preparatory Commission on 6 April 1983:[41]

The delegation of the USSR to the first session of the Preparatory Commission for the International Sea-bed Authority and for the International Tribunal for the Law of the Sea hereby transmits to the Commission the following information provided for in paragraph 5(a) of resolution II.

... the absence in resolution II of any provisions concerning reciprocal obligations of certifying States regarding the exchange of co-ordinates of areas for the purpose of determining the existence of conflicts has thus far precluded the possibility of initiating negotiations with other certifying States on the resolution of such conflicts. ...

The Soviet Union also assumes that all certifying States which by 1 May 1983 send such notifications to the Preparatory Commission, their enterprises or companies will, after the resolution of any conflicts that may arise, be registered as pioneer investors, that they will be allocated pioneer areas in pursuance of their applications and that these areas will in future be considered areas previously allocated as pioneer areas as specified in paragraph 5(a) of resolution II.

The USSR delegation requests that this letter be circulated as an official document of the Preparatory Commission.

(Signed) I.K. KOLOSSOVKSY
Chairman of the USSR delegation
to the first session of the Preparatory Commission
for the International Sea-bed Authority
and for the International Tribunal
for the Law of the Sea

The Soviet position and that of India, was opposed by France in a letter of the 28 April:[42]

Letter dated 28 April 1983 from the Permanent Representative of France to the United Nations addressed to the Chairman of the Preparatory Commission

My Government has taken note of the letter dated 24 April 1983 addressed to you by the Permanent Representative of India to the United Nations (LOS/PCN/7).

In that letter, the Government of India proposed that prospective certifying States should exchange by 1 May 1983 the co-ordinates of the areas in which pioneer investors would like to conduct pioneer activities within the meaning of resolution II governing preparatory investment and that negotiations should be initiated by that same date with a view to resolving any possible disputes. In addition, the Government of India stated that, if it did not receive any response on that matter by 1 May, it would feel free to proceed with the procedure laid down in resolution II. The Government of India thus suggested that it could already be registered at the current stage as a pioneer investor.

The French Government cannot accept such a position, with respect to which it has the same objections as those set out in the letter dated 27 April 1983 which it had the honour to send to you in response to the letter of 6 April from the Chairman of the delegation of the Union of Soviet Socialist Republics (LOS/PCN/8). It holds that no right or preemption can be based on the letter from the Permanent Representative of India or on any steps taken subsequently by India, acting either alone or with the Soviet Union or any other country.

I should be grateful, Sir, if you would have this letter circulated before 1 May as an official document of the Preparatory Commission.

(Signed) LUC DE LA BARRE DE NANTEUIL
Permanent Representative of France
to the United Nations

The French position was supported by Canada. In particular Canada was concerned to see the talks, which it had initiated in July 1982, on procedures for dealing with disputes about overlapping mining site claims, to be concluded before a state could register with the Preparatory Commission as authorised to approve mining operations.[43] In reply the Soviet Union disputed the French interpretation and commented as follows on the significance of the Canadian-initiated talks:

Preparatory Committee for the International Sea-bed Authority and for the International Tribunal for the Law of the Sea

Letter dated 29 April 1983 from the Permanent Representative of the Union of Soviet Socialist Republics to the United Nations Addressed to the Chairman of the Preparatory Commission[44]

The Soviet Union has studied the letter dated 27 April 1983 from the Permanent Representative of France to the United Nations addressed to the Chairman of the Preparatory Commission for the International Sea-bed Authority.

... an attempt is made in this letter to place on the same footing States which have signed the Convention and States which have not signed it, and to confer on the latter rights granted only to signatory States. ...

The Canadian initiative regarding consultations among interested countries for the purpose of drafting a 'Memorandum of understanding on the settlement of conflicting claims with respect to sea-bed areas', to which the Permanent Representative of France refers, does not and cannot impose any obligations on signatory States.

The Soviet Union also appreciates the usefulness of achieving the relevant 'gentleman's agreement' concerning such an understanding; however, it does not consider this to be essential, since all questions concerning conflict resolution are settled by resolution II. The procedure for the resolution of possible conflicts of this kind has long been established by international practice, to which paragraph 5 of resolution II refers *inter alia* . ...

During the exchange of letters, a number of states, including the United Kingdom,[45] Belgium and Indonesia formally reserved their position:[46]

Letter dated 27 April 1983 from the Representative of the United Kingdom of Great Britain and Northern Ireland addressed to the Chairman of the Preparatory Commission

The delegation of the United Kingdom have noted the letter dated 6 April 1983 from the Chairman of the delegation of the Union of Soviet Socialist Republics addressed to the Preparatory Commission for the

International Sea-bed Authority and for the International Tribunal for the Law of the Sea (LOS/PCN/4).

It is the view of the United Kingdom that it is in the interests of all States with deep sea mining interests that there should not be an overlapping of exploration areas in the deep sea-bed. In the absence of generally agreed arrangements for eliminating any possible overlaps, and having regard to its contingent interest, the United Kingdom reserves its position on the matters contained in that letter.

I request that this letter be circulated as an official document of the Preparatory Commission.

(*Signed*) PAUL FIFOOT
Leader of the United Kingdom delegation
to the Preparatory Commission

Following these exchanges the Indian note of 12 May indicated that co-ordinates had been exchanged with the Soviet Union, and both countries subsequently sought registration as pioneer investors:[47]

Note Verbale dated 12 May 1983 from the Permanent Representative of India to the United Nations addressed to the Chairman of the Preparatory Commission

The Permanent Representative of India to the United Nations presents his compliments to the Chairman of the Preparatory Commission for the International Sea-bed Authority and for the International Tribunal for the Law of the Sea and, in continuation of his note of 24 April 1983 (LOS/PCN/7) and upon instructions received from the Government of India, has the honour to state as follows.

The representatives of the Union of Soviet Socialist Republics and India met in New Delhi on 29 and 30 April 1983 and ensured themselves that, since the USSR intends to apply to the Preparatory Commission for registration and allocation of a pioneer area in the Pacific Ocean and India intends to apply to the Preparatory Commission for registration and allocation of a pioneer area in the central Indian Ocean, pursuant to the resolution governing preparatory investment in pioneer activities relating to polymetallic nodules, the areas in respect of which they intend to apply to the Preparatory Commission do not overlap one another. There is thus no conflict or controversy between the two countries in this regard. ...

Letter dated 20 July 1983 from the Acting Permanent Representative of the Union of Soviet Socialist Republics to the United Nations addressed to the Chairman of the Preparatory Commission[48]

... the Union of Soviet Socialist Republics, in accordance with resolution II of the United Nations Conference on the Law of the Sea, and as a certifying State, hereby submits to the Preparatory Commission on behalf of the Soviet enterprise Southern Production Association for Marine Geological Operations ('Yuzhmorgeologiya'), which is located in the town of Gelendzhik in the Krasnodarskiy district, and the General Director of which is Mr I.F. Glumov, an application for registration of the enterprise as a pioneer investor.

It is certified that this Soviet enterprise expended, before 1 January 1983, 40.9 million roubles on pioneer activities, as defined in resolution II, including 16 million roubles in the location, survey and evaluation of the area in respect of which this application is submitted. It is also certified that the list of coordinates of the area was submitted before 10 December 1982 by the Soviet enterprise concerned to the USSR Ministry of Geology as the State body with responsibility for issuing licences.

In accordance with paragraph 3(a) of resolution II, the application covers an area of the sea-bed 300,000 sq km having sufficient estimated commercial value to allow two mining operations. The area has been divided into two parts of equal estimated commercial value.

The data and information referred to in paragraph 3(a) of resolution II are being transmitted to the Preparatory Commission in a sealed packet in order to preserve their confidentiality as annex 1 to this application (5 maps).

The coordinates of the area, because of their strict confidentiality, are being kept by the Permanent Representative of the USSR to the United Nations in a sealed packet which will be transmitted immediately to the Preparatory Commission at your request as annex 2 to the application.

Memorandum

A memorandum is essentially a detailed statement of facts and related arguments. It resembles a note, but is stylistically far freer, has no opening or closing formalities and need not be signed. It may have a security classification and for convenience is often delivered with a covering letter, as in the following example:[49]

Letter dated 13 July 1981 from the representative of China to the Secretary-General

(Original: Chinese/English)
(14 July 1981)

I have the honour to transmit herewith the text of a memorandum of the Ministry of Foreign Affairs of the People's Republic of China on Sino-Vietnamese relations and request that this be circulated as an official document of the General Assembly and of the Security Council.

(*Signed*) LING QING
Permanent Representative
of the People's Republic of China
to the United Nations

ANNEX

Memorandum of the Ministry of Foreign Affairs of the People's Republic of China of 13 July 1981 on Sino-Vietnamese Relations

For some time the Vietnamese authorities have fabricated numerous lies and made unbridled slanderous attacks on China attributing to China the cause of the seriously deteriorated Sino-Vietnamese relations and of the turbulence in Indo-China and South-East Asia, in an attempt to confuse the right and wrong and cover up their acts of aggression and expansion so as to invent excuses for their intensified pursuance of the policy of regional hegemony. Therefore, the Chinese side deems it necessary to state the truth of the matter in order to set the record straight.

I. Why Sino-Vietnamese Relations Continue to Deteriorate

Since the end of Vietnam's war of resistance against United States aggression, the Vietnamese authorities have taken a whole series of measures to worsen Sino-Vietnamese relations. At present, they are stepping up these anti-China activities. Their professed willingness to improve Sino-Vietnamese relations is a sheer (sic.) gesture meant to deceive people. ...

II. The Root Cause of Tension in Indo-China lies in the Vietnamese Authorities' Attempt to Seek Regional Hegemony

The Vietnamese authorities assert that the present tension in Indo-China is caused by the so-called 'Chinese ambitions' rather than the policies of aggression and expansion they have pursued with the support of the Soviet Union. They even try to make people believe that the invasion and occupation of Kampuchea by 200,000 Vietnamese troops is for the purpose of dealing with the 'China threat'. However, the deeds of the Vietnamese authorities have provided an explicit answer as to who has single-handedly created turbulence and disaster in this region.

After the unification of Vietnam in 1976, the Vietnamese authorities went ahead with an ambitious plan in an attempt to establish their hegemonic rule in Indo-China. After it succeeded in gradually bringing Laos under its total control, Vietnam launched a large-scale war of aggression at the end of 1978, and occupied large parts of the Kampuchean territory and its capital Phnom Penh. At present, there are 50,000–60,000 Vietnamese troops and nearly 10,000 Vietnamese experts, advisers and secret police in Laos, controlling Laos' military, political, economic, cultural, propaganda and external affairs. ...

Modern usage of memoranda is very wide. For example, during the Iranian hostage crisis, the response of the United States Government of

8 November 1980 to the Iranian conditions set for the release of the US diplomatic hostages was delivered to the Iranian authorities by Algeria under a memorandum of 12 November 1980.[50] In 1970, Chancellor Willy Brandt and the GDR's Chairman of the Council of Ministers, Willy Stoph, held two historic meetings, first at Erfurt in March and then in Kassel. Following the Kassel meeting, Chancellor Brandt's twenty-point programme on the normalisation of inter-German relations was set out in a document which became known as the 'Kassel Memorandum'.[51]

The following illustrations indicate some further contexts within which memoranda have been used. In the first example, the Soviet Union delivered a memorandum to Japan on 27 January 1960, after the conclusion of the United States–Japanese Treaty of Mutual Co-operation and Security. The memorandum was a mixture of protest, warning and a statement of policy on the disputed northern islands:[52]

Memorandum from the Soviet Union to Japan, 27 January 1960

A so-called 'Treaty of Mutual Co-operation and Security' was signed between Japan and the United States on 19 January, this year. The contents of this treaty seriously affect the situation in the Far East and in the area of the Pacific, and therefore the interests of many states situated in that vast region, above all, of course, such direct neighbours of Japan as the Soviet Union and the Chinese People's Republic.

Under this treaty the stay of foreign troops and the presence of war bases on Japanese territory are again sanctioned for a long period with the voluntary consent of the Japanese Government. Article 6 of this treaty grants the United States 'use by its ground, air and naval forces of facilities and areas in Japan'. The treaty's reservations regarding consultations on its fulfilment cannot conceal the fact that Japan may be drawn into a military conflict against the will of the Japanese people.

The treaty perpetuates the actual occupation of Japan, places her territory at the disposal of a foreign power and alienates from Japan the islands of Okinawa and Bonin, and its provisions inevitably lead to the military, economic and political subordination of Japan. ...

The Soviet Government has repeatedly drawn the Japanese Government's attention to the danger of every step in international policy that increases the threat of a new war. It is obvious that at present there are particularly weighty grounds for such a warning. The conclusion of the military treaty by no means adds to Japan's security. On the contrary, it increases the danger of a catastrophe which would be the inevitable result of Japan becoming involved in a new war.

Is it not clear to everyone today that in conditions of a modern rocket-nuclear war the whole of Japan, with her small and densely populated territory, dotted, moreover, with foreign war bases, risks sharing the tragic fate of Hiroshima and Nagasaki in the very first minutes of hostilities? ...

Considering, however, that the new military treaty signed by the Government of Japan is directed against the Soviet Union, and also against the Chinese People's Republic, the Soviet Government cannot allow itself to contribute to an extension of the territory used by foreign armed forces by handling the aforesaid islands over to Japan.

In view of this, the Soviet Government considers it necessary to state that the islands of Habomai and Shikotan will be turned over to Japan, as envisaged in the joint declaration of the USSR and Japan of 19 October 1956 only on condition that all foreign troops are withdrawn from the territory of Japan and that a peace treaty is concluded between the USSR and Japan.

A common use of memoranda is in disputes to support a claim,[53] or establish a case, as in the Sino-Vietnamese example cited earlier. A particular line of policy of interpretation can be similarly set out to another government or organisation in a memorandum. During the Congolese Civil War, for example, the UN Secretary-General Dag Hammarskjöld issued a unilateral declaration of interpretation, in the form of a memorandum, on the controversial question of the nature and scope of the role of the UN peacekeeping force in the Congo and its relations with the central and provincial governments:[54]

Statement by Mr Hammarskjöld on the interpretation of paragraph four of the Security Council Resolution of 9 August, 12 August 1960

The Secretary-General, with reference to the Security Council resolution of 9 August 1960 (S/4426), has the honour to inform the Council of the interpretation which he has given to the Central Government of the Republic of the Congo, as well as to the provincial government of Katanga, of operative paragraph 4 of the resolution.

Memorandum on Implementation of the Security Council Resolution of 9 August 1960, Operative Paragraph 4

1. Operative paragraph 4 of the resolution of the Security Council of 9 August reads: 'Re-affirms that the United Nations Force in the Congo will not be a party to or in any way intervene in or be used to influence the outcome of any internal conflict, constitutional or otherwise'. The paragraph has to be read together with operative paragraph 3, which reads: 'Declares that the entry of the United Nations Force into the Province of Katanga is necessary for the full implementation of this resolution'.
2. Guidance for the interpretation of operative paragraph 4 can be found in the attitudes upheld by the Security Council in previous cases

where elements of an external nature and elements of an internal nature have been mixed. The stand of the Security Council in those cases has been consistent. It most clearly emerges from the policy maintained in the case of Lebanon which, therefore, will be analysed here in the first instance.

3. In the Lebanese question, as considered by the Security Council in the summer of 1958, there was a conflict between the constitutional President Mr Chamoun, and a group of insurgents, among them Mr Karame, later Prime Minister of the Republic. The Government called for United Nations assistance, alleging that a rebellion was fomented from abroad and supported actively by the introduction of volunteers and arms across the border. ...

8. Applying the line pursued by the Security Council in the Lebanese case to the interpretation of operative paragraph 4, it follows that the United Nations Force cannot be used on behalf of the Central Government to subdue or to force the provincial government to a specific line of action. It further follows that United Nations facilities cannot be used, for example, to transport civilian or military representatives, under the authority of their Central Government, to Katanga against the decision of the Katanga provincial government. It further follows that the United Nations Force has no duty, or right, to protect civilian or military personnel representing the Central Government, arriving in Katanga, beyond what follows from its general duty to maintain law and order. It finally follows that the United Nations, naturally, on the other hand, has no right to forbid the Central Government to take any action which by its own means, in accordance with the purpose and principles of the Charter, it can carry through in relation to Katanga. All these conclusions necessarily apply, *mutatis mutandis,* as regards the provincial government in its relations with the Central Government.

9. The policy line stated here, in interpretation of operative paragraph 4, represents a unilateral declaration of interpretation by the Secretary-General. It can be contested before the Security Council. And it can be changed by the Security Council through an explanation of its intentions in the resolution of 9 August. The finding is not subject to agreement or negotiation. ...

A further illustration of the use of a memorandum is the Finnish Government's proposal for the convening of a European security conference which was put to Western and other governments in its memorandum of 5 May 1969:[55] (extracts)

Memorandum from the Finnish Government on the Convening of a European Security Conference, 5 May 1969

The Government of the Soviet Union approached recently the governments of European countries in the matter of the arrangement of a

European security conference and of its preparations. This proposal concerning a special preparatory meeting was extended to the Government of Finland on 8 April 1969.

The Government of Finland has on several occasions stated that Finland considers a well prepared conference on European security problems useful. The Government of Finland considers well-founded the view of the Soviet Union that such a conference should be convened without any preliminary conditions. The participants should have the right to present their views and to make their proposals on European questions. ...

At the Foreign Ministers' meeting of Finland, Denmark, Iceland, Norway and Sweden, held in Copenhagen on 23 and 24 April 1969, a joint position was defined according to which 'preconditions for conferences on security problems are that they should be well prepared, that they should be timed so as to offer prospects of positive results, and that all States, whose participation is necessary for achieving a solution to European security problems, should be given opportunities to take part in the discussions. ...'

This is why the Government of Finland considers that the preparations for the conference should begin through consultations between the governments concerned and, after the necessary conditions exist, a preparatory meeting for consideration of the questions connected with the arrangements of the conference could be convened. ...

The Government of Finland is willing to act as the host for the security conference as well as for the preparatory meeting provided that the governments concerned consider this as appropriate.

The Government of Finland will send this memorandum to the Governments of all European States, to those of East and West Germany and to the Governments of the United States of America and Canada. ...

Finally, memoranda are frequently used in connection with treaties. In this usage the memorandum is to present to the other party a particular interpretation or understanding of a clause or section of the agreement. The memorandum may become the subject of a later exchange of letters. An interesting illustration of memoranda used in this way are the memoranda of the United Kingdom and the People's Republic of China, contained in the Draft Agreement on the Future of Hong Kong. The two memoranda set out the quite different interpretation each of the parties give to the definition and meaning of Hong Kong citizenship contained in the agreement.[56]

Aide-mémoire

The *aide-mémoire* is used widely and like a memorandum is extremely versatile in terms of the contexts within which it can be used. It is rather less formal, however, than a memorandum. In essence an *aide-mémoire* is drafted on the basis of discussions which have been held and is used to put forward new proposals such as a visit, conference, trade fair, an interpretation of policy or provide new information. Another use is in the sense of an *initiative*. For example proposals on the reform of the Security Council were put forward by France in the form of an *aide-mémoire* in December 1994.[57]

Extracts from the following three examples taken from United States practice indicate the wide variety of contexts in which an *aide-mémoire* can be used. The first example is from the United States dispute with Algeria over diplomatic property. The United States had acquired the property in 1948 and after Algerian independence carried out development work in 1962 on the site in order to build a new embassy. However, United States Embassy staff were subsequently refused entry to the site by the Algerian authorities. Later negotiations for an exchange of property for the Villa Mustapha Rais were inconclusive. In an *aide-mémoire* of 13 April 1979, the Department of State referred to discussions with the Political Counsellor of the Algerian Embassy, the essence of which was to link progress on the Algerian request for new chancery space in the International Centre in Washington to the United States claim regarding the Villa Mustapha Rais. The *aide-mémoire* in part reads:[58] 'The Department of State wishes to be responsive to the desire of the Algerian Embassy to obtain a suitable site for a new Chancery. At the same time, settlement of the United States claim, which dates from November 1964, remains a pressing concern of the United States Government.'

In the second example, the Department of State submitted an *aide-mémoire* on 6 March 1979 to the Soviet Embassy in Washington, in regard to the expiration on 31 March 1979 of the bilateral civil air transport agreement between them, signed orginally on 4 November 1966.[59] The *aide-mémoire* expressed United States dissatisfaction with the inequitable application of the existing agreement by the Soviet Union, and listed actions which it would have to carry out in order to preserve the current level of services permitted its carrier, Aeroflot, by the United States while negotiations for a more satisfactory, long-term air transport relationship were pending. A portion of the *aide-mémoire* follows:

There are several aspects of US–USSR air transport relations which continue to be unsatisfactory to the United States. Moreover, the basic equity of the current agreement is in question because of the one-sided nature of services now being provided.

Under these circumstances, the United States will wish to review the bilateral air transport relationship with a view to negotiating a more satisfactory long-term relationship at the appropriate time. Until such negotiations reach a new agreement, the US is not disposed to extend those current arrangements which expire on March 31, 1979.

Absent contrary action by the Civil Aeronautics Board, the foreign air carrier permit issued to Aeroflot provides only for two weekly roundtrip flights effective April 1, 1979. However, the United States does not wish to alter the status quo precipitously. Accordingly, the Civil Aeronautics Board is prepared to issue Aeroflot appropriate authority to continue to operate the level of services specified in the March 3, 1978 exchange of notes, that is, up to four flights during the summer season, subject to such change as the Board may order. Should a US airline propose to operate scheduled services to the USSR, the United States would expect the Soviet authorities to take comparable action.

The Soviet authorities should understand that the willingness of the United States to preserve the status quo for Aeroflot while negotiations are pending is dependent on the following Soviet actions:

1. Confirmation no later than March 30, 1979 that applications by US airlines, whether previously designated under the Civil Air Transport Agreement or whether they are scheduled or charter airlines, for charter flights between the United States and the USSR will be accepted and processed by the Ministry of Civil Aviation under the uniform procedural requirements presently applied to applications by Pan American World Airways.

2. Approval of charter flight applications presented by US airlines, whether previously designated under the Civil Air Transport Agreement or whether they are scheduled or charter airlines.

3. Satisfactory arrangements so that US airlines are able to participate on the basis of fair and equal opportunity in both scheduled and charter programs arranged by US tour operators, including the Russian Travel Bureau, in connection with the 1980 Olympic Games in Moscow.

Dept. of State File no. P79 0034-0754[60]

The third example is taken from the US–Canada Lockheed contract dispute. In 1976 Canada purchased eighteen long-range patrol aircraft from the Lockheed Corporation of the United States. Shortly before the purchase, the United States Government in an *aide-mémoire* to Canada of 29 April 1976, gave certain undertakings in the event of Lockheed insolvency, that Canada would receive advantage and considerations no less favourable than would the United States. The *aide-mémoire* also contained the US view regarding mutual security interests involved in Canadian acquisition of a modern long-range patrol capability:[61]

With respect to Lockheed's overall financial viability, its ability to continue as a corporation and to fulfil the terms of its proposed contract with the Canadian Government, the United States Emergency Loan Guarantee Board (ELGB) and the United States Department of Defense have recently reviewed Lockheed's financial position and have expressed confidence in Lockheed's prospects. ...

The United States Government shares with the Canadian Government a strong interest in the successful completion of the proposed Canadian procurement of eighteen Lockheed LRPA aircraft. In the view of the United States Government, the acquisition of these air-craft will substantially enhance Canada's ASW patrol capability, improve North American defense arrangements, contribute to NATO's overall security and thus is in the best interest of the United States. The pro-posed Canadian purchase will complement the purchase of a large number of Lockheed maritime patrol aircraft planned by the United States Government and should work to the mutual advantage of the two Governments. ...

If a situation were to occur under US bankruptcy laws involving voluntary or involuntary reorganization or bankruptcy of Lockheed which might affect Lockheed's contract performance, the United States Government, recognizing that it is in its best interest to do so, will act with Canada in all matters relating to the Canadian LRPA contract to obtain for Canada advantages and considerations no less favourable than those that might be obtained by the United States with respect to performance of its own defense procurement contracts. ...

Summary

Of the main means of diplomatic correspondence – notes, letters, mem-oranda and *aides-mémoire* – the note (*note verbale*) is probably the most formal despite the range of subject-matter it is used for. Exchanges of letters between heads of government have become an important element in the conduct of personal diplomacy. Written communication, in fact, whatever its form, is, despite developments in other forms of com-munication, still central to diplomacy. It is the means by which states put their position on record, explain the details of their policies, record protests, support claims, seek collective approval and carry out many other actions which make up the business of international relations.

References and notes

1. Security Council, S/1994/5/Add87, 5 December 1994.
2. Correspondence about the future of Germany, 10–25 March 1952, Cmd. 8501, March 1952. Reprinted by permission of the Controller of Her Majesty's Stationery Office.
3. Ibid., pp. 4–5.
4. Coral Bell, *Negotiations from Strength: A Study in the Politics of Power* (Chatto and Windus, London, 1962) p. 99.
5. Nuclear Test Cases, Vol. II, *New Zealand v. France,* ICJ, Pleadings, Oral Arguments, Documents, Annex III, p. 13, contains the list of notes exchanged.
6. Ibid., pp. 14–16.
7. Ibid., Annex IV, pp. 40–1.
8. See *Financial Times,* 20 October 1993.
9. *Documents on International Affairs* 1960 (Oxford University Press, London, 1964) p. 492.
10. S/1994, 24 August 1994.
11. *Security Council Official Records,* Supplement 1987 (New York, 1994), S/18818, 21 April 1987.
12. Case concerning the continental shelf, *Tunisia v. Libyan Arab Jamahiriya,* ICJ, Pleadings, Oral Arguments, Documents, Vol. 1, pp. 21–6.

13. Ibid., Annex 33, p. 260.
14. *Department of State Bulletin,* 23 May 1960, p. 818.
15. *Soviet News,* 11 May 1960.
16. *Department of State Bulletin,* 30 May 1960, p. 852.
17. See letter 13 Aug. 1981, from the representative of Cyprus to the Secretary-General, SCOR, 36th year, Supplement for July, Aug., Sept., S/14630, New York, 1983, pp. 40–1. Cf. SCOR, 1987, letter 2 Nov. 1987, protesting Turkish violation of Cypriot airspace.
18. Ibid., S/14694, p. 76.
19. Ibid., S/14632, pp. 41–2.
20. Iraq letter 29 Nov. 1994 to President of the Security Council, S/1994/1369, 1 Dec. 1994. See also identical letters of Kuwait and Saudi Arabia to the President of the Security Council, S/1994/980, 17 Aug. 1994.
21. This may take the form of an authorised statement. See for example Carlos Romulo's statement outlining the ASEAN position on Kampuchea, including the need for Vietnamese troop withdrawal and a UN-sponsored international conference, in SCOR, 36th year, S/14386, p. 51. The Vietnamese position, rejecting an international conference in favour of regional dialogue and consultation can be found in the collective letter of Laos, People's Republic of Kampuchea, and Vietnam, of 19 May 1981, in *Communist Affairs: Documents and Analysis,* No. 1 (Jan. 1982) pp. 134–5.
22. SCOR, 36th year, S/14384, pp. 49–50, and S/14362, pp. 35–6 for background information on the Peru–Ecuador dispute.
23. C.C. Schweitzer, D. Carsten, R.T. Cole, D.P. Kommers and A.J. Nicholls, *Politics and Government in the Federal Republic of Germany Basic Documents* (Berg Publishers, Leamington Spa, 1984) p. 305.
24. Gareth Porter, *A Peace Denied: The US, Vietnam and the Paris Agreement* (Indiana University Press, Bloomington, Ind., 1975) p. 74.
25. See for example Mr Macmillan's appeal for restraint to Mr Khrushchev in his letter of 19 July 1960, following East–West difficulties in the Committee of Ten on Disarmament, the second U-2 crisis and the Congo Civil War: 'I write to you now so plainly because I have the memory of our frank discussions with you in my mind. I simply do not understand what your purpose is today. If the present trend of events in the world continues, we may all of us one day, either by miscalculation or mischance, find ourselves caught up in a situation from which we cannot escape. I would ask you, therefore, to consider what I have said and to believe that I am writing to you like this because I feel it my duty to do so.' *Hansard,* House of Commons Vol. 627, Col. 253–6.
26. *The Sunday Times,* 16 Dec. 1984.
27. Edward Weintal and Charles Bartlett, *Facing the Brink* (Charles Scribner's Sons, New York, 1967) pp. 23–4.
28. Ibid., p. 24.
29. See Chihiro Hosoya, 'Japan, China, the United States and United Kingdom, 1951–2, The Case of the "Yoshida Letter" ', *International Affairs,* Vol. 60, No. 2 (Spring 1984) pp. 256–7.
30. See U Thant, *View from the UN* (David and Charles, London, 1977) Appendix I, pp. 466–7.
31. See Lawrence Freedman and Efrain Karsh, *The Gulf Conflict* (Faber and Faber, London, 1993) pp. 257–9.
32. SCOR, 36th year, S/14693, p. 76.
33. See for example the collective declaration of the Ministers for Foreign Affairs of the EC welcoming the peace plan adopted by the Presidents of Central American States, in Guatemala on 7 Aug. 1987, S/1928, 24 Nov. 1987.
34. S/1994/980, 17 Aug. 1994.
35. S/19389, 29 Dec. 1987.
36. Letter dated 5 Dec. 1994 from France, Germany, Russian Federation, United Kingdom and United States, to President of the Security Council, S/1994/1378, 5 Dec. 1994.
37. S/1994/1452, 28 Dec. 1994.

38. S/1994/1345, 8 Dec. 1994.
39. S/22558, 30 April 1991.
40. See *Financial Times,* 18 Feb. 1995.
41. LOS/PCN/4, 8 April 1983.
42. LOS/PCN/12, 29 April 1983.
43. LOS/PCN/15, 29 April 1983.
44. LOS/PCN/17, 29 April 1983.
45. LOS/PCN/13, 29 April 1983.
46. LOS/PCN/20, 12 May 1983.
47. LOS/PCN/21, 13 May 1983.
48. LOS/PCN/30, 24 Oct. 1983.
49. SCOR, 36th year, Supplement for July, Aug., Sept. 1981, S/14589, pp. 14–17. The Vietnamese reply is at S/14610, 22 July 1981, p. 28.
50. Pars News Agency, Tehran, 21 Dec. 1980.
51. Schweitzer *et al.,* op. cit., p. 381.
52. *Soviet News,* 29 Jan. 1960.
53. For example paragraph 3 of the Additional Memorandum of Morocco to the Secretary-General, of 14 Sept. 1960, on the dispute with France over Mauritania, states: 'The Notes which the Government of Morocco has dispatched since then, whenever France unilaterally changed the status of Mauritania, are eloquent in this connection. They place the Moroccan territorial claim in clear perspective and deny to the Government of France any exercise of competence in respect of Mauritanian territory.' GAOR, Fifteenth Session, Agenda item 79, Doc. A/4445/Add.1.
54. SCOR, 15th year, Supplement for July, Aug., Sept. 1960, S/4417/Add. 6, pp. 64–5, 70–1.
55. Finnish Embassy, London.
56. *A Draft Agreement on the Future of Hong Kong,* Misc., No. 20 1984, Cmnd. 9352, pp. 28–9.
57. Security Council 3483 meeting, 16 Dec. 1994.
58. *Digest of United States Practice in International Law,* 1979 (Department of State, Washington, 1983) pp. 576–7.
59. TIAS 6135; 17 UST 1909; entered into force 4 Nov. 1966 as amended, implemented, and supplemented.
60. *Digest of United States Practice in International Law* (Department of State Bulletin, 1983) pp. 1136–7; TIAS 6135; 17 UST 1909, 4 Nov. 1966.
61. *Digest of United States Practice in International Law,* 1976 (Department of State, Washington, 1977) pp. 746–8.

CHAPTER 5

Negotiation

Introduction

The aim of this chapter is to discuss both the nature of negotiation and the main characteristics of the negotiating process.

Negotiation can be defined as an attempt to explore and reconcile conflicting positions in order to reach an acceptable outcome. Whatever the nature of the outcome, which may actually favour one party more than another, the purpose of negotiation is the identification of areas of common interest and conflict.[1] In this sense, depending on the intentions of the parties, the areas of common interest may be clarified, refined and given negotiated form and substance. Areas of difference can and do frequently remain, and will perhaps be the subject of future negotiations, or indeed remain irreconcilable. In those instances in which the parties have highly antagonistic or polarised relations,[2] the process is likely to be dominated by the exposition, very often in public, of the areas of conflict. In these and sometimes other forms of negotiation, negotiation serves functions other than reconciling conflicting interests. These will include delay, publicity, diverting attention, or seeking intelligence about the other party and its negotiating position.[3]

The process of negotiation itself is sometimes conceived of in an 'across the table' sense. While the proceedings may take this form at some stage, the overall process, especially in a multilateral context, is better understood as including more informal activities leading up to or during negotiation, such as lobbying, floating a proposal through a draft resolution and exchanges of proposals and other consultations.[4] Negotiation too, of course, can be carried out 'at a distance', through formal or informal diplomatic correspondence, telephone, fax or e-mail.[5] The mode of negotiation itself may also change during negotiations from an 'across the table' working session, to correspondence between the parties about certain principles or detailed provisions of an agreement. Changes in the mode of this kind and other similar tactical demands for recess during negotiation can have either positive or negative effects on the process of reaching agreement. Change to negotiation by written means may serve to expedite the negotiating process, particularly if major principles and matters of substance have been resolved, reflecting substantial convergence over areas of common interest. If, however, unresolved issues remain from perhaps earlier rounds of exchanges, the possibilities for reopening these, uncertainty over the concession rate and the opponent's intentions, together with the effect of the delay, become important intervening considerations.[6]

Before we consider in detail particular definitions of negotiation, one further general observation is useful at this point. So far negotiation has been discussed in terms of the purpose and some features of the process; a third significant area relates to the changing forms of agreement which have been developed in more recent state practice. An important feature of modern practice, discussed at the end of the chapter, is the growth in 'unconventional' forms of agreement, in response to the complexity of issue areas and trend to multiparty agreements involving sovereign and non-sovereign actors.

Of the analytical literature,[7] Fred C. Iklé's book, *How Nations Negotiate* has had an important impact on the study of negotiation. Iklé has avoided a broad definitional approach which subsumes negotiation within the notion of bargaining or communication.[8] Such broader conceptions have tended to ignore or obscure features of the negotiating process, such as agenda setting, and the impact of the negotiating process on outcomes, in that they have focused on the wider context or setting of certain types of politico-strategic negotiation, involving warnings, threats and the use of coercive diplomacy.

In contrast, Iklé defines negotiations explicitly in terms of an exchange of proposals:[9]

negotiation is a process in which explicit proposals are put forward ostensibly for the purpose of reaching agreement on an exchange or on the realisation of a common interest where conflicting interests are present. It is the confrontation of explicit proposals that distinguishes negotiation from tacit bargaining and other forms of conflict behaviour.

Classification

A valuable aspect of *How Nations Negotiate* is the fivefold classification of international negotiation according to the purpose of the parties.[10] In the first of these, *extension* agreements (e.g. aviation landing rights, tariff agreements, renewal of a peacekeeping force mandate, renewal of leasing arrangements for an overseas military base), the purpose is to continue the existing state of affairs, and, as such, extension agreements are frequently, though not always, routine in nature. *Normalisation* agreements are intended to bring to an end conflict through, for example, cease-fire arrangements, a peace treaty or the re-establishment of diplomatic relations. Negotiations for the purpose of normalisation may involve a substantial degree of *redistribution* – the third category of negotiation. In a redistribution negotiation changes in the status quo or existing arrangements are sought in relation to, for example, territorial boundaries, voting powers in an international institution, budgetary contributions and similar matters. The fourth category is the *innovative* agreement. In negotiations on an innovative agreement the parties seek to establish different sets of obligations or relationships by transferring some degree of political and legal power to non-state institutions, as in the Treaty of Rome; devising new regulatory institutions such as the International Sea-bed Authority[11] or co-operative institutions as in the Mano River Declaration.[12] The Sino-British agreement of 1984 on the future of Hong Kong provides an interesting example of a normalisation and innovative agreement, setting out the status and powers of Hong Kong as a Special Administrative Region of the People's Republic of China.[13]

In the final category are negotiations for *side-effects*. In this type of negotiation one or more of the parties may seek objectives not directly related to reaching agreement. These can include putting on record statements of position, propaganda, gaining information about the negotiating position, strengths and weaknesses of the other party or undermining the resolve of an opponent.

The above categories provide a useful basic classification of negotiations, which can also be used to review changes in relations between states. The categories of course represent ideal types and in practice negotiations are often 'mixed' in character,[14] containing elements of pure bargaining,[15] normalisation and redistribution, because of factors such as the scope of the subject-matter or the extent of the differences between the parties. It is possible too for a party to misperceive or miscalculate the other's intention, regarding the negotiations, for example, as extension rather than redistribution.[16] Furthermore, in protracted and complex negotiations a party may change its strategy during the course of the negotiation from one of 'optimising' or seeking a high level of concessions to one of 'satisficing' in which more workable or less dramatic achievements are accepted, thus altering the form of the negotiation.[17]

While the basic fivefold classification scheme encompasses many types of negotiation, others are not so easily accommodated. These include: negotiations on communiqués ('textual', interpretative, ideological); inward or outward ministerial visits (bidding on dates, venues, agenda and matters of protocol); and draft articles in a working group of a multilateral conference (interpretative, with negotiations focusing on particular meanings, formulae and concepts). In addition, 'linked' negotiations have become a feature of bilateral negotiations between industrialised and developing countries in which the successful conclusion of one issue may be related to an entirely different political or economic issue. For example the government purchase of an item such as a naval vessel may be linked to changes in an air service agreement.

Classification by subject-matter

The basic scheme of classification discussed above can be complemented by considering negotiation in terms of the *subject-matter*. The

Table 5.1 Classification of subjects handled in international negotiations

Subject	Illustration
1 Political	Communiqués; draft resolutions; extradition; cultural agreement; boundary changes; exchanges of POWs; air highjacking; establishment of diplomatic relations; mediation; improvement or normalisation of relations
2 Development	Loan; bilateral aid (personnel, equipment); project finance; international capital market borrowing; inward investment; capital transfer; debt rescheduling
3 Contractual	Offshore exploration rights; sale/purchase of oil, LNG; equipment purchasers; hiring of foreign personnel
4 Economic	Trade agreement; balance of payments standby facility; tariff; anti-dumping; textile quota agreement; trade redistribution negotiation; sanctions
5 Security	Transit; overflight; establishment of border commission; arms purchase; bilateral security pact; joint development of weapons; mandate of peacekeeping force; base agreement; arms control
6 Regulatory	Convention against the use of mercenaries; law of the sea; flags of convenience, air services, fisheries; environmental; WTO; international commodity agreement; shipping; health; narcotics
7 Administrative	Inward/outward visit; acquisition of land or buildings for embassy; opening trade mission; visa abolition agreement; consular access to detained nationals; headquarters agreement; closure of international or regional organisation

indicative categories illustrating the range of modern negotiation are given in Table 5.1.

Multilateral negotiations

A third approach to considering differing types of negotiations is from the perspective of *process*. Using this perspective, which focuses on procedural influences and the roles of players and stakeholders, the following multilateral types can be distinguished for analytical purposes: (1) collegiate; (2) chair led; (3) fragmented multilateral; (4) technical specialist; (5) parliamentary; (6) informal. These categories can be used to complement the above two schemes (e.g. international negotiations on an innovative regulatory regime conducted on a collegiate basis).

Influences shaping negotiations

Broadly, three clusters of variables can be distinguished: the negotiating environment or setting, available assets and contingent variables. The first category – the setting – includes such factors as the location of the talks,[18] whether the negotiations are bilateral or multilateral; the extent to which the parties have regularised or friendly contact;[19]

abnormal or sensitive relations;[20] the amount of domestic support and the degree of directly or indirectly related international tension. The setting can influence:

1. The procedural conduct of negotiations as a result of the establishment of several working groups in a multilateral conference[21] or through institutional competence,[22] such as the Commission's responsibility for EU third-party fisheries agreements.[23]
2. The scope of negotiations (e.g. differences between external parties to a civil war can limit the mandate of a UN peacekeeping force).[24]
3. The content of a conference agenda.[25] A rotating presidency, conference chairman [or mediator] can attempt to structure a negotiation by putting forward proposals for an agenda, interpreting or articulating differences, as well as attempting to alter the pace of negotiation.[26]
4. Secrecy. Choice of setting can be used to promote the secrecy of talks and reduce or remove international media publicity. For example, the final Bosnian peace talks were held at a remote US airforce base near Daytona, Ohio, United States, where the principal protagonists and mediators were confined for a number of weeks. A further value of the site was that its tehnical computer facilities assisted the boundary and mapping aspects of the negotiations.

Other effects of setting can be seen in long-running bilateral and multilateral conferences in which decision-making becomes protracted because of repetitive statements of formal positions in plenaries and other meetings or the procedural need to agree regional positions. Indeed, some actors may have 'side effect' objectives or other personal stakes in simply keeping talks going without conclusion. Examples of inconclusive long-running negotiation fora include the 43-member UN Ad Hoc Committee on the Indian Ocean, which has held 438 meetings since 1971,[27] and the residual post UNCLOS negotiations on the Deep Seabed Mining regime from 1982 to 1992.[28] Routinised negotiations can sometimes be bypassed. For example the ritualised Israeli–Egyptian meetings at ambassadorial level in Washington DC were bypassed in 1993, in favour of secret talks involving Egyptian and Israeli non-diplomatic personnel, initiated and chaired by Norway.[29]

Second, there are those variables associated with the capabilities of the negotiating parties, such as the number and skill of diplomatic personnel,[30] the range of specialist expertise, proximity of negotiators to central power and the capacity to control the communications process in conflict.[31] Of these, negotiating style – that is, the characteristic ways in which national and international decision-makers approach negotiation, as a result of such influences as tradition, culture, bureaucratic organisation and perceptions of role – has received considerable attention. A number of studies have highlighted characteristics such as legalism,[32] attachment to declaration of principles, inflexibility[33] and crudeness.[34] In one case, the remarkable combination of meticulous deliberation and 'true grit' is seen as the hallmark of one particular national style.[35] A further, and indeed crucial component of negotiating capability is the range of deployable assets. These will include the extent of domestic approval, the nature and range of effective means, trade-off possibilities and the degree of external support.

The third category – contingent variables – consists first of all of such factors as the internal politics connected with the development and attainment of negotiating positions. Other contingent variables include the cohesion of a government or its delegation, how far 'opening' positions are re-evaluated, the concession rate, the impact of feedback and the influence of external events, such as a change of government, border clash or other incidents.[36]

The process of negotiation

Basic model

A basic model by which bilateral and some multilateral negotiation can be conceptualised is one in which the negotiations are seen as being a progression, in which the parties agree an agenda, outline and explore opening positions and seek compromises in order to narrow gaps between positions until a point of convergence is reached, which forms the basis for substantive agreement.[37] The model may be put schematically as follows:

1. Preparatory phase. (i) Preparation of national position; (ii) agree venue; (iii) outline agenda approved; (iv) level at which talks are to be conducted.
2. Opening phase (procedural). (i) Confirm credentials of the parties; (ii) re-establish purpose and status of the talks (e.g. whether they are informal or preliminary discussions, formal talks or whether any follow-up talks are envisaged and at what venue; (iii) working documentation; (iv) working procedures:
    (a) recess (if any);
    (b) language to be used;
    (c) rules of procedure;
    (d) agree which text or draft (if any) will be used as the basis for negotiation;
    (e) whether there is to be an agreed record.
3. Opening phase (substantive). (i) Confirm or amend agenda; (ii) exposition of opening position.
4. Substantive negotiation. (i) Exploration of areas of difference; (ii) construction of areas of agreement.
5. Adjournment of the negotiation for further rounds of talks (if appropriate).
6. Framework agreement reached.
7. Legal clearance and residual drafting amendments.
8. Initialling or signature of final agreement.
9. Statement on proceedings or communiqué.

Process

The preparatory and initial phases of a negotiation can take some considerable time. Thus matters such as the choice of the parties to be invited, for example the participation of the Vietminh at the 1954 Geneva Conference,[38] the National Liberation Front (NLF) in the 1968 Vietnam talks[39] and the Palestine Liberation Organisation (PLO) in the Geneva Middle East talks,[40] can be very contentious – so too can the content of the agenda[41] and even the shape of the negotiating table[42] became major obstacles to substantive progress in the initial phases of negotiation.

As far as procedural issues are concerned, the extent to which these may be dispensed with as routine or become contentious issues, depends very much on the closeness in the relations between the parties, the organisational setting and the kind of issues involved.[43] The early stages of the SALT I negotiations were taken up with the not uncommon problem of the ordering of items for discussion. In this case difficulties arose over whether to deal with an anti-ballistic missile (ABM) treaty first before moving on to offensive systems, or treat these in parallel.[44]

At the substantive phase, the negotiating process can take one of a number of forms. In 'polarised' negotiations, the process, as noted earlier, tends to be characterised by lengthy initial phases which involve exposition of positions and issues of principle.[45] In other forms of negotiation the progression can be conceptualised as one in which the parties move from opening positions, to seek compromises, narrow gaps between positions until a point of convergence is reached on an item or issue, which then forms the basis for the expansion of areas of agreement. This type of process might be incremental, or, less commonly, 'linear'. The latter form of progression is found for example in certain kinds of multilateral trade negotiations in which, ideally, a generally agreed 'across the board' tariff reduction is negotiated, so reducing the need for bilateral haggling. In practice, the 'linear' approach of the Kennedy Round was rapidly broken down as states attached lots of exceptions to their offers of tariff reduction.[46] A further illustration of the 'linear' approach can be found in the negotiating methods used by officials in the Committee on Trade and Tourism of ASEAN, which has progressively made percentage cuts or zero-rated categories of goods traded within ASEAN.[47]

Typically, the incremental process will involve attempts to narrow differences using one of a number of methods, such as establishing generally agreed principles; moving through an agenda by leaving areas which are sticking points on to other items upon which progress can be made; or trade-offs around blocs of concessions.[48]

A second element frequently involves the search for *referents*. These might include attempting to gain agreement for special rights such as fisheries access, transit landing or rights; acceptance of 'economy in transition status'; compensation or a pricing and specification formula in an international weapons supply contract. Other forms of referents may be of a conceptual nature such as the search to establish an agreed strategic 'language' in an arms control negotiation or mutually agreed conception of 'cost'. The search for and construction of referents forms a central part in negotiations of an incremental type. Without these negotiations tend to become bogged down or protracted. This type of difficulty can be seen for example in a number of international civil aviation renegotiations in which one of the parties attempts to revise route structures and schedules, but fails in the negotiations to reach mutually agreed definitions of cost.

Apart from these types, the substantive phase of certain bilateral or multilateral negotiations might be quite informal. Not all the phases outlined above would be gone through. Negotiators might confine themselves to broad general issues and leave details to a later date for officials to bargain over and clarify. Informal negotiations may also occur at the margins of *other* negotiations, particularly in regional organisations, for example the EU which perhaps may be addressing different issues. Furthermore, informal negotiations might lead to an agreement for example to adjust foreign or domestic policies (such as to intervene in currency markets or to apply drug laws more rigorously) in which nothing appears on paper. In these instances, the use of informal negotiations depends on the relations between the parties, the type of issue under discussion and other reasons such as the wish of the parties to retain some degree of flexibility and freedom of action.

Complex multilateral diplomacy

Apart from the above, a number of additional features of multilateral negotiations require comment. First, an important part of some multilateral negotiations is not a process of exchanges of concession which produces convergence, but rather exchanges and proposals which are part of information building;[49] concept development; establishment of principles, or, building up descriptive texts. Second, when issues concerning international standards or scientific processes arise,[50] convergence is often difficult, since 'purist' states refuse to accept 'dilution' of standards or procedures and insist on rigorous rules. Rules based on hard science, in this view, are preferable to flexible obligations or voluntary codes. In some instances, solutions can only be found in modifying not the standard but the terms of application.

Finally, in fragmented multilateral conferences with diffuse and highly complex agendas, deadlock has resulted in 'end run' negotiations, which seek formulae in the final sessions to avert the collapse of a conference. For example the collapse of the Intergovernmental Negotiating Conference on Desertification, which was divided on a number of major issues including financial arrangements for technical assistance, was averted by US proposals to defer solutions to financial arrangements until after the opening of the agreement for signature.[51]

Three areas of agreement

Three further features of the process of building up areas of agreement can be noted. First, structural complexity tends to be handled in one of several ways such as altering the level of responsibility in order to achieve a different perspective as well as flexibility (e.g. by changing the level of representative in a negotiation); frequent redefinition of the problem by building up information and revising draft texts, and the use of innovative negotiating structures.

In the second place, the diffusion of political power in complex multilateral conferences means that a number of states are able to wield a greater amount of influence than they normally would outside the context of such conferences. For example at the Law of the Sea Conference, Malta, Fiji, Cameroon, Peru and Venezuela have, through the skill and expertise of their individual representatives, played highly active roles.

For some states that influence may last only as long as their special area of interest remains unresolved; others, perhaps because of the chairmanship of a committee, specialist knowledge or skill in breaking deadlock, manage to play a consistently more important role on major issues. Minor powers like these have the capacity to block, delay or facilitate compromise like others, yet they have the advantage of far fewer domestic constraints. For larger powers constraints could stem, for example, from a large and divided delegation, pressure from a domestic 'constituency' or the need to appear frequently constructive. The representatives of minor states frequently enjoy a great deal of delegated power; in contrast, for the major powers the intervention in negotiation of a minister or senior adviser is not always appreciated by the technical negotiator, since the balance of initiative and decision shifts to the political élite.

Consensus

The second principal feature of the process of constructing consensus is that it is disjointed and fragmented. Substantial areas of disagreement remain as efforts are made to agree draft language in a text; trade blocs of issues or construct packages.[52] Packages in effect often have to be structured from the 'bottom up' as negotiators move through new terrain, assisted in some instances by referents and formulae from other contexts.[53] In practice too, there is considerable uncertainty as to the degree of support such efforts enjoy, since they are often made by the few or on a delegated basis, which then have to be presented and 'negotiated' as acceptable. During the process of structuring areas of possible agreement or packages, some difficult issues tend to be postponed to a later date or partially resolved, pending an overall settlement. The protracted nature of the negotiating process often means that issues which are only partially resolved can be reopened, thus temporarily halting or reversing the progress which has already been achieved. Examples of this occurred at the seventh session of UNCLOS when the United States reopened the question of the regime for marine scientific research, and, within the Uruguay Round, when France reopened the question of the intellectual property rights and electronic goods. In other instances efforts may be made to reinstate language from an earlier draft of a text, also risking reopening issues and unravelling of any emerging consensus.[54]

Issue learning curve

A third feature of multilateral conference diplomacy is the 'issue learning curve'. In complex innovative negotiation, negotiators progressively increase their knowledge of the issues at stake during the exploration of opposing positions and so gradually come to understand the ramifications of the problems as well as recognising potentially new dimensions for conflict or consensus-building.[55] The continued discovery of new facets of an issue presents negotiators with the opportunity to delay the search for agreements or maximise negotiating demands. A clear example of this phenomenon is provided by the negotiations on the issue of the regime for the international sea-bed which was probably the most complex and protracted issue at the UN Law of the Sea Conference. The construction of a regime for managing deep sea-bed resources brought together in a unique and novel manner an immense range of problem areas straddling private and public international law, involving such questions as the legal status of mining consortia, taxation, the rights of pioneer mining investors, the powers of the Global Mining Enterprise and the constitution of the Sea-bed Mining Council.

The process of reaching consensus on the regime was complicated further by the format of the regime. Unlike some international agreements establishing institutions which set out a general framework for the powers and functions of an organisation, the sea-bed regime has quite detailed provisions on production rates, taxation and so on. In the event, the overall regime which began to emerge gained the support of developing countries within the Group of 77 (G-77), but not the United States or a number of other sea-bed mining states.

Moreover, the proposals (e.g. taxation rates) were too detailed to be a basis for consensus, given especially the distant time-scale for cheap sea-bed mining. The level of detail was a reflection of the predominance of a small group of technical specialists from, for example, US, Canada, Germany, Australia, and expansion of negotiable issues, as the frontier of the issue learning curve was extended. Many of these provisions (e.g. taxation, transfer of technology, institutional arrangements) were overturned eventually in 1992–93 in the so-called 'compromise' Implementation Agreement, concluded as a supplement to the 1982 Law of the Sea Convention, to facilitate the accession of the US and other 'mining' powers to the Convention.

The dynamic of negotiation

The dynamic aspects of negotiation can usefully be understood through three concepts: focal points, the concession rate and momentum. Focal points may take a number of forms such as the British Government's demand for a policy of balance over the European Community budget and a specific reduction in contributions; blocs of policy issues, as in, for example, EU membership negotiations with Austria, Finland, Sweden and Norway, or particular assurances might be sought such as over the issue of guarantees on the political structure of Hong Kong, in the Sino-British talks on the future of the colony. As Iklé suggests:[56] 'focal points are like a notch where a compromise might come to a halt, or a barrier over which an initial position cannot be budged'.

Focal points therefore serve not only to reduce the options negotiators have to work within, but also act as a means of evaluating compromise. Secondly, the flow of negotiation will be influenced by the concession rate. In effect, the perceived extent to which a party makes a unilateral or reciprocal modification to its position serves to demonstrate *engagement* in or *commitment* to the negotiations. Concessions as such may be made either informally or formally. The possibility of a change of position can be indicated informally by modifications in negotiating style. In other instances a willingness to reach agreement may be signalled by not actually raising a sensitive item or by omitting it from conditions attached to a negotiating bid.[57] Conversely, delegations may signal continued dissatisfaction with a draft text by insisting on the retention of square brackets around parts or the whole of a draft article or section of an agreement. Formally, a concession may be indicated in several ways such as tabling a draft proposal, suggested modifications to an article in an agreement or contract, or withdrawal of a proposal.

The overall concession *rate* can be considered as consisting of sub-clusters of concessions, the pace of which will be influenced by several variables, including the degree of latitude in a decision-maker's instructions, whether parts of an issue remain 'closed' or non-negotiable and the extent to which decision-makers are operating under time constraints or deadlines. In bilateral negotiations, concessions tend to be more easily identified, unlike in complex multilateral diplomacy where the number of parties and scale of issues, some of which are quite often novel, make the construction of areas of agreement difficult. In multilateral negotiation, two elements in the concession rate need to be distinguished. First, there are those attempts at working group level to reach negotiated solutions. Second, there are the initiatives by the secretariat or specifically designated conference chairmen to construct so-called 'packages', or draft composite chairmen's negotiating texts, which link together broad areas of agreement or postpone partly resolved or contentious items. Another form of 'package' might entail a straight trade-off of concessions. The interplay between the low-level (working group) concession rate and the construction of overarching packages or composite negotiating texts is one of the main distinguishing features of complex multilateral diplomacy.

The third concept in terms of the dynamic of negotiation is the idea of momentum. Loss of momentum in negotiations may occur for several reasons such as the absence of a key negotiator, lack of movement on an issue or talks becoming bogged down in detail. Conversely, momentum may be sustained by regular negotiating sessions, the use of contact groups or third parties, as well as the concession rate discussed above.[58] Negotiators more rarely may seek to increase the momentum of negotiations by an ultimatum or setting a deadline. In the Sino-British talks on the future of Hong Kong, for example, the People's Republic of China set a deadline of 1 September 1984 for the conclusion of a framework agreement.

Characteristics of certain negotiations

The preceding sections of this chapter have looked at the negotiating process in general and some of the concepts which can be used to understand the processes of bilateral and multilateral negotiation. In the section on classification (Table 5.1) seven indicative categories were put forward as a way of grouping and reflecting the range of modern negotiation. Analysis of a number of negotiations in the categories would suggest that certain of the negotiations in the particular classes do have some broadly similar characteristics. In the first category, for example, negotiations on communiqués tend to be 'textual' in nature, with limited scope for trade-off, since the drafting is normally in the concluding phases of the proceedings.[59] As such communiqués are invariably negotiated under extreme time constraints, preferred positions tend to be either accepted or not, differences glossed to minimise public divergence and silence the norm on areas of major disagreement.

The effect of time constraints can also be seen in many other negotiations such as *ad hoc* law-making conferences, ministerial meetings of international organisations and multilateral conferences (category six), which have to be concluded by a specific date.[60] Closer to the conclusion of the conference the pace of negotiating (unless heavily polarised) tends to increase, with lengthy sessions and a not uncommon feeling of having to produce something – a joint statement, agreed text – or conclude the outstanding provisions of an agreement (despite differences), all of which may have varying effects on the degree of generality or precision of the terms of the agreement.

In category six, negotiations over regulatory agreements tend to be highly complex and structurally distinguished from other categories by mixed delegations of government and commercial interests, and high degrees of direct or indirect non-governmental group lobbying. Civil aviation negotiations (or more strictly renegotiations) tend to focus on one or two issues such as passenger capacity or new services. Agreements of the regulatory category are the least stable. Negotiations to change existing arrangements are normally lengthy, spanning several years of often inconclusive talks, as illustrated by Japan's unsuccessful efforts to revise the 1952 US–Japan Civil Air Transport Agreement from 1976.[61]

The international debt crisis has given rise to a new and unusual genre of financial 'rescue package' negotiations.[62] Debt rescheduling negotiations (category two) are multiparty negotiations involving heads of government, foreign and finance ministers, banking consortia, international banking officials and domestic economic, labour and banking interests in the rescheduling state. In these types of negotiations, political and economic élites in the rescheduling state are likely to be highly divided over strategies and policies, as the negotiations are conducted against a backdrop of shifting constraints in the form of deadlines, target dates and coercive pressures arising from the problems of meeting conditions attached to the rescue package. The pressures surrounding the rescheduling state were summed up by one director of a ministry of finance:[63] 'I go to New York and start ringing at one in the morning. The first hour to India and Singapore, the next hour I spend ringing the Middle East and then Germany, then Paris, then London and so it goes on.'

In category three, contractual negotiations tend to be handled at a specialist level. Contractual negotiations are also, unlike many other negotiations under discussion, distinct in that there is much less frequent ministerial or senior official involvement owing to the technical nature of the discussions, unless there is a major impasse. Negotiated agreements are frequently less stable, with renegotiation disputes arising out of the failure of a contracting party to purchase, for example, the amount of oil or gas agreed in a supply contract, or because price fluctuations in a commodity contract make the agreed pricing formula unattractive. The overall process of renegotiation can be quite lengthy, with the likelihood of adverse repercussions on other bilateral relations.

Multilateral conference negotiations

Collegiate style negotiations are characterised by the subdivision of negotiating issues into blocs or groups, which are allocated on a decentralised basis to sub-committees and working groups reporting to separate chairmen, subordinate to the conference president/plenary. In essence collegiate style negotiations involve building up of 'composite' single negotiating texts drawing on sub-committee drafts. The method was extensively developed during the law of the sea negotiations (1973–82)[64] and has been widely used subsequently, for example in the Uruguay Round. In contrast some multilateral conferences are predominantly chair-led, with texts filtered, refined and directed through the chair, usually assisted by a conference bureau, operating through lead delegations and private intercessional discussions with selected delegations. An example of chair-led negotiations is the UN conference on Straddling and Highly Migratory Fish Stocks (1993–96).[65]

Fragmented multilateral conferences generally have inconclusive preparatory phases; diffuse agendas and low political commitment by principal players to conference objectives, such as the World Population Summit, Cairo, 1994[66] and non or low-level attendance by principal players, as in the World Summit for Development (Stockholm, 1995).[67] These types of broad issue or thematic conferences contrast particularly with the standing or permanent technical meetings of UN specialised agencies such as IMO, FAO, IAEA, characterised by the co-ordinating and directing role of the lead core group, operating at sub-committee level and intercessional 'correspondence group' as a kind of sub-conference. Even in these types, extensive differences in technical conferences can emerge on central questions such as the economic cost of meeting enhanced international safety standards. For example, the 1995 diplomatic conference at IMO to revise the Safety of Life at Sea (SOLAS) Convention provisions on ro-ro passenger vessels, following the *Estonia* disaster, was deadlocked over higher international standards, and could only agree on a conference resolution permitting *ad hoc* additional regional agreements on specific stability requirements. Those arguing for world-wide implementation over a phased period of the lower existing ro-ro stability standards (SOLAS 90), rather than introducing revised higher standards to cover survivability with significant levels of water on deck, included the Russian Federation, Greece, France, Belgium, India, Egypt, Brazil, Spain, Cyprus and Panama. The group proposing higher international standards with special regional standards as only a last resort included United Kingdom, Denmark, Sweden, Finland, Norway, Estonia and United States. It is interesting to note that in this highly fragmented context, in the central debate over international as against regional standards, the regional approach was supported for different reasons both by the higher standards states (last resort) and by the maritime minimalists (e.g. Japan, Philippines, Indonesia, Bangladesh, Republic of Korea, China). For the latter, the regional argument was used ('special circumstances') to support the *non-application* of global higher international standards so as to *exempt* specific regions on geographical grounds, though in practice economic conversion or new building costs were the underlying reasons for the minimalists' position.[68]

Parliamentary style multilateral negotiations have been essentially influenced by the procedures, styles and practices of the UN General Assembly. These include extensive use of plenary debate; pluralism through one state one vote; and extensive numbers of multisponsored resolutions. Examples of parliamentary style negotiations are the proceedings of the preparatory Commission on the Status of Women[69] and the Assembly of the EU-ACP.[70] Finally, multilateral negotiations in informal meetings are generally not conducted on the basis of set rules of procedure.

Developments in international agreements

A number of important developments have taken place in the form and nature of modern international agreements. In the first place the increasing diversity of participants in the international system has led to the growth of agreements not just between sovereign states, but between states and a wide range of other actors ranging from international organisations, corporations, international credit banks, to shipping consortia. Secondly, these changes have been reflected in the growing informality of instruments which are negotiated and in particular the growth in usage of memoranda of understanding. The trend is in part influenced by national style, as well as convenience, since agreements and arrangements of this type avoid the requirement of constitutional approval. This usage, too, sometimes reflects the short-term intentions of the parties or incomplete nature of the agreement. Informal agreements have also been negotiated by states which do not have diplomatic relations to cover such matters as trade or fisheries regulation. In a third sense, the inability of states to finalise precise terms or reach definitive agreements has been reflected in the ways in which obligations are formulated. In this respect a number of novel forms of clauses giving effect to incompletely negotiated obligations have been developed such as the so-called 'gentlemen's agreement', barter or counter-trade agreements, 'implementation' agreements and voluntary or self-limitation clauses, covering, for example, ceilings on motor vehicle exports or steel production. These types of agreements or schedules in agreements have the advantage of flexibility and are intended to expedite the process of negotiation. On the other hand, the lack of durability of such arrangements and their potential for causing dispute has often offset the short-term advantages.

References and notes

1. Fred Charles Iklé, *How Nations Negotiate* (Harper and Row, New York, 1964).
2. See, for example, Robert L. Rothstein in *Global Bargaining* (Princeton University Press, Princeton, NJ) p. 150 *passim* on the polarised position during the integrated commodity negotiations at UNCTAD.
3. Iklé, op. cit., p. 31.
4. In a strict sense consultations are distinct from negotiation, although in practice the line between the two is blurred. Writing in the context of GATT, though applicable generally, Kenneth W. Dam notes: 'Although the carrying on of negotiations is to be distinguished from consultations, it is not clear to what extent the two exercises are to differ', in *The GATT* (University of Chicago Press, Chicago, 1970) p. 85.
5. Diplomacy by correspondence has been extensively used as a technique in conflicts by UN secretaries-general. The Secretary-General, perhaps rather more than national decision-makers, faces limitations on the amount of information he receives. In the 1968 El Al hijacking crisis for example the Secretary-General was not informed of the initiatives being made by the Italian Government. See U Thant, *View from the UN* (David and Charles, London, 1978) pp. 302–8.
6. In the Franco-American dispute on the removal of American military bases from France in 1966 the United States felt compelled eventually to end the exchange of diplomatic notes and move to direct discussion. As one American official put it: 'We

don't advance anything by making debating points in diplomatic notes.' Cited in Arie E. David, *The Strategy of Treaty Termination. Law Breaches and Retaliation* (Yale University Press, London, 1975) p. 121.

7. A review of this literature including labour and other economic relations can be found in Charles Lockhart, *Bargaining in International Conflicts* (Columbia University Press, New York, 1979) pp. 1–35.

8. For example, Lockhart, op. cit. and Thomas C. Schelling, *The Strategy of Conflict* (Oxford University Press, London, 1963), and *Arms and Influence* (Yale University Press, New Haven and London, 1966) pp. 131–41, for the concept of tacit bargaining.

9. Iklé, op. cit., p. 3, and Schelling's comment in *Arms and Influence,* p. 131.

10. Iklé, op. cit., pp. 26–58.

11. R.P. Barston, 'Law of the Sea Conference: Old and New Maritime Regimes', *International Relations* (David Davies Institute) Vol. VI, No. 1 (May 1978) pp. 306–10.

12. *UNTS*, Vol. 952, p. 264.

13. *A Draft Agreement between the United Kingdom and the People's Republic of China,* Misc. No. 20 (1984) Cmnd. 9352, especially Annex 1, pp. 14–23.

14. A similar difficulty arises over efforts to apply the distinction between the 'efficiency' aspects of negotiation (that is the search for mutually profitable adjustments) and the 'distributional' (the division of an object in favour of one rather than another party) to differentiate respectively innovative and redistributive negotiations. See Iklé's note on this, in Iklé, op. cit., p. 27.

15. 'Pure' bargaining is understood in terms of the relationship between demands and concessions. Demands are made, which may or may not be backed by coercive threats, with the aim or expectation of extracting concessions. Negotiation, at least in a co-operative sense, is distinct in that although demands are made the process involves adjustments, compromises, 'bridging' formula and other 'integrative' behaviour. As Knut Midguard and Arild Underdal note, 'pure' bargaining 'consists of trying to get the other party or parties to make the largest number of concessions, while making the smallest possible concessions oneself', 'Multiparty Conferences', in Daniel Druckman (ed.), *Negotiations: Social Psychological Perspectives* (Sage Publications, Beverly Hills, Calif., 1977) p. 332.

16. This can happen at the outset of an air service negotiation in which one of the parties regards the issue as a routine extension, while the other uses the opening negotiations for redistribution.

17. See Lockhart, op. cit., p. 9, and Robert D. Tollison and Thomas D. Willett, 'Institutional Mechanisms for Dealing with International Externalities: A Public Choice Perspective', in Ryan C. Amacher and Richard James Sweeney (eds), *The Law of the Sea: US Interest and Alternatives* (American Enterprise Institute for Public Policy Research, Washington, DC, 1976) esp. pp. 97–101 for a discussion of an optimal theory of negotiations.

18. Sofia was chosen by Moscow for the Soviet-Egyptian talks of November 1976, to re-appraise the Egyptian-Soviet Treaty of Friendship, as an appropriate 'neutral' location. See Ismail Fahmy, *Negotiating for Peace in the Middle East* (Croom Helm, London, 1983) p. 177.

19. For example US Secretary of State Warren Christopher brokered a reopening of Syrian and Israeli talks at ambassadorial level in Washington, DC (a route favoured to assist political leverage over the 'peace process'), after this strand had been broken off in February 1995 by Syria following the Hebron massacre. See *The Times,* 14 March 1995.

20. See G.R. Berridge, *Talking to the Enemy* (Macmillan, London, 1994), especially Chs 1 and 3, pp. 33–58.

21. See Ronald Barston, 'UN Conference on Straddling and Highly Migratory Fish Stocks', *Marine Policy*, March 1995, pp. 159–66.

22. See Volker Rittberger, 'Global Conference on Diplomacy and International Policy Making', in *European Journal of Political Research* (Special issue: Negotiation), Vol. 70, No. 11(2) (1983) pp. 167–82.

23. Michael Holden, *The Common Fisheries Policy* (Croom Helm, London, 1995).
24. For the influence of setting on the formation of the UN peacekeeping force in Cyprus (UNFICYP) see R.P. Barston, 'Problems in International Peacekeeping: The Case of Cyprus', *International Relations* (David Davies Institute, London, Nov. 1974) pp. 559–84.
25. See, for example, Henry Kissinger, *The White House Years* (Weidenfeld and Nicolson, London, 1979) p. 1205.
26. For an analysis of Kissinger's role in the Arab–Israeli disengagement after the October 1973 War see William B. Quandt, 'Kissinger and the Arab–Israeli Disengagement Negotiations', *Journal of International Affairs*, Vol. 29, No. 1 (Spring 1975) pp. 33–48, and William R. Brown, *The Last Crusade: A Negotiator's Middle East Handbook* (Nelson-Hall, Chicago, 1980). On mediators in the Arab–Israeli conflict from 1948 to 1979, see Saadia Touval, *The Peace Brokers* (Princeton University Press, Princeton, NJ, 1982).
27. See UN/IO/372, 30 March 1995; A/AC.172/157, 8 Aug. 1994, Annex 1.
28. For an account of the Secretary-General's consultations to resolve the impasse over the Deep Sea-bed Mining Provisions of the 1982 Law of the Sea Convention (Part XI) held from 1992–94, which produced the Agreement relating to the Implementation of Part XI of the United Nations Convention on the Law of the Sea of 10 Dec. 1982 (UN General Assembly Resolution 48/263), see *Law of the Sea Bulletin*, Special Issue IV, 16 Nov. 1994.
29. During 1993 the Israeli Foreign Minister Shimon Peres and Mahmoud Abbas (PLO), and other leading PLO officials held secret meetings in Norway and other locations under the brokerage of then Norwegian Foreign Minister Johan Jorgen Holst. The meetings ran parallel to the official talks which began in Madrid in November 1991 but were deadlocked. News of the breakthrough overshadowed the 11th round of 'official talks' at which there was no progress. The secret talks resulted in the Israel–PLO agreement of 13 September 1993. See *The Times*, 16 Sept. 1993; *Keesing* (Sept. 1993) 396 58.
30. See Arthur Lall, *Modern International Negotiation* (Columbia University Press, New York, 1966), pp. 323–44; Iklé, op. cit., Chs 6, 9 and 12; and P.J. Boyce, *Foreign Affairs for New States* (University of Queensland Press, St Lucia, Qld, 1977) esp. pp. 158–9 and 232–54.
31. The problem of establishing negotiating mechanisms to enable talks to be held with the Iranian authorities was perceived as a major constraint by United States decision-makers during the Iranian hostage crisis. See 'The Iran Hostage Crisis', *Report for the Committee on Foreign Affairs of the United States House of Representatives* (US Government Printing Office, Washington, DC, 1981) pp. 382–3, for details of the mediatory role of Algeria, and more generally, for a collection of some of the major developments.
32. Harold Nicolson, *Diplomacy* (Oxford University Press, 1963) pp. 18, 30–8.
33. For example see Kissinger on Soviet negotiating style, op. cit., pp. 1131–2, 1148–53, 1241. In his discussion of the negotiations to end the Vietnam War Kissinger provides an illuminating insight into the negotiating style of South Vietnam's President Thieu, which was strongly influenced by French diplomatic style: 'He (Thieu) fought with a characteristic Vietnamese opaqueness and with a cultural arrogance compounded by French Cartesianism that defined any deviation from abstract, unilaterally proclaimed principles as irreconcilable error', pp. 1322–8.
34. An account of Egyptian negotiations with the then Soviet Foreign Minister Andrei Gromyko can be found in Fahmy, op. cit., pp. 177–82. Fahmy notes the change in Soviet style from the tough formal approach session of the full delegation to that in the *tête-à-tête*.
35. Michael Blaker, *Japanese International Negotiating Style* (Columbia University Press, New York, 1977) pp. 54–8.
36. For example the grounding of the tanker *Amoco Cadiz* off Ushant, in 1976, causing major pollution damage, gave added weight to those seeking stronger anti-pollution measures at the Law of the Sea Conference. See R.P. Barston and Patricia Birnie (eds), *The Maritime Dimension* (George Allen and Unwin, London, 1980) p. 118.

37. See I. William Zartman, 'Negotiation: Theory and Reality', *Journal of International Affairs,* Vol. 29, No. 1 (Spring 1975) pp. 71–2.
38. Sir Anthony Eden, *Full Circle* (Cassell, London, 1960) pp. 115–16.
39. Gareth Porter, *A Peace Denied: the US, Vietnam and the Paris Agreement* (Indiana University Press, Bloomington, Ind., 1975) p. 77.
40. I. William Zartman and Maureen R. Berman, *The Practical Negotiator* (Yale University Press, New Haven and London, 1982) p. 139 on the efforts to devise a procedural formula for PLO participation in the proposed Geneva conference.
41. The scope of negotiations in terms of what is included or excluded on the agenda can be contentious. In the Sino-Indian boundary negotiations dispute arose over determining which sectors of the boundary should be discussed. China regarded *inter alia* the boundaries of Sikkim and Bhutan as outside the scope of the Sino-Indian boundary question. See *Reports to the Government of India and China on the Boundary Question* (Ministry of Foreign Affairs, India, 1961) pp. 37–9.
42. The US spokesman Cyrus Vance initially proposed two long tables (a two-sided conference) for the Vietnamese peace talks. The Democratic Republic of Vietnam (DRV) insisted on a square table with one delegation seated on each of the four sides, thus showing the NLF as an equal partner. The US then proposed a round table, which the DRV accepted, but which was rejected by the South Vietnamese Government. A compromise eventually emerged through a slight alteration to the formula of a round table: two rectangular tables were placed at opposite ends of the table. See Porter, op. cit., p. 78.
43. Procedural differences over the order of questions or items on the agenda can lead to the opening up of wider substantive matters. The fifth restricted session of the Geneva Conference on Indo-China, 24 May 1954, was taken up with discussion of whether military problems (cessation of hostilities, measures concerning regular and irregular forces, prisoners of war) should take priority over political problems (international supervision of agreement, guarantees) as the basis for further meetings. See secret telegram Secto 292, 25 May 1954, Smith (Head of Delegation) to State Department, in *Foreign Relations of the United States 1952–4. The Geneva Conference,* Vol. XVI (US Government Printing Office, Washington, DC, 1981) pp. 907 11.
44. Gerard Smith notes: 'Semenov claimed not to understand what I (Smith) meant by "in parallel" ', *Double Talk: The Story of the First Strategic Arms Limitation Talks* (Doubleday, New York, 1980) p. 250.
45. Rothstein, op. cit., pp. 148–57.
46. Johan Kaufmann, *Conference Diplomacy* (Sijthoff, Leiden, 1968) p. 181.
47. Interview (personal source).
48. Another important method involves the construction of formulae to bring the positions of the parties together or break an impasse. See Zartman and Berman, op. cit., esp. pp. 109–46 and 166–79.
49. For further discussion and illustration of the phenonemon of information and concept building in the initial stages of negotiations, see Chapter 8.
50. The issue of international standards versus national or regional exceptions is clearly illustrated in the debate within the international community over enhanced international standards of ferry safety against the background of continuing major ferry accidents such as *Herald of Free Enterprise* (Zeebrugge, 1987), *Donna Paz* (Philippines, 1991), *Estonia* (1995). More stringent international standards of passenger ferry stability (modifications to the 1990 Safety of Life at Sea Convention) were opposed by, for example, Greece, Morocco, Spain and Russian Federation. See International Maritime Organisation, MSC 65/25, 30 May 1995.
51. See Chapter 10.
52. Gilbert R. Winham, 'Negotiation as a Management Process', *World Politics,* Vol. 30 (1977–78), pp. 87–107.
53. The concept of 'structural uncertainty' is discussed by John D. Steinbruner, *The Cybernetic Theory of Decision* (Princeton University Press, Princeton, NJ, 1974), p. 18, *passim.*

102 *Modern diplomacy*

54. For example at the key April 1995 session of the UN Conference on Straddling and Highly Migratory Fish Stocks in New York, the veteran conference Chairman, Satya Nandan (Fiji) made an appeal in plenary for states not to reopen issues and so keep the conference moving towards some semblance of an agreement.

55. See Steinbruner, op. cit., pp. 40–4, 136–9, for a discussion of causal and cognitive learning.

56. Iklé, op. cit., p. 213.

57. Fahmy notes, in discussing the Egyptian–Soviet negotiations to reappraise the Treaty of Friendship, that Foreign Minister Gromyko did not raise the issue of Egyptian debt due to the Soviet Union in either the private meetings or full encounters of the two delegations. 'In fact this was the first time in any negotiation that the debt was not mentioned', op. cit., pp. 181–2.

58. See Kissinger, op. cit., p. 1137, and Zartman, op. cit., pp. 74–7.

59. See Fahmy, for an unusual example of bilateral communiqué negotiations held before a projected Egyptian summit conference, op. cit., p. 184. The practice of pre-communiqué negotiations is now, however, common in the run-up sessions to G-7 Summits. Indeed *leaking* of pre-conference draft G-7 communiqués has been used by leading G-7 states and/or host state to float ideas and gain endorsement for proposals, e.g. Halifax Summit proposals on reform of the IMF and cutback in UN agencies including UNCTAD.

60. An interesting account of the concluding phases of a GATT meeting is in 'Notebook: Behind the Scenes at the GATT Trade Talks', *New York Times*, 5 Dec. 1982.

61. Takayuki Hashizuma, 'US–Japan International Aviation Policies', in Aerospace: Asia and the Pacific Basin *(Financial Times*, London, 1984) pp. 18–22.

62. R.P. Barston, *International Politics Since 1945* (Elgar, Aldershot, 1991) pp. 115–21.

63. *The Observer,* 8 April 1984.

64. Barston, op. cit., Ch. 6 for a discussion of state practice after 1982, in comparison to consensus of UNCLOS, see also Ch. 6, footnotes 90, 91.

65. See Ronald Barston, 'UN Conference on Straddling and Highly Migratory Fish Stocks', *Marine Policy*, March 1995, pp. 159–66.

66. *UN Chronicle,* Vol. XXI, No. 3, September 1994. More than 900 NGOs were accredited to the inconclusive Preparatory Meetings in March 1991, May 1993, and April 1994. The World Population Conference had met previously in Rome (1954); Belgrade (1965); Bucharest (1974); Mexico City (1984).

67. Among heads of government not attending was the British Prime Minister, John Major. Several small and less developed countries cancelled on cost grounds, e.g. Malawi, preferring to allocate anticipated delegation costs to domestic poverty alleviation. See *The Guardian,* 7 March 1995.

68 See SOLAS/CONF.3/WP.2/Ad.1, 25 Nov. 1995; SOLAS/CONF.3/44, 28 Nov. 1995.

69. UN, WOM/825, 28 March 1995. Preparatory Commission on the Status of Women.

70. *The Courier,* November–December 1993.

CHAPTER 6

Diplomatic styles and methods

This chapter is concerned with the question of changes in diplomatic style and, secondly, discussing some of the main developments in diplomatic techniques. The concept of diplomatic style is a useful means of thinking about the characteristic ways in which states and other actors approach and handle their external policy. This is not of course to say that every decision will necessarily reflect features of the diplomatic style. Within diplomatic style are included negotiating behaviour, preference for open or secret diplomacy, the kinds of envoys used, diplomatic language, preferred institutions and types of treaty instruments such as memoranda or treaties of friendship. For international institutions, diplomatic operating style reflects the organisation's characteristic approach to problem-solving; the conduct of negotiations and the types of agreements normally associated with the institution.

Changes in diplomatic methods are looked at in five areas: (1) personal diplomacy; (2) East–West conferences; (3) bloc diplomacy; (4) associative diplomacy; (5) the use of consensus in multilateral diplomacy.

Diplomatic styles

To what extent have styles changed? Without doubt the rapid expansion of the international system since the 1960s has affected styles in a number of ways. Probably the most important effect has been the growth of personal diplomacy at head of state or government level, and the corresponding rise in regional diplomacy, through meetings, conferences and less formal gatherings of political, diplomatic and technical experts. The expansion of the state community has also brought with it a greater richness and variety in diplomatic styles, particularly at head of state level. This trend has been reinforced by the instability of governments, especially in Africa. One effect of this, at the level of diplomatic officials, has been an increase in the number of military personnel holding diplomatic appointments.[1] Embassies themselves, as a result, can become places of exile and the classical functions impaired or not carried out at all. This, in fact, may reinforce a further noticeable development in diplomatic style, which is a tendency for new actors to conduct their foreign policy from the centre rather than through their own foreign ministry and embassy channels, where these exist. This has important implications both for the process by which images and views about another party are formed, and the execution of policy. Embassies may not in fact be providing information or feedback which the usual explanation or models of diplomatic and foreign policy organisations suggest. Rather, the interface between parties may be short-circuited, the decision process truncated and decision-making personalised around the office of head of state and key advisers or agencies, and transnational corporate actors and international institutions in a national capital. As noted in Chapter 2 the foreign ministry, in some states, may rank third or fourth in the list of top five ministries behind the prime minister's department, treasury, and the economic planning unit (see Ch. 2).

The general characteristics of the diplomatic style of some newer states, discussed above, contrast with more established regimes. The latter tend to have a plurality of bureaucratic interests, greater degrees of functional decentralisation and conventional feedback mechanisms. A further difference is that the main elements in the operating style of established states have become stabilised, and, to some extent, built in as standard operating procedures. Thus a number of features of the overall operating styles of the United States, apart from variability in personal style at the executive level, have not greatly changed.

In United States diplomatic style, the presidential special envoy has been used in a number of ways, as illustrated by General Marshall's mission to China or the roving envoy role of W. Averell Harriman, and is a distinctive feature of American style.[2] The special envoy becomes the additional 'eyes and ears' of the president, acting as a fact-finder or trouble-shooter. For example, General Vernon Walters visited Colombo during the Sri Lankan Tamil separatist crisis in 1984 for talks with president Jayewardene.[3] Although the special envoy may provide the president with additional or competing assessments, as well as strengthen presidential control, the continued practice has been seen by some professional diplomatic service officers as an erosion of their areas of responsibility and influence. Other features of US style include the high use of memoranda of understanding and other informal instruments, endorsement by collective resolution and a preference for broad, package-type solutions in negotiations, the basis of which is not always conceptually clear. For example, the US notion of an 'umbrella' approach to the resumption of strategic arms control talks in 1984–85 gave Soviet officials the opportunity, publicly at least, to express puzzlement at the response of the US, while extolling the merits of their seemingly narrowly defined approach.[4] In at least one important respect, US operating style would appear to be undergoing change towards multilateral institutional diplomacy.[5] Dissatisfaction with certain multilateral fora has resulted in increasing US demands that international organisations get their house in order and increase their political and economic efficiency. There has also been preference for bilateral or small group diplomacy, coupled with a general quest for workable, smaller-scale arrangements with like-minded parties such as the North American Free Trade Agreement (NAFTA); US–South Pacific Forum fisheries agreement; Bering Sea Conservation agreements and ASEAN Regional Forum.[6]

Factors influencing diplomatic style

Of the other developments which have affected diplomatic styles, frequent changes of regime through a *coup d'état* or re-establishment of civilian or mixed regimes have been major factors which have prevented the emergence, with one or two exceptions, of any clear African styles.[7] Of note, however, is the re-emergence of Islamic or religious-based regimes. An immediate effect, in the case of Libya, was on the staffing and styling of Libyan embassies, which subsequently became retitled 'People's Bureaux'. In the case of Iran, the public presentational aspects of Iranian policy changed dramatically after the fall of the Shah, especially in terms of language, the use of revolutionary communiqués and frequent insistence on the use of reservations in international conferences dealing with the Palestine problem. A further change associated with the Iranian regime is the dualist nature of Iranian foreign policy, comprising government-to-people diplomacy as well as traditional government-to-government diplomacy. 'People's diplomacy' has involved establishing direct links with Islamic groups in other Islamic and non-Islamic states, as vehicles for promoting Iranian interests. The Islamic component has also involved the Iranian regime in international disputes such as that involving the *fatwa* on the writer Salman Rushdie.

Apart from questions concerning the style of old and new regimes, several changes have occurred in the representational aspects of diplomacy. The inseparability of political and economic issues in foreign policy has inevitably had repercussions on appointments at the highest, and indeed junior, levels of an embassy. The question, for example, of whether an ambassador to Washington should come from the career diplomatic service, or be a non-career appointment from the commercial sector is not uncommon. A number of senior ambassadors in the diplomatic service of the city-state of Singapore[8] are non-career officers from the business community. However, most established states continue to adopt a restrictive policy, relying on career officials. A change common to most states, nevertheless, is in the size and composition of delegations sent on trade-related missions overseas. It is now common practice for such delegations to be large, comprising of a mixture of businessmen, officials and political leaders, although the primary purpose for the delegation leader may be to resolve a political dispute. Even in such circumstances business coexists with politics.

The representational aspects of diplomacy have also been affected by the growth of multilateral diplomacy. Many new actors find it impossible to cope with the plethora of committees, regional groups and co-ordinating meetings at large-scale conferences. Given the range and complexity of issues, not all foreign ministries are able to provide sufficient instructions to their representatives. As a result, abstention or non-participation in voting has become an everyday feature of the diplomatic styles of some new states under these conditions.

Diplomatic style: international institutions

The concept of diplomatic style can also be applied to international institutions and other actors. As far as international institutions are concerned one of the major influences on operating style is that of the chief executive officer, who frequently may hold office for some considerable time.[9] The executive head will affect strategy, priorities and overall representation. The effect of change of chief executive can be seen, for example, in the case of the European Bank for Reconstruction and Development (EBRD), following the resignation of Attali. His less flamboyant successor, Jacques de Larosière, former Managing Director of the IMF, abolished the merchant banking (privatisation) and development banking departments and created Northern and Southern geographical departments,[10] to reduce duplication and provide some emphasis on public sector banking.

A second element of institutional diplomatic style is the characteristic procedures for negotiation and problem-solving. These might include the general use of inner, limited membership specialist working groups and intersessional correspondence groups (e.g. IMO); preparatory meetings and extensive 'definitional' legal reviews (e.g. Mediterranean Action Plan);[11] or financial 'rescue package' diplomacy conducted from the wings (e.g. IMF). A third element of institutional style involves the characteristic framing of problems, which includes types of treaty or informal instruments. An international institution may have, for example, an operating preference for informal instruments such as Action Plans, Codes and Guidelines, e.g. UNEP, which may be copied by other international fora to become part of a wider international idiom or practice.

Diplomatic methods

Personal diplomacy

Personal diplomacy has increased in importance as a feature of modern international relations. By using personal or direct diplomacy through visits, correspondence and telephone conversations, heads of government and other senior leaders establish contacts, promote their country's image or try and improve bilateral, official and other relations. Personal diplomacy through visits is also used frequently to put the seal of approval on a major project or agreement. Visits of this kind, whether they be ceremonial, psychological or have a substantive purpose, reflect the growing involvement in diplomacy of the head of state or government and a variety of key representatives of banks, corporations, regional institutions and other organisations.

In general, the growth of personal diplomacy has been brought about by changes in modern communications, and the spread of regional collaboration outside Europe, in Africa, Latin America, the Caribbean and Southeast Asia. Visits, too, have become synonymous with the presentational aspects of foreign policy – declarations, profile as well as problem-solving. In many instances visits, especially those to major powers, are undertaken with an eye on the domestic or electoral value in the home country. Another important reason for the continued use of personal diplomacy is that it may facilitate political transition. For example, in the former Soviet Union, the setting of the state funerals of Soviet leaders has been used as an opportunity for brief but important contacts between the new leadership and foreign politicians. Similarly, a personal visit by one head of state or government to another, following a *coup d'état*, can be used to open up new relations.

Personal diplomacy plays an important part in alliance and other collaborative relations. In the European Community, twice-yearly summits have become the norm in Franco-German relations, symbolising the importance each accords the other, whereas annual summits are held by France with Britain and Italy. France extended the system of summits to Spain, following agreement on its accession into the Community, in a co-operation agreement signed during the official visit of King Juan Carlos in July 1985. The agreement provided for annual meetings of the French president and Spanish Prime Minister, the setting up of joint consultative committees on international and strategic issues and annual meetings of the defence ministries.[12] Regular, though far less formal meetings have long been a feature of Anglo-American relations.

French and British practice has differed in terms of the methods used to develop relations with their former colonies. In contrast to Britain, France in terms of its African diplomacy (as well as elsewhere) has relied heavily on presidential and foreign ministerial visits to both francophone and non-francophone states. A frequent purpose of such visits is to reassure allies of continued support. For example, the 1984 African-French summit in Burundi, attended by President Mitterrand and the French Foreign Minister, was preoccupied with the question of Chad and French policy *vis-à-vis* Libya. The occasion also gave M. Mitterrand an opportunity to engage in some pre-summit 'old'-style personal diplomacy, when he held private talks with President Mobutu aboard the latter's presidential yacht on the Congo.[13]

The projection of national images and export promotion are the other major purposes of personal diplomacy. For example, at the end of 1984, the former British Prime Minister, Mrs Thatcher, travelled 250,000 miles in 130 hours, principally for the formal signing of the Hong Kong agreement in Beijing with the People's Republic of China. The journey also took in meetings in Bahrain, Moscow, Delhi and Hong Kong, returning via Guam, Honolulu and Washington.[14] An economic mission was undertaken the following year to Southeast Asia. It is not surprising that the political geography of heads of government sometimes becomes confused in these circumstances. It is in fact worth while contrasting the *pace* of modern diplomacy with that shortly after the Second World War. For example, P. C. Spender (Australia) and British Foreign Secretary, Ernest Bevin, travelled to the United States aboard the liner *Queen Mary*, in September 1950. Bevin was travelling to the UN in New York, while Spender's mission was to gather support for a Pacific security pact. Spender sought to win the approval of the British Foreign Secretary, but at the end of a personal meeting recounts:[15] 'I felt that when I left Bevin's stateroom that despite the warm personal hearing, I had again failed to penetrate the United Kingdom indifference, if not opposition to the idea.' Within less than a decade shortly after that the first modern exponent of air travel in diplomacy, US Secretary of State John Foster Dulles, became one of the most travelled post-war secretaries of state covering some 560,000 miles and attending 50 conferences in little more than six years.[16] The tradition has been carried on, with the addition of 'shuttle' diplomacy, as used by Secretaries Vance in the Cyprus crisis, Kissinger after the 1973 Arab–Israeli War, Haig in the Falklands conflict and Christopher in the Middle East.

Summits and conferences

In post-war diplomacy summit conferences have been increasingly used since the 1970s by a wide variety of states other than major powers for traditional high-level meetings. Summits serve one or more of the following purposes: (1) symbolic effects; (2) gaining information/exchange of views; (3) discussion of side issues; (4) defining strategic policy; (5) resolution of disputes; (6) diffusing crises; (7) negotiation and ratification of final stages of agreements. The diversification in the use of summits has been influenced particularly by the growth of economic diplomacy following the Algiers summit in 1973 on the New International Economic Order (NIEO) and subsequently through the expansion of regional and sub-regional groups post Cold War. The term 'summit' has lost accordingly some of its sense of high occasion and special purpose, as a venue for decisions of critical importance, becoming a term in diplomatic vocabulary for relatively routine meetings at head of state or government level. The term 'summit' has also been adopted for some *ad hoc* UN global conferences, e.g. Copenhagen World Social Summit (1995). Periodic summit meetings of economic and other groupings, such as Asia-Pacific Economic Forum (APEC) or G-7, should be distinguished from special occasion summits of the more traditional type. An example of the latter is the meeting of Western hemisphere leaders at Miami in 1994, for the Summit of the Americas, to agree plans for a future free trade area. The summit last met at Punta del Este in 1967. The Summit of the Americas was also used for a side issue: the announcement by the US, Canada and Mexico of their decision to admit Chile to NAFTA.

Some further general comments may be made on the above developments. While it has been argued that the use of summits has widened in terms of action and content, an exception to this development is the decline and reduction in significance of US–Russian Federation summits. The lessening of the significance of US–Russian Federation summitry contrasts with the importance of the primary powers in managing East–West and global security. In the Cold War period East–West relations were handled through four-power conferences (US, UK, France and the Soviet Union), limited membership conferences on specific issues such as Indo-China in 1954 and bilateral personal visits or summits. United States–Soviet bilateralism was a dominant feature of the classical period of *détente* from 1971–76,[17] and, 'revived' *détente* from 1985–90. Some indication of the pluralism in the diplomatic methods which were to feature after 1990 in the handling of East–West relations and broader international security were foreshadowed in the pan-European Helsinki Conference, and 1990 Paris CSCE summit.[18] Subsequently the increasing number and blurring of security roles, institutional responsibility, and concepts ('security pluralism') in Europe, was influenced and accentuated by conflicts on the European and Central Asian rimland of the Russian Federation.[19]

Apart from the decline or reduced significance of primary power summits as vehicles for international security after 1992,[20] the widening usage of 'summits' for relatively *routine* matters raises questions about purpose and effectiveness. It can be argued that frequent or regularised meetings styled as 'summits' undermine the concept of summit as a vehicle for resolving (or not) at the highest level critical issues, *after* they have been explored and examined at other levels (e.g. foreign minister) to the greatest extent possible. The *non-routine* value of a high-level summit is best seen in the cases of *emergency* or unscheduled summits. The dramatic recall or reconvening of heads of government in the context of a crisis underlines the potential importance of summits as emergency or non-routine methods of last resort. An example of an emergency summit meeting was that reconvened by Egypt and Israel in 1995 in Cairo to try and resume the Israeli–Egyptian 'peace process' following attacks in the Gaza Strip.[21] Finally, we should note that in terms of diplomatic protocol, decisions to convene or not a scheduled summit conference are both sensitive matters and indicative of the state of relations between states.[22]

Russian Federation and the CIS

The diplomatic style and methods of the Russian Federation are distinguished by three features: increasing volume and importance of bilateral negotiations;[23] decline in multilateral conference role; reconstruction of the Federation's treaty network. The loss of its global diplomatic-economic-military alliance grouping,[24] which followed the break-up of the former Soviet Union and dissolution of the Warsaw Pact severely weakened the Russian Federation's capacity to act internationally. Changes in the style of conducting foreign policy reflect a fundamental shift in orientation towards local and regional perspectives (the so-called 'near abroad') following the December 1991 Minsk Declaration establishing the CIS, and subsequent CIS trade, economic co-operation and security agreements.[25] Efforts to build up the CIS have involved the Russian Federation in extensive visits to individual member states to negotiate bilateral agreements (e.g. Russian Federation and Ukraine on the Black Sea fleet and nuclear weapons)[26] and summits of the CIS.[27] The domestic economic reform programme of the Russian Federation has contributed to the inward orientation; the lessening of the connections between technical ministries and the influx (some of it short term) of Western corporate entities and international institutions representative offices and *ad hoc* delegations from the IMF and World Bank for example.[28] In addition, on its immediate periphery Russian Federation diplomacy has had to assess and respond to Western governmental and transnational corporate economic activity, particularly the oil sector, in the Central Asian republics.[29]

Extensive bilateralism which is one of the main changes in Russian Federation diplomatic methods has been largely brought about by the need to reconstruct the former Soviet treaty network,[30] and the end of the Comecon–Warsaw Pact alliance system. Bilateralism has meant an enhanced roving role for the Russian Federation foreign minister as negotiator, spokesman and interlocutor. Special envoys have also assumed increased importance, for example, on the Yugoslav conflict to support the active Russian Federation interests and role in the G-5 Contact Group negotiations.[31]

Among the revised bilateral agreements are those with India[32] and China. The Russian Federation–Chinese agreement on border security and incident reduction, December 1994, was initialled during the symbolic visit of President Jiang Zemin, the first Chinese visit to the Soviet Union or Russian Federation since that of Mao in 1957.[33] Other bilateral agreements of note are increasing *ad hoc* arms sales and nuclear materials agreements, e.g. Iran,[34] Malaysia.[35] At a multilateral level, Russian Federation involvement in social-economic (G-77) or Rio (environmental) type diplomacy, never a great feature of Soviet diplomacy,[36] has further declined. Moreover, the Russian Federation orientation in multilateral diplomacy has altered to take on a more limited or local rather than global power perspective. For example at the 1994 Intergovernmental Conference to negotiate an agreement to combat desertification, particularly in Africa, much of the Russian Federation's diplomatic efforts were directed towards securing a special reference in the chapeau of the agreement to the desert areas of the Russian Federation.[37]

Western economic summits

An important innovation in Western diplomatic co-ordination is the creation of the Western economic summits. The summits began at Rambouillet in 1975 and have been held annually since. It was not until the London summit of 1977, however, that it was agreed that the summits should become regular features on the diplomatic calendar of the major industrialised countries – the United States, United Kingdom, France, Italy, West Germany and Japan. Membership was subsequently extended to Canada, the European Community, and (for the political discussions of the summit) to the Russian Federation.

The initial Rambouillet summit was a product not only of United States political concerns about the cohesion of the Western alliance but also of a series of oil, monetary and trade crises. Two Western political leaders – Giscard d'Estaing and Schmidt – were important in bringing the summit about. Their co-operation also reflected a strong wish to create a more effective European voice both in alliance matters and more generally on wider international issues. As Cesare Merlini notes: 'The real innovation is that the leaders of the seven industrialised democracies now meet on a regular basis and with a consolidated membership, in a forum which has more or less direct and effective relationship with the existing institutions and alliances that link the participating countries among themselves and with others.'[38]

A striking feature of the early summits was the attention given to economic questions. After Rambouillet an agenda was identified comprising six broad areas: the international economic situation; trade problems; East–West trade; relations with developing countries; energy and monetary problems. Although the focus of the summits was initially economic, the agendas have been extensively broadened to incorporate a wide range of global issues. The Bonn summit (1978) was the first to make non-economic decisions, with a special declaration on air piracy, committing the participant governments to halt flights to and from countries that refused to extradite or prosecute hijackers or return hijacked aircraft. Following the example of the Bonn summit, the communiqué after the Tokyo summit (1979), which agreed among other things oil import quotas, also included a statement on the plight of refugees from Kampuchea and Vietnam. The Venice summit in 1980, overshadowed by the Iranian hostage crisis, included discussion on the seizure of diplomatic personnel and hijacking, and the communiqué reiterated the participants' concern over the Vietnamese 'boat people'. The Williamsburg summit (1983) is unusual in that, in addition to decisions on monetary policy and East–West trade, security issues were included for the first time.

While there may be doubts about the substantive achievements of the summits, they nevertheless have served as a convenient framework in which the major Western leaders can establish personal contact, exchange views and take these into account when formulating their future policies. Apart from this, the summits have linked Japan, and to a lesser extent the Russian Federation, institutionally with the Western powers. The summits thus provide an arena for initiation and endorsement of policies, criticism of other members and a stage from which to project national policies to the international press. In this connection the summits are also a forum for European–American exchanges, in which the Europeans have been careful to maintain their independence both individually and as a grouping. The summits too are a means of presenting new initiatives or raising on to the agenda new problems, such as special debt relief terms for the least developed (Toronto, Naples), anti-terrorism (Lyon summit), or establishing control on the export of nuclear materials from the Russian Federation.[39]

The operation of the summits since Rambouillet suggests a number of limitations. Considerable loss of focus has occurred as a result of the extension of the agenda to include political and security questions. Related to this is the increasing tendency for the grouping to be seen as a general clearing-house for US policy on a variety of European security, arms control and global issues. The inclusion of Japan, in this respect, has caused concern among the smaller NATO members, particularly Belgium and the Netherlands, which are excluded from the seven-nation framework.[40] France has remained critical of the dominance of US over the G-7 agenda and proceedings.

The loss of focus coincided with a change of the style in US foreign policies at G-7 summits coinciding with the 1981 Ottawa summit, away from a detailed agenda, specific agreements and lengthy communiqués to stressing more personal contact and declarations of intent. Related to this is the impact of the external setting on the summit agenda, particularly the tendency for events immediately prior to or during the summit itself to intrude on the proceedings. For example, the Bonn summit in 1985 was overshadowed by the US President's visit to the Bitburg war cemetery, and the timing of the announcement of US sanctions against Nicaragua, while collective action against Libya and the Chernobyl nuclear accident diverted the Tokyo summit from what Japan had hoped would be a summit devoted largely to economic matters.[41] More generally, the tendency for the summits to be overloaded is reinforced through the continued practice of having two separate declarations (political and economic) at each summit. In this context it is difficult to sustain any concerted efforts, as the summits move from theme to theme ('Building World Partnership'; 'Sustainable Development' and 'The Reduction of Employment') each year.[42] As such the summit communiqués have tended to become lengthy UN General Assembly style documents ('attach importance to'; 'call for greater efforts'). Without reform the summits are likely to have largely symbolic and perhaps some limited sectoral importance (e.g. debt, nuclear materials, treaty ratification). Reform of the summits could include (1) format and style of communiqué; (2) reduction in agenda; (3) follow-up mechanisms/initiatives.

The EU and developments in diplomatic methods

One of the most striking features of developments in diplomatic methods is the emergence of the EU as a bloc actor in multilateral technical diplomacy. While the Maastricht Treaty set out in the Title V of the Treaty provisions for a common foreign and security policy,[43] it is within the field of technical diplomacy rather than traditional foreign policy that the EU has increasingly acted *au communitaire* on the basis of the Treaty of Rome, Single European Act and decisions of the European Court of Justice, within areas of Community competence. These areas include the Common Fisheries policy, transport and some international trade and environment policy. In areas where the Community has competence, member states are represented by the Commission in international negotiations. In certain residual policy areas, for example some international trade policy in the Uruguay Round framework, there is mixed or joint competence. Difficulties have arisen over definitions of what matters fall within Community competence between member states and the Commission, in areas such as trade policy, including restrictions on exports, civil aviation and immigration. In the civil aviation sector, for example, disputes have occurred over bilateral air transport agreements under negotiation or concluded by non-Community members with individual Community members (e.g. US–UK, US–Finland, Austria, Sweden). The Commission opposed bilateral agreements and sought a mandate from EU transport ministers to negotiate air transport agreements on a bloc basis.[44]

What are the implications of Community competence in technical diplomacy for diplomatic methods of the EU? First, the negotiation of a bloc common line or position generally involves a lengthy clearing process before and during daily sessions of a multilateral conference or meetings of an international or regional institution. Similar consultations may be undertaken intersessionally. Thus, the balance of EU diplomatic effort tends to be shifted to intra-bloc negotiations. The cleared position is invariably on a lowest common denominator basis. In the second place, representation by the Commission in effect reduces the negotiating capacity of individual member states, and potentially effectiveness, in that negotiations are not conducted by a professional diplomatic service. Thirdly, in areas of Community competence member states cannot take part in plenary or other debates of a conference, initiate proposals, or broker compromise in open session. In practice, the effect is to take out of plenary and informal conference processes European players with varying interests, diplomatic skills and traditional roles. The effect is well illustrated by Sweden's non-role at the third session of the UN Conference on Straddling and Highly Migratory Fish Stocks following entry into the EU in January 1995.[45] Prior to that Sweden, as an active neutral power, had played a prominent role at the conference. The effective removal of individual European players from parts of the processes of negotiations has altered the dynamic of multilateral conferences in a number of respects.

As a bloc actor, the EU cannot easily perform broker or moderator roles, especially in debates during 'fluid' plenary or working group sessions, or initiative flexible proposals. Multilateral conferences also lose the drafting input of individual European states. As a bloc, the EU tends to be susceptible to general attack if it opposes or appears intransigent on particular issues, and as a result therefore often does not adopt a position, consequently appearing passive or quiescent, for the sake of its bloc image. One of the other reasons for EU non-positions, is as noted the internal clearing debate the EU undertakes on a daily basis during multilateral conferences. The excessive diplomatic time devoted to these 'internal' debates means that not only is the EU conducting a conference within a conference, but its positions are often out of phase with other conference initiatives. The EU's bloc composition also means that its negotiating style is one of tabling its own lowest common denominator amendments rather than acting strategically.

An indirect effect of these developments is to allow wider latitude for small or non-traditional players in multilateral conferences, e.g. Papua New Guinea, Morocco and Uruguay. The EU's 'bloc' presence has not led to obvious counter-blocs so far but the bloc approach has been imitated to some extent, for example, by the South Pacific Forum.

Group of 77

Within the United Nations system the G-77 is the largest grouping or bloc of states concerned with international economic aspects of development. The G-77 was launched in June 1964 at the conclusion of the first UNCTAD conference.[46] Although it is the major co-ordinating forum for developing countries and others, the increasing size of the Group – the membership rose to 131 with the admission of the Federated States of Micronesia, South Africa and Bosnia in 1995 – has effectively meant the Group has found it difficult to mobilise its membership along common themes. Historically, the main platforms of the G-77, formulated during the 1960s in an ideologically less complex international system, were the establishment of a New International Economic Order (NIEO) and South–South Cooperation (Caracas Programme of Action 1981).

Despite the G-77's size and scale of operation as an international institution, relatively little has been written about the Group's diplomatic methods, which rely extensively on personal diplomacy and closed informal preparatory meetings at UN Headquarters and other centres. Organisationally, the G-77 is headed by an elected chairman, rotating annually, assisted by a voluntary secretariat seconded from, for example, Algeria, Columbia, Panama, Nigeria, India and Republic of Korea.[47] Beneath the office of chairman, the G-77 is mainly run through five groupings called 'chapters', meeting at ambassadorial level in Geneva, Rome, Paris,[48] Nairobi and Vienna. The chapters prepare G-77 inputs into the programmes of the technical UN agencies for which each chapter has a special responsibility, such as UNDP, FAO,

UNESCO, UNEP and UNIDO. A sixth chapter, the G-24, which has few links with the other chapters, meets in Washington, DC, to monitor the IMF and IBRD. The G-24's generally more conservative orientation often puts it at odds with the social and economic development programme approach of other G-77 chapters, and, is indicative of the difficulties the G-77 has in reaching compatible positions between these different pillars of international development diplomacy.

Apart from the G-24, the G-77 has one further sub-group – the G-27, which is a working group of the whole at ambassadorial level.[49] The increasing use of G-27 as a sub-group for co-ordinating positions is also indicative of the problems the G-77 has in co-ordinating overall group positions. The G-27 in fact was originally set up with nine countries from Africa, Asia and Latin America in 1974 to prepare for the seventh special session of the General Assembly. Its composition is no longer limited to 27 states but fluctuates. The proliferation of multilateral conferences since 1990, coupled with the diplomatic practice of interim implementation of international agreements, permanent meetings of conferences of the parties to treaties (e.g. Biodiversity Convention, Climate Change Convention, Law of the Sea) has made it virtually impossible for leading G-77 states (historically Algeria and Latin American representatives) to come up with overarching positions given the myriad of interests and levels of development of the 131 members. The tendency for the G-77 to fragment or splinter was illustrated at the Barbados Conference on Small Island Developing States in 1994, where the G-77 was unable to agree a bloc position and the lead role was ceded to the new South Pacific Alliance of Small Island States.[50] In other instances internal divisions on issues can lead to bargaining over whether an item appears on a multilateral conference agenda or is postponed to a different conference, with loss of momentum and effect. For example, the G-77 was divided over UNDP and similar proposals for a commitment of 20 per cent of GNP to social policy, and the proposals were shifted from the Cairo Population Conference (1994) to the Copenhagen Social Summit in 1995.[51]

Two further aspects of the functioning of the G-77 can be noted. The first concerns the question of overlap between the Non-Aligned Movement (NAM) and G-77. Following the end of the Cold War, the NAM lost much of its *raison d'être*. However, NAM efforts to shift their activities to include greater attention to economic issues, brought NAM on a collision course with the G-77. Although a Joint Coordinating Committee was set up in 1995, the relationship between the two institutions in the long term remains problematic. Second, an issue of concern for the G-77 has been the revitalisation of its central ideology and programmes since 1990 given the complexity of contemporary diplomacy, the decline in international economic assistance and international fragmentation. In developing new concepts, the G-77 has sought to build on the success of its campaign to reform the Global Environment Facility (GEF), with other specific campaigns on the developed world meeting commitments of 0.7 per cent of GNP to ODA. Other elements of the revised G-77 central themes are (1) strengthening international co-operation for development (Agenda for Development); (2) revival of South– South trade co-operation; (3) defending UN agencies with development functions threatened with closure (e.g. UNCTAD, UNIDO); (4) shifting the balance of UN financial effort from peacekeeping to development; (5) altering sustainable development programmes to development co-operation.[52] In effect, these five themes represent an attempt to shift the UN's development role away from the Rio Commission on Sustainable Development (CSD) approach.

Associative diplomacy

One of the more striking aspects of the evolution of modern diplomacy is the relations which regional organisations develop with *other* regional organisations, international institutions, groups of states and individual states. The attempts by individual states or groups to develop significant links within a treaty and institutional framework with other states or groupings beyond merely routine transactions can be described as 'associative diplomacy'. Associative diplomacy serves one or more of a number of purposes, including the creation of a larger grouping, the co-ordination of policies and mutual assistance within the grouping. Other purposes are maintenance of the political, economic or security influence of the 'primary' grouping, limiting the actual or potential coercive power of other groupings ('damage limitation'), and enhancement of the identity of individual members in the grouping.

There are generally four main elements in associative diplomacy. These include the institutional and treaty framework, regular meetings of senior political leaders and officials, some measure of co-ordination of policies, and schemes to promote economic relations of the groups, such as trade credits, generalised scheme of preferences (GSP) project aid and financial loans. Associative diplomacy can involve one or more of the major sectors of public policy, including socio-cultural exchanges, economic (trade, technical and financial assistance), political and security relations. It is possible to distinguish, therefore, various types of associative diplomacy, such as, for example, aid-project dominated (e.g. EC–African, Caribbean and Pacific countries (ACP)); mixed economic-security (e.g. ASEAN dialogues); economic (e.g. EU-associate members); security (e.g. NATO extension via Partnership for Peace).

In this section two examples – the ASEAN dialogues and the Lomé Convention – have been chosen to illustrate the working of associative diplomacy, starting with the ASEAN dialogues.

ASEAN

The ASEAN case illustrates associative diplomacy in transition from one of initial concerns with development projects to international trade and security issues. ASEAN was established in 1967, although formal links with other states and international institutions did not develop significantly until after the Bali summit of ASEAN heads of government in 1976.[53] Prior to this, ASEAN had established formal dialogues, meeting regularly at official and ministerial level with Australia in 1974 and New Zealand the following year, to discuss trade and development projects. Relations with other groupings, such as the EEC were *ad hoc* up to the Bali summit and ASEAN did not follow up the European Commission's offer of a co-operation agreement, similar to that concluded with India in December 1973.[54] The 1976 Bali summit not only reformed the institution of ASEAN, giving them greater economic emphasis but also gave the impetus for enhanced ASEAN co-operation with third countries and international organisations. During 1976–77, in a period of intense diplomatic activity, ASEAN concluded a framework agreement on future project assistance with the United Nations Development Programme (UNDP) and formalised dialogue arrangements with Canada and Japan. The prime ministers of Japan, Australia and New Zealand met with ASEAN heads of government in August 1977 in Kuala Lumpur, which confirmed their position as core dialogue partners. The first formal meeting of the US–ASEAN dialogue was held in Manila in September 1977. These meetings were complemented by the discussions held between the ASEAN ambassadors to Brussels and the Committee of Permanent Representatives (COREPER), which led to the first ministerial meeting between the Community, including the Commission, and ASEAN in Brussels in November 1978. A co-operation agreement was signed with the European Community in March 1980.[55]

The associative diplomacy of ASEAN is conducted at four levels – the annual dialogue meeting, ministerial meetings with individual dialogue partners or international organisations, and at the level of officials dealing with particular projects, which are co-ordinated by the Joint Coordinating Committee (JCC) in each country. An unusual fourth level involves the encouragement of non-governmental contacts. Within ASEAN itself a noticeable feature is the effort to promote regional development through private sector co-operation. ASEAN private or non-governmental associations have been set up in traditional areas such as chambers of commerce, as well as others such as the ASEAN Bankers Association, Shippers' Council, jurists and journalists.[56] As part of ASEAN associative diplomacy at a non-govermental level, business councils have been established between ASEAN private sector groups and their counterparts in Japan,[57] the EC and the United States.

ASEAN's associative diplomacy has been concerned with both political and economic issues, though the latter have commanded the most attention. An important aspect of the economic dimensions is the development project assistance provided by individual dialogue countries. By 1981 some 150 projects were being jointly implemented in areas such as food production, nutrition, agricultural development, fisheries, forestry and communications. To co-ordinate co-operation with third countries ASEAN has devised a system of designated responsibility among its members: Indonesia speaks for ASEAN in its dialogue with Japan; Malaysia with Australia; the Philippines with the United States and Canada; Singapore with New Zealand; and Thailand with UNDP, Economic and Social Commission for Asia and the Pacific (ESCAP) and the EC. This does not, however, limit or prevent individual ASEAN members from conducting bilateral relations outside the scope of the 'dialogue'. In addition ASEAN maintains a collective presence in each of the dialogue countries and other capitals. These are termed 'Asean committees in third countries', and include the committees in Brussels, Bonn, Geneva, London, Paris, Canberra, Tokyo and Wellington, made up of the chiefs of mission.

From an ASEAN perspective, the dialogues have contributed to the wider recognition of ASEAN's growing status and importance in international relations. For the dialogue partners, the importance attached to the dialogues varies according to the nature and degree of their regional involvement. Thus, unlike other dialogue partners except Japan, the primary interest of the European Community is economic, with ASEAN viewed in terms of the general Community policy of extending its formal links with other regional groupings for economic purposes. ASEAN, moreover, is institutionally 'recognisable' and familiar to the European Community, fitting in, if not mirroring, some of its own styles of decision-making. In contrast, the dialogues provide the United States with an opportunity to put across US policies on regional security, including the ASEAN Regional Forum (ARF), wider groupings such as APEC and issues before the WTO.

ASEAN has periodically reviewed the format and usefulness of the dialogues. Dissatisfaction within ASEAN was influenced by the growing number of trade disputes, particularly between ASEAN and the United States over the application of the US GSP,[58] as well as similar difficulties with the European Community GSP. The take-off of some of the ASEAN economies in the late 1970s meant that increasingly ASEAN preoccupations were with trade access and less with conventional development assistance.[59] The ASEAN review of the dialogues in other words reflected the classical debate between trade-orientated development as against agriculture-based development assistance.[60] Ironically, ASEAN's appeal for greater trade access for its products had been enshrined some years earlier in ASEAN's major treaties, the Declaration of ASEAN Concord (section 3 (iv)) and in article 6 of the Treaty of Amity and Cooperation in Southeast Asia, though these objectives had not been collectively pursued to any significant degree until the review of the dialogues.

Apart from trade access, dissatisfaction with the project aspect of the dialogues lay in two areas. First, over half of the 150 projects initiated since 1975 have been undertaken by international or regional institutions, rather than the dialogue partners, including those by UNDP (42), ESCAP (14) and IMO (5).[61] The take-up by individual dialogue countries has been low, with Japan setting up 9 projects, Canada 11 and the United States 13,[62] as against New Zealand 7, Australia 12 and the European Community 19.[63] More than half of the projects are low-level development schemes such as livestock rearing and aquaculture.[64]

A third general area of dissatisfaction has been with the lack of focus or clear priorities in the dialogues. As the dialogues progressed a number of member states began to feel that the content had become broad and the institutional procedures somewhat ritualised. There were doubts too on the part of some of the dialogue partners as to whether this form of associative diplomacy added anything over and above that which could be achieved through normal diplomatic and other channels. For example, there were no dialogue meetings at the level of officials between Canada and ASEAN between 1977 and 1981, although there were bilateral contacts outside the 'dialogue' framework.[65]

As a result of the review the dialogues with existing countries have subsequently concentrated more on market access, international economic problems, commodity problems and socio-cultural co-operation. Other countries have been added to the dialogue, e.g. India, and Vietnam and Laos were admitted to ASEAN as observers.[66] In addition, following the initial but limited easing of tension in Southeast Asia after the ending of the Cold War, and regional readjustments, ASEAN concluded a Special Consultative Relationship with the People's Republic of China in 1993, covering trade and scientific co-operation. Furthermore, Vietnam was admitted as a full member of ASEAN in 1995. ASEAN too has had to adjust to other regional and pan-regional groupings following, for example, APEC, and has sought revised relations with the EU.

The EC and Lomé

A notable feature of the expanding role[67] of the European Community is its associative diplomacy based on co-operation agreements. Many of the early agreements were little more than trade agreements.[68] They were often limited in scope, for example to essentially French-speaking Africa, such as the Yaoundé agreement of 1963,[69] or were put together on an *ad hoc* basis after painstaking and arduous negotiations, as with the Maghreb and Mediterranean agreements between 1963 and 1980. The conclusion of the Lomé I Convention in February 1975 between the Community and 46 independent states in the ACP countries marked a major stage in the development of its associative diplomacy.[70] It has extended the political, economic and institutional links of the Community to the Caribbean and Pacific, and eventually to most of Africa. Significantly, Asia and Latin America were omitted from the original Lomé framework. No doubt in the case of Asia, exclusion was based on a concern for the long-term challenge posed by textiles and other manufactured goods from the 'heartland' of the newly industrialised countries' revolution. In October 1979, Lomé II was signed with 57 ACP countries and the convention further renewed in December 1984, Lomé III, and in 1989 (Lomé IV) by 68 ACP states.[71]

During the Lomé I negotiations,[72] a number of ACP political leaders, along with others including Commonwealth Secretary-General Ramphal, felt that the South should develop their own institutions for co-ordinating their policies and promoting development. The Lomé framework offered some opportunity to develop South–South institutions. For the North (Western Europe), the convention was seen as one of the few successful parts of the generally weakened North–South dialogue. Subsequently the ACP states have developed a parallel institutional structure to the joint EC–ACP institutions, which include the Council at Ministerial Level, the ACP–EC Committee of Ambassadors, the Joint (Parliamentary) Committee and Consultative Assembly.[73] At the Georgetown (Guyana) meeting in June 1975 the ACP states established an ACP council, the Committee of Ambassadors, and a secretariat was set up the following year in Brussels. The main work of the ACP Committee of Ambassadors is conducted through specialist sub-committees on, for example, commercial co-operation. Other joint sub-committees have been set up on sugar and banana exports, which are areas of particular concern in the diplomacy of a number of the Commonwealth Caribbean members of the ACP.

Within the ACP, the sugar producers have formed a sub-group of producing countries, which has met periodically to co-ordinate policies, for example, at the Georgetown conference in February 1985,[74] which was attended by fourteen of the eighteen signatories to the Sugar Protocol attached to the Lomé Convention.

Since Lomé II, the institutional machinery of EC–ACP associative diplomacy has been strengthened through what has become known as the 'Article 108 Committee'. The committee, which meets at ministerial and technical working party levels, is responsible for assessing the effectiveness of the financial and technical assistance provisions of the convention. In response to ACP criticism, the procedure of the 108 Committee, which is composed of equal numbers of representatives was further revised in Lomé III reducing the role of the European Commission and enhancing that of the ACP states in joint financial decision-making.[75] Prior to this the annual review and assessments of projects had in practice been mainly undertaken by the Commission. These changes have helped to reinforce the principle of joint administration on finance and improve the intergovernmental rather than technical aspects of EC–ACP associative diplomacy.[76]

How far EC–ACP associative diplomacy can develop through institutional and other changes seems broadly dependent on four sets of considerations. In the first place there is the problem of reconciling increasingly competing interests. As the membership has expanded, so the range of interests to be listened to, if not accommodated, has broadened. Should greater attention be given to the smaller Pacific states? Should the Community promote regional integration, or would particular national projects offer a more modest but arguably more effective route given resources? In this respect, the availability of EEC funds will be a major determinant of EC–ACP orientation.[77] Export stabilisation schemes such as Stabex raise expectations, but clearly cannot cope with major crop failure.[78] Again, while many of the Caribbean and Pacific states have low populations their integrative project requirements, such as ports, security, fisheries and shipping services are capital intensive.

In response to growing demands on EC financial resources, the EIB has extended its operations so as to become an important instrument in EC–ACP projects by providing risk capital.[79] The disbursement does, however, favour resource related projects, e.g. petrochemicals. Continued shortage of development funds and disputes over distribution would have the effect of turning the Lomé Convention more into a conventional trade co-operation agreement. Related to this, the inability of the Community itself to provide sufficient project aid and other funds under Lomé has led to financial relations being developed between EC–ACP institutions and other financial sources such as the World Bank, Arab funds and private capital. Other factors which have led to restrictions on EU financial resources to Lomé, include the effect of expanded membership, and preference for bilateral assistance by some EU members, notably Germany, United Kingdom, Sweden, Finland. The introduction also of 'human rights' and good governance clauses has been a major source of conflict in Lomé IV renegotiation.

The evolution of EC–ACP diplomatic methods is influenced by the institutional arrangements linking the two groups. The establishment of parallel ACP institutions alongside the joint EC–ACP institutions has caused considerable strain on ACP political and diplomatic resources. As might be expected the record of the joint committee is mixed. At the ACP level, the South–South diplomat still has to be persuaded about the career benefits of serving in an overseas secretariat. Another area of difficulty for ACP organisation concerns the powers of the office of secretary-general. Reaching agreement on an acceptable candidate has proved time-consuming and divisive. As in the OAU,[80] the inability of ACP members to agree a candidate has seriously impaired the office of secretary-general and led to calls for the revision of the election procedures.[81] In general, internal organisational problems within the ACP have acted as a limitation on the effectiveness of the ACP component of South–South diplomacy, as well as the joint EC–ACP institutions.

Multilateral diplomacy

The growth of consensus decision-making is one of the developments in multilateral diplomatic methods worth particular comment. The post-war period saw the continued shift away from decision-making based on unanimity. However, more recently, there appears to be some return to the notion of unanimity with the growth in the practice of decision-making by consensus. Writing on unanimity, I. L. Claude notes:

Traditional international law contributed the rule which served as the historic starting point for international voting and still serves as its basing point: the rule that every state has an equal voice in international proceedings and that no state can be bound without its consent. The ingredients of sovereign equality and sovereign immunity from externally imposed legislation were combined in the rule of unanimity.[82]

Nevertheless, the changing composition of the UN, including the emergence of the G-77 and the introduction of G-77 procedures into international institutions, has influenced the search for procedural solutions to avoid or at least lessen the confrontational aspects of majority–minority clashes. The rule of consensus is one such method. Others include weighted voting, as in the International Postal Union, and the rule that governments may 'opt out' of participation as in the Nordic Council of Ministers.[83] In the United Nations, other than strict abstention, the practice of non-participation in proceedings or voting is widely used.

The use of consensus decision-making in the UN dates particularly from the early 1970s. Consensus decision-making is distinct from unanimity in that unanimity implies that there is no opposition or request for a vote. Decision-making by consensus has come to mean the exhaustive search for widely acceptable solutions. In the UN system the consensus method has been widely used, e.g. at the UN Disarmament Commission[84] and the Law of the Sea Conference.[85] Elsewhere, consensus has been used in the CSCE and meetings of the G-77 non-aligned, although the practice of the G-77 also allows for opting out and reservations. In order to avoid undue delay and make decision-making more effective other variations have been developed, such as combinations of consensus, 'cooling-off' periods for consultation and voting, as in the 1975 and 1980 Non-Proliferation Treaty review conference.[86] In UNCTAD a combination of consensus and voting has been used. For example, the United States proposal for an International Resources Bank was voted on at UNCTAD IV at Nairobi and rejected.[87] In the IMF, meetings of the Executive Board are generally conducted on the basis of consensus. Occasionally opposition may be expressed after proposals have been formally agreed. For example, during the second Mexican financial rescue package negotiations in 1995, the United Kingdom, Germany and a number of other countries asked the IMF Managing Director to record their positions as for abstentions, even though at the time they had not voted against the rescue proposals.[88] Finally, it should be noted that in international agreements, provisions relating to the negotiation of the agreement, e.g. consensus, should be distinguished from those governing the *implementation* of the agreement. Implementation arrangements, for example, on financial contributions, may, following the first conference of the parties, be set up on the basis of majority voting rather than consensus.

Consensus in practice: some issues

The practice of consensus would seem to have been widely adopted recently as a means of responding to the problem of dissatisfaction at majority voting and the difficulties created by the emergence of opposing blocs or groups in multilateral conferences.[89] Consensus decision-making clearly has advantages for the great powers in that lengthy decision-making, which is a feature of the consensus method, provides opportunities for advancing and protecting their policies through lobbying, supporting draft proposals and forming support groups, without the threat of being frequently voted down. Ultimately, however, the consensus method may break down and voting take place, as, for example, in the Law of the Sea Conference in 1982, when a majority of the participants felt that continued US opposition to the sea-bed mining provisions was holding up the finalisation of the overall convention.[90] But the advantages do not lie solely with the great powers. Minor powers and small states in some respects have enhanced opportunities for protecting their positions in the drafting process of a consensus system. Put differently, consensus may be a convenient political fiction which is maintained during a conference to prevent premature break-up or postpone a decision. States subsequently may choose to interpret the meaning of a text in different ways, and, indeed, implement it, if at all, in quite divergent ways.[91]

Other reasons for voting taking place include testing the legitimacy of a consensus, or pressure from dissatisfied states who wish to place on record their position, knowing that key states are unlikely to support the declaration or resolution. The latter was well illustrated in the debate in the International Maritime Organisation (IMO) in which a group of states led by Spain, and opposed by the United States, United Kingdom and Japan, sought to obtain a majority vote prohibiting the dumping at sea of radioactive waste.[92]

One of the major disadvantages of consensus decision-making in international institutions and conferences is the protracted nature of the process. Decision-making is exhaustive and exhausting, as attempts are made to achieve compromise texts. At a procedural level, secretariats of international institutions and working group chairmen have, however, become important in searching for and in developing their own and others' compromise formulae. The method has also led to the development of innovative negotiating techniques to overcome deadlock and maintain momentum. For example, at the seventh session of the Law of the Sea Conference the impasse in negotiations was broken by defining the remaining core issues (e.g. the system for the international administration of deep sea-bed mining) and setting up seven new negotiating groups on these issues. Again, at the eighth session in 1978, the establishment of a Working Group of 21 on deep sea-bed questions was a further procedural innovation. Unlike previous formal groups, membership was restricted and drawn from ten developed industrialised states, including the United States, United Kingdom, France, FRG, Canada, Australia and the former Soviet Union and ten developing countries, represented *inter alia* by Brazil, Peru, Mexico and the People's Republic of China.[93]

Apart from the length of the decision-making process, a further related criticism which has been made is on the kinds of agreements which result from consensus decision-making. Often the lowest common denominator dictates that the outcome may be a set of obligations with a very high degree of generality or one steeped in qualifications. The technique of putting square brackets round parts of the text where there is no consensus can sometimes produce a labyrinthine set of brackets, resembling more an algebraic equation than a draft treaty article.[94]

Finally, there is the question of whether decisions reached using consensus are likely to be more or less implemented, than those reached on the basis of majority voting or other methods. While it might be assumed that a consensus decision formally should command wide support, in practice the degree of support a set of proposals commands may be uncertain, as in other forms of negotiation. That uncertainty or ambiguity may never be tested by vote or ascertained until after the conference, when the state may feel it does not wish to be bound by the terms of the consensus reached. Writing in the context of UNCTAD, Krishnamurti notes: 'many recommendations adopted by consensus in UNCTAD on trade, finance, least developed countries and other areas, remain only meagrely fulfilled'.[95] A frequently used term in discussion of the concept of consensus negotiations is the notion of a 'package deal'. In large-scale and complex multilateral diplomacy such a concept may not be a particularly exact means of understanding the negotiating processes. The 'package' may in fact be a political illusion.

In order to safeguard against some of these difficulties, modifications to the consensus role have been incorporated into implementation provisions. For example, in the General Scheme of Trade Preferences Among Developing Countries (GSTP), provisions are made for consensus or voting if requested when there is no consensus.[96] The rules of procedure require a two-thirds majority on matters of substance and a simple majority on procedural issues.

In order to speed up implementation and modification, the Montreal Protocol[97] introduces express tacit acceptance procedures for *adjustments*, which enter into force six months from notification for parties, as distinct from *amendments*, which are subject to ratification. The tacit acceptance procedure is one important method to reduce some of the ambiguity surrounding entry into force of agreements negotiated on the basis of consensus.

Conclusion

Contemporary diplomacy has undergone several significant changes in methods in recent years. The growth and frequency of personal diplomacy by heads of state or government has confirmed a general shift in the involvement and responsibility of chief executives for external policy. In the main this has been at the expense of foreign ministers, who nowadays often tend to be overshadowed by their counterparts from finance and trade. A related development has been the undoubted spread of bilateral diplomacy. At a commercial level governments have become much more involved in the management of bilateral trade on an intergovernmental basis as well as with non-state entities. Politically, high-level visits serve a number of purposes, not least of which are the bypassing of conventional organisational channels and the establishment of personal contact. In multilateral diplomacy a number of different methods have been attempted, including associative diplomacy, North–South 'bridging' diplomacy and large Pan-European security conferences, with varying degrees of success. While large-scale multilateral conferences have continued to be successful at a sectoral level in establishing regulatory regimes such as law of the sea, world health or telecommunications, global-style conferences with vast, redistributive agendas have not. A common feature, especially with global negotiations, is not only with the range of the agenda but the size of the negotiating groups, which have necessitated extensive efforts at constructing representative negotiating groups which are politically acceptable. These and the other changes in diplomatic methods discussed in the chapter suggest that the international community is in a period of transition in terms of diplomatic methods as it seeks to find workable arrangements for its expanded membership.

References and notes

1. P.J. Boyce, *Foreign Affairs for New States* (University of Queensland Press, St Lucia, Qld, 1977) pp. 62–5.
2. Elmer Plischke (ed.), *Modern Diplomacy – The Art and The Artisans* (American Enterprise Institute for Public Policy Research, Washington, DC, 1979) p. 177.
3. *The Guardian*, 10 Dec. 1984.
4. In an effort to resume arms control negotiations the United States renewed its offer to hold 'umbrella talks' with the Soviet Union in Oct. 1984. *The Guardian*, 16 Nov. 1984.
5. See John Gerrard Ruggie, 'The United States and the United Nations', *International Organisation*, Vol. 39, No. 2 (Spring 1985) pp. 343–56. On the US withdrawal from UNESCO, announced in Dec. 1983, see *Hearings*, Sub-committee on Human Rights and International Organisations of the Committee on Foreign Affairs, House of Representatives, 27 Sept. and 3 Oct. 1983; *US Withdrawal from UNESCO*, Report of a Staff Study Mission, Committee on Foreign Affairs, US House of Representatives, April 1984; *Assessment of US–UNESCO Relations 1984*, Report of a Staff Study Mission to Paris–UNESCO, Committee on Foreign Affairs, House of Representatives, 1985; *Hearings*, Sub-committees on Human Rights and International Organisations and International Operations, Committee of Foreign Affairs, House of Representatives, 26 July, 13 Sept., 6 Dec. 1984.
6. See M. Delal Baer and Sidney Weintraub, *The NAFTA Debate* (Lynne Rienner, Boulder, 1994); Convention on the Conservation and Management of Pollock Resources in the Central Bering Sea, June 1994; and *UKTS*, No. 46, 1982, Cmnd. 8685, for the Interim Agreement on Deep Sea Bed Mining between the US, Britain, France and Germany, prior to entry into force of the Law of the Sea Convention.

7. Timothy M. Shaw and Solar Oja, *Africa and the International Political System* (University of America Press, New York, 1982) pp. 22–3. On the decline of personal diplomacy and the evolution of South African foreign policy style see Deon Geldenhuys, *The Diplomacy of Isolation: South African Foreign Policymaking* (Macmillan, Johannesburg, 1984) pp. 17–19, 241–3.
8. Interview. For an account of a Singapore diplomat-MP see Lee Khoon Choy, *An Ambassador's Journey* (Times Books International, Singapore, 1983).
9. For example, Tolba (UNEP), Srivastava (IMO), Beltrano (International Coffee Organisation).
10. *Financial Times*, 9 Nov. 1993.
11. See *MEDWAVES*, No. 31 (Winter 1994–95), pp. 5–6 on the revision of the Barcelona Convention.
12. *Financial Times*, 10 July 1985.
13. *The Guardian*, 10 Dec. 1984.
14. *Sunday Times*, 23 Dec. 1984.
15. Sir Percy Spender, *Exercises in Diplomacy: The Anzus Treaties and the Colombo Plan* (Sydney University Press, Sydney, 1969) p. 35.
16. See Elmer Plishke, 'The New Diplomacy', in Plishke, op. cit., p. 70.
17. The 1963 US–Soviet direct communications link ('hotline') was renewed in an updated agreement of 30 Sept. 1971. John H. Barton, *International Arms Control* (Stanford University Press, Stanford, California, 1976) pp. 330–7.
18. The Paris summit was a landmark in the end of the Cold War. The summit endorsed the series of preceding negotiations on European troop reduction, force levels and frontiers.
19. Karen Dawisha, *The Russian Federation and the New States of Central Asia* (Cambridge University Press, Cambridge, 1994).
20. Since 1989, bilateral US–Soviet/Russian Federation summits at head of state level have been held in Malta (2–3 Dec. 1989, Bush–Gorbachev); Helsinki (9–10 Sept. 1990, Bush–Gorbachev); Moscow (30–1 July 1991, Bush–Gorbachev); Maryland (1 Feb. 1992, Bush–Yeltsin); Vancouver (3–4 April 1993, Clinton–Yeltsin); Moscow (6–7 May 1995, Clinton–Yeltsin meeting at 50th anniversary of Allied Victory over Nazi Germany).
21. *Times*, 4 Jan. 1995.
22. The 11–13 Feb. 1991 US–Soviet summit was postponed because of the Gulf War and Baltic crisis, until 30–1 July 1991.
23. For the main Soviet treaties with the Middle East and Asian states, see Zafar Iman, 'Soviet Treaties with Third World Countries', *Soviet Studies*, Vol. XXXV, No. 1 (Jan. 1983), pp. 53–70.
24. For historical origins and structure of the post-war Soviet economic-military alliance, see Michael Kaser, *Comecon* (Oxford University Press, London, 1967); Kurt Weisskoff, *Progress of the COMECON Integration Programme* (NATO, Directorate of Economic Affairs, Brussels, 1977); Vladimir Sobell, *The Red Market: Industrial Cooperation and Specialisation* (Gower, Aldershot, 1984).
25. 31 *ILM* 138 (1992).
26. *Times*, 3 April 1995.
27. *Keesing* (1994) pp. 39876 and 40201.
28. See IMF *Survey*, 17 April 1995.
29. See *Times*, 7 Jan. and 5 May 1995 on Western oil company involvement in Central Asia, and Russian Federation response. For economic union of Kazakhstan, Uzbekistan and Kirghizia see *Economist*, 15 Jan. 1994.
30. See Zafar Iman, op. cit., pp. 124–6.
31. For G-5 Contact Group negotiations with Serbia on conditions for relief of UN sanctions, see *Times*, 15 Feb. 1995.
32. *Keesing* (1994) p. 40103 for Moscow Declaration.
33. *Financial Times*, 1 March 1995.
34. Agreements with Russian Federation have included the Bushehr nuclear power plant, and aircraft sales agreements, see *Times*, 17 March 1995.

35. *Keesing* (1994) pp. 40199–200.
36. See Robert M. Cutler, 'East–South Relations at UNCTAD: Global Political Economy and the CMEA', *International Organisation*, Vol. 37, No. 1 (Winter 1983), pp. 121–42.
37. See Chapter 10.
38. Cesare Merlini (ed.), *Economic Summits and Western Decision-Making* (Croom Helm, London, 1984) p. 193.
39. See Economic Declaration, Munich Summit, 8 July 1992, para. 2.
40. An emergency NATO ministerial meeting was held on 15 Oct. at the request of Belgium and the Netherlands. *Financial Times*, 3 and 16 Oct. 1985. Italy and Canada were brought into the G-5 framework at Tokyo in a compromise which allowed the G-5 to hold its own meetings. See *Financial Times*, 6 May 1986.
41. *Financial Times*, 3 May 1986.
42. See for example Tokyo Economic Declaration and Political Declaration, 9 July 1993, paras 5 and 4–6 respectively.
43. See Maastricht Treaty, Title V, Provisions on a Common Foreign and Security Policy, Article J. 1–6.
44. *Financial Times*, 2 March 1995.
45. See R.P. Barston, 'The UN Conference on Straddling Stocks and Highly Migratory Fish Stocks', *Marine Policy*, Vol. 19, No. 2, 1995, pp. 159–66.
46. *Journal of the Group of 77*, Vol. 7, No. 5, May 1994.
47. The volunteer members in 1995–96. See *Journal of the Group of 77*, Vol. 7, No. 2, Feb. 1994, p. 1.
48. *Journal of the Group of 77*, Vol. 7, No. 5, May 1995.
49. *Journal of the Group of 77*, Vol. 7, No. 5, May 1995, p. 15.
50. See Chapter 10.
51. See *Journal of the Group of 77*, Vol. 17, No. 9, Sept. 1994, p. 7.
52. *Journal of the Group of 77*, Vol. 8, No. 1, Jan. 1995, p. 7.
53. For the Declaration of ASEAN Concord, the Treaty of Amity and Cooperation in South East Asia, and other documents from the Bali summit, see *10 Years ASEAN* (ASEAN, Jakarta, 1978) pp. 111–25.
54. *Europe Information External Relations* (16 Feb. 1979) p. 5.
55. *Europe Information External Relations*, X/68/83–EN (Feb. 1983) p. 4.
56. For a list of ASEAN non-governmental and private organisations, see *10 Years ASEAN*, ASEAN *Newsletter*, March–April 1984, pp. 2–4.
57. *Annual Report of the ASEAN Standing Committee 1982–3* (ASEAN Secretariat, Jakarta, 1983) p. 66.
58. See statement by Carlos P. Romulo at the 15th ASEAN Ministerial Meeting, 18 June 1982 (ASEAN Secretariat, Jakarta, 1982) p. 84.
59. See *Annual Report of the ASEAN Standing Committee 1982–3*, pp. 64 and 71.
60. See 15th ASEAN Ministerial Meeting, 14–16 June 1982, Joint Communiqué, p. 56, para. 54.
61. The project figures for dialogue partners have to be offset by financial contributions to the Asian Development Bank (ADB) made by dialogue partners.
62. For United States projects and objectives see ASEAN *Newsletter*, Jan./Feb. 1985, p. 9.
63. The Netherlands has two ASEAN projects, including setting up an ASEAN promotion centre in Rotterdam and on ASEAN export promotion. Details of other EC projects with individual ASEAN members can be found in *Europe Information External Relations*, X/68/83–EN, Table IV, pp. 11–12.
64. Details of the projects can be found in ASEAN *Newsletter*, Vol. 2, No. 2 (July 1981) pp. 4–5, 10.
65. See remarks by Dr M. MacGuigan, Canadian Secretary of State for External Affairs, 15th ASEAN Ministerial Meeting, p. 69. An ASEAN–Canadian Cooperation Agreement was, however, signed on 25 Sept. 1981 in New York.
66. See ASEAN *Update*, Sept. 1993, p. 1; and on Vietnam's admission July 1995, see ASEAN *Update*, Oct. 1995, p. 5.

67. The Community has developed a number of working arrangements for Community participation in international organisations and agreements. In some instances Community participation is higher than observer status, as in the OECD, as provided for in the Supplementary Protocol. In others the working arrangements are structured, as with the joint working parties in UNESCO. Since many organisations deal with issues falling within the jurisdiction of member states, Community representation sometimes takes the form of 'dual representation'. Under this system the Community is represented by both the Commission and the member state holding the presidency, with the Commission normally acting as spokesman on matters falling within Community jurisdiction, e.g. UN General Assembly, ECOSOC, UNCTAD. Other formulae include a single declaration of the Commission and member states, with the Commission acting as spokesman, as in the negotiation for the 1971 International Wheat Agreement, the 1973 International Sugar Agreement and the 1975 International Cocoa Agreement. The differences in the forms of representation reflect the evolution of Community competence, as well as its recognition in international fora. For details of the status of the Community in international institutions and regional intergovernmental organisations, see *The European Community, International Organisations and Multilateral Agreements*, 3rd rev. edn (Commission of the European Communities, Luxembourg, 1983) pp. 15–29. For the respective roles of the Commission and member governments in different negotiations, see Paul Taylor, *The Limits of European Integration* (Croom Helm, London, 1983) pp. 124 *passim* and p. 129.
68. On the arrangements with East Africa (Kenya, Tanzania and Uganda) see *Official Journal of the European Communities*, L282/55, 1970.
69. 2 *ILM*, 971.
70. *Official Journal of the European Communities*, L25/1, 1976; *UKTS*, No. 105, 1979, Cmnd. 7751.
71. The Third ACP–EEC Convention, signed at Lomé, 8 Dec. 1984, ACP–EEC Council of Ministers, BX-43-85-377-EN-C, 1985. See the special issue of *The Courier*, No. 89, Jan.–Feb. 1985, and *Lomé III, Analysis of the EEC–ACP Convention*, X/123/1985 (Commission of the European Communities, Brussels). The ACP include: Antigua and Barbuda, Bahamas, Barbados, Belize, Benin, Botswana, Burkina Faso, Burundi, Cameroon, Cape Verde Islands, Central African Republic, Chad, Comoros, Congo, Djibouti, Dominica, Equatorial Guinea, Ethiopia, Fiji, Gabon, Ghana, Grenada, Guinea, Guinea-Bissau, Guyana, Ivory Coast, Jamaica, Kenya, Kiribati, Lesotho, Liberia, Madagascar, Malawi, Mali, Mauritania, Mauritius, Mozambique, Niger, Nigeria, Papua New Guinea, Rwanda, St Christopher and Nevis, St Lucia, St Vincent and the Grenadines, Sao Tomé and Principe, Senegal, Seychelles, Sierra Leone, Solomon Islands, Somalia, Sudan, Suriname, Swaziland, Tanzania, Togo, Tonga, Trinidad and Tobago, Tuvalu, Uganda, Western Samoa, Vanuatu, Zaïre, Zambia and Zimbabwe.
72. Carol Cosgrove Twitchet, *A Framework for Development: The EEC and the ACP* (George Allen and Unwin, London, 1981).
73. The Joint Committee and Consultative Assembly (256 parliamentary representatives) were merged under Lomé III because of the overlap between the two institutions. See *The Courier*, No. 88 (Nov.–Dec. 1984) p. 3.
74. *The Courier*, No. 90 (March–April 1985).
75. Although still referred to as the 'Article 108 Committee', the relevant article in Lomé III is 193.
76. Article 220(6) of Lomé III.
77. For the geographical distribution of EIB finance in ACP states, see *Annual Report of the ACP–EEC Council of Ministers, 1993*, Table 6, p. 79.
78. Stabex is a compensation scheme for loss of export earnings from agricultural products caused by falls in prices. Under Lomé II, minerals, which were excluded from Stabex, are covered by a scheme known as 'Sysmin'. This is designed to provide assistance to improve mining production. In contrast to Stabex which has been heavily used, Sysmin has not yet been drawn on much except by Zaïre and Zambia. See Hamini Kibola, 'Stabex and Lomé III', *Journal of World Trade Law*, Vol. 18 (1984) pp. 32–51.

79. On the EIB see Arnold Heertje (ed.), *Investing in Europe's Future* (Basil Blackwell, Oxford, 1983); *The Courier*, No. 83 (Jan.–Feb. 1984) pp. 7–14.

80. Election to the post of Secretary-General of the OAU has been a source of considerable controversy within the organisation. At the Mogadishu summit in 1974, twenty ballots were required before Eteki Mboumoua (Cameroon) was elected. The 1983 and 1984 summits were similarly deadlocked and an interim Secretary-General (Onu, Nigeria) was installed. See *West Africa*, 15 July 1985, p. 1409.

81. ACP Council, 37th meeting in Lomé, Dec. 1982.

82. Inis L. Claude Jr., *Swords into Plowshares* (University of London Press, London, 1964) p. 112.

83. See Klaus Tornudd, 'From unanimity to voting and consensus. Trends and Phenomena in Joint Decision Making by Governments', *Cooperation and Conflict*, Vol. 17 (1982) p. 165.

84. Rule 18, Rules of Procedure of the Committee on Disarmament, *The United Nations Yearbook* (United Nations, New York, 1979) Vol. 3, 1978, p. 487.

85. Appendix to 1974 Rules of Procedure, 27 June 1974. The agreement to use consensus was reached on 16 Nov. 1973.

86. See Tornudd, op. cit., pp. 170–1.

87. TD/2 136. See UNCTAD IV, Vol. 1, pp. 53–4. For other examples of voting in UNCTAD, see R. Krishnamurti, 'UNCTAD as a Negotiating Instrument', *Journal of World Trade Law*, Vol. 15, No. 1 (Jan.–Feb. 1981) pp. 14–18.

88. Following the decision on the Mexican package, the UK, Germany, Belgium, Switzerland, the Netherlands, and Norway, representing over forty countries, asked for their position to be recorded as abstention. Belgium later revoked its abstention. See *Financial Times*, 16 Feb. 1995.

89. Ibid., pp. 18–29.

90. See R.P. Barston, 'The Law of the Sea. The Conference and After', *Journal of World Trade Law*, Vol. 17, No. 3 (May–June 1983) pp. 208–10.

91. See R.P. Barston, 'The Third UN Law of the Sea Conference', in G.R. Berridge and A. Jennings, *Diplomacy at the UN* (Macmillan, London, 1985) pp. 158 *passim*.

92. See IMO, LDC 9/12, 18 Oct. 1985, p. 37 *passim*.

93. See R.P. Barston and Patricia Birnie (eds), *The Maritime Dimension* (George Allen and Unwin, London, 1980) pp. 155–6.

94. As an example see the selected documents of the second Non-Proliferation Treaty (NPT) review conference, in Stockholm International Peace Research Institute (SIPRI), *Yearbook, 1981*, pp. 346–65.

95. Krishnamurti, op. cit., p. 7.

96. 27 *ILM* 1204, 1988, Article 7 2 (b).

97. 26 *ILM* 1541, 1987, Article 2 9 (c).

CHAPTER 7

International financial relations

Within the past decade questions to do with international financial relations have increasingly moved to the forefront of the international agenda. A noticeable feature of this development is the rise in importance of the International Monetary Fund (IMF) and the International Bank for Reconstruction and Development (IBRD) as international institutions responsible for the co-ordination and management of international liquidity and development finance. This chapter explores two areas: the main developments in the organisation and work of the Fund after 1973, and the management of the international debt crisis, including the role of the Fund.[1]

Historical background

The IMF and the World Bank were formally set up on 27 December 1945, following the Bretton Woods conference, attended by 44 countries.[2] Bretton Woods in fact was one of several major conferences held during the closing stages of the Second World War on the establishment of post-war institutions, including the United Nations conferences on food and agriculture at Hot Springs, Virginia, in May 1943, which culminated in the San Francisco conference of April 1945, setting up the United Nations. The Havana Charter, which was intended to establish an international trade organisation (ITO) to complement the IMF and the Bank, was, however, never ratified. It was not until 1947 that a much reduced version of an ITO in the form of the GATT was established at Geneva.

The framing and drafting of the Bretton Woods agreements was strongly influenced by the wartime setting and the need to prevent the recurrence of a collapse of the international monetary system similar to that of the 1930s.[3] The themes of reconstruction and the transition from a wartime to a peacetime international economy dominated the original conception of the Fund and the Bank. In this respect too the original conception of the Bank was weighted in favour of the reconstruction of the economies of the war-torn European states, rather than addressing the economic concerns of developing countries. It is interesting to note in this context that the Indian proposals at Bretton Woods to include specific reference to the need for assistance for developing countries in the articles of agreement made little headway.[4]

The Bretton Woods system

The Fund's main tasks, as set out in article 1, were the provision of international liquidity and assistance to members with balance of payments difficulties. Associated with these functions was the aim of promoting the orderly development of trade by discouraging direct controls, such as import quotas or discriminatory tariffs, to influence the balance of payments, but the failure of states to ratify the Havana Charter, partly because of uncertainties caused by the scale of post-war reconstruction, meant that institutionally the IMF and the Bank were weakened since trade matters were not closely grouped with the work of the Fund or the Bank.

A key element of the Bretton Woods system was the maintenance of orderly exchange rates. An initial par value for the currencies of individual members was agreed, which could only be altered in the event of fundamental disequilibrium. The resources which the Fund has at its disposal for extending balance of payments assistance to member countries are derived from subscriptions equal to their quotas (ordinary resources) and borrowing from official institutions. Subscriptions are paid partly in an acceptable reserve asset and partly in a member's own currency. Apart from their reserve position in the Fund, members have access to Fund credit in four tranches or segments of 25 per cent of their quota up to a limit of 100 per cent of quota. This is not necessarily an absolute limit and may be exceeded depending on the type of programme, assessed needs and the current guidelines on access.[5] Drawings (purchases) above 25 per cent of quota are subject to increasing *conditionality*. This involves Fund consultations with the member on performance criteria and reviews of its macro-economic policies.

The functions of the Fund can be summarised as: regulatory (exchange rates), financial (providing additional liquidity) and consultative (providing a forum for the collective management of monetary and financial relations). As Cohen notes: 'For the first time ever, governments were formally committing themselves to the principle of collective responsibility for the management of the international monetary order.'[6]

The institutional arrangements were based on the clear distinction in principle that the IMF was to be a revolving fund lending surpluses to deficit countries on a temporary basis. The IBRD, on the other hand, was to be responsible for long-term lending. In more recent times, however, the blurring of this distinction is especially noteworthy.

Institutional arrangements

Under the articles of agreement, the principal decision-making body in the Fund is the Board of Governors (article XII). It consists of one governor and one alternate governor appointed by each member of the Fund, who is usually the minister of finance or governor of the central bank and who serves for five years, subject to the approval of the appointing member. The Executive Board, which conducts the day-to-day business of the Fund, consists of both appointed and elected members. The members with the five largest quotas are each empowered to appoint an executive director, while the remainder are elected on a group basis. Elections are normally held every two years. In addition, the two members with the largest reserve positions in the Fund over the preceding two years may also each appoint an executive director, unless they are already entitled to do so by virtue of the size of their quotas. The Executive Board is chaired by the managing director, an office which has increasingly acquired significant, if discreet, political importance.[7] The Board of Governors have a number of powers not shared by the Executive Board, including the admission of new members, the determination of quotas and the distribution of the net income of the Fund. Since 1953 the governing bodies of both the Fund and the World Bank have held consecutive meetings in Washington, DC, and every third annual meeting is in a member country other than the United States.

In many respects the original aims and purposes of the Bank were not dissimilar from those of the Fund. As originally conceived (article 1) the Bank's purposes were to facilitate the investment of capital for productive purposes, including the restoration of economies destroyed by war, the conversion of productive facilities to peacetime needs and, only thirdly, encouraging the development of productive facilities in less developed countries. These aims were to be achieved through Bank guarantees and loans, although in practice the greater contributions to capital flows have not been through guarantees but direct lending. The Bank was established as a joint-stock bank, initially capitalised at $US 10 billion. Under article 5 (section 3) each member has 250 votes plus one additional vote for each share of the stock held. Whereas in the Fund quotas were the bench-mark for drawing rights, in the Bank, the ability to borrow was independent of capital contributions.

The institutional arrangements of the Bank closely follow those of the Fund. These provide for a board of governors, executive directors and president, supported, like the Fund, by an international staff. Some 23 countries have traditionally provided ten or more staff to the Bank, with the largest concentration being made up of nationals from the United States, United Kingdom, Germany, Japan, Australia, Canada, Pakistan and India.[8] There are three main institutional differences between the Bank and the Fund. In the first place the Bank's articles of agreement provide for an advisory council, although in practice this rapidly fell into disuse. Unlike the Fund, the Bank, secondly and most importantly, contains no jurisdictional provisions which limit the sovereignty of its members in the financial field. As such the Bank's power of supervision, formally at least, is related to control over its own loan operations. The other difference relates to requirements for information. The Fund contains provisions on a wide range of information which members are obliged to provide on their payments, reserves and import–export positions. These have no counterpart in the Bank's articles of agreement, except for information required about projects financed by the Bank.

A special organisational feature of the Bank is the strong position of its president, who, as the chief executive, is responsible for recommending the terms and conditions of loans to the governing directors, as well as organisational questions relating to the staffing and running of the Bank. In practice the office of president has acquired importance, from the latter period of Eugene Black's presidency through that of Wood and particularly Robert McNamara, when the Bank's role changed from being a bank *per se* to become the central international development agency with a philosophy geared to project lending rather than more general programme aid.

Apart from operating as a development finance agency, the Bank has also acted in a dispute settlement role as well as providing financial and other consultancy services to members. For example President Wood acted as a mediator in the negotiations after the Suez crisis which led to the financial settlement between the United Arab Republic and the Suez Canal Company shareholders.[9] The Bank subsequently acted as fiscal agent for funds contributed by various governments towards the cost of clearance of the canal. A further example of the successful mediatory role of the Bank can be seen in the long-running negotiations involving the Bank, India and Pakistan over the development of the Indus waters, which culminated eventually in the Indus Waters Treaty of 1960.[10] With the creation of the International Finance Corporation (IFC) in 1956 and the International Development Association (IDA) in 1960, the three institutions became known as the 'World Bank Group'.

The evolution of the fund

The impact of the Fund and the Bank during the late 1940s and early 1950s was limited in view of the scale of post-war reconstruction. For the most part reconstruction finance was channelled from 1947 through the Marshall Aid Programme. Apart from the loans of 1947, the IMF made no further major loans until 1956. The shortage of Fund liquidity in effect meant that the United States became the residual source of international liquidity through the dollar, with the dollar acting as the major vehicle for international trade and investment and a reserve asset for central banks. However, a number of developments in the late 1950s and early 1960s served to alter the focus of operations of both the Fund and the Bank as well as lessen the influence of the United States. In particular, from 1961 to 1963, there was an unprecedented increase in the accession of new members to the Fund, largely because of the rapid decolonisation in Africa, which raised the membership to 102.[11] The expansion in membership inevitably brought an extended range of interests into the Fund, and radically altered the scale of potential demands on

Fund resources. Apart from this, the period from the late 1950s, saw the
major Western European powers emerge as a leading decision-making
group on international and financial and monetary matters. By this stage
European and Japanese recovery had moved out of the post-war reconstruction phase. Above all, the convertibility of Western European
currencies (Japan followed in 1961) symbolised this transition, which
was accompanied by a rapid development of the European capital markets. In contrast, serious balance of payments deficits after 1958 led not
only to concern in the United States about international confidence in the
dollar, but the overall role of the United States in the Bretton Woods system, as the leading banker and aid donor. Commenting on the changed
monetary relationships, Solomon, for example, contrasts the visit of
Treasury Secretary Robert B. Anderson and Under-Secretary of State
Dillon, to Europe in 1960, to discuss with European officials ways of
reducing the strain on the American balance of payments, especially the
relief of US troop costs in Germany, with the visit eleven years earlier of
Treasury Secretary John W. Snyder bringing with him in almost imperial
style US proposals for a devaluation of sterling and other European currencies.[12]

Against this context, the Group of 10 (G-10) made up of Belgium,
Canada, France, FRG, Italy, Japan, the Netherlands, Sweden, United
Kingdom and the United States began to play an increasingly central
role in negotiations on financial and monetary matters. The importance
of the G-10, as the leading group within the Fund, can be seen institutionally in the borrowing arrangements, exclusive to G-10 members,
known as the General Arrangements to Borrow (GAB).[13] The GAB,
which was agreed by the G-10 after the Paris negotiations in December
1961 and approved by the Fund's Executive Board in January 1962,
commenced with a US$6 billion credit line. Although this was a valu-
able source of supplementary finance for the Fund, the GAB could only
be called upon to finance drawings from the Fund by the participants.
Unlike other Fund arrangements, major amendments to the GAB require
the approval not only of the Executive Board but the agreement of all
ten original participants.[14] The arrangements for the GAB remained
essentially unaltered until 1982. The exclusivity to the G-10 of the
GAB, coupled with the undermining of collective decision-making, led
to criticism by industrialised countries outside the arrangements, as well
as less developed countries.

SDRs

The influence of the G-10 was particularly illustrated during the negotiations to create a new reserve asset (later termed 'special drawing rights'
or SDRs) from 1966 to 1968.[15] Much of the preparatory work was conducted within the G-10 framework. However, the position of the Fund
was asserted by the then Managing Director, Pierre-Paul Schweitzer,
who sought to broaden the framework of discussions beyond the G-10.

In this Schweitzer was supported by the United States, which preferred the discussions to be held within the framework of the IMF, rather than face the possible concerted position of the EC. Four meetings of the deputies of the G-10 and the executive directors of the IMF, ten of whom represented groups other than the G-10, were subsequently held during 1966–67. A further feature of the SDR negotiations was the close Franco-German collaboration, which has become a feature of the conduct of diplomacy on major international financial questions. Although the Fund itself did not in this instance take a leading role, the SDR negotiations did contribute to its technical status, through the secretariat work carried out by Fund staff. The SDR facility came into existence in July 1969, when sufficient approval was received (three-fifths of the members of the Fund having four-fifths of the total voting power) for the amendment to the Fund Articles of Agreement to come into force. The Fund made an initial allocation of SDRs the following year.

Other facilities

Two further facilities in the period under review, the establishment of the compensatory financing facility (CFF)[16] and the buffer stock financing facility, illustrate new areas of operations reflecting the Fund's expanded membership. The CFF, which was set up in 1963, was established to provide assistance mainly for the exporters of primary products who were experiencing payments difficulties due to fluctuations in export earnings. The CFF was complemented in June 1969 by the buffer stock facility, through which funds are made available to assist members in meeting their contributions under approved international buffer stock agreements, such as the international sugar, tin, cocoa and natural rubber agreements.[17] Unlike the CFF, this latter facility has not been greatly used owing to the problems of setting up and managing buffer stocks.

End of Bretton Woods

The Bretton Woods system of par values and convertibility of the dollar was in effect brought to an end in August 1971 by the package of measures taken by the United States, which included the temporary suspension of dollar convertibility and a 10 per cent additional import tax, in response to the exchange rate crisis.[18] The dollar was further devalued in February 1973 and shortly afterwards most major currencies were allowed to float.

What form a future international monetary system might take was entrusted in July 1972 to the IMF's Committee of the Board of Governors on Reform of the International Monetary System and Related Issues (known as the 'Committee of 20'). In the event the Committee of 20 achieved few of its long-range tasks, being overtaken by the events of the Arab–Israeli War and the subsequent oil crisis, which narrowed the committee's focus of negotiation to more immediate concerns. The problems of conducting complex multilateral negotiation on monetary reform are summed up by Fleming in this observation on the Committee of 20:[19]

Very few of the major countries established coherent national positions over the whole range of these issues, and only the United States brought out a fairly comprehensive statement of its position. ... The Europeans handicapped themselves by trying to agree issue by issue on a joint EEC position. The less developed countries made great efforts to agree a common programme of reform through the Group of Twenty-Four, but this agreement was inevitably confined to a few isolated matters of common interest such as the nature of the link between SDR creation and development finance.

A number of immediate measures, however, set out in the second part of the committee's report, *Outline for Reform*, were later adopted by the Fund. These included the setting up of an oil facility and extended borrowing arrangements which are discussed separately below. The need for a broad-based advisory committee was also recognised and the Committee of 20 was continued as a committee of the Fund, under the title 'Interim Committee'.

Post-Bretton Woods

Following the exchange rate crisis of 1971–73 a number of broad changes took place over the next decade in the structure and roles of the Fund. With exchange rates for major currencies floating, the Fund's regulatory functions received less emphasis. The second of the Fund's functions, the provision of international liquidity, began to assume greater importance, particularly through the provision of standby arrangements. However, as the scale of lending operations increased in the 1970s, the Fund found it could no longer rely on the resources derived from members' subscriptions and subsequently had to negotiate additional bilateral arrangements ('borrowed resources') with individual states, notably oil producers and large industrial countries. Borrowed resources have been used to establish temporary facilities for members with large balance of payments imbalances in relation to their quota and requiring large resources for long periods over and above the normal limits of borrowing. The supplementary financing facility (SFF) was set up in 1979 and broadly similar arrangements continued under the enlarged access policy from 1981–92 after the funds had been committed under the SFF. Following the second oil crisis of 1979, the Fund became an important financial intermediary *vis-à-vis* central banks, development agencies, the Bank for International Settlements (BIS) and creditor governments, as multi-funding operations were developed to meet enhanced payments difficulties. With this development, the Fund's third function, as a co-ordination and decision-making centre, came to assume more importance, especially after the onset of the debt crisis in 1982, although the Fund did not become the principal source of balance of payments support, since multilateral restructuring of debt and other financial support increasingly involved the central and commercial banks and other development institutions.

Institutional developments

In the main the formal and informal structural changes in the Fund's central institutions have had the effect of broadening the participation in decision-making by introducing a wider range of states into the processes of dialogue and negotiation. Some of these changes, however, have been pragmatic appreciations of alterations in the political or economic importance of states. Thus Saudi Arabia and the People's Republic of China have been added as single constituency members of the Executive Board. Saudi Arabia has appointed an executive director since 1978, which raised the executive directors to 21. In September 1980 the Board of Governors approved the increase in the number of elected members from fifteen to sixteen, which enabled China to elect a director with only that country as the constituency, bringing the total number of executive directors to 22. The Russian Federation joined the IMF in 1991.[20]

Interim Committee

The establishment of the Interim Committee as the successor to the Committee of 20 in October 1974 was an important addition to the formal decision-making machinery of the Fund. The committee brings together at the level of Fund governor, ministers or equivalent rank 24 representatives, each of whom may appoint associates, plus the Fund managing director, and observers from international and regional organisations. Switzerland also had observer status, until full IMF membership in 1992.

The Interim Committee, which meets usually twice a year, normally in conjunction with the IMF's annual meeting, and again in the spring, is responsible for the provision of advice and recommendations to the Board of Governors and Executive Board in three broad areas. These are: (i) the proposals of the Executive Board to amend the articles of agreement; (ii) measures to deal with sudden disturbances that pose a threat to the international monetary system; (iii) supervising the management and adaptation of the international monetary system. Between 1974 and 1976, for example, the Interim Committee had under its first and second areas of responsibility been concerned with the amendments to the Fund's articles to permit floating and setting up and operation of the oil facility. Under the third area, the Interim committee has examined the issue of SDR allocation, the Fund's enlarged access policy, and made recommendations on quota limits.[21] The Interim Committee continues to operate under its anomalous title since its intended successor, the council, envisaged as having decision-making powers rather than advisory ones like the committee, has never commanded sufficient political support to enable it to be set up.[22]

Development Committee

The Development Committee, the second of the two committees established as part of the recommendations of the Committee of 20, was intended to carry on its work on the transfer of real resources to developing countries. Unlike the Interim Committee it is a joint committee of the Fund and Bank. The committee consists of 22 members, generally ministers of finance, appointed in turn for successive periods of two years by each of the countries or groups of countries that nominates or appoints a member of the Bank's or IMF's Board of Executive Directors. In the main the Development Committee has lacked a clear set of tasks given its very broad mandate. The Development Committee's large size, with anything up to 150 participants, has also contributed to the committee having little impact. The Development Committee conceivably could have occupied a more central role, other than as a discussion forum, as a link between the Fund and the Bank. However, in practice it has tended to occupy an area covered by other international institutions such as UNCTAD, and straddled the borderlines between orthodox IMF functions, trade and development finance.

In recognition of the need to clarify the mandate and improve the effectiveness of the committee, a number of changes to its procedures were made in April 1979.[23] A more novel approach was taken in September 1984 in response to initiatives from the June 1984 London seven-nation economic summit, the Cartagena group of foreign and finance ministers and the September 1984 meeting of the Commonwealth finance ministers, which called for a special extended meeting of the Development Committee on specifically defined finance, trade and debt issues. A number of changes subsequently were made for the informal session of the Development Committee held in April 1985, including the curtailment of the heavily attended plenary sessions, which had tended in the past to be largely taken up with prepared statements. The agenda of the informal sessions was also co-ordinated with the parallel Interim Committee meeting. These and other changes have had the effect of moving the Development Committee somewhat more in the direction of the second of the two types of roles noted above, that is, as a vehicle for facilitating links between the Fund and the Bank.[24]

Group of 24

Apart from the Interim and Development Committee, the establishment of the Group of 24 in November 1971, known officially as the Intergovernmental Group of 24 on International Monetary Affairs (G-24), should be noted. The stimulus for the creation of the group, which is a ministerial committee of the G-77 and not an official committee of the Fund, came from the virtual exclusion of developing countries from the main negotiations conducted by the G-10 on the creation of the SDR and the 1971–73 exchange rate crisis.

The G-24 comprises eight members each drawn from Africa, Asia and Latin America. The People's Republic of China also attends as an invitee. The group has steadily increased its effectiveness, especially from the late 1970s, but it has not yet been able to develop the level of contact and co-ordination of the G-10. In fact since 1973 the G-10 has intensified its extensive network of ministerial and official contacts, through regular meetings of its finance ministers, the subdivision into the G-5 and meetings of the G-7 deputies, normally in Paris in conjunction with officials from OECD's Working Party 3. The G-24, however, has gradually developed from being simply a co-ordinating body to a forum for the preparation and presentation to the Fund and other institutions of its own concerted programmes, such as the 1979 Plan of Immediate Action. Meetings of the G-24 at deputy and ministerial[25] level usually take place prior to those of the Interim Committee.[26] The Fund provides secretariat support. Although the size and disparate range of interests has limited the degree of co-ordination, a core group has emerged, made up of Argentina, Mexico, Brazil, India and Pakistan, whose ministers and officials individually play important roles inter-governmentally and as staff in international financial institutions.

Development of fund facilities

The Fund has been concerned with six broad issues since 1973:

1. The problems generated by fluctuations in commodity prices, such as petroleum, or shortfalls in commodity export earnings from, for example, cereals, sugar, tin, rubber and other commodities;
2. Long-term arrangements to assist structural adjustment;
3. The enlargement of the resources of the Fund;
4. Increases in quotas;
5. The extended payments crisis;
6. Post-communist economic reconstruction in Russia, Eastern Europe and Central Asia.

In the main the Fund's approach, particularly on the first of these issues, has been based on augmenting the existing facilities, that is, standby arrangements, with a number of temporary facilities including those for oil, as well as the supplementary financing facility and enlarged access policy (see Table 7.1). To a large extent the use of short-term facilities has been influenced by the third of the issues, that is, the problem of enhancing the Fund's resources over and above that derived from members' subscriptions.

Underlying the debate about enlarging the access to Fund resources are a number of different issues. As regards *borrowed* resources, some of the larger Western industrialised countries felt that the Fund might become unduly dependent on OPEC, although this view has to some extent been modified out of reluctant necessity. A separate issue has been whether there is actually a need for larger access on a continuing

Table 7.1   IMF arrangements in effect at end of financial years ended April 30, 1953–95

Financial Year	Number of Arrangements as of April 30					Amounts Committed Under Arrangements as of April 30 (in millions of SDRs)				
	Stand-by	EFF	SAF	ESAF	Total	Stand-by	EFF	SAF	ESAF	Total
1953	2				2	55				55
1954	3				3	113				113
1955	3				3	113				113
1956	3				3	98				98
1957	9				9	1,195				1,195
1958	9				9	968				968
1959	11				11	1,013				1,013
1960	12				12	351				351
1961	12				12	416				416
1962	21				21	2,129				2,129
1963	17				17	1,520				1,520
1964	19				19	2,160				2,160
1965	23				23	2,154				2,154
1966	24				24	575				575
1967	25				25	591				591
1968	31				31	2,227				2,227
1969	25				25	538				538
1970	23				23	2,381				2,381
1971	18				18	502				502
1972	13				13	314				314
1973	12				12	282				282
1974	15				15	1,394				1,394
1975	12				12	337				337
1976	17	2			19	1,159	284			1,443
1977	17	3			20	4,673	802			5,475
1978	19	3			22	5,075	802			5,877
1979	15	5			20	1,033	1,611			2,643
1980	22	7			29	2,340	1,463			3,803
1981	22	15			37	5,331	5,464			10,795
1982	23	12			35	6,296	9,910			16,206
1983	30	9			39	9,464	15,561			25,025
1984	30	5			35	5,448	13,121			18,569
1985	27	3			30	3,925	7,750			11,675
1986	24	2			26	4,076	831			4,907
1987	23	1	10		34	4,313	750	327		5,391
1988	18	2	25		45	2,187	995	1,357		4,540
1989	14	2	23	7	46	3,054	1,032	1,566	955	6,608
1990	19	4	17	11	51	3,597	7,834	1,110	1,370	13,911
1991	14	5	12	14	45	2,703	9,597	539	1,813	14,652
1992	22	7	8	16	53	4,833	12,159	101	2,111	19,203
1993	15	6	4	20	45	4,490	8,569	83	2,137	15,279
1994	16	6	3	22	47	1,131	4,504	80	2,713	8,428
1995	19	9	1	27	56	13,190	6,840	49	3,306	23,385

Source: Annual Report IMF 1995

basis. Lack of agreement on this within the Fund has in turn prevented wider agreement on quotas versus borrowed resources to finance access. The issues of quota increases and other aspects of enlarged access, including SDR allocation are returned to at the end of the chapter.

As regards structural adjustment facilities, the Fund has implemented a number of the ideas discussed in the Committee of 20 including an additional permanent facility known as the extended fund facility (EFF), which was set up in September 1974. The EFF is intended to provide support for member countries willing to undertake medium-term structural adjustment programmes which are experiencing payments difficulties for structural reasons such as production difficulties, changing patterns of trade, or weakness in their payments position because of development-related imports. The EFF facilities normally run for three years for amounts greater than the members' quota.

Modifications have also been made to other permanent facilities. For example, the CFF was extended in August 1979 to include fluctuations in receipts from travel and workers' remittances in the calculation of the export shortfall. A further modification was made to the CFF in May 1981, partly on the initiative of the UN Food and Agricultural Organisation (FAO), to extend the CFF to provide coverage for cereal crop failure or a sharp increase in the cost of cereal imports. Purchases under the CFF between 1979 and 1981 amounted to nearly SDR 1 billion, almost one-third of total purchases from the Fund.[27]

The CFF has been progressively expanded in 1979 and again in 1990 as a result of the Gulf conflict, to widen the range of services to include loss of earnings from pipe lines, canal transit fees, shipping and insurance. A contingency financing component was subsequently added and the facility was retitled Compensatory and Contingency Financing Facility (CCFF).

Short-term facilities

Between 1974 and 1981 three short-term Fund facilities were set up using *borrowed* resources. These were the oil facilities (1974 and 1975) and the SFF. Both schemes were later augmented by special low-interest subsidy accounts for countries, defined by the UN Secretary-General and Fund staff, which were worst affected by oil price increases or other special factors.[28] The Fund's experience in establishing these facilities suggests a number of general difficulties with regard to the negotiation of borrowed resources. In the first place, the schemes have encountered political opposition. The first oil facility was opposed by the United States in response to OPEC policies, which after the outbreak of the October 1973 War classified countries for the purposes of the oil embargo on the basis of whether they were friendly to Arab interests (e.g. Britain, France and Spain), 'neutral' (e.g. Japan and Germany) or hostile (e.g. United States and the Netherlands). Although the embargo ended in March 1974, oil price rises (the marker for Gulf crude rose to $11.65 after January 1974) had long-reaching effects on the economies of non-oil exporting developing countries, IMF facilities and the source of IMF funds.[29] United States opposition in the Interim Committee was later withdrawn through a compromise that modifications to the Fund's articles would make it possible for the Fund to use a wider range of member-country currencies, in conformity with Fund policies, so increasing the liquidity of the Fund.[30] A second general problem arises from the need to secure a pool of contributions. The first oil facility was extended in 1975 when the Interim Committee recommended borrowing up to SDR 5 billion. To reach the target the Fund had to conclude agreements with fourteen countries, seven of whom (mainly oil exporters) had contributed to the 1974 facility.[31] The United States was noticeably absent from the list of contributors.[32] Borrowing under the oil facilities was confined to 1974 and 1975. The oil facility was dissolved after 1983, which coincided with the softening of petroleum prices, by which stage outstanding repayments had been cleared.[33]

Not dissimilar difficulties were encountered over the establishment of the SFF (1977), although in this case the United States contributed to the financing of the facility. The scheme called for borrowing up to SDR 7.8 billion to provide additional support to countries with standby or extended arrangements, for adjustment programmes of up to three years. The facility took a considerable time to enter into operation (February 1979), a point criticised by the Interim Committee at its meeting in April 1978 in Mexico City.[34] To raise the required SDR 7.8 billion the Fund had to negotiate contributions, and later terms, with fourteen countries, plus the Swiss National Bank. Not only was the group amorphous, but it included a significant number of small contributions including those made by Qatar, Abu Dhabi, Kuwait, Belgium and somewhat curiously, Guatemala. The major contributions were on an 'on-call' basis and as part of the liquid reserve assets of the donor could be called or expire before being drawn down. Furthermore, as part of the terms and conditions, purchases were at US commercial rates at OPEC insistence which, with conditionality, made the facility less attractive.[35] Yet, the SFF was virtually fully drawn and no new commitments were permitted after February 1982.

Enlarged access policy

The unsatisfactory nature of the borrowing arrangements for the oil facilities and the SFF influenced a move away from individual OPEC countries to a more stable and cohesive donor group. From 1981 the Fund has relied heavily for borrowed resources on a group made up of the central banks, the BIS,[36] the Saudi Arabian Monetary Agency (SAMA) and Japan. Saudi Arabia's enhanced role in the Fund (analogous to that of Japan in the World Bank), as a major contributor of borrowed resources, is perhaps one of the most marked recent features in the development of the Fund. In May 1981 an agreement was concluded by the Fund with SAMA to borrow up to SDR 8 billion over six years. This enabled the Fund to continue lending operations using a mixture of ordinary and borrowed resources after the phasing out of the SFF in 1982. In order to provide continued funding for the enlarged access policy, four new borrowing arrangements for SDR 6.8 billion were concluded with SAMA, the BIS, Japan and the National Bank of Belgium in April 1984. Although the enlarged access policy is properly regarded as a short-term arrangement, it has however been extended *ad hoc* on an annual basis from 1984 to 1992, using short- and medium-term borrowed resources.

Quotas and Fund resources

The enlarged access policy was terminated in November 1992, as a result of quota increases becoming effective under the Ninth General Review of quotas. The eventual agreement on quota increases in effect enabled the Fund to switch over to a policy of reduced dependence on borrowed resources.[37] The cost, however, was achieved largely by IMF members drawing down on SDRs, leading the Managing Director to call for a new issue of SDRs. Other facilities developed since 1982 in addition to stand-by arrangements have mainly been of an *ad hoc* kind. An exception is the Extended Fund Facility (EFF) which has been continued as a vehicle for providing medium-term programmes over three to four years aimed at overcoming structural balance of payments problems. Countries which have used the EFF include Lithuania, Jordan, Egypt, Philippines. Examples of *ad hoc* concessional facilities include the Structural Adjustment Facility (SAF) 1986–93, and the Enhanced Structural Adjustment Facility (ESAF), based on the IMF's Trust Fund for low income member countries.

The inability of the IMF to agree on appropriate long-term facilities, rather than a series of *ad hoc* arrangements, reflects the divisions among industrialised countries,[38] and between industrialised countries and the G-24 over the expansion of IMF resources.[39] Substantial differences have continued since the onset of the debt crisis over (1) the need for a general issue of SDRs and the effect of this on global inflation; (2) the need for and scale of increase in IMF quotas; (3) the means of funding for special facilities for those poorest heavily indebted countries with little prospect of repaying or restructuring public (mainly Paris Club) official debt or debt to commercial banking sources. One of the proposed solutions was to open up the conditions for access to General Arrangements to Borrow (GAB).[40] However, although the GAB has been progressively liberalised since 1983, this solution has been regarded as inadequate by the G-24 and other developing countries, who have preferred a package of measures, including general quota increases, rather than emergency Mexican influenced rescue schemes.[41]

Multilateral debt restructuring

The international debt crisis which developed in mid-1982 posed major problems of management for the international community. Not only were there no established institutional arrangements to cope with the scale of debt restructuring or renegotiations, but also no single institution or state group was capable of providing unaided the necessary financial resources to meet the needs of deficit countries. Prior to 1982, restructuring of official and commercial debt was generally on a small scale. Banks, too, preferred to avoid formal renegotiations. Such restructuring as took place was generally of a conventional refinancing kind. Between 1975 and 1982, only a minority of negotiations (7 out of 28) rescheduled over $US300 million.[42] However, five official debt reschedulings from 1982 to 1985 were for more than $US1 billion (Mexico, Morocco, Brazil, Zaïre, Argentina) and over half of the 36 cases involved more than $US300 million.[43]

Another distinctive feature of the debt crisis was the suddenness with which the position of the major borrowers such as Mexico, Brazil, Venezuela, Chile and Yugoslavia (see Table 7.2) deteriorated. The near-simultaneous loss of credit-worthiness by several large borrowers as a result affected perceptions of regional risk. For example the development of the Polish debt crises in 1981[44] created uncertainty about financial and commercial relations with other parts of Eastern Europe, especially Hungary and Romania. With the onset of the Mexican crisis in mid-1982, a similar regionalisation of risk took place. By the time the IMF met at Toronto in the autumn of 1982, it seemed

Table 7.2   Countries reviewed ranked by debt to banks at the end of December 1982 (in millions of US dollars)

1. Mexico	62,888	15. Sudan	1,119
2. Brazil	60,453	16. Bolivia	940
3. Venezuela	27,474	17. Zaïre	873
4. Argentina	25,681	18. Dominican Republic	866
5. Chile	11,610	19. Nicaragua	814
6. Yugoslavia	9,821	20. Zambia	590
7. Nigeria	8,527	21. Jamaica	521
8. Peru	5,353	22. Honduras	469
9. Ecuador	4,488	23. Senegal	410
10. Romania	4,243	24. Madagascar	299
11. Turkey	3,971	25. Togo	253
12. Morocco	3,882	26. Malawi	202
13. Uruguay	1,531	27. Guyana	129
14. Costa Rica	1,261		

Source: Bank for International Settlements, *The Maturity Distribution of International Bank Lending.*

that the international community was faced with 'rolling over' one massive debt crisis after another.

Paris Club

Prior to 1982, multilateral official debt renegotiations were conducted mainly though by no means exclusively within the framework of the Paris Club. Other fora which have been used include aid consortia (e.g. for India and Pakistan) or special creditor groups, as in the cases of Mexico and Morocco. States have also approached major creditor 'sources' on a bilateral basis to restructure some parts of their official debt.

The Paris Club, which mainly consists of OECD creditors,[45] is a forum within which countries negotiate the restructuring of official debt, that is loans from creditor governments and private export credits guaranteed or insured by export credit agencies in the creditor countries. The origins of the Paris Club date to 1956, when several European countries met in Paris to discuss rescheduling Argentina's foreign debt, and similarly in 1961 and 1962, when certain Brazilian debts were rescheduled. The Paris Club meets at the French Treasury.

Initial responses to the debt crisis

In the absence of any formal international machinery for dealing with the debt crisis, the initial responses of necessity took the form of *ad hoc* rescue packages, or what has been called the 'fire brigade' approach. In the main, such operations involved stop-gap financial support, selectively orchestrated to a large extent by the United States, together with, in some cases, short-term balance of payments finance via bridging loans, arranged mainly through the Basle-based central bank organisation, the Bank for International Settlements (BIS). In October 1982, for example, the US Treasury provided a US$1.23 billion 90-day loan to Brazil, though this was not formally announced until President Reagan's visit to Brazil in December 1982.[46] The US$1.23 billion loan was also supported by a trade package, allowing for the relaxation of controls on Brazilian sugar exports to the United States and the continuation of Brazilian subsidies on steel exports for a further two years.[47] In addition, Brazil secured US$600 million bridging finance from its six major bank creditors. Further short-term finance of US$1.2 billion was provided by the BIS in December 1982, pending attempts to agree a financial rescue package involving the IMF and commercial banks.[48]

The Mexican and Brazilian crises highlighted what were to become four central problems in the management of the debt question: the need to mobilise internationally very large amounts of finance on a recurring basis; the complexity of the negotiating process owing to the number of secondary banks and other agencies; the need to co-ordinate the respective involvement of the IMF and commercial banks, and the inadequacy of IMF resources to meet the financial requirements of debtor countries over and above balance of payments financing.[49]

The experience of the Mexican and Brazilian debt negotiations laid the basis for the subsequent development of the IMF's co-ordinating role. Thus, by mid-December 1982, Brazil had reached substantial agreement with the IMF for a Fund-supported programme, which was put to the Brazilian bank creditor group meeting in New York on 20 December 1982, attended by some 125 bank representatives and the IMF's then Managing Director, Jacques de Larosière. Nevertheless, the position remained precarious,[50] dependent on bridging operations, the maintenance of interbank lines and the mobilisation of large amounts of commercial and international institution funding.[51] Subsequently the ideas underlying the IMF's approach to assembling financial packages became based on what was known as the 'critical mass' doctrine.[52] In essence, the doctrine, which shaped IMF policy until its modification in 1986, required commercial bank commitments to have reached a critical amount, normally over 90 per cent of that required, before IMF funds would be committed.

Following the Mexican and Brazilian crises, the debt position of a number of other developing countries also worsened substantially. In 1983–84, 23 countries sought debt relief within the framework of the Paris Club.[53]

Apart from the Paris Club agreements referred to above, 32 restructuring agreements were reached in principle by 26 countries through bank advisory committees, which were an important innovative feature of the debt crisis, during 1983–84.[54] Since 1982 some 20–30 bank advisory committees have been set up. Each is chaired by a lead bank (with a deputy), generally with the largest country exposure, and is nominated by the debtor country – such as Citibank, Bank of America and Manufacturers Hanover for Argentina, Bolivia and Chile respectively; trade factors, accounting for example for the German bank representation on the Polish committee; or thirdly, traditional or specialist banking services, for example Manufacturers Hanover/Bank of Tokyo for the Philippines. The advisory committee for Ivory Coast is chaired by Banque Nationale de Paris (BNP), again illustrating the third factor. The advisory committee liaises and co-ordinates terms, conditions and the scale of commercial bank contributions to financial packages. While some bank advisory committees, particularly those dealing with the bank debt of smaller African and Caribbean countries, have remained informal and *ad hoc,* being revived as and when necessary, those dealing with major Latin American countries have become highly institutionalised. (Four countries – Brazil, Mexico, Argentina and Venezuela – account for 80 per cent of US banks' exposure.)

Personal diplomacy

In this context the IMF's co-ordinating role has involved the Fund's Managing Director in extensive personal diplomacy.[55] This has included personal interventions with foreign commercial banks to exert pressure in order to mobilise the required commercial bank funds to 'fit' alongside those of the IMF.[56] Apart from this, the strain on Fund liquidity has also involved the IMF Managing Director in extensive diplomatic efforts to secure a more stable base of borrowed resources.[57] Following the 1973–74 oil crisis the Fund was forced to rely on a diverse group of 14 countries, half of which were OPEC members, to augment its borrowed resources to establish the second oil facility (1975–83), which caused the IMF management considerable concern.[58]

In order to widen the lender base to continue funding under the enlarged access policy, four new borrowing arrangements for SDR 6.8 billion were concluded with the Saudi Arabian Monetary Agency (SAMA), the BIS, Japan and the National Bank of Belgium in April 1984, confirming the move away from OPEC.[59] A further agreement was concluded between the Fund and Japan in December 1986 for SDR 6 billion, effective until March 1991.[60]

The debt restructuring process

From the 32 restructuring agreements noted above a number of particular features require comment. First, the range of parties makes the negotiating process highly complex. In an extreme case such as Mexico over 500 banks (apart from governments, institutions and other agencies) have had some degree of involvement.[61] Certainly in the cases of the larger debtor countries considerable strain has been placed on the co-ordination and communication resources of the bank advisory committees. While the establishment of the advisory committees was an important and innovative concept in international diplomacy,[62] the serial or cyclical nature of debt rescheduling, with debtor countries renegotiating fresh arrangements generally within two years, has led to questions being raised about the effectiveness of advisory committee procedures and approaches to the debt crisis. At a substantive level a major policy-related difficulty which has emerged is over the degree of financial participation in loan packages required of smaller and regional banks. In this respect the extended number of banks involved in major debtor countries has meant that the task of gathering in banks for the required critical mass has had to be delegated to individual banks on the advisory committees, which have been given responsibility for national or regional co-ordination. The 'distancing' of smaller banks from the central decision-making process has been a contributory factor in the growing difficulty in gathering sufficient financial commitments, particularly as banks have sought to reduce loan risk exposure. The increasing difficulties in putting together loan packages were underlined with schemes such as so-called 'exit' bonds, designed especially to secure the one-time commitment of smaller banks before their withdrawal. A related procedural issue has concerned the over-representation of major US banks on advisory committees. Difficulties of this kind, for example, caused delay in the Nigerian negotiations during 1987–88, when Japanese banks were reluctant to commit resources because of non-membership on the lead advisory committee.[63]

A further distinctive feature of restructuring negotiations is in respect of the availability of information. Frequently the exact scale of debt is not available to bank advisory economic committees or secondary banks. A particularly difficult issue is estimating the financing gap required for the maintenance of short-term interbank lines. Brazil, for example, established 16 Brazilian banks abroad, as part of its development strategy, with a total of 104 branches and outstanding deposits in 1982 of US$10 billion.[64] Other liabilities may be incurred by airlines, parastatal agencies and other sub-national actors operating transnationally in, for example, development finance, manufacturing, defence,[65] or service sectors such as shipping.[66] It is worth noting that, in response to these types of difficulties, Sri Lanka ceased to allow state corporations and government supported enterprises such as Air Lanka, and the steel and shipping corporations, to raise loans from foreign sources.[67]

Third, debt negotiations are extremely sensitive to *domestic* events in the debtor country, such as labour unrest, inflation rate movement, the removal of key players such as the central bank governor or finance minister, and changes of government.[68] Externally too, international developments such as shifts in major creditor financial policy and, increasingly, hitherto unrelated trade disputes impinge on debt negotiations, making them distinct from other forms of technical negotiations, which generally tend to be much more 'insulated' from domestic and external pressures.

Fourth, although banks in theory approach negotiations on a case-by-case basis, it is not a line which is always easily maintained. An important corresponding development is the co-ordination between major Latin American debtors at bilateral and multilateral levels in the Cartagena and other fora on general debt strategy and approaches to particular negotiations. The Cartagena Group, which comprises Mexico, Bolivia, Chile, Colombia, Dominican Republic, Ecuador, Peru, Uruguay and Venezuela, has met regularly at foreign and finance minister level since 1984.[69] Linkages between negotiations have tended to occur because of the overlap of bank representatives on advisory committees and the leakage of information on terms. Furthermore one negotiation may help or hinder another. For example, banks were unwilling to deal with Bolivia's concessionary finance demands in late 1985 because of the onset of further negotiations with Mexico.[70] In the Nigerian debt negotiations, Japanese banks participated reluctantly because of earlier US Federal Reserve pressure over Mexico in late 1986. In contrast, the unwillingness of banks to have difficulties simultaneously with the 'big three' Latin American debtors was a factor hastening the 1987 Argentine bank restructuring agreement.[71]

The above four characteristics have meant that debt rescheduling negotiations have become some of the most complex and technical in contemporary multilateral diplomacy. Moreover, as far as the fourth feature, the linkage aspect, is concerned, a further distinctive development is the growing fusion of debt questions with other issues which have hitherto been treated separately. Debt negotiations in a number of instances have become tied up with such matters as measures to combat the narcotics trade, tariff rates and trade disputes, such as that between Brazil and the United States over the Brazilian Informatics Law which restricted US computer exports to the reserved Brazilian market.[72]

Transition

The period 1986–89 marked an important point of transition in the management of the debt crisis. Up to that point, bridging loans,[73] retiming of interest, securitisation[74] and trade financing[75] had stabilised the debt problem. However, the resurgence of payments difficulties during 1986–87, along with the October 1987 stock crash brought short-run financing techniques full circle with the re-emergence of temporary bridging loan operations initiated by the United States for selected Latin American debtor states.[76] A further feature of the crisis was the impact of the collapse of oil prices, in undermining the Baker proposals outlined at the October 1985 IMF/World Bank meeting in Seoul, which had called for wider commercial lending of US$20 billion to the entire group of heavily indebted countries.[77] The uncertainty and instability caused by the crisis was reflected in the negotiations surrounding the 'Jumbo' debt package of April 1987;[78] the unilateral US bridging loans of US$500 million to Argentina in late 1988 and Brazil's request for a US$3 billion 'trade liberalisation' facility, which caused surprise and alarm in the international financial community, given the relatively short time lapse since the 1982 crisis.

The main effect of the 1986–89 crisis was to accelerate moves by major creditor commercial banks to reduce exposure to Third World lending and seek ways of writing off debt. In this regard the Citibank decision in May 1987, on reserve allocation for debt write-off signalled a major change in strategy. The crisis underlined the severe differences between the US and European banks over debt management strategies. In general, European banks resented US pressure in the 1987 and 1995 crises, to participate in mammoth rescue operations for Mexico.

Lack of co-ordination between the US and Europe on debt strategy and policies has remained a feature of US–European financial relations. A further effect of US unilateral action, based on the primacy of regional economic interests, is on eroding the IMF guidelines which required a debtor country to have in place, at least in outline, an IMF programme before tranches of debt relief funds could be released.

The search for solutions

Since the 1986–89 financial crisis, efforts to find solutions to the debt crisis have moved away from strategies which attempted to blend new money with restructuring packages. Rather, the introduction of debt-reduction concepts in effect broke the psychological barriers by formally accepting the need to write off debt or find other ways of substantially reducing overhangs of interest or principal.

Efforts to find solutions to the debt crisis within the framework of the Paris Club for official debt should be distinguished from commercial bank debt-reduction operations. As regards the Paris Club, moves towards debt reductions initially were confined to greater flexibility over repayment and grace periods. For example, Paris Club agreements with Mauritania, Uganda and Zaïre were rescheduled for repayment between 15 and 20 years, with a ten-year grace period. Since the Toronto economic summit (1988) and Trinidad Commonwealth Finance Ministers meeting in 1990, the Paris Club terms for qualifying countries and types of debt have been gradually eased on a selective basis. For example, in line with the Houston G-7 summit, more favourable debt-relief terms were targeted at lower-middle-income countries. However, only four countries (El Salvador, Honduras, Morocco and Congo) concluded negotiations on the basis of the revised terms. Further revision of the Paris Club terms have focused on provisions for least-developed countries for write-off of up to two-thirds of debt payments falling due. Paris Club agreements were reached with Cambodia, Guinea, Togo, Guinea-Bissau and Uganda.[79]

In terms of commercial bank debt restructuring 32 countries restructured bank debt between 1987 and 1997. This group, which includes Argentina, Mexico, Brazil and Nigeria, accounted for some 80 per cent of the bank debt of developing countries in the 1990s. Debt to commercial banks was reduced in real terms by US$50.3 billion at a cost of US$17.9 billion.[80] The agreements are in the main complex packages with restructuring, debt reduction and debt service reduction components, involving extensive negotiations over anything up to two years. These negotiations have rarely achieved completed agreements in that the package often deals with only part of the *overall* debt, or, may be conditional on interest arrears repayment.[81] For example, in the Dominican Republic case, a lengthy stalemate over the issue of partial repayments was broken following the resumption of payments by the Dominican Republic which facilitated preliminary agreement on terms of the package.[82]

The restructuring agreements concluded after 1987 have been based, in part, on an acceptance by commercial banks of the principle of steep discounts for low-income countries as part of 'exit' operations, while a complex range of instruments have been developed for middle-income countries where banks have long-term interests. In addition, a limited number of low-income countries have liquidated commercial debt via the World Bank International Development Agency (IDA) debt facility, e.g. Bolivia, Guyana, Sierra Leone. The World Bank (IDA) has also participated in multilateral donor consortia agreements with low-income debtor countries such as Uganda.[83]

New facilities and challenges

The central problem for the IMF – the matching of resources against the continuous expansion of its operations since 1982 – can be illustrated through three issue areas. These are the question of quotas and arrears; the provision of financing for new facilities; and the allocation of resources for existing short-term facilities for least-developed countries.

Quotas and arrears

The question of increases in the allocation of resources through quota increases has also become linked to arrears. Under the third amendment of the Articles in November 1992, the IMF tightened provisions on arrears at US insistence and is empowered to suspend members with overdue obligations. The Interim Committee approved a rights accumulation programme in May 1990, to assist those members with protracted arrears. The selective nature of donor group assistance was underlined with Japan's support for Vietnam and Cambodia. Suspended states include Zaïre and Sudan.

Additional facilities

As regards additional facilities, the most significant was the introduction of the temporary Systemic Transformation Facility (STF) to assist the Russian Federation and other economies in transition. More than ten countries which were either part of the former Soviet Union or socialist group made extensive drawings under the STF[84] (equal to over half of the purchases under the basic stand-by facilities, and four times the amount drawn down by least-developed countries under the EFF).[85] In addition, the entire stock of Russian Federation debt existing in 1991 – estimated at some US$24 billion was rescheduled in 1993, together with a US$6.8 billion stand-by credit in 1995.[86] The expanded membership of the IMF (17 countries joined the Fund after 1992) has not only increased extended demands on resources, but has also shifted to some extent the strategic focus of the IMF.

Disputes on renewal of facilities

Disputes over the renewal of short-term facilities have occurred over the extension of the STF and the extension and enlargement of the Enhanced Structural Adjustment Facility (ESAF). For example, the G-7 failed to agree at the Halifax summit (1995) on financing modalities for the ESAF. United Kingdom proposals for the sale of part of the IMF's gold holding to finance the ESAF were opposed by Germany.[87] It is worth adding that eligibility for ESAF funds is restricted and enlargements are agreed by the Executive Board. Other proposals, including those of Managing Director Michel Camdessus for a 36 billion SDR issue have not been supported by industrialised countries, indicating the quite divergent views over temporary facilities and allocation of resources.

Summary

Since 1973 the role of the Fund has changed in a number of important ways. In particular, its second function as a source of international liquidity has increased in importance. Yet in establishing new facilities the Fund has, because of the limitations on its ordinary resources, had to negotiate borrowed resources with different sets of donor groups. However, more recently the Fund has been able to develop a more stable basis for its borrowed resources through formal links with the BIS, central banks, Japan and Saudi Arabia. Saudi Arabia itself has emerged as a major financial actor within the Fund, formally through association with the GAB and via other support operations carried out by SAMA.

The onset of the debt crisis coincided with the revised arrangements noted above. While these provided a medium-term basis of borrowed resources, the scale of the debt crisis put the Fund's overall resources under severe strain. Since 1982 the Fund has been involved in perhaps its most intensive period of post-war financial diplomacy. The management of the debt crisis has involved highly complex multilateral diplomacy, in which a new type of debt negotiations has emerged, involving creditor groups, bank liaison committees, central financial institutions, the BIS, governments and large numbers of non-governmental groups. The process of internationally mobilising large volumes of financial resources has led also to increased institutional linkage, in which the Fund has played an important part. An underlying assumption behind this process has been the common concern to reduce the risk of default. In this sense financial risk has been shared through aggregation.[88]

This can be seen particularly in the use of cross-default clauses and the extensive growth of bridging and syndicated loans. The Fund itself has assumed a significant role in terms of the co-ordination of rescue packages, the mobilisation of resources and, through both formal and *de facto* certification of the economies of Fund members. The Fund's role is changing too, in part through increased membership after the Cold War, which has affected priorities and programmes. Relations with the World Bank have required continued adjustment. Demands for an enhanced role for the World Bank in a way mirror the blurring of concepts associated with orthodox balance of payments support operations and development finance, which has occurred because of the very high levels of debt faced by some countries. Whatever changes take place, it is clear that the three issues of quotas, access to Fund resources and the availability of borrowed resources will continue at the centre of the Fund's international financial relations. The Fund's multifaceted role has been aptly summed up by de Larosière as 'part credit union, part referee and part economic adviser'.[89]

References and notes

1. For a Selected bibliography on the Fund, see various IMF Staff Papers, e.g.Anne G.M. Salda, *The International Monetary Fund*, IMF Staff Papers, Vol. 31, Supplement (Dec. 1984).

2. Of these 29 countries signed the agreement, which rose to 35 at the inaugural meeting of the Board of Governors at Savannah on 8 March 1946. The Soviet Union, which was present at Bretton Woods subsequently did not join the Fund. Three countries have subsequently left the Fund: Poland on 14 March 1950; Czechoslovakia on 31 Dec. 1954; and Cuba on 2 April 1964. Of the countries outside the United Nations, Italy became a member in 1947, and the FRG and Japan followed in 1952. On the Bretton Woods conference, see, for example, J. Keith Horsefield, *The International Monetary Fund 1945–65, Volume 1: Chronicle* (IMF, Washington, DC, 1969) Ch. 5.

3. For the role of Keynes in the negotiations see John Morton Blum, *From the Morgenthau Diaries: Years of War, 1941–4* (Houghton Mifflin, Boston, 1967) p. 273 *passim*.

4. Horsefield, op. cit., p. 93.

5. For example the Fund concluded a stand-by arrangement in April 1985 with the Dominican Republic over twelve months, for purchases of up to the equivalent of SDR 78.5 million, which is equivalent to 70 per cent of the Dominican Republic's quota of SDR 112.1 million in the Fund. The stand-by arrangement is financed from the Fund's original (subscription) resources. See IMF, *Survey*, 29 April 1985, p. 140.

6. Benjamin J. Cohen, *Organising the World's Money* (Macmillan, London, 1978) p. 93.

7. Managing Directors have been: Camille Gutt (Belgium) 1946–51; Ivor Rooth (Sweden) 1951–56; Per Jacobsson (Sweden) 1956–63; Pierre-Paul Schweitzer (France) 1963–73; H. Johannes Witteveen (the Netherlands) 1973–78; Jacques de Larosière (France) 1978–87. See Margaret Garritsen de Vries, *The International Monetary Fund 1972–78*, Vol. 2 (IMF, Washington, DC, 1985) Ch. 52 for portraits of Fund staff.

8. See for example staff distribution of IBRD/IDA, Table H-7, Appendix H, in Edward S. Mason and Robert E. Asher, *The World Bank Since Bretton Woods* (The Brookings Institution, Washington, DC, 1973) pp. 879–80.

9. Ibid., p. 566.

10. In the nine years of negotiations the Bank played a prominent role in putting forward a number of proposals to bridge the gap between the two sides. For Black's personal correspondence with Nehru, see Mason and Asher, op. cit., p. 625.

11. Horsefield, op. cit., p. 496.

12. Robert Solomon, *The International Monetary System 1945–81* (Harper and Row, New York, 1982) p. 33.

13. See Michael Ainly, *The General Arrangements to Borrow*, Pamphlet Series No. 41 (IMF, Washington, DC, 1984).

14. Switzerland, which was not a member of the Fund, was associated with the GAB in June 1964. See exchange of letters between the Ambassador of Switzerland to the United States and the managing director of the Fund, 11 June 1964, in *Selected Decisions*, 10 (1983) pp. 148–52. Switzerland joined the IMF in 1992.

15. The currency value of the SDR is determined daily by the Fund by summing the values of a basket of five currencies, based on market exchange rates in US dollars according to the following amounts: US dollar (0.57); Deutsch mark (0.46); French franc (0.80); Japanese yen (31.0); pound sterling (0.0812). *Annual Report* (1995).

16. See Louis M. Goreux, *Compensatory Financing Facility* (IMF, Washington, DC, 1980) esp. pp. 25–50.

17. See A.I. MacBean and P.N. Snowden, *International Institutions in Trade and Finance* (George Allen and Unwin, London, 1983) Ch. 6.

18. For an evaluation of the Bretton Woods system, see W.M. Scammel, *International Monetary Policy: Bretton Woods and After* (Macmillan, London, 1975) Ch. 7.

19. Marcus Fleming, cited in Solomon, op. cit., p. 237.

20. The membership was subsequently increased to 24 as a result of the admission of the Russian Federation, Eastern European and Central Asian states to the IMF. A single constituency seat was created for the Russian Federation.

21. Interim Committee communiqué, IMF *Survey*, 15 Oct. 1984, pp. 292–4.

22. A possible reason for this is that less developed countries feel that they have greater influence through the executive directors of the Fund, and that a council would weaken the Executive Board. See Solomon, op. cit., p. 628.

23. *Select Decisions of the IMF*, 11 (30 April 1985) pp. 367–8.

24. See Fritz Fischer, 'The Spring 1985 Meeting of the Development Committee', *Finance and Development*, June 1985, pp. 8–9.

25. The membership of the G-24 in 1985 comprised Algeria, Argentina, Brazil, Colombia, Egypt, Ethiopia, Gabon, Ghana, Guatemala, India, Islamic Republic of Iran, Ivory Coast, Lebanon, Mexico, Nigeria, Pakistan, Peru, Philippines, Sri Lanka, Syrian Arab Republic, Trinidad and Tobago, Venezuela, Yugoslavia, Zaïre.

26. See *The Times*, 18 Jan. 1983.

27. IMF, *Annual Report, 1981*, p. 84.

28. The 18 identified were: Bangladesh, Cameroon, Central African Republic, Egypt, Haiti, India, Ivory Coast, Kenya, Mali, Mauritania, Pakistan, Senegal, Sierra Leone, Sri Lanka, Somalia, Tanzania, Western Samoa, Democratic People's Republic of the Yemen, IMF, *Annual Report, 1977*, p. 65.

29. Solomon, op. cit., p. 281. OPEC met in Kuwait on 16 Oct. 1973 and decided the following day to cut oil supplies by 5 per cent each month and to impose a total ban on certain countries supporting Israel. It was also agreed to raise posted prices from $US3 to $US5.12 per barrel. An extremely good analysis of OPEC including the embargo can be found in Albert L. Danielson, *The Evolution of OPEC* (Harcourt Brace Jovanovich, New York, 1982) pp. 159–99.

30. The entry into force of the second amendment to the Fund's articles made it possible to add to the total of usable currencies about SDR 1 billion in currencies that had previously not been used or sold only on an irregular basis. The Fund's holding of eleven currencies totalled about 85 per cent of all usable currencies at the end of April 1978, with the US dollar accounting for 50 per cent of the total. See IMF, *Annual Reports, 1995*, p. 55 and *1978*, p. 234. In practice, however, the bulk of the Fund's usable currency holdings is represented by a small number of currencies. At the end of 1980–81 the Fund's holding of five currencies accounted for a little over 70 per cent of its total usable resources, IMF, *Annual Report, 1981*, p. 88.

31. See IMF, *Annual Report, 1976*, p. 54.

32. See IMF, *Annual Report, 1975*, pp. 54–6.

33. See IMF, *Annual Report, 1975*, pp. 54–6.

34. For the communiqué see IMF, *Annual Report, 1978*, Appendix IV.

35. See Solomon, op. cit., pp. 280–1 and MacBean and Snowden, op. cit., p. 54.

36. *The Times*, 12 Dec. 1983.

37. Private Market Financing for Developing Countries IMF (December 1993), p. 1.

38. See the debate, for example, within the G-5 and G-10 conducted at the Toronto, Frankfurt and Paris meeting from December to February 1982–83, on emergency measures to deal with the debt crisis, including the first modification of access to the GAB. During the discussions, large quota increases were supported, for example, by Japan; in contrast, the United States favoured modifying access to the GAB, rather than quota increases, which were opposed by the US Congress. The G-7 Halifax Summit (June 1995) agreed eventually to further modify the GAB, in the wake of the renewed Mexican crisis, with the proposal to establish an Emergency Financing Mechanism. The UK plan to raise liquidity for the least developed through the sale of IMF gold was opposed by Germany, France and Japan. See *The Times* 10, 13 Dec. 1982; *New York Times*, 9 Dec. 1992; *The Times,* 10 Feb. 1983; *The Times*, 16 June 1995.

39. IMF *Survey*, September 1995, pp. 11–14.

40. The G-10 met in Paris on 17 Jan. 1983 in the context of the debt crisis and formally approved a number of proposals which substantially altered the GAB. These entailed increasing the credit lines from SDR 6.4 billion to SDR 17 billion and, in a major

departure, opening the GAB, under well-defined circumstances to non-participants. Arrangements were also made for the participation of Switzerland in lending operations and a lending agreement was reached with Saudi Arabia on 8 Jan. 1983. See *The Times*, 10 Jan. 1983; and Michael Ainley, *The General Arrangements to Borrow* (IMF, Washington, DC, 1984) pp. 49–51.

41. *Annual Report,* 1995. Mexico borrowed 5.3 billion SDR, the largest sum in the history of the IMF.
42. See K. Burke Dillon *et al.*, *Recent Developments in External Debt Restructuring*, IMF Occasional Paper 40 (Oct. 1985) p. 20.
43. 'Multilateral Official Debt Rescheduling 1975–1985', in Dillon *et al.*, op. cit., Table 4, p. 8.
44. See William R. Cline, *International Debt: Systemic Risk and Policy Response* (Institute for International Economics, Washington, DC, 1984) pp. 273–81; *Hearings*, US Senate, Committee on Banking, Housing and Urban Affairs, second session, 22 Feb. 1982, esp. pp. 77–80; *Hearings*, US Senate, Committee on Foreign Relations, Sub-Committee on European Affairs, second session, 27 Jan. 1982, pp. 8–12.
45. Members of the OECD Development Assistance Committee (DAC) include, Australia, Austria, Belgium, Canada, Denmark, Finland, France, FRG, Italy, Japan, the Netherlands, New Zealand, Norway, Sweden, Switzerland, United Kingdom, United States and the Commission of the EEC.
46. *New York Times,* 3 Dec. 1982.
47. *New York Times,* 8 Dec. 1982.
48. *New York Times,* 13 Dec. 1982.
49. IMF, *Annual Report, 1985,* p. 65.
50. See testimony of Henry C. Wallich before the House Sub-Committee on International Trade, Investment and Monetary Policy, April–May 1983, pp. 75–99.
51. IMF *Survey,* 7 March 1983, pp. 65, 76.
52. See Azizali F. Mohammed, 'The Case by Case Approach to Debt Problems', *Finance and Development* (March 1985) especially pp. 27–30.
53. K. Burke Dillon *et al.*, *Recent Developments in External Debt Restructuring,* IMF Occasional Paper 40 (Oct. 1985) p. 19; Table 116, p. 47 and Table 17, pp. 47–62.
54. Ibid., p. 14.
55. See Joseph Kraft, *The Mexican Rescue* (New York: The Group of Thirty, 1984) pp. 27–8.
56. For example, de Larosière intervened with the Italian bank Istituto Mobiliare Italiano and sent a telegram to the Minister of Commerce seeking 'fullest co-operation'. See Kraft, *The Mexican Rescue* (New York: Group of Thirty, 1984) pp. 27–8.
57. *The Times,* 12 Dec. 1983.
58. IMF, *Annual Report, 1976,* p. 54.
59. IMF, *Annual Report, 1985,* p. 69.
60. The agreement took effect on 24 Dec. 1986 and ran for four years. There is provision for a two-year extension depending on the Fund's liquidity and borrowing needs. IMF *Survey,* 12 Jan. 1987.
61. Kraft, *The Mexican Rescue,* p. 54.
62. See remarks by William R. Rhodes, Chairman of the Restructuring Committee, Citibank, Citi Corp, at the Group of 30, London, 3 Nov. 1983.
63. See *Financial Times,* 3 April 1987 and 6 Jan. 1988. Japanese corporations on the informal bilateral Japan–Nigeria Committee include C Itoh, Kawaho, Marubeni, Miusui, Mitsubishi, Sumitomo, Suzuki Motor, Toyo Menka Kaisha and Nishizawa.
64. See Carlos G. Langoni, 'The Restructuring Experience of Brazil', in Khadiga Haq (ed.), *The Lingering Debt Crisis* (Islamabad: North South Round Table, 1985) p. 113.
65. On the problem created for the IMF of the impact of undisclosed arms purchases on their assessments, see *The Times,* 4 Feb. 1983; the relationship between Third World debt and arms purchases is discussed in M. Brzoska, 'The Military Related Debt of Third World Countries', *Journal of Peace Research,* Vol. 20, No. 3 (1983) pp. 271–7.
66. Of the debt accumulated by Pemex, the Mexican state oil company, shipping purchases particularly were a significant component of the total Mexican debt amounting to some US$20 billion. See Kraft, *The Mexican Rescue,* pp. 27–8.

67. See *Financial Times*, 24 Jan. 1986.
68. See Table 17, fn. 1, p. 49 in K. Burke Dillon *et al.*, *Occasional Paper 40* (IMF Oct. 1985) on renegotiation of agreements by new governments.
69. The text of the Caragena Consensus, 22 June 1984, can be found in *Hearings, Committee of Foreign Affairs, House of Representatives*, second session, 1 and 8 Aug. 1984, pp. 62–72.
70. See *Occasional Paper* 43 (IMF Feb. 1986) Table 40, fn. 5, p. 107, and p. 112 for details of the Mexican agreements and type of debt rescheduled.
71. *Financial Times*, 4 Jan. 1988.
72. *Financial Times*, 14 Oct. 1987.
73. See BIS, *Annual Report* (1983) pp. 146–66.
74. For details of the Hungarian agreement concluded in 1986, which used US Treasury Bonds as collateral, see Maxwell Watson *et al.*, *International Capital Markets*, IMF (January 1988) p. 62.
75. See *Occasional Paper* 43 (IMF 1986) Table 40, p. 120 and Bank for International Settlements, *Recent Innovations in International Banking* (1986).
76. BIS, *Annual Report*, 1987, p. 1984.
77. The proposals by US Secretary of the Treasury Baker were outlined at the October 1985 IMF/World Bank Seoul meeting and called for new lending by commercial banks of US$20 billion over the following three years to the entire group of heavily indebted countries. Included in the group were Argentina, Bolivia, Brazil, Chile, Colombia, Ivory Coast, Ecuador, Mexico, Morocco, Nigeria, Peru, Philippines, Uruguay, Venezuela and Yugoslavia. See IMF/IBRD press release no. 13, 8 Oct., and statement by Secretary Baker before the Bretton Woods Committee in *Treasury News*, Department of the Treasury, Washington, DC, also found in IMF *Survey*, 3 Feb. 1986.
78. *International Capital Markets*, IMF (Jan. 1988) Table 37, p. 91.
79. *Financial Times*, 1 March 1995; IMF *Survey*, Sept. 1995 on Naples terms.
80. *Private Market Financing for Developing Countries*, IMF (Dec. 1993), p. 7.
81. See *Private Market Financing*, Table 3, p. 8 and Table A2, p. 52 *passim*.
82. See *Private Market Financing*, p. 10.
83. On Feb. 26 1993, Uganda completed a buy-back of commercial debt comprising of mainly trade and suppliers' credits. The operation covered US$153 million of claims (89 per cent of total eligible principal) at a price of 12 cents per dollar of principal. The $18 million cost was met by contributions from a consortia made up of IDA (US$10 million); the Netherlands (US$2.7 million); Switzerland (US$0.7 million) and bridging loan of US$5 million from Germany/EC. See *Private Market Financing*, Table A3, pp. 60–1, for other examples of the range and composition of buy-back arrangements.
84. IMF *Survey*, Oct. 1993, p. 3; *Annual Report*, 1995, pp. 125–6.
85. IMF *Survey*, Aug. 1994, p. 14.
86. IMF *Survey*, April 1995, pp. 24–5.
87. *Financial Times*, 6 Oct. 1994.
88. David Folkerts-Landau, 'The Changing Role of International Bank Lending in Development Finance', IMF, *Staff Papers*, Vol. 32, No. 2 (June 1985) pp. 326–30.
89. Remarks by J. de Larosière to the Los Angeles World Affairs Council, 19 March 1986. Cf. comments of Michel Camdessus, de Larosière's successor as managing director, in IMF *Survey*, 20 April, 1987, p. 114.

CHAPTER 8

Trade, foreign policy and diplomacy

Trade has traditionally been a concern of diplomacy. Trade interests and trade policies are generally part of the central preoccupations of most states. Ideally, trade policy and foreign policy should support each other, in the same way that defence and foreign policy have a mutually supportive relationship. Yet trade policy, rather more than defence has tended to pull in divergent directions from foreign policy, unless, as is sometimes the case, economic issues dominate external policy. As a result an additional task for diplomacy is dealing with external problems arising from the consequences of differing lines of external policy. Divergency between trade and foreign policy can sometimes arise from the practice of having separate diplomatic and trade missions, reflecting the tendency to treat the political and economic aspects of foreign policy separately. Trade and foreign policy may also diverge because of demands made by established trade interests within states.[1]

Trade interests may of course be acquired for a number of reasons such as long-standing commercial links, entrepreneurial exploitation of overseas markets or successful domestic lobbying as in the case of European, Japanese[2] or US farming interests. Such interests which either tacitly or formally become part of trade policy may create strains or ambiguity in foreign policy, such as calls for the ending of sanctions against the Soviet Union by US grain farmers. Put differently, foreign policy decision-makers may consider that particular trade interests are incompatible with foreign policy, for example the US Government's attitude to oil operations by Chevron in Angola or Conoco with Iran.[3] Under these circumstances, the task of diplomacy is to reconcile or explain divergent interests to appropriate external actors, or, bring the trade policy and interests into line with foreign policy. The process of bringing trade and foreign policy into alignment can be difficult if trade interests, broadly defined, secure either sufficient economic importance, or official support to conduct trade separately or even at the expense of foreign policy. The latter is well illustrated by the long-running diplomatic dispute between the EC and the US over the protective aspects of the EC's Common Agricultural Policy (CAP).

Apart from the questions of divergence and primacy, trade policy may become a direct instrument of foreign policy. In this sense trade is used to support or further objectives which are not exclusively economic but political or military. The political uses of trade involve diplomacy in initiatives to develop goodwill, promote regional co-operation, gain political influence or strategic assets (e.g. bases) within another state, through to coercive sanctions and other forms of punitive behaviour.

The international trade setting

In international trade, the classical functions of diplomacy, other than strict commercial promotion are evident in four areas. These are: (i) multilateral rule-making or rule-changing; (ii) the creation of a favourable political setting or legal framework at a bilateral or regional level; (iii) resolution of disputes; (iv) the creation of innovatory agreements. To these a fifth area, 'coercive' diplomacy, should be added.

The setting itself for international trade diplomacy has been distinguished by the post-war growth in the number of multilateral institutions with direct or indirect responsibility for trade (e.g. GATT\WTO, UNCTAD, ECOSOC, UNIDO, IFC, ILO). This institutional pluralism reflects the growth in the membership of the international community, as well as other factors such as the developing country dissatisfaction with seemingly Western-dominated institutions, continued North–South disputes over market access and the resulting attempts by developing countries to create new trade and development arrangements within a South–South and pan-regional context. Trade issues themselves have progressively moved up the international agenda as the promotion and regulation of trade became extensively politicised through growing direct and indirect governmental involvement, privatisation, increasing protectionism and other problems such as price uncertainties which have affected a wide range of key commodities. Apart from the continued North–South trade conflict, marked by the overall feature of trade and technology redistribution (the UNCTAD goals), the growth of regional economic co-operation organisations has accelerated after the Cold War. In addition, the institutional transformation of GATT into the UN system marks a fundamental change at a multilateral level in the management of international trade. The other feature of note is trade conflict between the United States, EU and Japan, which has become a permanent structural feature of the international trade setting. In the remainder of the chapter the focus is on the World Trade Organisation (WTO); regional and pan-regional trade organisations, and, the trade in bilateral relations. The final section of the chapter examines some of the principal categories of trade conflict.

Multilateral institutions: the World Trade Organisation (WTO)

The establishment of the WTO in 1995 as part of the triad of international institutions (Security Council, IMF/IBRD, Trade (WTO)) was an important shift in the organisation at a multilateral level of trade relations.[4] Prior to WTO, international trade had been regulated on an intergovernmental basis from 1948 to 1994 under the General Agreement on Tariffs and Trade (GATT), an intergovernmental body set up after the failure to establish a WTO in 1945–46, via so-called trade 'rounds' of multilateral negotiations.[5] The rounds included Annecy (1948); the Dillon Round (1960–62); Kennedy Round (1964–67); Tokyo Round (1973–79) and Uruguay Round. The Tokyo Round was particularly important in terms of the breadth of negotiations.[6] Although modest tariff cuts were agreed, the Round more importantly entered new ground with agreements on non-tariff areas in the form of codes to the GATT agreement.[7] The codes included those on subsidies and countervailing duties;[8] customs valuations;[9] anti-dumping;[10] government procurement;[11] trade in civil aircraft;[12] import licensing and standards.[13]

There are nevertheless limitations arising from this form of rule-making. Thus the United States has been prepared to extend the benefits of particular codes only to those states which are signatories to the code in question and not to free riders. Furthermore the use of agreements of this type introduces selectivity in terms of participation and application. Negotiation of what is politically possible inevitably means that there are gaps or ambiguities in texts. In the subsidies and countervailing duties code, for example, what precisely constitutes 'unjustifiable' use of countervailing measures was left undefined. In the code on government procurement, which aimed to liberalise non-military procurement to competitive bidding, discussions on the inclusion of state-owned authorities such as public utilities gave rise to considerable dispute. The issue was well illustrated in the closing stages of the Tokyo Round, in the dispute between Japan and the United States over the opening up of the Japanese telecommunications market, which has remained unresolved. The United States has subsequently used the GATT civil aircraft code to try and gain access to the European civil aircraft market.

Challenges to GATT

GATT has faced a number of constraints in its efforts to liberalise world trade. In particular the principle of non-discrimination has suffered major erosion. The use of variable import levies and other restrictions, for example, by customs unions and similar groupings, has become a major source of friction, especially in the context of North–South trade relations. Another example of the GATT having to accept a patchwork of bilateral tariffs and quotas was in the textile field, which was governed under the Multiforce Arrangement (MFA). A second area of protectionism, which increased with the deterioration in the climate of world trade after 1979, involved *ad hoc* bilateral measures of a non-tariff kind such as orderly marketing arrangements (OMAs) and voluntary export restraints (e.g. on Japanese and EC steel exports to the

United States). Other forms of trade restrictions in widespread use by both developing and developed countries include import licensing procedures, demands for compensatory exports, currency restriction, differential taxes to protect newly established industries in NICs. Qualitative restrictions have been increasingly introduced on a wide range of developing country exports through standards, certifications, hygiene, and environmental import procedures.

But by far the largest gap in the Tokyo Round was the failure to reach agreement on improving the Article XIX safeguard system, authorising emergency action against suppliers of disruptive imports. Agreement was prevented because of the fundamental disagreement over European Community demands for the right to apply discriminatory safeguard action with limited GATT surveillance, which was opposed by developing countries, joined in this instance by Japan. As Olivier Long notes, 'the debate on the safeguard clause reveals a classic dilemma between, on the one hand, insistence on application of the rules at the risk of making the legal instrument unworkable and, on the other, a degree of tolerance which weakens the value of the instrument and the protection which member governments expect from it'.[14]

The issue of subsidies and corresponding charges of unfair competition have emerged as major sources of international trade conflict. The main area of export subsidy competition is export credits. Government intervention in differing forms of export credits has now become highly institutionalised. In the aid field the traditional concept of aid has become blurred with trade credit, so much so that the former is now almost without meaning except perhaps in a humanitarian sense. The so-called 'Pergau Dam' affair involving conflict between the UK and Malaysia over the financing of the Pergau dam, classically illustrated the diplomatic and other domestic difficulties which can occur when aid, trade and defence budgets and operations become mixed up.[15]

Apart from subsidies and mixing of trade and aid issues, managed trade has become a noticeable feature of international trade practice in response to increased trade competition and protectionism. Within this category are unilateral import restrictions on goods and services and bilaterally agreed pricing arrangements. Other bilateral arrangements have included greater use of long-term trade agreements and bilateral and regional free trade areas (e.g. United States–Israel). Although some of these arrangements may be of limited economic effect because of their short-term nature, low trade value or because the countries involved have little traditional direct trade, taken with other developments they suggest a general weakening of multilateralism, in favour of bilateral and regional arrangements.

The developments discussed above have created an increasingly complex environment for international regulation. Many of the non-tariff restrictions have distorted trade, as in the case of VERs on steel, which have merely led to redirection and the transference of distortion to other markets.[16] New networks of commercial links have been developed by governments and their commercial entities, with trade diplomacy geared to avoiding restrictions through the negotiation of quota-swapping agreements, relocation of production to non-quota affected states and agreements with third states for transhipment and indirect entry into regional trade groupings either through cross-membership (e.g. Chile–NAFTA) or 'client' third countries (e.g. Ireland or UK for EU access). Inevitably, trade disputes have tended to increase.

World Trade Organisation (WTO)

The functioning of the WTO has been influenced firstly by the Uruguay Round legacy. The broad scope of the Uruguay Round continued the approach of the Tokyo Round but added new sectors[17] (agriculture, services, textiles),[18] new issue-areas (intellectual property rights,[19] trade-related investment measures)[20] as well as streamlining of GATT dispute procedures.[21]

The changes introduced by the Uruguay Round in effect lay the framework for the interim operation of the WTO.[22] These include the traditional area of tariff reduction, with an agreed tariff reduction of 38 per cent on the pre-Uruguay Round tariff average of 6.4 per cent in developed countries. The agriculture negotiations focused on three areas: market access, domestic price support and export competition. The incorporation of agriculture, previously largely excluded under GATT, was of only limited success. The Cairns Group, which includes Canada, Australia, Argentina, New Zealand, remained dissatisfied at the staged quantitative reduction in the volume of subsidised exports as the multilateralisation of thinly disguised voluntary export restraint negotiated between the US and EU.[23] For the Cairns Group these provisions in the accord tended to confirm the unsatisfactory duopoly of the US and EU in world agricultural markets. In the provisions on trade-related investments (TRIMS), the Uruguay Round broke new ground, mainly at US insistence, although opposed by large developing countries such as India and Brazil. The final agreement bans TRIMS which are inconsistent with Article II (national treatment), such as domestic content requirements, and Article XI (quantitative restrictions). The agreement, which does not cover subsidies and grants, was largely aimed at investment restrictions in developing countries. The provisions on trade aspects of intellectual property rights (TRIPS) covers patents, trademarks, copyright and trade in counterfeit goods. It is primarily aimed at the pharmaceutical, agrochemical, computer software and designer clothing markets. In one estimate the United States assessed that it had lost over US$24 billion in illegal copying of microchip design and software counterfeiting.[24] Counterfeit trade accounts for at least 6 per cent of world trade and will prove difficult to eradicate. The Uruguay Round compromise reflects this with weak phase-in provisions for developing countries and 'economies in transition'. In the third new area, trade in services, the Uruguay Round was unable to reach substantive agreement with differences over sectors, and demands for exceptions, such as audio-visual services, maritime transport and selective reciprocity in financial services, telecommunications and air transport. The concept of selective reciprocity, introduced because of US–EU differences, and US dissatisfaction with the lack of market opening in Japan, the NICs and developing countries, marks a departure from previous GATT multilateral provisions on MFN.

The development of the WTO

In this section, four aspects of the WTO will be examined to show the issues arising in the evolution of the WTO. The first of these concerns the office of Director General of the WTO.[25] Prior to the entry into force of the WTO, member states were deadlocked for twelve months over three 'bloc' candidates before the US withdrew its opposition to Renato Ruggiero, former Italian minister of foreign trade. A further aspect of the compromise, which has weakened the office of Director-General compared with GATT, is the appointment of a further post of Deputy Director General in addition to three existing deputies. The understanding that the Director General would only serve one term and that the successor would not be a European further politicised the office. The election process reflects the transition from GATT as an intergovernmental treaty organisation to a body within the UN system. The more transparent and politicised WTO decision-making style, reminiscent of the UN General Assembly, contrasts with the arcane bureaucratic-technical deliberations of its predecessor.

Second, the membership of the WTO is now nearly universal. GATT achieved that only in the last few years of its existence. The WTO is now potentially more open to cross-influences from other UN institutions, and, enhanced politicisation given the expansions of membership. A third related factor concerns the revised dispute settlement procedures. Under the WTO accelerated procedures, greater potential for use of dispute settlement is encouraged by the express procedures under which after 60 days the WTO disputes settlement body can establish an independent panel. In essence, the difficulty for the WTO is that partial or apparent use of the procedure through threats to file a dispute before the WTO tends to lead eventually to *ad hoc* bilateral arrangements, so undermining the authority and marginalising the WTO. For example, the United States threatened to file a formal complaint against Japan over the car import dispute in 1995, though in practice the issue has remained at a bilateral US–Japanese level.[26] Fourth, emphasis in the WTO on services and major bloc trade disputes means that, although the WTO is near universal, trade issues relevant to small powers, particularly those in Africa with commodity problems, are relegated or remain low on the WTO agenda.

Finally, the establishment of WTO has raised issues about the role and future of the United Nations Conference on Trade and Development

(UNCTAD). Those seeking institutional revision have argued that the WTO makes UNCTAD redundant. UNCTAD has, however, been defended by a number of members of the G-77.

Regional and pan-regional groupings

At the trade co-operation level a striking feature is the growth since the 1980s of a variety of regional economic institutions. Regional economic organisations (REOs) differ in geographic area, membership and levels of co-operation. Examples of regional economic organisations include the North American Free Trade Agreement (original members US, Canada, Mexico) (NAFTA). The NAFTA agreement is unusual in that it was supplemented by separate additional instruments on labour co-operation, and environmental co-operation in September 1993. An agreement establishing a tri-member secretariat located in Mexico City, was concluded in July 1994.[27] A further interesting feature of the secretariat agreement was the obligation on secretariat staff not to receive or seek instructions from any government or authority external to the NAFTA commission, and that each party is required to respect the international character of the secretariat.[28] NAFTA was augmented by Chile, extending NAFTA's regional economic access, in 1995.

Regional economic organisations have been developed particularly in Latin and Central America. Examples include the G-3 (Colombia, Mexico, Venezuela) and Mercosur (Argentina, Brazil, Paraguay, Uruguay) set up in 1991. The international debt crisis led to formation of the G-8 in 1987. Within Asia, the Economic Co-operation Organisation (ECO) (Iran, Afghanistan, Pakistan, Turkey) was augmented following the break-up of the former Soviet Union with the admission of the five Central Asian Republics.[29] Examples of ambitious but loosely structured free trade area groupings are the Asia Pacific Economic Co-operation (APEC) and the *ad hoc* Summit of the Americas, meeting in December 1994 in Miami.

International trade disputes

In this section of the chapter, a number of illustrations of international trade disputes are given to show the range of conflict. Resource disputes, for example, have become much more complex, in part, because of the break-up of the former Soviet Union and loss of control over part of its oil resources and pipelines. For example, the Russian Federation has refused to accept the Caspian Sea offshore oil exploration agreement reached by Azerbaijan with a nine-company multinational consortium.[30] Territorial claims, linked to oil exploration, have meant that the Spratly Islands remain sources of considerable conflict with multiple claims and periodic tension or clashes. For example the Spratly dispute intensified following the Chinese occupation in 1994 of the appropriately named Mischief Reef, claimed by the Philippines, 200 kilometres off Palau.[31]

The Philippines formally protested against the Chinese action in February 1995, referring to the Manila ASEAN Declaration. The Philippines protest note introduced a new geographical concept in maritime disputes: 'nearest country stewardship', as the basis for the Philippines' claim.

In a second category, disputes over market access are common and lead to varying degrees of conflict. A marked feature of Japanese–United States trade conflict, for example, is the recurrence of trade disputes which have been apparently wholly resolved (e.g. semi-conductors) or have only been partly resolved. A characteristic example of the latter, extensively favoured in Japanese negotiating style and methods, was the conclusion of a last minute agreement in the negotiations on opening Japan's markets to specified goods and services to avert US retaliation. However, no agreement was reached on access for motor vehicles and vehicle parts which then became the focal point of dispute in 1995–96.[32]

Bilateral trade access disputes in fact take many forms and are experienced at some point by most states. For example, the Malaysian–Singapore petrochemical dispute (put to the WTO by Singapore) centred on Malaysian local content and licence restrictions on Singapore petrochemical products exported to Malaysia, introduced to limit Singapore petrochemical products.[33] Trade access disputes can also involve weak regional economic organisations in disputes over membership and relations with other organisations.[34] For example relations between the Caribbean community (CARICOM) and the Organisation of Eastern Caribbean states (OECS) remain limited. On membership, Surinam was accepted as the fourteenth full member of CARICOM in 1995. Similar applications to convert observer states to full membership by Haiti and the Dominican Republic were rejected.

A number of different types of disputes have arisen in the aid-trade category. The category includes disputes over the percentage of subsidies in aid packages; aid offset agreements; quota challenges and periodic reviews of trade development funds within regional trade organisations. Disputes involving offset agreements (e.g. mixed military-aid packages) usually occur because of internal opposition within the donor state to the agreement from a competing agency or affected opposing interest groups. For example the dispute over the Pergau dam funding noted earlier involved opposition by UK development NGOs to the use of parts of the UK aid budget for a complex dam construction and weapons deal in Malaysia. Disputes over the amount of increase in trade development packages are well illustrated in the Lomé IV review context. The intervention of *political conditionality* (e.g. human rights, good governance) provisions fundamentally transformed the character of the negotiations, changing them from traditional financial-technical discussion on the amount, scale and phasing of disbursements to more politicised exchanges.

One of the growing categories of trade conflict involves non-tariff restrictions on exports. Some of the most extensive of these involve environmental and hygiene provisions applied to the entry of goods.

Environmental criteria have been introduced into trade relations, for example in the context of regulations regarding dolphin bi-catch in tuna fishing (US–Mexico). In the hygiene and phyto-sanitary category, disputes have led to extensive new provisions being included in the WTO covering procedures and safeguards in these areas. A low regulated area, with poor or lax enforcement, in which there are quite frequent disputes is international veterinary standards and conditions for live animal exports. Environmental clauses have been attacked by developing countries as a form of trade restriction.

Finally, a new category of trade dispute has developed over the significance of the concept of sustainable development for the trade opportunities of developing countries. Developing countries including Malaysia, Indonesia, India, and Colombia have opposed in debate over the application of sustainable development, concepts such as 'sustainable human development', 'human security' and so-called 'social clauses' techniques, as a form of means to undermine the competitiveness of the South.

Summary

Trade is a central feature of diplomacy, rather than a discreet or distinct area of activity as under traditional diplomacy. For the diplomat, the task is to assess constantly the relationship between national trade interests and the country's foreign policy; reconcile as necessary conflicting trade and foreign policy interests, and ascertain the prospects and possibilities for external trade co-operation and promotion. The expansion of international trade issues requires foreign ministries to recruit or co-opt additional technical and multi-disciplinary personnel.

At an international level, one of the most striking features of modern diplomacy over the past decade is the resurgence or establishment of an increasing number of trade-based economic organisations at a sub-regional, regional and global level. The continued emergence of economic regionalism has, however, posed challenges for global trade order through the WTO. The use of protective tariffs, qualitative and other restrictions on access and the closure of strategic sectors such as services and petrochemicals by regional trade organisations and other groupings, has served to undermine multilateral trade rule-making. Apart from the regional–global dichotomy, three further related features of the trade setting with important continuing implications for the conduct of diplomacy are the intensification of the North–South economic and financial division; political conditionality in trade, and divisions within the international community about the need for trade-related UN specialised agencies such as UNCTAD, following the establishment of the WTO.

References and notes

1. For a discussion of the role of the China lobby in changing British Policy to one of checking Japan and preserving South China in a sphere of influence, see Stephen

Lyon Endicott, *Diplomacy and Enterprise: British China Policy* (Manchester University Press, Manchester, 1978).

2. In the trade dispute between the United States and Japan over US exports of beef and citrus products, Japanese farming interests strongly lobbied the Agriculture Ministry and the Liberal Democratic Party's parliamentary farm committee to limit any quotas increase. The dispute brought the Japanese Agriculture and Foreign Ministries into dispute. In this instance, the tough line recommended by agriculture prevailed. See *Financial Times,* 4 April 1984.

3. *Financial Times,* 30 Jan. 1986.

4. Final Act embodying the results of the Uruguay Round, Marrakesh, 15 April 1994, UK, Misc. No. 14 (1994) Cmnd. 2570.

5. BISD Vol. III (Geneva) p. 3.

6. Olivier Long, Law and its limitations in the GATT Multilateral Trade Negotiations (GATT, Geneva, 1979).

7. The Tokyo Round of Multilateral Trade Negotiations (GATT, Geneva, 1979) and Vol. II, Supplementary Report (GATT, Geneva, 1979).

8. Misc. 21 (1979), Cmnd. 7658.

9. Misc. 26 (1979), Cmnd. 7663.

10. Misc. 27 (1979), Cmnd. 7664.

11. Misc. 25 (1979), Cmnd. 7662.

12. Misc. 24 (1979), Cmnd. 7661.

13. Misc. 20 (1979), Cmnd. 7657. The revision to these codes in the Uruguay Round, together with other amendments were carried over to become the main elements in the WTO system.

14. Olivier Long, op. cit., p. 60.

15. The Pergau Dam Crisis arose after domestic criticism by UK aid agencies of the use of the UK aid budget to offer a loan on concessional terms for the construction of the Pergau Dam in Malaysia. For the Foreign Secretary's evidence to Parliament see *The Times,* 3 March 1994.

16. See Kent Jones, Politics v. Economics in World Steel trade (Allen and Unwin, London, 1986) p. 125.

17. Misc. 28 (1994), Cmnd. 2556; Misc. 17 (1994) Cmnd. 2559.

18. Misc. 18 (1994), Cmnd. 2561.

19. Misc. 29 (1994), Cmnd. 2557.

20. Misc. 20 (1994), Cmnd. 2565.

21. Misc. 15 (1994), Cmnd. 2571.

22. See Ronald P. Barston (ed.), *International Politics Since 1945* (Elgar, Aldershot, 1991) pp. 224–42; *Finance and Development,* March 1995, pp. 24–7.

23. See Annual Report Foreign Affairs and Trade (Canberra, 1994) pp. 83–93.

24. See Barston, op. cit., p. 232.

25. *Financial Times,* 22 and 24 March 1995.

26. *Financial Times,* 12 May 1995.

27. Personal Communication Ministry of Foreign Affairs, Secretariat Agreement, Ottawa, 14 July 1994.

28. Secretariat Agreement, 14 July 1994.

29. Kazakstan, Kirghizia, Tadjikistan, Turkmenistan, Uzbekistan joined the ECO. *Keesing* (March 1995) 40483.

30. *Times,* 7 Jan. 1995.

31. *Keesing* (1995) 40403.

32. *Financial Times,* 3 Oct. 1994.

33. The Malaysian Singapore dispute was the first case put to the WTO. *Financial Times,* 23 Feb. 1995.

34. Richard Bernal, 'Regional Trade Agreements in the Western Hemisphere', *American University Journal of International Law and Policy,* Vol. 8, No. 4, Summer 1993, pp. 683–714.

CHAPTER 9

Environmental diplomacy

In this chapter we shall be looking at some of the main characteristics of environmental diplomacy which have become apparent in the course of the increasing international attention directed at environmental questions over the past decade. Environmental issues have continued to move up the international agenda since the mid-1980s. As part of this process an increasing number of bilateral, regional and global agreements and arrangements have been concluded by states, international institutions and other agencies. The characteristics of the negotiations will be discussed under four main headings: setting, the main players, process and the form of agreements.

Setting

The first major post-war high-level global conference to discuss environmental questions was held in Stockholm in 1972.[1] Prior to that environmental matters had in the main been handled through limited agreements, such as the 1911 Bering Sea fur seal agreement (United States, Britain, Japan, Russia)[2] or regionally as in the case of the 1964 European Fisheries Convention.[3] At an international level examples of agreements include the International Convention for the Prevention of Pollution of the Sea by Oil (1954)[4] and the Ramsar Convention concluded in 1971,[5] which deals with protection of habitats. Most of the agreements concluded in the early pre- and post-war years contained only two or three of the five necessary parts for effective conservation and management: jurisdiction, regulation or enforcement provisions and not scientific advice or institutional implementation.

An important and continuing influence on the development of environmental diplomacy, apart from the Stockholm conference, was the convening of the third United Nations Conference on the Law of the Sea in 1973.[6] Although environmental issues were one of a number of complex issues before the conference, their inclusion within the jurisdictional context of the territorial sea, exclusive economic zone (EEZ) and the seabed beyond the EEZ, known as the international area, furthered the process of considering environmental problems in the context of other multiple sea uses, such as navigation, fisheries, leisure, disposal and offshore oil exploration. In contrast, that part of the Stockholm process under the auspices of UNEP[7] has mainly tended to promote the negotiation of a number of regional and sectoral agreements such as regional framework conventions with specific regional protocols, e.g. on combatting oil pollution[8] or setting up special areas;[9] and sub-regional marine scientific research projects.[10] At the international level initiatives and guidelines have included migratory species;[11] the Montreal Guidelines on Land Based Pollution;[12] ozone[13] and transboundary movement of waste.[14]

International attention began to be increasingly focused on environmental regulation again at a global level from the mid-1980s. As in previous phases, renewed international activity is often brought about and influenced by major disasters. The short-run effect of adverse external events in catalysing diplomatic activity is in fact one of the main features of safety-related environmental diplomacy. Major incidents such as Chernobyl and *Exon Valdez* have the effect of dramatising a problem, galvanise non-governmental groups and influence calls for the revision of international codes and rules. Second, state practice as evidenced in national administration, international guidelines and agreements, began increasingly to adopt a broader and more cautious approach to environmental conservation and management. This change reflected in part the shift in land planning and coastal zone management approaches in some countries to incorporate integrative and multiple use concepts. As a result, international agreements in this period are distinguished from most of those in the first decade after the Stockholm Conference by relating obligations to a variety of precautionary type principles (e.g. best technology, environmental restoration, precautionary transfer and impact assessment) and changing procedures for the disposal of dangerous and toxic substances.[15] The extent and consistency of implementation does, however, vary quite considerably; new disputes, mainly of an economic kind, have arisen over developed country obligations; categories of most affected countries and institutional control over economic assistance.

A third factor is the effect of scientific advancement on environmental initiatives and negotiations. The identification of serious new environmental problems associated with the ozone layer and ozone depletion, along with the problem of global warming have received widespread scientific acceptance within the international scientific community and given environmental issues a heightened urgency.[16] The issues raised further major questions about the distribution of international responsibility and what assistance might be given to developing countries. Fourth, the United Nations Conference on Environment and Development (Rio Summit, 1992)[17] despite limitations, has, nevertheless, brought high-level attention to environmental issues. The follow-up process of national reporting and review meetings of the parties which are a requirement of Rio agreements[18] and similarly other related instruments, added to the momentum of environmental diplomatic initiatives, ensuring the issue areas are kept to the forefront of international relations. In addition, the problem of inadequate environmental controls, for example over dumping at sea and defence-related waste, has been underlined in societies undergoing major political transition (e.g. Russian Federation).[19] Further, environmental destruction has been used as a politico-military technique in war and armed conflict, as in the destruction of Kuwait oil-fields in the 1991 Kuwait occupation and the Iraqi destruction of the southern marsh Arabs' habitat, raising international concern over this form of environmental warfare.[20]

Multilateral conference typology

Within the range of environmental diplomatic conferences, five broad types of process may be distinguished: (1) Collegiate; (2) Chair-led; (3) Fragmented – multilateral; (4) Technical specialist core group; (5) Informal. In the collegiate category, the law of the sea negotiations 1972–82 have provided a basic master or model for much of subsequent contemporary multilateral environmental and other large-scale conferences.[21] The stages of a collegiate-style conference can be represented schematically as follows:

Conference president/chairman (election)
Conference officers (Bureau) (election)
Chairmen of main committees (appointed)
Plenary meetings
Formal working groups (reporting to chairs of main committees, president or plenary)
Informal working groups
Ad hoc groups of the conference (e.g. to address core outstanding issues, made up of selected states representing key interests)
Intersessional negotiations
Draft texts (e.g. informal negotiating text; revised composite negotiating text; draft convention)
Final closure sessions
Formal opening for signature

The concept of a collegiate conference is drawn from the idea of the amount of delegation given to the chairmen of the principal committees to create and promote draft texts within the committees, which are then put together to create a composite text for revision in order to create a single draft convention. This type of format has been adapted and used at general diplomatic conferences, like the London conference on the Convention for the Prevention of Pollution of the Sea by Oil (MARPOL)[22] and most UN specialised agencies, e.g. UNEP, UNDP. The main modifications to the UNCLOS format have been the introduction of brief organisational and preparatory meetings, and, in a few instances, provision for ministerial negotiation.

Of the other indicative types the fragmented multilateral conference is characterised by the absence of clear coalitions, limited bloc influence, and large numbers of uncommitted states. Major powers involved in fragmented negotiations will attempt to dominate as single actors rather than in coalitions, by influencing the agenda, and through specific interventions. An example of negotiations encompassing many of these features are the Montreal negotiations for a new agreement to replace the Montreal Guidelines on land-based sources of pollution.[23] Technical/ specialist styled negotiations managed by a core group are most frequently found in the negotiations conducted in the standing conferences and working groups of functional organisations such as the International Maritime Organisation (IMO), Food and Agriculture Organisation (FAO), International Civil Aviation Organisation (ICAO), International Atomic Energy Agency (IAEA). For example at the IMO, the specialist core group, common to Plenary Sessions of the Marine Environment Protection Committee (MEPC) and Working Groups, is made up of United States, United Kingdom, Norway, Holland, France and Germany. In general, the G-77 as a co-ordinating body does not operate in these fora and involvement by other states is mainly to protect or secure special interests (e.g. Turkey on the Turkish Straits or Brazil to obtain exemptions or modified terms for older type tanker tonnage).[24]

In informal multilateral diplomacy, negotiations are conducted without extensive rules of procedure. Under these conditions, states tend to participate more on an individual rather than coalition or sub-regional group basis, as happened in the World Bank–Caribbean negotiations in 1993 to extend the Global Environment Facility (GEF) to the wider Caribbean area.

Players in environmental diplomacy

Environmental diplomacy has involved an increasingly wide range of actors, including new intergovernmental organisations, UN and other international institutions, secretariats, elected conference officials, NGOs,[25] as well as states.[26] The expansion of state members of the international community to nearly 190 means that, as in other forms of multilateral negotiations which have universal or near universal participation, the number of accredited delegates could be over 700, some two or three times the size of multilateral conferences in the first phase of multilateral environmental diplomacy (1972–79). Modern universality places major constraints on interpretation and other conference facilities,[27] location of meetings, and logistics. Very few conference facilities at UN headquarters in New York can handle multilateral conferences of this size at a time when New York is becoming a centre for non-standing multilateral conferences. In a sense, the United Nations is at breaking point. The physical effect of size on conference facilities has also affected the process of negotiations. This will be discussed below.

However, unlike earlier multilateral conferences, the actual accredited participation of nominally universal environmental conferences varies in practice quite considerably. In some instances conferences on what might be considered issues of global importance, have participation in the *negotiation* process of as few as 20–50 states (e.g. Vienna Convention for the Protection of the Ozone Layer[28] or UN intergovernmental negotiations on a land-based pollution convention),[29] although the participation level may rise during later negotiating phases as a convention or other instrument nears conclusion and at the implementation stage itself as non-negotiating states accede to conventions. Those negotiations which have attracted high levels of accreditation and participation have generally been resource-related multilateral conferences, such as the UN Conference on Straddling and Highly Migratory Fish Stocks, or development-related, like the UN Conference on Sustainable Development of Small Island States.[30]

Format

In the main international environmental negotiations are conducted at a bureaucratic and technical, rather than ministerial or political leader level. Ministerial involvement in ongoing technical level negotiations is confined to buttressing up a country's case; restating the negotiating position (particularly for domestic audiences); announcing a major change of policy, or negotiating broad policy objectives. In major international or global negotiations, ministerial involvement tends to be carefully orchestrated to provide for some involvement in the final phases leading up to signing an agreement. Exceptions with sustained ministerial involvement occur in those cases in which states are involved in serious regional disputes or have vital specific interests (e.g. Canada – Grand Banks fisheries; Russian Federation – overfishing; Sea of Okhotsk). Occasionally too ministers may play important brokering roles in the event of impasse (e.g. Germany at Rio on financial provisions).[31] Since Rio, a further development has been the attempts to enhance heads of government or ministerial involvement by making provision for a heads of government general debate on current and long-range issues during a special section of the negotiations. This technique, styled the 'high level segment', was used, for example, at the 1994 Barbados session of the Global Conference on Sustainable Development of Small Island Developing States,[32] taking the theme 'Forging Partnerships for Sustainable Development'. So far the technique, which has been mainly used in Rio-related multilateral diplomacy, has had only limited success because of non-participation by some major players,[33] differing *levels* of ministerial participation and the tendency for this type of forum to become a *de facto* plenary for restatement of known positions.

Stakeholders

In multilateral diplomacy one way of understanding the differing interests and degrees of involvement is through the concept of 'stakeholder'.

Stakeholders are those states and other actors which seek to safeguard or enhance particular concerns or sets of interests over and above general or minimal interest in the proceedings of a conference. Stakeholders may seek negative or positive outcomes. Five types of stakeholders can be distinguished: personal; international institutional; treaty; special interest; substitution interests. In the first category are stakeholders who are national diplomatic representatives or international civil servants who regularly act as multilateral conference office-holders or in secretariats. Diplomatic representatives of a number of smaller countries such as Cape Verde, Fiji, Tanzania, have been particularly associated with ongoing or long-running conferences. The Law of the Sea Conference, for example, continued in reduced form with meetings on the disputed deep sea-bed mining provisions (Part XI)[34] in the Preparatory Commission, for ten years after the opening for signature of the Convention in 1982 until the major overhaul of UN activities undertaken by the UN Secretary-General Boutros-Ghali. Second, international institutions through their permanent secretariat staff develop a variety of agenda-setting, financial, budgetary and project stakes. In the third category, states may develop stakes as a result of initiating or hosting an initial diplomatic conference which negotiates an agreement that is subsequently either amended or reviewed. For example, Canada was active and hosted the Montreal Protocol negotiations on ozone depleting substances (CFCs),[35] as well as other related environmental negotiations. An interesting example of an unsuccessful Canadian initiative is provided by the 1994 review negotiations for an international convention on land-based sources of pollution. The initial negotiations, which produced best practice guidelines for dealing with land-based pollution (Montreal Guidelines), had been hosted, and actively influenced, by Canada in 1985. However, Canada was unable during the review negotiations to prevent the United States forcing the Montreal Guidelines to be abandoned as a basis for negotiation,[36] and had to accept US pressure to alter the agenda to one of financial mechanisms for assisting developing countries.

Fourth, states often approach environmental negotiations with *special interests*. These might include problems arising from a nuclear power plant in a neighbouring state, desertification, transboundary pollution, or, conversely powerful domestic lobbies such as petrochemical, chemical or logging industries which seek to limit or modify environmental legislation. An example of a new alliance of special interests is provided by the Vatican, Saudi Arabia and Iran set up to oppose or block population control proposals at the UN Global Conference on Population, held in Cairo in 1994.[37] In the fifth category of stakeholder, are those actors which seek substitution goals. These might be negative, as in the previous example. Alternatively, substitution goals can take the form of attempting to focus the agenda of a diplomatic conference away from primary regulations or regime-building issues, to implementation questions such as review conferences, institutional arrangements or financial mechanisms. These tactics feature heavily in Swedish diplomacy, which has consistently sought in specialised standing technical diplomatic conferences and other fora to redirect the agenda to technical assistance mechanisms (consultants, studies, working groups, financial funds) in support of Sweden's high national interest in development diplomacy.[38]

Delegations

A notable feature of environmental diplomacy in non-standing international conferences is the considerable variation in the size and composition of delegations, which is more accentuated than in other types of multilateral diplomacy. In part, this is due to the fact that environmental questions tend to be handled at an international level by representatives from diverse ministries such as fisheries, parks and recreation, tourism, scientific research institutes, rather than by fully-fledged environment ministries. This tends to have the effect of narrowing perspectives and restricting contributions, particularly from developing country participants, who are generally more active and comfortable on broader issue-based rather than environmental diplomacy, such as international declarations and programmes on sustainable development.

Which ministry is the lead ministry for sessions of a conference can be a source of dispute. In those instances in larger delegations where the departmental leadership of a delegation changes there is often an alteration of style and emphasis in the way negotiations are conducted. Thus the foreign ministry may place greater emphasis on national security considerations, political relations with other states and the tactics of diplomacy, than the specialist ministry. Changes between lead *specialist* ministries are less frequent and will affect priorities and interests. During negotiations, for example, at the Marine Environment Protection Committee of the International Maritime Organisation (IMO) on special areas, the lead changed from the US coastguard (usual delegation leader), to National Oceanic and Atmospheric Administration (NOAA). As a result the United States position became for a brief period much more sympathetic to the concept of marine special areas.[39]

The overall impact of a delegation will vary depending on factors such as negotiating past history, diplomatic skills, contribution to the intellectual process of negotiation and formal or informal committee roles. In some instances, limited resources may mean that a delegation's input is deliberately restricted, for example to the legal field (e.g. Kenya, Singapore). Larger states such as the United States, United Kingdom and the Netherlands have acquired roles, in addition to their traditional technical input, as treaty-drafting specialists,[40] invariably serving on drafting committees. In other instances, impact is achieved by acquiring the role of roving envoy or regional spokesman.[41] For example, Indonesia's roving ambassador Hasim Djalal, who has responsibility for all maritime issues in international fora, has an acquired diplomatic reputation for performing with some skill the role of interlocutor, probing the meaning of draft international agreements, while avoiding discussion of Indonesia's position.

Finally, we should note the phenomenon of nominal or symbolic accreditation. Although a diplomatic conference may have, for example, one hundred states accredited, the actual *participation level* (measured by attendance throughout the conference and input) by accredited representatives will vary considerably. Minimal or token participation is usually associated with delegations exclusively made up of representatives of a permanent mission accredited to an international organisation.[42]

International institutions: stakes and influence

In environmental and other diplomacy international institutions carry out a number of roles. These include agenda-setting; liaison; initiating studies; assisting working groups; sponsoring draft articles; brokering compromises and overseeing the administration, review and amendment (if any) of conventions.

These roles, which amount to more than oiling the wheels of diplomacy, are often of decisive importance, and are generally undertaken in conjunction with elected or nominated conference chairmen or presidents, the chairmen of the principal committees of a conference and elected office-holders (e.g. regional group conference vice-presidents). The latter constitute the bureau of a diplomatic conference, which may be expanded on an *ad hoc* basis with the addition of other states.[43]

In the course of the evolution of contemporary environmental diplomacy, international institutions have developed through their officials and chief executives, interests, doctrines and programme stakes. Such interests are analogous in some ways to departmental stakes in bureaucratic politics theory. They are only in rare circumstances (e.g. a very narrow technical subject on which there is consensus) epistemic[44] but rather personal, technical, managerial and linked to the generation of international institutions' funding and programme budgets. In personality terms, leading figures such as Mostapha Tolba (UNEP) have done much to promote ideas about the international management of the environment, and to promote major programmes, as well as harness support for the negotiations of a specific convention, such as Tolba's role in the Vienna and Montreal Protocol negotiations.[45] Specific international institutional interests are seen most clearly in pre-conference discussions over which international institutions should have responsibility for initiating and managing negotiations. At the pre-conference and initial phases of negotiation international institution interests are seen in secretariat-sponsored draft compilation or negotiating texts.[46] Nevertheless, secretariats are not always successful in having their texts used as a basis for further elaboration or negotiation, and in the Forest Principles negotiations at Rio, for example, the secretariat text was not used by the intergovernmental working group.[47] Third, international institution interests are evident in those parts of negotiations which are concerned with ongoing funding arrangements for a convention, including programme and permanent secretariat measures, which are generally among the main sources of conflict between North and South. Fourth, international institutions have become increasingly associated with the implementation of conventions. The institutional responsibility for and control of the management of the Barcelona Convention (Mediterranean) was a source of considerable acrimony between FAO and UNEP.[48] In a similar sense, international institutions may seek to use their existing competence within one convention to challenge and acquire responsibilities which come under another international organisation. For example the Basel Convention secretariat, with responsibility for aspects of transboundary movement of hazardous waste[49] in seeking to broaden its jurisdictional boundaries came into conflict with the International Atomic Energy Authority (IAEA) and International Maritime Organisation (IMO).

Multilateral process

Before we look at some of the specific features of the dynamic of environmental conference diplomacy two general features of the process will be discussed: the effects of the rule of consensus and the growing pluralism of actors and interests.

Consensus

For the most part multilateral conferences since the 1970s have been conducted on the basis of the rule of consensus rather than unanimity or voting. The rule allows for voting only after all attempts to reach agreement on the basis of discussion have been explored. Thus the consensus rule operates on the fiction that there is an emerging measure of support for a proposal or elements of a draft text. Negotiations continue on the basis of attempting to create wider consensus and construct *apparent* areas of agreement. In this way the operation of the rule of consensus sometimes tends to disguise or postpone significant areas of disagreement. This inevitably means that negotiations are lengthy even *within* fixed time frames or deadlines. As a result under the consensus rule more and more business has tended to be conducted within the informal conference plenary, with fewer working groups and greater reliance on chairman's consultations and so-called contact groups. A second, related fiction is that of broad consultation with delegations by the conference chairman to reduce differences. In practice consultation may be selective and unequal for reasons of time and momentum. This tends to reinforce one of the central paradoxes of the consensus rule: that negotiations appear to be based on widespread agreement, whereas the depth of support at a multilateral conference is never really known.

Blocs and groups

The development of multilateral diplomacy has been marked by increasing pluralism and the decline of large traditional groups or blocs. Negotiations tend to be more personal, technical and pluralistic. In only relatively few instances can they be conceptualised as being epistemic, such as the initial ozone negotiations.[50] This is because of the complexity of issues, differing levels of representation at multilateral conferences, and the growing tendency as noted above to use representation to conferences from permanent missions. While traditional UN groupings continue such as the Afro-Asian bloc, these have lost much of their significance as vehicles for substantive caucus or co-ordination, as regions splinter and redefine their membership and purposes. However, North–South divisions within multilateral conferences remain marked, but the groupings within these have changed over the past decade. In the South, the G-77 has found it increasingly difficult to operate as a clearing and co-ordinating group in environmental and other diplomacy in the past because issues have become more technical and scientific and less susceptible to political brokerage or politically derived 'package' solutions. New sub-regional interests have emerged, like the Alliance of Small Island States, which disputed the process and agenda promoted by 'established' (Latin American) members of the G-77 in the run-up to the Barbados Conference on the Sustainable Development of Small Island States in 1994. Other alliances have been created across regional groups such as at Rio by Malaysia, India and Brazil to defeat a legally binding international agreement on forest management. While the G-77 has retained much of its co-ordinating structure, which is principally made up of the active core G-77 permanent mission ambassadors in Paris, Rome, Geneva and New York, the agenda co-ordinated by these chapters tends to focus now on periodic large-scale UN conferences, such as Sustainable Development or Habitat II, rather than detailed clearing of texts on South–South trade or technical co-operation negotiations.[51]

Within the developed states, loose informal consultation on environment and maritime related matters has continued since the initial law of the sea negotiations, with annual meetings and intersessional exchanges between members of the G-5 (now plus Germany).[52] Of the former Soviet Union allies, the socialist bloc itself has ceased to exist and is no longer a grouping for representation and other purposes in the UN system and in international agreements, following the collapse of the Soviet Union. Although some consultation continues on non-near abroad issues, the break-up of the bloc has weakened Russian Federation diplomatic capabilities. Concern over this led the Russian Federation to try and retain separate representation for Eastern Europe in the International Seabed Authority, during the final negotiations in 1994 to revise the Law of the Sea Convention to facilitate the adherence of the major maritime powers.

In contrast the EU has emerged as a bloc actor in multilateral conferences. The role of the EU Commission, to negotiate on behalf of member states, in areas in which it has competence has progressively expanded since the Maastricht agreement into an increasing range of functional diplomacy. In general, the capacity of individual EU member states to conduct international environmental and other negotiations has as a result been severely constrained. Unless there is mixed or joint competence, EU members are represented by the Commission. In multilateral diplomacy, individual EU member states cannot initiate draft proposals, intervene in plenary debate, propose clarifications during debate, broker compromise or deviate from the public position which is frequently lowest common denominator.

It can be argued that the expansion of the role of the EU Commission, corresponding to changes in its competence, has fundamentally altered the dynamics of those multilateral conferences in which it participates in this form by negating individual EU member input and removing from the process key European players. An indirect effect of this is that the focus of interaction has shifted to middle-rank and lesser known actors and non-EU powers, such as Canada, Brazil, Norway, Australia, Mexico, Chile, and Morocco who play much greater roles in environmental diplomacy.

The dynamic of environmental negotiations

The momentum of an international conference is the function of several factors such as the role of conference and committee chairpersons, the drafting and refining role of *ad hoc* and formal working groups in identifying compromise formulae on focal points or providing draft text on specific areas of difficulty, and the concession rate.

The chairperson of a multilateral conference, with the support of the secretariat, can influence the momentum of negotiations in a number of ways such as agenda-setting, the conference timetable, drafting texts and consultations with delegations. One of the main difficulties the chair faces in the course of chair-led negotiations is developing a distinctive or personal negotiating text which is seen to be sufficiently neutral or distinctive from any text sponsored by a lead delegation or other group. Failure to maintain 'neutrality' can lead to substantial conflict and deadlock. In loose collegiate and fragmented multilateral conferences, the chair is generally less able to carry out the kind of roles discussed.

Other techniques developed to assist momentum are the use by the chair and states of reference points (e.g. provisions of Agenda 21) or borrowing from concepts and definitions from other agreements or codes. In some instances, however, the reference point or 'transferred' definition has had the opposite effect. Rather than unify or expedite it has become a source of controversy.

Another notable feature of recent multilateral conference diplomacy is the use of non-papers and informal conference papers in part in response to the complexity of environmental diplomacy. The use of non-papers and informal papers also coincides with the transformation and general loosening of group and bloc structures to more individual diplomacy and non-traditional links. Most importantly from the perspective of process, informal papers have to a considerable extent replaced the technique of individually or collectively sponsored draft articles which typified multilateral negotiation up to the early 1980s. The technique assists particularly in the preparatory phase of negotiation in that provision for informal technical studies, outline agenda of priorities and other similar informal papers enables participants to have their ideas annotated in either the formal draft agenda or in a composite secretariat text. In the course of negotiations informal papers submitted by delegations assist momentum in that parts of the informal paper may be periodically incorporated into an evolving draft text, possibly by the conference chairman, keeping participants committed to the consensus process.

Concession and compromise

One of the main causes of lack of momentum and deadlock in environmental diplomacy is the tendency to rely heavily on bracketing throughout the course of negotiations to indicate that certain parts of a text are unacceptable.

Another important related source of difficulty in environmental negotiations is the potential range and complexity of issues over which there is disagreement. These might be single issues such as the conflict between African states and other members of the G-77 over priority for Africa in desertification negotiations (INCD), or one of several critical sub-areas of disagreement on a list of outstanding issues. Environmental negotiations too have recurring focal points of critical disagreement, such as financial arrangements, including eligibility for access to special funds, and control regimes for implementing environmental agreements. For example the draft financial provisions of Agenda 21 came from the preparatory working group to Rio with over 40 G-77 amendments. Focal points too may often be quite specific. Protracted disputes have occurred over the meaning of a single word, such as the effect or meaning of inserting the word 'including' in the financial mechanisms section of Agenda 21. A further distinctive feature of environmental diplomacy is that financial disputes have led to the *extension* of disputes over 'categories of countries' or special cases.

Loss of momentum or deadlock can also occur as a result of the effect of increased political and technical knowledge about issues, and other delegations' positions, gained during the course of negotiations. This is evident especially in those parts of a negotiation in which attempts are being made to develop new concepts or international institutions. As the ramifications of proposals are better understood, delegations re-appraise positions and as a result table amendments or perhaps withdraw earlier proposals.

In the event of deadlock techniques have been developed in multilateral diplomacy to attempt to construct widely acceptable solutions. These include the appointment of a specific delegate to broker compromise formulae; contact groups; closed sessions of heads of delegations; and innovative revised texts sponsored by the chair. In addition, the constraints on the frequency and duration of non-standing multilateral conferences have meant that in a number of environmental conferences several all-night sessions have become the norm and several crucial issues have been postponed or deferred to the final meeting, or, if permitted, a follow-up 'implementation' or review conference.

It is also interesting that package deal type approaches are seemingly inappropriate or not particularly evident in environmental diplomacy. In part this results from the time constraints noted previously. In so far as some environmental negotiations have become 'end run' (i.e. crucial issues stacked for the final meetings or postponed) it is difficult or impossible to use 'bottom-up' or package deals strategies because of the complexity of issues and time constraints. Nor indeed may the idiom be understood by some delegations in a pluralistic and heavily divided North and South negotiating environment. Rather, the process of 'soft' law-making increasingly relies on codes; variations of framework agreements; or simply language which defers a solution.

International environmental agreements and other measures

A variety of formal instruments such as treaties, agreements, conventions and protocols, as well as informal instruments such as codes, guidelines and declarations, have been used in order to create binding and non-binding rules. The choice of instrument is generally determined by such factors as the context of negotiations, purposes, number of parties and above all the nature of the obligations undertaken. The growing use of qualified language in international environmental agreements has given rise to the distinction between so-called 'hard' and 'soft' law. The use of phrases such as 'as appropriate', 'according to developing country capabilities',[53] and 'as far as possible'[54] reflect the need for accommodation, compromise and meeting particular interests especially in a North–South context without which international agreements in these areas would be less likely or impossible to reach. The process of balancing conflicting interests also underlines the point that the negotiation of environmental agreements, as with other forms of treaty negotiation, is essentially a *textual* process, of attempting to have incorporated in draft agreements the interests and agendas of the respective protagonists.

Apart from the above developments, environmental diplomacy is also distinguished by the increased use of informal administrative or good governance type instruments such as declarations, codes, guidelines and Action Plans. These are generally non-binding and their growing use has been influenced by several features of current environmental diplomacy.

First the non-binding nature of the instrument facilitates reaching agreement on a lowest common denominator basis. That is, some states which would not have accepted obligations in binding treaty language nevertheless are prepared to go along with non-obligatory documents, which are no more than a set of, for example, administrative recommendations on best practice, like the Authoritative Statement of Forest Principles.[55] Only rarely are codes upgraded into formal treaty instruments such as the International Maritime Organisation Dangerous Goods Code.[56] Even then it is not clear which existing parties to the convention are applying the code in a mandatory manner through appropriate national legislation and enforcement. Implementation of soft law is generally weak.

Second, the use of informal instruments has been particularly influenced by the operating styles of international institutions and other agencies within the UN system. The United Nations Environment Programme (UNEP) has frequently used the formula of preparatory meetings followed by Action Plans. UNEP has also influenced the use of the concept of 'framework' conventions which depend for implementation on subsequent sectoral agreements by the parties. Framework conventions have the advantage of laying the groundwork or 'kick-starting' environmental co-operation, and have become a feature of UNEP operating style, as in the Barcelona Convention. The growing practice of using framework conventions is further illustrated in the Rio Convention on Climate Change, which incorporates the term 'framework' within its title.[57] In this instance the use of 'framework' reflected the reluctance of some countries, e.g. United States to see (at least at Rio) specific timetables and commitments, favouring other fora and an 'all sources, all sinks approach'.[58] Third, codes and guidelines are being used as good governance instruments, which can be applied to problems quickly, rather than treaty instruments which may be delayed through slow entry into force. Such thinking lay behind Canadian and other support for the 1993 FAO Code of Conduct on Responsible Fishing,[59] in view of acute overfishing problems of the Newfoundland Grand Banks area.[60] Fourth, the process of selecting and adopting environmental agreements is influenced by the use of reference points, similar to focal points in negotiations, which become an authority or guide for negotiations, in that they create parameters and have spill-over effect. Examples of documents, codes and guidelines in this category are UN General Assembly Resolutions (e.g. Resolution 47/180) convening a conference on Human Habitats (Habitat II)[61] and Agenda 21.

References and notes

1. Report of the United Nations Conference on the Human Environment (UNCHE), Stockholm, 5–16 June 1972 (New York, 1973), UN Doc. A\CONF. 48/14/Rev.1. The Declaration of Principles, Action Plan and Resolution on Institutional and Financial Arrangements are reproduced in 11 *ILM* (1972) 1416, 1421, 1466. The 27th session of the UN General Assembly approved the measures 116 in favour, none against and 10 abstentions.

2. 104 BFSP (1911) 175.
3. See R.P. Barston and P.W. Birnie, *The Maritime Dimension* (George Allen and Unwin, 1980).
4. International Convention for the Prevention of the Pollution of the Sea by Oil, 1954.
5. Convention on Wetlands of International Importance, 3 Feb. 1971, held at Ramsar, Iran, *ILM*, 11, p. 963. For an outline of the work of the Convention, see P.W. Birnie and A. Boyle, *International Law and the Environment* (Clarendon Press, Oxford, 1992) pp. 465–70.
6. See J.K. Sebenius, *Negotiating the Law of the Sea* (Harvard University Press, 1984); Robert L. Friedhiem, *Negotiating the New Ocean Regime* (University of South Carolina Press, 1993).
7. For an assessment of the significance of the Stockholm Conference, see Lawrence Caldwell, *International Environmental Policy: Emergence and Dimensions,* 2nd edn (Durham, 1990), Chs 2 and 3; and Louis Sohn, 14 *Harv ILJ* (1973) pp. 423–515.
8. In the Mediterranean, Barcelona Convention, 16 Feb. 1976, in force 12 Feb. 1978; Persian/Arabic Gulf, Kuwait Regional Convention, 23 April 1978, in force 1 July 1979; Gulf of Guinea, Abidjan Convention, 23 March 1981, in force 5 Aug. 1984; in the Southeast Pacific, Lima Convention, 12 Nov. 1981, in force 19 May 1986; in the Red Sea and Gulf of Aden Environment (with Protocol Concerning Combating Pollution by Oil and Other Harmful Substances in Cases of Emergency, Jeddah, 14 Feb. 1982, in force 20 Aug. 1985; in the Caribbean, Cartagena Convention, with Protocol, 24 March 1983, in force 11 Oct. 1986; in the Indian Ocean and East Africa, Nairobi Convention, with Protocols (Protected Areas and Wild Fauna and Flora) and Combating Marine Pollution in Cases of Emergency, 21 June 1985, not yet in force, and in the Southwest Pacific, the Noumean Convention, with Protocols (oil pollution and dumping), 25 Nov. 1986.
9. See R.P. Barston, 'Weighing the Risks and Changing the Rules', *Seaways,* Aug. 1993, pp. 8–10.
10. See, for example, Monitoring Programme of the Eastern Adriatic Coastal Area, *Report* 1983–1991, MAP Technical Reports, Series No. 86, UNEP, Athens, 1994. In 1989 at the 6th Ordinary meeting, Athens, the Barcelona contracting parties agreed to abandon the monitoring and research approach carried out from 1976–89, which had included programmes on e.g. oceanographic processes; eutrophication; plankton blooms; and pollutant transfer processes, instead shifting the emphasis to effects and techniques useful for establishing environmental quality criteria; measurement, modelling and prevention controls. See *Final Report* on Research Projects Dealing with Toxicity of Pollutants on Marine Organisms, MAP Technical Reports Series No. 79, Athens 1994. The limitations of regional monitoring are discussed in MAP Technical Reports Series No. 81 (pp. 4–11), which notes low participation, lack of regularity and weakness in sampling procedures.
11. Bonn Convention on Migratory Species (1979).
12. Montreal Guidelines on Land Based Pollution, UNEP General Council Decisions 13/18 (II), 24 May 1985; revised as Washington Global Action Plan, 1995.
13. Vienna Convention for the Protection of the Ozone Layer, 1985. See D. Freestone and R. Churchill (eds), *International Law and Global Climate Change* (Graham and Trotman, London, 1991); B. Benedict, *Ozone Diplomacy* (Cambridge, Mass., 1991); J. Brunée, *Acid Rain and Ozone Depletion* (Dobbs Ferry, NY, 1988), pp. 225–54.
14. Cairo Guidelines on Waste Management, UNEP General Council Decision 14/30, 17 June 1987.
15. For a discussion of this and other external factors shaping coastal zone management, see R.P. Barston, 'International Dimensions of Coastal Zone Management', *Ocean and Coastal Management,* 23 (1994), pp. 93–116.
16. Burton Benedict, op. cit., Ch. 1.
17. For commentary and documents see Stanley P. Johnson, *The Earth Summit* (Graham and Trotman, London, 1993); M. Grubb, *The Earth Summit Agreements* (Royal Institute of International Affairs, London, 1993).
18. The Rio agreements and instruments comprise the Framework Convention on Climate Change, A/AC 237/18 (Part II) Add. 1, 18 May 1992 (Johnson, op. cit., pp. 59–102);

Convention on Biological Diversity, 5 June 1992 (Johnson, op. cit., pp. 82–102); Rio Declaration on Environment and Development, A/CONF.151/5 Rev. 1, 13 June 1992 (Johnson, op. cit., pp. 118–22); Authoritative Statement on Forest Principles, A/CONF.151/6 Rev. 1, 13 June 1992 (Johnson, op. cit., pp. 59–102). Agenda 21 (Programme of Action for Sustainable Development) is reproduced, along with the Rio Declaration and Authoritative Statement of Forest Principles, *Agenda 21* (UNDPI, E.93.1.11).

19. See David Scrivener, 'Environmental Co-Operation in the Euro-Artic', *Environmental Politics,* Vol. 4, No. 2, Summer 1995, on Norwegian–Russian Federation bilateral environmental co-operation, pp. 320–7.

20. Following the Gulf War the Security Council set up a Compensation Commission under Security Council Resolution 692 (1991) to review compensation claims resulting from Iraq's invasion and occupation of Kuwait. The first major large claim of $950 million was submitted by the Kuwait Oil Company for reimbursement of the costs of extinguishing hundreds of oil wells set ablaze by Iraqi forces. See UN/IK/2367/25 Aug. 1994.

21. See UNEP/MG/IG/1/1/Add. 1, 6 April 1994.

22. International Convention for the Prevention of Pollution from Ships (MARPOL 73/78) (International Maritime Organisation, London, 1992).

23. UNEP/MG/IG/I/3, 29 April 1994; UNEP/MG/IG/I/L/I, 9 June 1994. See Chapter 10 for case study of the Montreal review negotiations.

24. See Chapter 5 for further discussion of this point on special interests in the context of the international negotiations at the IMO on international standards for ferry safety.

25. For a valuable discussion of transnational actors and international institutions, see Peter Willetts, *Transnational Actors and Changing World Order,* International Peace Research Institute, Meigaku, Occasional Paper Series, No. 17.

26. See Report of the Secretary-General, A/C.5/48/26 and Add. 1, and Report of the Advisory Committee on Administrative and Budgetary Questions, A/48/7/Add. 7; A/RES/48/259, 1 Aug. 1994 on the request to the Secretary-General to keep special representatives and envoys to a minimum.

27. A 1993 survey of 52 UN bodies that meet regularly in New York, Geneva and Vienna. The *Ad hoc* Committee on the Indian Ocean; Commission on Sustainable Development; Commission on Human Rights, held 1143 meetings. These were respectively New York 441; Geneva 629 and Vienna 93. See A/AG.172/159, 8 Aug. 1994, Annex 2, p. 21.

28. 26 ILM (1987) 1516, 1529; Benedict, op. cit., p. 44 and p. 69.

29. Global Programme of Action, UNEP/LBA/IG. 2/7 (1995) (chap. 10).

30. A/CONF.164/INF 11, 18 April 1994.

31. The then German Environment Minister Klaus Töpfer chaired the Ministerial Level negotiations on Forests Principles. See Johnson on Töpfer's role, op. cit., pp. 109–10.

32. A/Conf. 167/3, 31 March 1994, para. 15.

33. At the Barbados Conference, those states not sending heads of Government or Ministers to the High Level Segment included France.

34. United Nations Convention on the Law of the Sea 1982. United Nations Sales No E83 V5. The Prep. Comm discussions included topics such as financial arrangements for the start up of the Authority; licence arrangements; transfer of technology provisions and constitutional questions relating to representation and voting. For a summary see *Ocean Policy News,* Vol. xi, No. 1, March 1994; and Vol. xi, No. 3, June 1994. The modification to Part xi of the 1982 UNCLOS, known as the so-called 'Implementation Agreement', which made it possible for major powers such as United States, Germany, United Kingdom, to accept the overall Convention, can be found in Fiji's draft resolution on the Agreement relating to the implementation of Part xi, A/48/L60, 22 June 1994.

35. Canada was a member of the IG 'inner group' of heads of delegations convened by UNEP's Mostapha Tolba to formulate proposals on CFC controls during the negotiations prior to Montreal. See Benedict, op. cit., p. 72.

36. The initial agenda for the land-based pollution negotiations had been drawn up by UNEP with the clear intention of the Conference using the Montreal Guidelines (1985) as a base text for the creation of a new agreement. See UNEP/MG/IG/1/2, 29 April 1994.

37. *The Times*, 15 Aug. and 5 Sept. 1994.

38. At the opening session of the newly established International Maritime Organisation (IMO) Flag State Implementation Committee in 1993, Sweden threatened to withdraw its contributions to IMO, if the work of the new committee did not principally focus on technical assistance, rather than other questions such as reforming classification societies, favoured by Germany, Norway, United Kingdom and United States.

39. For an outline of the role of the environmental NGOs at IMO, including the special areas debate, see G. Peet, 'The Role of Environmental Non-governmental Organisations at the Marine Environment Protection Committee (MEPC) of the IMO and at the London Dumping Convention', Ocean and Coastal Management, Vol. 22, No. 1 (1994) pp. 3–18.

40. See Jill Barrett's account for example of the United Kingdom role in preparing the 'Base Negotiating Text' for the Washington session of the intergovernmental negotiating committee of the Climate Change Convention, in Churchill and Freestone (eds) op. cit., pp. 187–93.

41. At the August 1994 session of the UN conference on Straddling Stocks and Highly Migratory Species, Ambassador Djalal lobbied, with support from the conference chairman Nandan (Fiji), to have the date of the fifth session of the conference altered to put it back to back to the formal opening of the new United Nations Deep Sea-bed Mining Committee.

42. For example, at the third session of the UN Conference on Straddling Stocks and Highly Migratory Fish Stocks, 14–31 March 1994, 38 of the states accredited were represented by diplomats from their permanent missions. Of these nine (Barbados, Belarus, Cape Verde, Congo, Côte d'Ivoire, Estonia, Madagascar, Zambia and Zimbabwe) were not represented at the fourth session (15–26 August 1994). See A/CONF.164/INF 11, 18 April 1994.

43. The functions of the conference bureau include the strategic management of a diplomatic conference; consultation with contact groups and promoting compromise proposals. For example at the final session in Paris, 6–17 June 1994 of the intergovernmental negotiating committee for the elaboration of an International Convention to Combat Desertification (INCD), the expanded bureau established a contact group of eight developed and eight developing countries to try and resolve the deadlock over the provisions in the draft text on international financial resources for combating desertification, A/AC.241/2.19, 7 June 1994.

44. See Emmanuel Adler, *International Organisation*, Vol. 46 (1992) p. 101; M.J. Petersen, 'Whalers, Cetologists, Environmentalists and the International Management of Whaling', *International Organisation*, Vol. 46 (1992) pp. 148–86; Peter M. Haas, 'Banning Chlorofluorocarbons: Epistemic Community Efforts to Protect Stratospheric Ozone', *International Organisation*, Vol. 46 (1992) pp. 187–224.

45. See Benedict, op. cit., pp. 41–3.

46. For example the secretariat to the intergovernmental negotiations on desertification (INCD) prepared the draft text for the Convention, which was discussed at the third session of the INCD, held in New York, 17–28 Jan. 1994. See A/AC.241/15.

47. Johnson, op. cit., p. 126 and pp. 213–14.

48. On the conflict between which secretariat (FAO or UNEP) should run the Barcelona Convention, see Peter H. Sand, *Marine Environmental Law and UNEP* (Cassell Tycooly, London, 1988), Note V, p. xvii. See also J.E. Carroz (who later became Assistant Secretary-General of FAO for fisheries), 'Institutional Aspects of Resources Management in the Mediterranean', *Ocean Management*, 3, (1978) pp. 235–51.

49. On the issue of co-operation and competing documentation between the Basle convention and other institutions see SBC No. 94/008, Geneva, June 1994, Decision I/18, p. 56, for the records of relevant Basle decisions.

50. See INC, A/AC. 237/Misc.l/Add. 1, 22 May 1991. See also Jill Barrett, 'The Negotiation and Drafting of the Climate Change Convention', in Churchill and Freestone (eds), op. cit., p. 187.
51. See *Journal of the Group of 77,* Vol. 7, No. 5, May 1994, p. 9 on the Paris G-77 Chapter which in its programme working party focused on the World Summit for Social Development and Final Communiqué, 18th Meeting of Chairmen/Co-ordinators of the G-77, Geneva, 15 March 1995.
52. D.H. Anderson, 'Legal Implications of the Entry into Force of the UN Convention on the Law of the Sea', *International and Comparative Law Quarterly,* Vol. 44 (April 1995) p. 313 *passim.*
53. See e.g. Articles 6 and 20 on the provision of financial resources.
54. The expression 'as far as possible and as appropriate' is used extensively through the Convention on Biological diversity, 5 June 1992. See for example Articles 5, 7, 8, 9, 10, 14.
55. Stanley Johnson argues that the Forest Principles document was weakened in that it emanated from the Prep-Com, rather than using the UNCED Secretariat/Working Group draft. However, the degree of opposition from large developing newly industrialised countries including Malaysia, India and Brazil illustrated in fact the political inappropriateness of trying to raise the 'level' of the agreement, which would have been required if the Secretariat/Working Group text had been used. See Johnson, op. cit., p. 126, and Ch. 7, and Ch. 9, pp. 213–14.
56. International Maritime Organisation, IMDG Code, was made mandatory through incorporation with the 1974 Safety of Life at Sea Convention (SOLAS) in 1991.
57. United Nations Framework Convention on Climate Change, in Report of the Intergovernmental Committee for a Framework Convention on Climate Change, A/AC.237/18 (Part II), Add. 1, 15 May 1992.
58. Johnson, op. cit., p. 58.
59. See FAO, CCRF: TC/94/Inf. 11 Aug. 1994.
60. See Douglas Day, 'Tending to the Achilles' Heel of NAFO: Canada Acts to Protect the Nose and Tail of the Grand Banks', Marine Policy (Special Issue) Vol. 19, No. 4 (July 1995) pp. 257–70.
61. A/CONF. 165/PC/2, 2, 22 Feb. 1993.

CHAPTER 10

Environmental diplomacy: case examples

Introduction

Four conferences have been selected to illustrate some of the main issues and processes involved in multilateral negotiation introduced in the previous chapter. The conferences are on desertification, land-based pollution, a new regime for highly migratory and straddling stock fisheries, and the construction of an action plan for small island developing states. The *modus operandi* of the four conferences is typical of that developed in multilateral environmental diplomacy since 1990. The case studies address two aspects of multilateral negotiations: questions of authority and influence using concepts such as stakeholders; substitution interests and agenda-setting, and secondly, various aspects of the dynamic of the negotiation process (focal points, issue learning curve, issue expansion, momentum and structuring compromise).

INTERNATIONAL CONVENTION TO COMBAT DESERTIFICATION

The Convention to Combat Desertification was concluded over a thirteen-month period in five substantive two-week sessions during 1993–94, chaired by Sweden with the concluding session held at UNESCO headquarters in Paris from 6 to 17 June 1994.[1]

In addition to the Plenary, the conference established two working groups on finance (co-chair Canada and The Gambia) and regional annexes (chair France) and a legal committee (Tanzania). Overall, the conference was heavily divided both within and across North–South lines, reflecting the multiple range of competing interests. The G-77, chaired by Algeria, found it extremely difficult to reach co-ordinated positions for example over priority for Africa, finance and other regional agreements. This case study focuses on two issues before the conference: claims to special status, and responsibility for international funding.

Claims to special status

Although the main features of a convention had been outlined by the fourth session, a number remained bracketed.[2] Major outstanding issues

185

included the priority for Africa and annexes for other regions; financial sources and mechanisms; categories of countries and institutional questions. In the course of the negotiations, African states as potentially principal stakeholders were keen to retain the priority accorded to the region in the 1992 General Assembly resolution 47/188. The African position however had been weakened at the initial meeting which was partly devoted to an exchange of scientific and other information on desertification. As a result, rather than unifying participants on causes and technologies, it had the effect of widening the number of 'bids' by delegations claiming desertification or drought status. Other stakeholders which attempted to claim special status included the Russian Federation, which was opposed by the G-77. In an initial compromise, the Russian Federation gained special mention in the Preamble to the draft convention. However, the Russian Federation re-opened the issue in the final plenary, opposing the formula contained in the draft Preamble: 'Central Asia and Southern Caucasus', favouring 'Central Asia and *trans-*Caucasus' (emphasis added), in order to include Russian Federation territory. Of the other stakeholders, Saudi-Arabia, for example, had *substitution* interests in that a primary Saudi concern was not desertification but to weaken references to the development of renewable energy resources in the draft convention.

Financial issues

Of the outstanding issues, the provisions of the conference on financial resources and mechanisms remained deadlocked until the final hours, and in fact seemed likely to prevent the conclusion of a convention. The financial issues included conflict over formulations to cover 'new and additional resources'; the commitments to the target of 0.7 per cent GNP for ODA; and which international institution should have overall responsibility for co-ordinating and dispersing funds to combat desertification. A number of members of the G-77 favoured a new Global Fund, although this was opposed by the United States, EU and Africa. Sweden for example opposed the idea on the grounds of high administrative cost.

The financial provisions of the convention also created a number of specific focal points of disagreement within the overall 'categories of countries' dispute. The first of these involved differences over the drafting of Article 6 (developed country obligations), which also led to further loss of momentum and eventual deadlock as a result of a lengthy and inconclusive procedural debate over linkage between Article 6 and Articles 20–1 (Financial Resources and Mechanisms). In an attempt to break the impasse on financial resource issues, discussions based on an informal text prepared by the Working Group co-chairman were transferred to a smaller contact group, which had only partly completed its work by the final day.

Among the other issues raised in the Working Group and contact group were those of a 'threshold kind', concerning which countries would qualify for concessionary assistance. In addition a new issue which arose late in the negotiations was the realisation that under the draft text in Article 20(3) it was unclear whether a country might be a financial *donor* or recipient (or both). In the final plenary meeting (18 June 1994) Malaysia, India, Brazil and Bolivia indicated that Article 20(3) as drafted would turn a developing country into a donor. The drafting the Malaysian group objected to stated: 'Affected developing country Parties, taking into account their capabilities, undertake to mobilise adequate financial resources for the implementation of the Convention.' A Saudi Arabian amendment was accepted which replaced 'the implementation of the Convention' in draft of Article 20(3) with 'for their national action programmes'.

The deadlock on Article 6 (financial obligations of developed countries) was incompletely resolved through an unusual drafting formulation 'developed country Parties', which creates an unsatisfactory precedent of formally allowing for non-acceptance by some developed states. The differences generally between the OECD and G-77 on financial obligations had been foreshadowed in the earlier long-running dispute over whether obligations were 'as agreed' (G-77) or in the OECD language 'as *mutually* agreed' (emphasis added).

Of the outstanding institutional issues at the fifth session, the title for the secretariat (Article 23) responsible for co-ordinating implementation remained bracketed. The EU, Japan, and Norway opposed the term 'Permanent Secretariat' formally on the grounds that the expression is not found in similar conventions. Other concerns were to keep the secretariat small and not, as African states wanted, develop into an implementing agency, though the bracketing was eventually removed partly as a result of an opinion by the UN Legal Office.

The question of a global financial fund to counter desertification in effect remained unsolved. No direct formula could be agreed and the conference eventually accepted a United States proposal to defer identification of a 'global mechanism' for funding until the first conference of the parties (Art. 21(5)).

LAND-BASED SOURCES OF POLLUTION

The purpose of this case study based on UNEP negotiations to revise and create new international guidelines on land-based sources of pollution is to illustrate how the agenda and purposes of an international conference can be fundamentally altered and taken over by lead delegations. Conversely the case illustrates how an international organisation and host government can lose control as stakeholders.

The Montreal Guidelines for the Protection of the Marine Environment from Land-based Pollution were adopted on 19 April 1985, after two years' negotiation under UNEP auspices by an *Ad Hoc* Working Group of Experts.[3] The Guidelines are of a recommendatory nature based upon prevailing concepts such as classification of substances; levels of protection; multiple use of the sea and levels of protection. Since then a number of different essentially more precautionary ideas such as preventive action in the absence of full scientific information and the precautionary principle, have been developed at a national, regional and international level, in for example the Oslo–Paris Commission, Helsinki Commission, revised London Convention and UNCED.

In response to Agenda 21 (para. 17.29) UNEP authorised[4] the Executive Director to direct a preparatory process with two initial meetings to review selected regional seas programmes (Nairobi, 1993); a one-week meeting of government-designated experts focusing on the Montreal Guidelines (Montreal, 1994); a final preparatory meeting of government-designated experts on the draft of the Programme of Action (Reykjavik, March 1995) and a two-week intergovernmental conference in Washington (November 1995) to revise and adopt the Programme of Action.[5]

The Montreal meeting (6–10 June 1994) was attended by representatives of 73 states and several international institutions and NGOs. Although the primary purpose of the Montreal meeting as set out in the UNEP authorising decision was to focus on the Montreal Guidelines, in the event the conference did not do so but substantially abandoned the Guidelines as an approach and discussed instead the outlines of an Action Plan to assist developing countries to tackle marine pollution from land-based activities.

The switch of emphasis in the Montreal agenda represented a major failure of UNEP since the Montreal Guidelines were one of the links to the UNEP Regional Seas Programmes. How did this occur when Canada, as a so-called 'Montreal Power', had built up extensive interests in environmental diplomacy? These interests had involved hosting a number of conferences and active involvement as a coastal state main player in the law of the sea negotiations; Arctic interests, including the land-mark Arctic Waters Act (1970);[6] international fisheries,[7] and, marine-based development diplomacy. Canada too has been active in negotiations on global climate change and hosted the Montreal Protocol on substances that deplete the ozone layer.[8]

As a major stakeholder, Canada aimed to bring the Montreal Guidelines up to date in the form of a new agreement, backed by an Action Plan. To achieve this an intergovernmental meeting of selected experts had been held in Halifax, Canada in May 1991, although these discussions were overtaken by the broader UNCED preparatory process. Following the UNEP decision to hold an international conference on land-based sources of marine pollution, Canada, in liaison with UNEP officials, agreed to host a second preparatory meeting, focused on the Montreal Guidelines. In line with traditional Canadian diplomacy of hosting informal meetings of like-minded states, specialists and NGOs, a preparatory meeting was held in Ottawa in January 1994, with a core group of nine countries, plus Green Peace International.

Failure of the Canadian initiative

There are five main reasons for the failure of the Canadian diplomatic initiative. In the first place, Canada was unable to prevent the United States, led by the Department of State (Office of Ocean Affairs) and NOAA, shifting the focus of the meeting to the capacity building aspects of Montreal, Agenda 21 and UNCLOS, during the first main plenary. Second, Canada was unable, despite having the largest delegation and conference chairmanship, to re-focus the meeting back to the Montreal Guidelines (Agenda Item 5). The highly disparate range of delegates, included lawyers, scientists and officials from foreign ministries, environment, water and merchant marine departments, comprising single-member delegations, many with limited backgrounds, if any, in land-based pollution. The G-77 did not function as such nor did it produce any co-ordinated position papers. In addition some major players were absent or represented at embassy or junior official level.[9] In this context few, apart from Finland and a small number of other states, were prepared to take on a seasoned United States delegation, especially at the very outset of the meeting and probably without instructions on the matter. Moreover, three of the Ottawa group meeting (Australia, Sweden and the Netherlands) supported in the first plenary the United States position, which criticised the Montreal Guidelines and sought to shift the conference attention instead to focus on capacity and technical assistance building measures.

A third important factor in the failure of the Canadian initiative concerned the availability of conference documentation. In contrast to standing multilateral technical conferences with advance documentation circulation rules of procedure, informal *ad hoc* multilateral conferences often face critical problems in preparatory document distribution. The documentary problem was compounded by the limited relationship of the preparatory meetings on Regional Seas Programmes to the primary aim of reviewing the Montreal Protocol. The UNEP Secretariat concept of the way in which the conference would develop was based on a key article by article review of the Montreal Guidelines. However the article-based critique prepared by UNEP was not available until shortly before the opening meeting, preventing national appraisal. It also made it difficult or impossible for the conference chair to move the conference in the direction of a detailed article by article review in the plenary, following the UNCLOS method over the RNT and ICNT. Such procedures would have required substantial pre-sessional meetings.[10] The UNEP Secretariat incorrectly assumed that the Montreal meeting could move into the UNEP's text containing proposed changes to the Montreal Guidelines[11] without adequate notice of the proposed detailed changes.

Fourth, Swedish policy, which aimed primarily to turn the Montreal meeting into a framework for external technical assistance projects indirectly assisted the United States position[12] of moving off a review of the existing Montreal Guidelines. An interesting aspect of Sweden's strategy was its use of an NGO (Advisory Committee on the Protection of the Sea) to promote its central aim of external assistance for land-based pollution reduction projects.[13]

Finally, an unusual feature of the Montreal meeting was the decision by the conference chairman to use four Working Groups, in view of the limited and varied expertise, as well as relatively low participation[14] of states. It can be argued that the use of four Working Groups was excessive given the low total participation at the Montreal conference and the high number of single-member delegations. Together these factors enabled the United States as a principal stakeholder to move the Montreal meeting towards an Action Plan in the more recent style of UNEP, rather than review and update the 1985 Montreal Guidelines.

STRADDLING AND HIGHLY MIGRATORY FISH STOCKS

The question of straddling and highly migratory fish stocks is one of a number of important gaps left over from the 1982 convention on the law of the sea (UNCLOS). The convention failed to address adequately in, *inter alia*, Articles 63(2) and Articles 114–20 appropriate requirements for straddling and highly migratory fish stocks which transit through or straddle EEZs. The issue of straddling and highly migratory stocks in EEZ/High Seas areas began to attract increasing political attention from the late 1980s because of the emergence of a number of conflicts between coastal and distant water fishing states as pressures on stocks increased. This case study examines two notable features of the UN straddling and highly migratory fish stocks conference (1993–95): the phenomenon of issue expansion in the process of regime negotiation, and the methods used by the conference chairman in a chair-led multilateral negotiation.

Background

Straddling and highly migratory fish stocks such as tuna, squid, and mackerel account for around 10 per cent of the world food supply, reaching a peak of around 13.7 million tons in 1989.[15] Problems associated with the fisheries began to command international attention from the late 1980s because of stock depletion connected with high seas drift-net fishing and conflicts involving coastal and long-range fleets in the Northeast Atlantic (Canada/EU off the Grandbanks), Bering Sea, Southwest Atlantic and Pacific. The issues have been addressed within the FAO and at UNCED (Chapter 17, Agenda 21). Technical consultations have been held within FAO, which led to the 1993 Agreement to promote far stricter flag state control over fishing vessels and prevent re-flagging.[16] The 47th session of the General Assembly approved on 29 January 1993 an intergovernmental conference on straddling and highly migratory fish stocks.[17] An initial technical consultation was

held under FAO auspices on 7–15 September 1992 and the UN conference subsequently met at UN headquarters on 19–23 April 1993, 12–30
July 1993, 14–31 March 1994 and 24 July–4 August 1995.

Players

The substantive phases of the UN Conference have been influenced
essentially by three groups of states: the extreme coastal states group
(Chile, Colombia, Ecuador and Peru) linked with activist coastal states
(Canada, Argentina and Norway); the high seas fishing group (Japan,
Korea, Poland, together with China); and the moderate reformist
coastal states (Australia, New Zealand). In a fourth group are entities
(the United States, Russian Federation, EU) with perhaps divided interests, or, as in the case of the Russian Federation, very particular
concerns, e.g. over the Bering Sea. Fifth, there is a large number of
developing country coastal states, which are unorganised, whose
spokesmen are almost exclusively India and Indonesia. The extreme
coastal state group encompass a coalition of disparate interests ranging
from predominantly straddling stock concerns, to migratory, or, a combination of migratory/straddling stock fisheries issues in and beyond the
EEZ.

While one of the main issues for Canada in its dispute, particularly
with the EU, is control over straddling stocks in areas adjacent to its
EEZ, such as the Grand Banks grounds,[18] some of the Latin American
members have a second or wider agenda of securing international
acceptance of coastal state rights over resources beyond the 200 mile
EEZ, based on 'presencial sea' type doctrine articulated for example by
Chile.[19] The group remains linked by certain common tenets such as
unambiguous sovereign rights of coastal states over resources within
the EEZ; recognition of the special interests of coastal states in areas
outside the EEZ for management and conservation; flag-coastal State
agreements to allow coastal state inspection and arrest of foreign flag
vessels; and the application of national standards in the EEZ in the
event of no consensus in a regional organisation on minimum international standards.

In contrast, the high seas fishing States group (Japan, Korea, Poland)
has taken a fundamentally opposing position based on *inter alia,* the
concept of 'due regard' for the interests of both flag and coastal states;
the coherence of measures across the whole of the migratory range of
straddling stock (these measures may differ); and the scientific priority
of the regional organisation over the coastal state. In addition, the group
has sought to maintain the principle of flag state responsibility and no
arrest of vessels on the high seas (e.g. by coastal states). As regards the
form of the outcome of the UN conference, the high seas group has
argued for a non-binding instrument. A number of aspects of the
groups' position have also been supported in extreme form by the
People's Republic of China.

Of other interests at the conference, New Zealand and Australia have played active roles as moderate reformist, regional actors, and as spokesmen of the micro-state South Pacific Forum. Other large regional powers like Mexico, Brazil, Indonesia, Philippines, and Malaysia, have, despite substantial high seas fisheries interests as either fishing and/or transit states, adopted low-key, passive roles. The Australian and New Zealand approaches have been distinguished by emphasis on establishing concepts such as biological unity of stocks; scientific data-gathering, and above all, effective enforcement. Strong monitoring too has formed one of the main elements (along with the promotion of the FAO 'flagging' agreement and dispute settlement) in the overall line taken by the United States. In general, the United States occupied, publicly at least, an uneasy position, seeking an international instrument which balances coastal and high seas fishing interests, though its private diplomacy has been shaped strongly by regional interests such as fisheries arrangements with the Russian Federation, e.g. Sea of Okhotsk,[20] and access agreements with the South Pacific Forum, rather than wider international interests. The Russian Federation itself has attempted in its open diplomacy to promote through a variety of draft proposals special provisions for enclaves in enclosed and semi-enclosed seas in view of foreign overfishing which have brought about the collapse of the fishery industry in the Sea of Okhotsk, and difficulties in the Bering Sea.[21]

A particular feature of the Russian Federation's contribution to the conference has also been on conceptual and definitional issues, through one of the few working papers on the definition of straddling stocks; proposals for greater precision of the term 'adjacent area', and unified interpretation of main terms.

Issues: building regimes

The polarised nature of the UN conference on Highly Migratory and Straddling Fish Stock (HMSS) negotiations can be illustrated through at least four major areas.[22] The first of these concerns the geographic area of application or extent of the regulations outside the EEZ. This issue posed difficulties because of the lack of a precise definition in UNCLOS Article 63(2) of the extent of areas on the boundaries 'adjacent to the zone'. Proposals on adjacency have been put forward or reintroduced at successive negotiations sessions of the conference since 1993, particularly by the Russian Federation. The Russian Federation proposals[23] envisaged the adjacent area as a narrow area of some 20–70 nautical miles beyond the EEZ, which might be a migration route through which a stock passes. The conference, however, was heavily divided and reluctant to move to precise definitions, given the very wide range of views from coastal states to high seas distant water fishing states. In contrast, within the coastal state group, Canada and some Latin American states, for example, have wanted the area of application for regulation and enforcement outside the EEZ to be equivalent to the area covered by a regional fisheries organisation (e .g. NAFO).[24]

Compatibility of conservation measures

The question of compatibility of conservation and management measures inside and outside the 200 mile EEZ has remained one of the central issues before the conference. As the exchanges have progressed, it is also clear that several other new issues have been recognised such as the *primacy* or not of management measures taken outside the EEZ over coastal state measures, which have added both to the complexity and competing interpretations of the respective working papers and draft articles. In other words as the conference attempted to refine and give precise meaning to the earlier third session draft provisions on management measures in and outside the EEZ, the participants increasingly began to appreciate various ramifications which had previously not been understood or considered. A good example of one of the negotiating difficulties in this context of *issue expansion,* was the problem of operationalising bridging formulae such as 'minimum international standards'. While that formula had been put forward as a possible compromise to authorise fisheries enforcement outside 200 mile EEZs, particularly in the absence of a regional organisation or agreed fish stock management measures, the proposal made little headway because of the problem of establishing what was actually meant by a minimum international standard. At the fourth session in August 1994, difficulties over this question then triggered further exchanges on the biological unity of stocks and whether conservation measures would apply throughout the range of stocks outside the EEZ, rather than stocks only in narrow adjacent areas to the EEZ.[25]

The ramifications of regional regulation increasingly caused concern for several larger developing and newly industrialised countries such as Thailand, India, Indonesia, Chile and Mexico, because of possible restrictions on their freedom of action to develop commercially their fisheries. This new issue of externally imposed quotas influenced by high seas factors impacting on coastal states' fisheries operations in its EEZ was seen as a fundamental challenge to one of the major benefits developing countries obtained from UNCLOS: the 200 mile EEZ. The Indian delegate, reflecting this concern, aptly coined the new concept of 'reverse creeping jurisdiction'.[26]

Enforcement

As might be expected, enforcement issues (authority for enforcement; temporary measures; the registry or flag of a vessel and arrest) were the questions which most divided the conference. Canadian Fisheries Minister Paul Tobin summed up the general consensus that 'the best conservation measures, supported by all states, will fail without effective enforcement'. Although there was apparent consensus at this general level of formulation, nevertheless widespread and fundamental differences continued over enforcement methods and the 'pieces' in the overall regime. The major focal point of dispute, however, was detention and arrest outside the EEZ, which divided the distant water fishing states (Japan, Poland, Korea, Panama, and some EU members (France, Spain, Italy) from the active coastal and other reformist states.

Negotiation process

The UN conference on straddling and highly migratory fish stocks is a classic example of a modern chair-led multilateral negotiation. The complex negotiations were orchestrated under the chairmanship of veteran law of the sea negotiator Satya Nandan (Fiji). The complex nature of the conference was underlined by the extensive range of interests: distant water fishing, coastal reformist, flag registering countries, developing coastal states, newly industrialised import or transit states (e.g. Malaysia), FAO, intergovernmental fisheries organisations (e.g. International Commission on North Atlantic Tuna) and a variety of NGOs. Nandan exercised overall influence in three main areas: on the content of the agenda, both prior to and during sessions; consultations with delegations, and, chiefly through compiling, drafting and editorially revising the chairman's draft negotiating texts. Nandan's negotiating *authority* lay in his long experience of law of the sea negotiations, particularly since the establishment of UNCLOS and his formal position as conference chairman.

As chairman, Nandan especially cultivated the concept of a channel of private access to the chairman, through which delegations were encouraged to submit draft articles, non-papers and other conference documents, on the understanding that these would be sympathetically received and dealt with in an even-handed manner. In a similar way the chair benefited from receiving the texts of recent bilateral or multilateral fisheries agreements from delegations which were not widely available. For example, the chairman drew upon as a model a number of sections of the United States–Russian Federation Bering Sea Pollock Agreement.[27] The documentary/drafting channel in effect served to create an inner track of delegations; the process also helped to varying degrees to lock in inner track delegations to the chairman's negotiating text.

As noted above, influence over the agenda and focus of negotiations is important to chair-led multilateral negotiations. It is by no means absolute or unlimited. Examples of Nandan's influence on the agenda included keeping off the agenda as long as possible definitional questions of a controversial nature such as the meaning of 'adjacency', and which fish species would be counted as straddling or highly migratory. The chairman also delayed as long as he could the critical question of deciding the *form* of any agreement. By leaving the question open, the chairman hoped to keep the dynamic of the conference moving ahead, resolving or partially settling issues, without reaching conclusions on whether the agreement would be in the form of guidelines or a legally binding treaty. Examples of the chairman's influence on the focus of the conference are found in many areas, including summary reports of sessions, attendance at informal intersessional meetings (e.g. Geneva, January 1994) and definition of critical outstanding negotiating issues at the fourth session (August 1994).

The limitations on the chair's influence in multilateral negotiations occur as states attempt to insert into the agenda sub-issues of particular concern, which could distort or fragment (as in the desertification negotiations) the overall process. For example, at the UN straddling stocks conference, the Russian Federation at the fifth session (March 1995) threatened the chair that without satisfactory provisions on enclaves, the Russian Federation would be unable to sign an agreement.

A final area worth comment is the question of consensus in chair-led negotiations. In this case, the negotiations were relatively unusual in that the conference was conducted through the plenary (or the plenary as an informal working group of the whole) with little use of sub-working groups. Informal consultations were held before and during each session in order to define and take issues forward. These consultations were based on the *consensus fiction* that they were held with as wide a number of delegations as possible. In practice, up to the fourth session, consultations were limited to a relatively small number of lead delegations from the coastal state, moderate reformist and distant water fishing groups. That fiction formally lasted until the closing stages of the fourth session. The issuing of two chairman's texts[28] – a calculated gamble by the chair to shift to treaty form in the final days critically focused attention on consensus. It was clear that to break down the polarised positions on key issues such as form and high seas arrest, not only had further substantive alterations to the text to be negotiated, but also a broader consensus had to be achieved. However, the extended informal consultations (Geneva, February 1995), while contributing to further concessions, illustrated the problem of widening informal groups at the expense of consultations of the whole.

Conclusion

The UN Conference on Straddling and Highly Migratory Fish Stocks provides a number of insights into chair-led multilateral negotiations. As an exercise in regime building, to cover the gaps left by UNCLOS, the conference had in effect to break new ground in several areas. Much of the negotiating was of a highly polarised form. The early phases were also typically characterised by information or descriptive texts and non-papers, similar to the multilateral negotiations such as desertification as efforts were made to construct possible regimes. Another feature exhibited by the SSHMS and other multilateral negotiations was the borrowing of concepts from other regimes (e.g.

port state control on ship safety and pollution) and, in this example inappropriately seeking to transplant them into other regimes without appropriate modifications. However, *fisheries* practice in the form of bilateral and other multilateral agreements provided models which were drawn on. Finally, a relatively unusual feature of the conference was that in contrast to the desertification or land-based pollution negotiations, it did not generally subdivide on a collegiate basis into sub-working committees but throughout most of its main sessions met in informal consultations involving the chair or hosted by lead players. The greater emphasis on the use of informal working groups of the whole may become more extensively used as a model for global negotiations even of a specialist kind.

SMALL ISLAND DEVELOPING STATES

The UN Global Conference on the sustainable Development of Small Island Developing States met in Barbados from 25 April to 6 May 1994. The aims of the conference included reviewing the special problems of small island developing states; establishing priorities for sustainable development; management of resources and national capacity building. The conference was attended by 120 states, international institutions, intergovernmental organisations, NGOs, as well as 40 heads of state and government, and other representatives who attended the special High Level round-table discussion in the final days. This case study examines one of the players in the process – the Alliance of Small Island States (AOSIS) – a new small state pressure group, in conflict with the G-77.

Background

The UN Conference on Sustainable Development of Small Island Developing States was authorised under UN General Assembly resolution 47/189. The conference has its roots in a number of regional conferences held by small states on problems of vulnerability, and international conferences on climatic change. At Rio small island states registered their special claims in chapter 17 of Agenda 21. The Barbados conference held a preparatory session in New York (15–16 April 1993) on organisational matters, at which Australia was elected as chair, and a disparate group of four vice-chairs (Japan, Romania, Antigua and Barbuda, and Cape Verde). The preparatory phase was limited to week-long regional meetings for the Indian and Pacific Oceans in Vanuatu and Trinidad, prior to the first session of the Preparatory Committee on the Programme of Action, 30 August–10 September 1993 in New York. During the process of negotiating the 15 Chapter Programme of Action, AOSIS differed substantially with leading members of the G-77. In addition, large parts of the Preamble and Chapter 15 on implementation of sustainable development measures remained square bracketed, reflecting differences both within AOSIS and G-77, and between these groups and industrialised countries,[29] particularly over financial mechanisms, and relevant international agreements.[30]

Alliance of Small Island States

The Alliance of Small Island States was formed in 1990 at the Second World Climate Conference in Geneva, with 36 members and five observers, bringing together as a new grouping island states from the Pacific, Indian and Atlantic oceans.[31] The idea for the grouping originated at the Small Islands Conference on Sea Level Rise, in Male in November 1989, to promote international attention on small island states and their vulnerability to threats such as global sea-level rise. For example, few of the Maldives 1,196 islands rise above 3.5 metres. Similar difficulties face Tuvalu, Tokelu, Marshall Islands and Kiribati.

Barbados preparatory committee

The preparations for the UN Barbados conference underlined two features of post-1990 diplomatic methods – the reduced ability of the G-77 to harmonise a collective position in multilateral conference of a technical rather than social-ideological nature, and the continued emergence of new groupings. At the initial Prep.-Com the G-77, through its predominantly Latin American leadership, attempted to assume responsibility for preparing the draft Programme of Action for the forthcoming session.[32] The G-77 text was rejected by the AOSIS group. The differences were outlined by Vanuatu, on behalf of the AOSIS group. In essence AOSIS considered that the G-77 text introduced by Peru did not sufficiently take into account the concerns and critical threats faced by small island states at the lower levels of development. Issues underestimated, in the view of AOSIS, included administrative capabilities and small states drowning in paper and consultants; the need for more early warning systems; promotion of new technologies to combat water shortage; and compensation for small states for hosting 'environmental tourism'.

Many of these ideas were incorporated into the revised G-77 with reluctance. The balance though had shifted, with the G-77 ceding the role of co-ordinator to AOSIS.

Development of AOSIS

The future development of AOSIS as a negotiating group will be affected particularly by the influence of logistical factors on group co-ordination, in view of the diverse range of membership; the existence of other groups which cross-cut the membership (e.g. South Pacific

Forum) and above all the calibre of its diplomatic representatives. It is an axiom of modern diplomacy that small states frequently through the skill of the diplomats make greater contributions to *creating* rather than implementing international agreements.

Conclusion

Contemporary international negotiations on environmental questions are distinct above all by the highly complex range of subject-matter, and the corresponding diffuse range of interests. North–South divisions remain a strong feature, although within that overall division, extensive subdivisions have developed. While the North has relatively well established co-ordination and consultation mechanisms, developing countries within the South have found it increasingly difficult to negotiate collective positions within such traditional groupings as the G-77. Environmental negotiations too, more than other types of negotiations, contain both a high degree of technical content and extensive issue learning. Follow-up implementation is generally weak, especially with Action Plans.

References and notes

1. A/AC.241/15, Rev. 7, 1994.
2. International Convention to Combat Desertification, A/AC.241/15, Rev. 7, 1994.
3. UNEP, Decision 13/18/II, Governing Council of UNEP, 24 May 1985.
4. UNEP Decision 17/20, 17 May 1993.
5. UNEP/MG/IG/1/1 Add. 1, 6 April 1994.
6. See R.R. Churchill and A.V. Lowe, *International Law of the Sea* (Manchester University Press, Manchester, 1988) p. 245.
7. See, for example, Evelyne Meltzer, 'Global Overview of Straddling and Highly Migratory Fish Stocks: The Nonsustainable Nature of High Seas Fisheries', *Ocean Development and International Law*, Vol. 25, 1994, pp. 255–344; R.P. Barston, 'UN Conference on Straddling and Highly Migratory Fish Stocks', *Marine Policy*, March 1995, pp. 159–66.
8. 26 *ILM* 1541, 1550, 1987.
9. For example Germany and Japan.
10. See the final case study on the procedures adopted at the UN Straddling Stock and Highly Migratory Fish Stocks Conference, which went through an extensive 'Knowledge extending' stage, draft non-papers, conference working papers and draft articles before it moved onto a text in draft treaty form.
11. UNEP/MG/IG/1/3, 29 April 1993.
12. 'The aim should be to identify sources of funding of, in particular, developing country projects. This should be done in the preparatory process for the Washington Conference, at the Conference itself or in the UNCED review of the Oceans Chapter of Agenda 21.' Swedish Position paper, 30 May 1994, p. 15.
13. See statement by Dr Per Wraamner, head of the Swedish delegation to the UN Straddling Fish Stocks Conference. Sweden's entry into the EU in January 1995 removed Sweden as an independent development assistance player. For example, Sweden was unable to speak independently at the March 1995 session of the UN Conference on Straddling Fish Stocks as a result of EU entry.
14. See Chapter 5.
15. United Nations Convention on the Law of the Sea, Annex 1 (United Nations publication, sales No. E.83.v.5). The highly migratory species listed in Annex I are: Albacore tuna; Bluefin tuna; Bigeye tuna; Skipjack tuna; Yellowfin tuna; Blackfin

tuna; Little tuna; Southern bluefin tuna; Frigate mackerel; Pomfrets; Marlins; Sail-fishes; Swordfish; Sauries; Dolphin; Oceanic sharks; Cetaceans.

16. Agreement to Promote Compliance with International Conservation and Management measures by Fishing Vessels on the High Seas, FAO, Rome, 1993.
17. Report of the Secretary-General, A/48/451, 1993.
18. FAO Technical Paper 337, Rome 1994, pp. 54–9.
19. See Jane Gilliland Dalton, 'The Chilean Mar Presencial: A Harmless Concept or a Dangerous Precedent', *Marine and Coastal Law,* Vol. 8 No. 3, August 1993, pp. 399–403.
20. See for example joint US–Russian Federation paper on the Sea of Okhotsk, A/CONF.164/L33, 28 July 1993.
21. A/CONF.164/L.25, 26 July 1993.
22. The UN Conference on Straddling and Highly Migratory Fish Stocks, see R.P. Barston, 'The Draft UN Convention on Straddling Stocks and Highly Migratory Fish Stocks', *The Ocean Governance Study Group,* University of Hawaii, Jan. 1995.
23. See Barston, 'United Nations Conference on Straddling and Highly Migratory Fish Stocks', *Marine Policy,* March 1995, pp. 163–4.
24. See draft articles of Argentina, Canada, Chile, Iceland and New Zealand, A/CONF.164/L11/Rev.1, 26 July 1993.
25. A/CONF.164/3/Rev.1, 30 March 1994.
26. Barston, 'United Nations Conference on Straddling and Highly Migratory Fish Stocks', p. 164.
27. United States–Russian Federation Bering Sea Pollock Agreement, 1994. For parties and details see ILM Vol. 34, No. 1 January 1995.
28. The first text was styled the so-called 'Fish Paper', because of the design of the cover depicting fish straddling an imaginary EEZ.
29. Report of the Preparatory Committee for the Global Conference on the Sustainable Development of Small Island Developing States, UN General Assembly, A/48/36, New York, 1994.
30. A/48/36 (New York, 1994). The United States at the first and second preparatory meetings put the whole of the Preamble of the draft agreement into square brackets. See the General Assembly, Official Records, 48th Session, No. 36 (A/48/36).
31. Geoffrey Lean, *Our Planet* (UNEP) Vol. 26 (1994).
32. A/CONF. 164/13/Rev. 1, 30 March 1994.

CHAPTER 11

Diplomacy and security

Defining security

The relationship between diplomacy and security is complex and evolving. The question of what constitutes security can be addressed from three perspectives – the international system, nation-state and the individual. Internationally, security can be thought of in terms of the stability of the international system, defined as the level of tension or violence and the corresponding extent to which actor interests can be accommodated through diplomacy, without recourse to violence, on the basis of mediation, rule and norm setting. In the event of violence occurring, the task of diplomacy is ultimately peaceful settlement, through the negotiation of cease-fires, withdrawal and other measures of a longer-term nature. From a quite different perspective violence may be a preferred end in itself and diplomacy the means of orchestrating violence rather than bringing about a negotiated solution.

At a national level, security has traditionally been considered in terms of responses to essentially external threats of a military kind. From this perspective diplomacy features as the state craft of force, involving such actions as deterring aggressors, building up coalitions, threatening or warning an opponent and seeking international support of legitimacy for the use or control of force.

However, the advent of large numbers of new states into the international community, many with preoccupying internal economic problems, underlined the inadequacy of traditional strategic theory or guerrilla war type definitions and perspectives.[1] The range of security threats from an advanced country perspective was highlighted in a Japanese study, which identified earthquake control as a central national security objective.[2] Other examples of 'domestic' security interests include food security, population control and water security (which frequently has an external threat dimension). Thus, security can be considered as the pursuit of policies, using diplomatic, military and other means in relation to one or more of the following: (1) external threats; (2) regime maintenance; (3) achievement of an acceptable level of economic viability, including avoidance of excessive economic dependence; (4) ethnic stability; (5) anti-terrorism; (6) environmental threats; (7) transnational sources of instability and (8) access to physical resources.

At a third level security can be thought of in terms of the individual – the diplomat and the private citizen. Security threats to diplomatic personnel and embassies have continued to increase as 'spill over' from Middle Eastern conflicts and transnational ethnic group conflict. At the level of the individual citizen, individuals tend to enjoy varying degrees of protection depending on state capabilities and conceptions of national security. On occasion, states may have to take up exposed diplomatic positions in order to plead for their nationals.

Some implications for diplomacy

Security interests of states and organisations are seldom static, except for a limited number of core values. New interests are acquired and marginal values are either elevated or discarded. At an economic level, continued access to overseas markets for key exports, the availability of raw materials and the protection of the overseas assets of its nationals are frequently ranked as important security considerations. Conversely, security interests may be downgraded or contracted, as may happen with foreign bases or particular security agreements being allowed to lapse. States generally also face entirely novel and far-reaching threats from, for example, maritime fraud,[3] international economic fraud, narcotics groups and transnationally organised crime.[4] The purpose of diplomacy is to contribute to the process of recognising and identifying new interests at an early stage through continuous reporting and assessments, facilitating adjustment between different interests and contributing to policy implementation.

Secondly, the internal aspect of national security has a number of implications for diplomacy. In those states in which national security is essentially internal, security policy-making tends to be highly likely to be conducted *internally*, rather than through the country's embassies abroad or other external channels, with representatives of international organisations, non-governmental organisations (NGOs) , foreign corporations on such issues as food aid, disaster relief and project implementation. Other domestic/international security concerns could involve threats such as financial fraud, refugee influx, hostage-taking, urban sabotage by cults, and the activities of transnational religious groups. Dual-security states encounter problems concerning the balance of emphasis between internal and external security requirements and, in their external diplomacy, the need to compromise on pragmatic grounds with ideological opponents. For example, those states with insurgency problems may find it necessary to attempt policies of political co-operation with an insurgent group's protecting power. Writing albeit largely in an external context, Arnold Wolfers notes: 'security covers a range of goals so wide that highly divergent policies can be interpreted as policies of security'.[5]

A third feature for many weaker states is the problem of establishing suitable regional security arrangements. A noticeable feature of recent diplomacy is the high priority attached by some states which perceive themselves weak or vulnerable in a local or regional context to enhancing their security through declarations and treaties, frequently negotiated within the framework of the United Nations. In other instances, such as resulting from the break-up of the former Soviet Union, a security vacuum has led to a corridor of weak states in Northern and Central Europe attempting to seek NATO membership or associate status.

Finally, it should be recalled that the nexus between security and diplomacy can be broken in a number of circumstances. As we noted earlier, diplomacy may be directed entirely to the execution of violence. In other instances a shift to the use of force might reflect dissatisfaction with the failure of diplomacy. For example, during the Tehran hostage crisis, President Carter terminated the labyrinthine negotiations with Iran and authorised an attempted rescue mission of US diplomatic personnel. He recounts in his memoirs: 'We could no longer afford to depend on diplomacy. I decided to act.'[6]

Security and the international system

The founding concept of post-war international security within the UN framework was intended to be based on the idea of collective security. The UN Charter envisaged collective action to forestall or limit the action of a potential aggressor, through military and other measures. Thus the UN Charter concept of security was one of states acting in concert to control or limit force. Such collective action clearly required universality of membership or something close to that, and the willingness of members to provide appropriate military forces on a suitable scale as envisaged under article 43 of the Charter. Although UN membership expanded rapidly in the 1960s an adequate agreement could not be reached to provide the UN with sufficient military force of a permanent nature. The closest the UN came to a collective security action against an aggressor was in the Korean War (1950–53) with the establishment of a UN force under US command. The Korean crisis provided the context for the wider role of the General Assembly on security matters when it passed the Uniting for Peace Resolution in November 1950 in response to the stalemate in the Security Council caused by the Soviet veto.[7]

The failure, however, to achieve collective security has meant that approaches to security within the UN system have been developed on an *ad hoc* basis, with the negotiation and establishment within the limits of what is politically possible of UN observer, truce and peace-keeping forces. The operating experience of the UN Military Observer Group in India and Pakistan, the United Nations Observation Group in Lebanon (UNOGIL) (1958), the United Nations Emergency Force

(UNEF) (Suez, 1956) and Opération des Nations Unies (ONUC) in the Congo (1960–62), however, formed the basis for the subsequent development of the concept of preventive diplomacy set out by Secretary-General Hammarskjöld.[8] Central to the idea of preventive diplomacy was putting UN forces into areas of potential superpower conflict, to forestall direct involvement, with the aim of limiting the scale of the conflict. Writing in 1960, Hammarskjöld noted:[9] 'Those efforts must aim at keeping newly arising conflicts outside the sphere of bloc differences. Further, in the case of conflicts on the margin of, or inside the sphere of bloc differences, the United Nations should seek to bring such conflicts out of this sphere through solutions aiming, in the first instance, at their strict localization. ...'

Preventive diplomacy, to which the efforts of the United Nations have to a large extent been traditionally directed, is of special significance in cases where the original conflict may be said either to be the result of, or to imply risks for, intervention by the main powers.

In this way the success of preventive diplomacy depends on the interrelationship between the peacekeeping operation and the related diplomatic efforts to resolve the conflict. Operating experience in the Congo, Cyprus (United Nations Force in Cyprus (UNIFCYP), 1964–) and the Lebanon (1978–) suggests that there are a number of particular conditions which influence the effectiveness of preventive diplomacy.[10] In the first place, states must be prepared to put the matter before the UN. Successive secretaries-general have criticised one or more parties to a conflict for their unwillingness to allow UN involvement. Other than this the cases under review indicate the importance of the initial and continued consent of the host government and the primary powers. The operation of ONUC especially brought the UN into major crisis. The United States and the Soviet Union not only had very different views on the legality and mission of ONUC, but the Soviet Union attacked the 'impartiality' of the Secretary-General. In the troika proposal the Soviet Union called for substantial changes including the establishment of three secretaries-general.[11] The controversy over the operation directly precipitated the financial crisis over the funding of UN peacekeeping operations. As a result of the dispute over the purposes of the force, the Soviet Union and a number of other states refused to finance the force. Following the Congo experience, subsequent operations have been funded in differing ways, such as voluntary contributions as in the case of UNFICYP. The accumulating debt arising from peacekeeping operations, rose to nearly $400 million by 1985–86.[12]

While preventive diplomacy remains one of the important tasks or functions of the UN, the number and type of UN operations has subsequently expanded considerably under the Boutros-Ghali *Agenda for Peace* (see Table 11.1). Some of these operations are close in character to earlier UN missions such as border observations, while others are distinctive, resembling 'governance' operations, e.g.. UNTRAC or

Table 11.1   UN Peacekeeping Operations 1990–96

UNIIMOG	United Nations Iran–Iraq Military Observer Group	August 1988–February 1991
UNAVEM I	United Nations Angola Verification Mission I	January 1989–June 1991
UNTAG	United Nations Transition Assistance Group	April 1989–March 1990
ONUCA	United Nations Observer Group In Central America	November 1989–January 1992
UNIKOM	United Nations Iraq–Kuwait Observation Mission	April 1991–To Present
UNAVEM II	United Nations Angola Verification Mission II	June 1991–To Present
ONUSAL	United Nations Observer Mission In El Salvador	July 1991–To Present
MINURSO	United Nations Mission For The Referendum In Western Sahara	September 1991–To Present
UNAMIC	United Nations Advance Mission In Cambodia	October 1991–March 1992
UNPROFOR	United Nations Protection Force	March 1992–To Present
UNTAC	United Nations Transitional Authority In Cambodia	March 1992–September 1993
UNOSOM I	United Nations Operation In Somalia I	April 1992–April 1993
ONUMOZ	United Nations Operation In Mozambique	December 1992–To Present
UNOSOM II	United Nations Operation In Somalia II	May 1993–To Present
UNOMUR	United Nations Observer Mission Uganda–Rwanda	June 1993–To Present
UNOMIG	United Nations Observer Mission In Georgia	August 1993–To Present
UNOMIL	United Nations Observer Mission In Liberia	September 1993–To Present
UNMIH	United Nations Mission In Haiti	September 1993–To Present
UNAMIR	United Nations Assistance Mission For Rwanda	October 1992–To Present
UNASOG	United Nations Aouzou Strip Observer Group	May 1994–June 1994

Source: United Nations

relief-enforcement operations (e.g. UNPROFOR). Although governance missions had been a subsidiary component of earlier UN operations, the authorisation of 'governance' forces whose primary tasks are for police, electoral and transfer of power functions, raised important issues concerning the negotiation of resources, sovereignty in civil war and the potential longevity of operations.

What are the implications for the relationship between security and the conduct of diplomacy at an international level? Firstly the practice of modifying or extending peacekeeping forces on an *ad hoc* basis means that diplomacy, particularly in the context of post-Cold War *civil wars,* is perpetually chasing or following events, e.g. breaches of Danube sanctions or attempts to protect enclaves in the Yugoslavia conflict. In contrast an unusual example of *deterrent* diplomacy was the rapid establishment of the small UN force (UNFIM) in Macedonia (FYRM).[13] Second, delay in securnng agreement on the texts of Security Council resolutions is often a product of divisions among external powers as much as local parties. In addition, concern over a further problem – lack of consultation in two areas – between the Security Council and troop providers to peacekeeping forces, and between 'host' parties and the Council, has led to the introduction of a number of reforms in 1995–96 to the Security Council's procedures. Among these are the regular consultation sessions between troop providers and Security Council members, and improved access to the Council for non-permanent members.[14]

Third, the expansion of UN peacekeeping and related operations – more than 20 operations have been mounted since 1990, has put increasing pressure on the authority and effectiveness of the UN Secretary-General. These constraints include the introduction of revised budgetary auditing procedures, the political effects on the office of Secretary-General of ineffective or failed UN operations and the multiple initiatives in intra-state conflict, which may conflict with those of the Secretary-General. This contrasts with the earlier period of preventive diplomacy during the Cold War in which the Secretary-General was more easily able to exert influence.

The increased *volume* of UN activity has brought with it greater use by the Secretary-General of special representatives or envoys. However, it can be argued that excessive or inappropriate use of envoys in effect weakens or displaces personal diplomacy by the Secretary-General, reducing the impact of the office.[15]

Fourth, the financial crisis of the UN has impaired its ability to link diplomacy with sustained peacekeeping leading to operations being curtailed, withdrawn or not expanded at critical moments, e.g. Somalia, Bosnia. Finally, development of UN operations hinges on the UN's ability, based upon an agreed mandate, to have on call adequate military capability, integral to a peacekeeping operation, or available in support of a revised enforcement operation with clear lines of politico-military command and control.

Rules and international security

Apart from preventive diplomacy and peace enforcement approaches as an approach to security in the international system, a further important dimension of internationally derived security is the development of tacit and formal rules. Rules may take the form of treaties or agreements, less formal means including declarations, through to informal tacit arrangements such as customary restraints, or accepting the spirit of an agreement.[16] In general, rule setting involves lengthy procedural and definitional diplomacy, especially within international organisations, in view of the high interests at stake. In the UN extensive diplomatic efforts have been devoted to such issues as definitions of aggression,[17] the legal status of mercenaries[18] and the principles of international law concerning friendly relations.[19] Related to these rule-setting conferences are investigations into, for example, challenges and threats to international security from new sources such as internationally organised crime,[20] the use of chemical weapons in particular conflicts and war crimes. These and other similar inquiries and UN special missions frequently form the basis for UN resolutions and formal legal instruments.

A noticeable feature of internationally sourced security are the efforts sponsored particularly, though not exclusively, by weaker states to establish regimes to regulate the status and use of particular territory. For example, the 1959 Antarctic Treaty reserves (article 1) Antarctica for peaceful purposes.[21] Other attempts to neutralise territory or limit the use or placing of weapons include Austrian neutrality (1955),[22] the Rappaki plan for zonal disengagement in Europe (1957–58)[23] and the creation of the Saudi Arabian–Iraq neutral zone.[24] Since then, attempts to designate international areas for peaceful purposes have increased.[25] For example the non-aligned movement discussed the Indian Ocean region at the Lusaka conference in 1970. In December 1971 the issue was taken up by the UN General Assembly, which declared the Indian Ocean a zone of peace and formed the Ad Hoc Committee on the Indian Ocean.[26] A number of regional treaties, including the Treaty of Tlatelolco (1967)[27] have declared nuclear-free zones. In Southeast Asia, ASEAN issued a declaration in 1971 intended to secure recognition of Southeast Asia as a zone of peace, freedom and neutrality (ZOPFAN),[28] while the Valletta declaration of September 1984 made peaceful use claims for the Mediterranean as a closed sea.[29] The security debate too has become widened to include opposition by regional actors to the carriage of hazardous cargo such as processed nuclear materials by sea through areas such as the Caribbean and Pacific. These and similar declarations suggest that states continue to find value in committing very significant amounts of their diplomatic time to establishing rules, declarations and regimes by international diplomatic conferences despite the remoteness of the objectives.

Allies, alliances and diplomacy

The foregoing has looked at the scope and limitations on internationally sourced security in the form of preventive diplomacy and internationally agreed rules. Of the other national actions undertaken by states in the pursuit of security, three broad areas of diplomatic activity have been devoted to the enhancement of security, the redefinition of security interests and the maintenance of freedom of action.

In seeking to *enhance* security, states have traditionally had at their disposal methods such as negotiation of arms supplies and security arrangements with a protecting power. Other options are avoidance of direct involvement in conflicts, maintenance of a low diplomatic profile, or conversely seeking international support. Failure to achieve a wide basis of support was seen as a major source of weakness by the Iranian government during the long drawn out Iran–Iraq war. As Khomeini bitterly complained, Iran could count its allies on the fingers of one hand.[30] In the Yugoslav conflict, the inability of the Bosnian Muslim government to gain the unequivocal support of a major power, coupled with divisions among Western powers, severely hampered Bosnian policy of securing weapons and military backing.

For many states, nevertheless, reliance has continued to be placed on bilateral arrangements. Such arrangements have been between local powers, e.g. the Sudan–Egyptian security co-operation agreement against Libya. More often than not a major external power has featured in an agreement. Between 1970 and 1980, for example, some ten countries signed bilateral treaties of friendship and co-operation or similar arrangements with the former Soviet Union which were renegotiated from 1992 by the Russian Federation.[31]

In bilateral arrangements involving a larger central power demands by the smaller power for advanced weapons systems or replenishment of equipment are periodically a source of diplomatic dispute in that concessions by a major power on *supply* may sometimes conflict with the other foreign policy interests. Supply remains the essential lever over an ally. The failure of the former USSR to refurbish the Egyptian army both before and after the October 1973 War was a major factor in the reorientation of Egyptian foreign policy after 1975.[32] The *ability* (or loss of) to supply particular types of weapons, dual use technology or restricted defence or nuclear materials can be seen by supplying powers as an important indicator of status (e.g. Russian Federation–Iran nuclear materials supply).

Relatively few formal multilateral security alliances have been concluded in recent years. The period since 1972 has, outside Europe, been largely one of alliance demise. An exception is the creation of the Gulf Co-operation Council (GCC) in 1981. Diplomatic co-operation among GCC members (Bahrain, Kuwait, Oman, Qatar, Saudi Arabia and the United Arab Emirates) has increased considerably since then. However, security arrangements remain embryonic, despite the Iraqi invasion of Kuwait and the Gulf war. It is interesting to note in comparison that the Association of Southeast Asian Nations (ASEAN) has remained an essentially *economic* organisation, following the winding up of the South-East Asia Treaty Organisation (SEATO). Factors working against alliance transformation were the differing defence orientations of the principal ASEAN members before 1990, bilateral defence links with external powers, notably the US and UK, and concerns that one of the larger members of ASEAN might seek to dominate regional security.

Different dilemmas have been posed for ASEAN members in the post-Cold War era as a result of United States diplomatic initiatives to create wider pan-regional Asia–Pacific economic and security institutions. For some ASEAN members, particularly Malaysia, the establishment of wider pan-regional bodies, like the ASEAN regional forum and Asia–Pacific Economic Council (APEC) has blurred traditional security threats, and created new economic security challenges from rival institutions within which it has far less influence.[33] In the GCC case, the effect of the Gulf War on alliance transformation, has been mainly diplomatic. The GCC has been extended to include Egypt and Syria, to form an additional grouping known as the Damascus Declaration States, meeting separately from the GCC at ministerial level on territorial issues. However, the group has been unable to agree on the creation of an Arab peacekeeping force, envisaged in the Damascus Declaration.[34] The Gulf War is of interest additionally in that the war against Iraq was fought via an *ad hoc* US-led multinational force, under Security Council Resolution 686. Although not a formal permanent alliance, diplomatic links among the coalition members continued in the context of Security Council follow-up resolutions on Iraq.

Within Europe, a security vacuum was created with the collapse of communism, and the accompanying dissolution of COMECOM and the Warsaw Pact. Former members of the Warsaw Pact including the Czech and Slovak republics, Hungary and Poland, rejected a sub-regional quadripartite alliance, in favour of defence links with Nato. It is interesting to note that the Russian Federation approach to security, apart from the CIS, and bilateral agreements, e.g. the 1994 Treaty of Friendship with Georgia, has preferred pan-European OSCE structures as a counter to an expanded Nato. Pan-regional structures have featured in European and Asian–Pacific economic security restructuring.

Security of small states

While there appears to have been reluctance among states to enter into formal multilateral alliance commitments, interest, nevertheless, has increased in regional arrangements of a lesser nature. A good example is the South Pacific Forum, which brings together Australia, the Cook Islands, Fiji, Kiribati, Nauru, New Zealand, Niue, Papua New Guinea, Solomon Islands, Tonga, Tuvalu, Vanuatu and Western Samoa. The grouping has been drawn together on a number of issues, including problems connected with extended maritime boundaries under the Law of the Sea Convention, dumping of waste at sea, illegal fishing by distant water fleets and nuclear testing.

Other small actors have sought security through a deliberate policy of joining as many regional and international organisations as possible, e.g. Baltic states. The new central Asian states have joined, for example, both the European Bank for Reconstruction and Development (EBRD) and the Asian Development Bank (ADB), despite dual membership clauses which limit duplicate economic benefits.[35] In this instance *membership* alone without drawing rights is seen as a symbolically important element of security. For some the membership cost of a multi-international institution policy is too high, e.g. Uzbekistan, forcing a shift in strategy to one of enhancing *inward representation* by international organisations and corporate bodies, rather than maintaining a larger external presence. Uzbek policy, for example, has been to encourage the opening of missions in Tashkent, including an integrated UN regional office, corporate bodies such as IBM, and other institutions such as the Red Cross. Sensitive geo-strategic location and limited diplomatic resources has also meant that Uzbek policy has placed great importance on non-involvement in conflicts such as that between Azerbaijan and Armenia over Karabakh, and that involving Tadjikistan. Traditional diplomacy is seen as inadequate or even dangerous in the context of ethno-clan conflict.

A further aspect of the security of small states is the growing recognition of the range of threats faced by small states in the highly vulnerable category. For example, the UN conference on the Protection and Security of Small States identified three groups of threat:[36] (1) international drug/currency networks; (2) policing of the territorial sea and exclusive economic zone; (3) piracy, mercenaries and terrorism.

In addition, intergovernmental conferences have addressed other specific areas of vulnerability including global sea-level rise and other ecological problems such as desertification. In fact most of the above threats require high degrees of international co-operation via international institutions rather than low-level regional responses. Commenting on this problem the representative of the Maldives noted:[37] '... for the small state, diplomacy will always remain the first line of defence, no matter what steps are taken to strengthen its national defence capabilities.'

Security: embassy and diplomat

Concern over the growing risks faced by diplomatic personnel, officials accredited to international organisations and to diplomatic and consular premises has intensified considerably since the conclusion of the Vienna Convention on Diplomatic Relations in April 1961.[38] The Vienna Convention provisions relating to security deal *inter alia* with the inviolability of the mission and the special duty of the receiving state to take all appropriate steps to protect the premises of the mission against any intrusion or damage and prevent any disturbance or impairment of the dignity of the embassy (article 22). The archives and documents of the mission are also inviolable (article 24), as is the person of a diplomatic agent. The receiving state must take all appropriate steps to prevent any 'attack on his freedom, person or dignity'. Other relevant international agreements are the Vienna Convention on Consular Relations of 1963 (with Protocols) and the Convention on the Prevention and Punishment of

Crimes Against Internationally Protected Persons, including Diplomatic Agents of 1973. In the event of a breach in relations or other serious conflict, the Vienna Convention on Diplomatic Relations allows for the operation of protecting powers, acceptable to the host country. For example British interests in Iran were assumed by Sweden from 1980 to 1988 for security reasons despite the maintenance of diplomatic relations between the two countries.[39]

In 1980, in view of continuing violations of the Vienna Convention, the UN General Assembly passed Resolution 35/168 establishing reporting procedures for incidents against embassies and diplomatic personnel.[40] States have used the reporting procedures for two different purposes, either to report violations regarding their own missions and representatives, or to submit information on incidents in their own territory, whether the incidents had or had not been previously reported by the other state concerned. The reports provide information on incidents ranging from assassination, bomb attacks, violent attacks on diplomatic buildings, including occupation through to demonstration.[41] Several of the incidents are extensions of ongoing regional conflict or civil war. Others involve breaches of travel restrictions in prohibited zones or security areas (article 26). A further question which has arisen concerns the status of a representative office. For example, Sweden argued that an attack on the Turkish Tourist office in Stockholm did not fall within the 1961 Vienna Convention, since the Turkish office did not enjoy diplomatic status.[42]

Redefining security

Efforts to redefine the purposes and benefits of security arrangements have now become an almost everyday feature of international relations. Why does redefinition arise? What issues are raised by redefinition and how are they resolved? Major redefinition of security interests, rather than routine adjustments, is likely to occur for one of a number of reasons such as change of government; a desire to decrease dependency; dissatisfaction with a major 'guarantor'; and to acquire enhanced economic benefits. Only very rarely does redefinition occur because of alliance or bloc collapse or disintegration, as in the case of the Warsaw Pact.

For example, the issue of stationing, presence and use of nuclear weapons has been a source of dispute within the ANZUS alliance[43] (Australia, New Zealand, United States) between New Zealand and the United States, while the presence of US warships carrying nuclear weapons in Japanese ports has become increasingly sensitive for Japanese governments.[44] The Japanese and other governments in the Pacific region and elsewhere viewed with alarm the French government's decision to resume nuclear testing in the Pacific in 1995.

In ANZUS, New Zealand redefined its security interests in 1985 with the refusal to allow port facilities to United States warships with potential nuclear capability.[45] In response the United States initially cancelled joint exercises, meetings of communications officials and the sharing of joint intelligence. With no modification of New Zealand policy, the United States suspended its security arrangements under ANZUS with New Zealand in August 1986.[46]

Redefinition of security has occurred for a number of other reasons. In redefining security, states have sometimes sought to diversify their sources of security. For example, Malta has experimented with various security arrangements with differing countries including Libya, since the 1970s, and in an exchange of notes with Italy declared itself to have neutralised status in 1981.[47] In other instances, unfulfilled economic and military commitments can lead minor powers to switch protecting states rapidly, for example, Somalia and the former Soviet Union. The arms-supply policies of an external power by definition have security implications for neighbouring states and can create perceptions of vulnerability. Thus the Egyptian abrogation of the Egyptian–Soviet treaty in 1976[48] was influenced not only by the former Soviet failure to build up the Egyptian armed forces but also by the former Soviet Union's rearmament of Libya.[49] In their economic actions external powers are generally more sensitive to the security implications of cuts in budgetary and other assistance to former colonies. In some instances reductions in budgetary assistance by an external power have led to efforts to find a new economic *patron*. The Central African Republic and Benin, for example, have attempted to diversify from France, yet these exercises have generally been short-lived and often led to a *coup d'état*.[50]

In the main, African states have found it difficult to develop effective regional security arrangements.[51] The contribution to regional collective security of organisations such as the OAU has on the whole been very limited.[52] This situation seems for the most part to have been tacitly accepted and the Organisation's role confined largely to political and economic questions. In relatively rare cases some states have taken the step of actually withdrawing from a regional organisation. Morocco, for example, withdrew in 1985 from the OAU,[53] and Nigeria withdrew from the Organisation of the Islamic Conference (OIC) in 1991.[54] It is clear that withdrawal tends to be an action of last resort because of fears of diplomatic isolation. Although a regional organisation might be ineffective in military terms, it is nevertheless a diplomatic *milieu* for contact, discussion and lobbying, which are in themselves essential ingredients to continued perceptions of independence, legitimacy and security well-being by the member states.[55]

Summary

In modern international relations the nature of security and the security requirements of states have strikingly changed from the kinds of issues traditionally thought of as comprising threats. Many modern threats are however of a non-military nature and require diplomatic or other appropriate responses. Diplomacy, too, is an essential element in the continual process of defining, maintaining and enhancing security. In the main, security through United Nations peacekeeping and other quasi-military forces has been a relatively important though declining contribution to national and international security. In contrast, states have placed importance on using the United Nations as a forum for the generation and establishment of rules and regimes such as nuclear-free zones, and zones of peace, environmental security and resource management. The economic dimension of security finds its expression in moves outside Europe in the Middle East, Asia, the Pacific and Latin America to increase regional co-operation, and promote stability through the establishment of groupings within which to promote trade, extradition, fisheries and Exclusive Economic Zone (EEZ) management and other co-operation. Many of these are as yet embryonic, but they are an important indication of the differences in perceived needs and emphases of states. Overall, the security threats faced by modern states have become increasingly diverse and continue to pose additional complex challenges for diplomacy.

References and notes

1. R.H. Ullman, 'Redefining Security', *International Security*, Vol. 8, No. 1 (1983) pp. 129–33.
2. See J.W.M. Chapman, R. Drifte and I.T.M. Gow, *Japan's Quest for Comprehensive Security* (Francis Pinter, London, 1983) pp. xiv–xviii, for a discussion of the concept of comprehensive security in a Japanese context.
3. On maritime fraud see for example the UNCTAD studies, *Maritime Fraud* (status of the work of non-governmental organisations to combat maritime fraud) TD/B/C.4/9, 22 Aug. 1985, and the UNCTAD Secretariat's report on maritime financial fraud, TD/B/C.4/6, 27 June 1985, esp. pp. 6–14.
4. See Report of the Secretary-General, 'Progress Report on United Nations Activities in Crime Prevention and Control', UN Doc. E/AC/57/1986/3, 28 Nov. 1985, para. 15, Economic and Social Council, UN Doc E/AC/57/1986/4, 20 Feb. 1986, paras 51, 72, 80.
5. Arnold Wolfers, *Discord and Collaboration* (The Johns Hopkins Press, Baltimore, 1962).
6. Jimmy Carter, *Keeping Faith* (Collins, London, 1982) p. 506.
7. Inis L. Claude Jr., *Swords into Plowshares*, 3rd edn (University of London Press, London, 1964) pp. 245–8; Hans Kelsen, *Recent Trends in the Law of the United Nations* (Stevens and Sons, London, 1951) pp. 953–90.
8. Alan James, *The Politics of Peace-Keeping* (Chatto and Windus, London, 1969) esp. Chs 7 and 8.
9. *Public Papers of the Secretaries-General of the United Nations*, Vol. V (Dag Hammarskjöld) 1960–61 (Columbia University Press, New York, 1975) pp. 131–2.
10. See R.P. Barston, 'Problems in International Peacekeeping: The Case of Cyprus', *International Relations* (David Davies Memorial Institute of International Studies, London) Vol. III, No. 11 (May 1971) pp. 928–40.
11. Claude, op. cit., pp. 297–8.
12. The projected deficit as at 31 Dec. 1985 was $US390.7 million, of which $US116.3 million related to withholding, or delay in payments to the regular budget and the balance to peacekeeping activities. See A.40/1102, 12 April 1986, paras 11 and 15. See also *UN Chronicle*, Vol. XIX, No. 5 (May 1982) pp. 65–70.

13. Following the 9 Dec. 1992 Report of the Secretary-General (S/24293) the Security Council acting under Ch. VII of the UN Charter expanded UNPROFOR by one battalion, and 35 UN military observers to form the UN force in Macedonia, *UN Monthly Chronicle,* March 1993, p. 10.
14. S/PV 3483, 16 Dec. 1994.
15. See for example the General Assembly resolution which requested the UN Secretary-General to keep to a minumum special envoys and representatives, A/RES/48/259, 1 Aug. 1994 and Review of the Efficiency of the Administrative and Financial Functioning of the UN, General Assembly A/49/310, 12 Aug. 1994.
16. Raymond Cohen, *International Politics* (Longman, London, 1981) p. 156.
17. UN General Assembly Resolution 3314 (XXXIX) 29 UN GAOR, Supp. (No. 31), 142 UN Doc A0631 (1975).
18. *UN Chronicle,* Vol. XIX, No. 5 (May 1982) p. 6.
19. John F. Murphy, *The United Nations and the Control of Violence* (Manchester University Press, Manchester, 1983) pp. 89–90.
20. See statement by Giuseppe Di Gennaro, outgoing chairman of the UN Committee on Crime Prevention and Control, and Executive Director of the UN Fund for Drug Abuse Control, in *UN Chronicle,* Vol. XIX, No. 5 (May 1982), p. 60.
21. *UNTS,* Vol. 402, p. 71; *UKTS,* No. 97 (1961) Cmnd. 1535.
22. Austrian State Treaty, 15 May 1955, *UNTS,* Vol. 217, p. 223; *UKTS,* No. 58 (1957) Cmnd. 214. Austrian neutrality was promulgated as a constitutional law on 26 Oct. 1955.
23. F.S. Northedge, *Descent From Power* (George Allen and Unwin, 1974) pp. 244–5.
24. Henry W. Degenhardt, *Treaties and Alliances of the World* (Longman, London, 1981) pp. 3, 6.
25. See Study on the Naval Arms Rate, Report of the Secretary-General, UN Doc A/40/535, 17 Sept. 1985, pp. 50–70.
26. See Resolution 2832 (XXVI) 16 Dec. 1971, and Philip Towle, 'The United Nations Ad Hoc Committee on the Indian Ocean: Blind Alley or Zone of Peace', in Larry W. Bowman and Ian Clark (eds), *The Indian Ocean in Global Politics* (Westview Press, Boulder, Colo., 1981) pp. 207–22. The committee is composed of these member states: Australia, Bangladesh, Bulgaria, Canada, China, Djibouti, Egypt, Ethiopia, Germany, Greece, India, Indonesia, Iran, Iraq, Italy, Japan, Kenya, Liberia, Madagascar, Malaysia, Maldives, Mauritius, Mozambique, the Netherlands, Norway, Oman, Pakistan, Panama, Poland, Romania, Russian Federation, Seychelles, Singapore, Somalia, Sri Lanka, Sudan, Thailand, Uganda, United Arab Emirates, United Republic of Tanzania, Yemen, Yugoslavia, Zambia, Zimbabwe.
27. UN Doc A/40/535, para. 238, p. 65.
28. Alison Broinowski, *Understanding ASEAN* (Macmillan, London, 1983) Appendix E, p. 294.
29. See Final Declaration of the first ministerial meeting of the Mediterranean members of the non-aligned movement, Valletta 10–11 Sept. 1984, UN Docs A/39/526 S/16758, and A/40/535, para. 253, p. 69.
30. Khomeini, quoted in Dilip Hiro, *The Longest War* (Grafton Books, London, 1989) pp. 154–5. The July 1984 Iranian offensive was proposed for diplomatic reasons. Failure the following year of Iran's March 1985 offensive in the Haur al Hawizeh marshes to seize the Basra–Baghdad road, softened Tehran's attitude to relations with the Gulf Co-operation Council, and the Saudi foreign minister was invited to Teheran, prior to the GCC Muscat summit. Hiro, p. 156.
31. Zafar Iman, 'Soviet Treaties with Third World Countries', *Soviet Studies,* Vol. XXV, No. 1 (Jan. 1983) pp. 53–70. For revision of the treaties see Ch. of Chinese treaties in Grant F. Rhode and Reid E. Whitlock, *Treaties of the PRC 1949–78* (Westview Press, Boulder, Colo., 1980) pp. 15–43. Revised military co-operation agreements have been concluded for example with Iran (*Times,* 17 March 1995); Sudan (*Keesing,* April 1995, 40492); Yugoslavia (FRY) (*Keesing,* March 1995, 40476), and India, with the Moscow Declaration (*Keesing,* July 1994, 40281). New agreements were concluded by Malaysia (arms counter purchase) *Times,* 7 June 1994: and

with the PRC which included a border agreement and non-targeting (*Keesing*, Sept. 1994, 40181).

32. Ismail Fahmy, *Negotiating for Peace in the Middle East* (Croom Helm, London, 1983) pp. 145–7, 172, 176.
33. *Financial Times*, 1 March 1995.
34. *Middle East Economic Digest*, 21 Jan. 1994.
35. Basic documents of the European Bank for Reconstruction and Development (EBRD), Agreement Establishing the EBRD 29 May 1990, Article 13 (vii).
36. Report of the Secretary-General, A/46/339, 18 Sept. 1991.
37. Ibid., para 11(d), p. 35.
38. UN Doc A/CONF.20/13, 16 April 1961, 55 *AJIL* 1961.
39. See 57 *British Yearbook of International Law* (1987), p. 568.
40. See UN GA RES 35/168, 15 Dec. 1980; and A.RES/49/49, 17 Feb. 1995.
41. For details of incidents see A/49/295, 5 Aug. 1994.
42. See Ibid., p. 21 for the Swedish Note Verbale arguing that the attack on a tourist office fell outside the reporting requirements of Resolution 42/154.
43. See J.G. Starkes' discussion of the special issues confronting ANZUS, including the US guarantee, in the ANZUS Treaty Alliance (Melbourne University Press, 1965) esp. pp. 228–42. The text of the treaty is at pp. 243–5.
44. See J.W.M. Chapman and I.T.M. Drifte, *Japan's Quest for Comprehensive Security* (Frances Pinter, London, 1983) pp. 120–3.
45. The port access issue came to a head in early Feb. 1985 when the New Zealand Government declined to approve a requested visit by an American warship, USS *Buchanan* on the grounds that it was unable to satisfy itself that the vessel was not nuclear armed. See *Report of the Ministry of Foreign Affairs*, March 1985 (Wellington, 1985) pp. 21–2.
46. *The Times*, 13 Aug. 1986.
47. Exchange of notes on Malta becoming a neutralised state, with Italy, 15 Sept. 1981. See *Italian Yearbook of International Law* (Napoli, Editorial Scientifica, 1983) pp. 352–7 for the texts of the two notes.
48. Fahmy, op. cit., p. 172.
49. Ali E. Hillal Dessouki, 'The Foreign Policy of Egypt', in Bahgat Korany and Ali E. Hillal Dessouki (eds), *The Foreign Policies of Arab States* (Westview Press, Boulder, Colo., 1984) p. 137.
50. I. William Zartman, 'Africa and the West: the French Connection', in Bruce E. Arlinghaus (ed.), *African Security Issues* (Westview Press, Boulder, Colo., 1984) p. 50, and Timothy M. Shaw and Olajiode Aluko, *The Political Economy of African Foreign Policy* (Gower, Aldershot, 1984).
51. See, for example, Tom Imobighe, 'ECOWAS Defence Pact and Regionalism in Africa', in R.I. Onwuka and A. Sesay (eds), *The Future of Regionalism in Africa* (Macmillan, Hong Kong, 1985) pp. 110–23.
52. John M. Ostheiner, 'Cooperation Among African States', in Arlinghaus, op. cit., pp. 157–70, and Mark W. Zacher, International Conflicts and Collective Security 1946–77 (Praeger, New York, 1979) pp. 121–60.
53. *The Annual Register 1984* (Longman, London, 1985) pp. 219, 362; *Revue Générale de Droit International* Public (A. Pedone, Paris, 1986) p. 460. Morocco officially ceased to be a member of the OAU on 12 Nov. 1985.
54. On this point see Zacher, op. cit., p. 155. Zacher also notes that the OAU's major function is now more one of creating a consensual African foreign policy on extra-African issues rather than acting as effective agent for collective security.

CHAPTER 12

Diplomacy and mediation

One of the central tasks of diplomacy at an international level is contributing to the pacific settlement of disputes between or involving states and other actors. The continued proliferation of disputes and armed conflict in the Cold War and post-Cold War period, many marked by their seeming insolubility, ethnic and nationalist nature or associated with the break-up of the former Soviet Union have meant the constant adaptation of diplomatic methods. This chapter will focus especially on one of these methods – mediation, and will examine the nature of mediation, the mediators, methods used in mediation and the limitations or success of mediation efforts.

Mediation: meaning and definitions

Traditionally, the methods used for the pacific settlement of disputes have included inquiry, negotiation, conciliation, arbitration, mediation and judicial settlement. This range of methods has received formal importance in both the League of Nations Covenant and United Nations Charter.[1] Although the UN Charter distinguishes the pacific settlement of disputes in Chapter 6 from enforcement under Chapter 7, mediation, of course is possible during the course of armed conflict or war.

In a strict sense mediation should be distinguished from conciliation and arbitration, although there are a number of features common to all three. The essence of conciliation is more on facilitating communication between the parties and clarification of opposing positions, rather than necessarily proposing substantive solutions. Conciliation has been particularly used in domestic disputes, while in international diplomacy a number of initiatives under UN auspices in the 1950s and 1960s were of the conciliation type such as the UN Commission on India and Pakistan, drawn from security council members, or individual envoys such as Sir Owen Dixon in the Kashmir dispute.[2] Intermediary functions under UN authorisation have been carried out by named individuals (e.g. Count Bernadette, Palestine); a named group (e.g. the Good Office Group on Korea, 1951); Secretary-General (Pérez de Cuellar, Gulf, 1987) and more frequently by persons designated by the Secretary-General (e.g. Secretary-General's special representative for

Angola and representatives of three observer states).[3] The increasing use of envoys of differing types and varied missions has tended to blur the distinction between conciliation, good offices and mediation.[4]

Arbitration is properly distinguished from mediation in that it is generally juridically based. Moreover, the solution proposed by an arbitrator may not necessarily be reached on the basis of a balance between conflicting interests but on criteria such as arbitrators' interpretations and application of principles or precedents. Arbitration may be binding or non-binding. It is noticeable that compulsory dispute settlement provisions through arbitration have been a feature of several recent resource-related treaties.[5]

Mediation is distinct from conciliation or arbitration in that the mediator is either indirectly or directly attempting to promote a temporary or permanent solution based on a conception of outcomes likely to receive joint or widespread acceptance by the parties in dispute.[6]

A mediator is thus concerned with strategies to affect both the process and content of possible solutions. In other words the aim of mediation is to change four elements: perception, approach, objectives and behaviour. In a useful definition of mediation Kissinger put these four elements as follows: 'the utility of a mediator is that if trusted by both sides he can soften the edge of controversy and provide a mechanism for adjustment on issues of prestige'.[7] The issues, however, need not necessarily be ones of prestige.

Mediation is undertaken by third-party representatives mainly from states and international institutions but also by individuals, NGOs and informal actors. The mediator should in some sense be external to the dispute, thought he could be an ally of one of the parties. In order not to broaden or confuse the concept, 'mediation' by a formal office-holder in multilateral conferences is better understood by other concepts such as the 'brokering' of compromises or initiatives, negotiation initiatives or facilitating roles.

Two further points concerning the definition of mediation can be made. The first concerns the perception of the nature, status and purpose of an envoy's mission. In some instances one or more parties may misperceive the status or purpose of a visit or talks. For example, during the Chile–Argentine dispute over the Beagle Channel, with Argentinian and Chilean warships hours apart from confrontation in the Straits of Magellan, the Pope's special envoy, Cardinal Samore made it clear that his mission to both countries was not to mediate a settlement but rather seek restraint: 'I speak rather of a mission and not of mediation, in a technical sense, because mediation is a juridical term that gives to the mediator, if not authority, at least the possibility of making proposals, not only to listen or to invite the parties. But we are still not in that phase.'[8]

A further important point, which is often ignored in mediation literature, partly because of the emphasis on mediation in bilateral conflict, is that there may be multiple levels of mediation occurring in a multiparty dispute. Multiple layers or types of mediation occur particularly in multilateral conflict if one of the main protagonists is diplomatically isolated, or has limited diplomatic machinery. In these circumstances there is a tendency to use multiple or perhaps informal channels of communication and conduct several levels of mediation negotiations. Again, in civil war cases in which there is extensive external intervention by major powers and international organisations, some disputants attempt to play off various mediation initiatives linking them to battlefield developments to perhaps delay mediation pending battlefield progress or seeking other concessions.

The mediators

Mediation is carried out by a wide range of actors including formal office-holders of states, international institutions, special representatives, envoys and groups. In the informal category the range is extensive with actors such as business, labour organisations, opposition politicians, aid workers, religious leaders and other 'citizen' diplomats being called in to perform on an invited basis (and sometimes not) mediation functions to varying degrees.[9] It is also notable that a third category of mediator – the senior former office-holder, e.g. ex-US president Jimmy Carter, has become more prominent. Former president Carter carried out missions, for example, to North Korea, Haiti, Bosnia and Romania during 1994–95, seemingly for all intents and purposes, at least in the first three instances, as a secretary of state. It is not always clear, however, what precisely is the status of an 'unofficial' mediator. Confusion can arise when established diplomatic services and procedures have broken down during periods of significant political transition, periods of high tension resolution or war.[10] In other instances revolutionary or 'pariah' regimes seem to attract foreign domiciled nationals who inhabit the grey area or *demi-monde* of 'representative' or contact channels and thrive on intrigue and crisis.[11]

Apart from questions to do with the status of mediators, it should be remembered that although juridically and analytically distinctions are made between inquiry, conciliation and mediation, diplomatic methods used in dealing with conflict may contain, in practice, elements of inquiry, conciliation and mediation, which are not always easy to distinguish. It is worth noting too that mediation may be undertaken on a collective or group basis.

Why have different categories of mediators developed?

As regards the second category probably one of the main reasons is the growth in the role of the private commercial and financial sector as an adjunct of government when states seek to improve relations or reduce tension with other states. Second, as part of the growth of contacts in international society, large-scale post-war ethnic movements have created a new kind of trans-urban international relations in some regions, for example the Hispanic community relations in NAFTA in which domestic and international politics are fused over issues such as emigration, unemployment, banking, trade and environmental standards. Trans-urban international relations have influenced the emergence of new players, especially 'domestic' (e.g. city mayors or chief executives) procedures and institutions.[12] Third, informal mediators have been used in crises as a means of *supplementing* official channels to provide reassurance that the intended message or proposals are getting through. Fourth, informal mediators, particularly in the third category, have been used in cases of breaches of relations or periods of high international tension (e.g. hostage release).[13] Fifth, informal mediators (category 2) have sometimes been used to conduct secret negotiations parallel to official negotiations in order to make a breakthrough.

Mediation strategies

Mediation strategies can be employed to influence the setting, process and content of a dispute. Strategies concerning the setting include choice of location, the means of communication, which parties to invite and whether the discussions are conducted in public or private. Inventive locations have included the headquarters of a London antique company;[14] a desert tent in no-man's land between opposing armies;[15] and the splendour of papal palace.[16] More often though, *initial* or pre-negotiation contacts will be made at the margins of international or regional conferences or meetings.

While not decisive, location can have positive or negative effects in facilitating progress, or alternatively becoming an arena for sterile or routine exchanges. Ultimately, the outcome of mediation, particularly undertaken intensively over short periods of time in third country locations, has to be taken back to national organisations for consideration, assessments and response.

Process

Mediation activities which address the process aspects of conflict are typically aimed at the perceptual and attitudinal approach of disputants and seek to develop *engagement* and commitment to the negotiations. Mediation techniques in this area can be conceptualised as generally falling into two categories: procedure and approach. In the procedural group are proposals relating to the frequency of meetings, construction of an agenda, order of items and introduction of new texts. Within the approach group, techniques focus on developing rapport; the framing of the problem; creating commonly held conceptions about what the outcome might broadly look like and willingness to progress from initial negotiations to substantive exchange and agreed solutions.

One of the main process techniques is that of clarification. For example, during the Beagle Channel dispute between Argentina and

Chile noted earlier, the officially nominated papal mediator Cardinal Samore and his team devoted six months in the initial phase of the mediation (the talks ran intermittently from 1979 to 1984) gathering information and hearing both sides' positions.[17] The use of the technique of clarifying and 'unpacking' the elements in the positions of the respective parties at any stage of negotiations makes this aspect of mediation similar to conciliation.

It is worth noting that other techniques have been developed in multilateral conference diplomacy to broker solutions between opposing blocs or groupings on focal points of disagreement through altering the structure of the decision-making group to redefine the problem. Committees of the whole or large working groups can be reduced to a more manageable size by creating a small group of 'representative' states under an *ad hoc* chairman. For example at the third conference on the Law of the Sea an *ad hoc* group was formed under Ambassador Castenada (Mexico) to try and reach a compromise solution on the intractable question of the outer limit of the continental shelf.[18] As we have argued in Chapter 5,[19] the tendency to use smaller groups has to be matched by methods which make the output widely acceptable to the conference as a whole. Other methods include process techniques which attempt to alter the pace of mediation negotiations, re-scheduling talks, keeping talks going and deadlines. Deadlines have, however, tended not to be greatly used by mediators for fear that undue use or failure to be met weakens the credibility of the mediator.[20] Mediators may, nevertheless, encounter deadlines set by the *parties,* arising from domestic or other contexts such as a disputant's fear of running out of time, the perceived cost of political failure, or inability to complete a mediation because of an impending election.[21] Concern over the completion of a mediation mission is evident too in the best known, though not frequently used example of mediation methods, 'shuttle' diplomacy.[22] As a form of high risk strategy, shuttle diplomacy depends critically on momentum to maintain the *engagement* of the principal protagonists.

Content

At the level of content mediation initiatives can be conceptualised in terms of whether the proposals are framework; integrative; incremental or compensatory.[23] Framework proposals aim to establish the overall basis for talks by, for example, agreeing general principles[24] or a time-table on which the dispute may be settled.[25] In this type of approach a high premium is placed on rapport between opposing states and *engagement* in the process of finding acceptable solutions and subsequent implementation. Other strategies aim to establish common ground. These might be through proposals which reflect a generally held conception of the outcome or promote agreement by reducing the *areas* of substantive negotiation. Differences are narrowed[26] and outstanding issues are relegated to bilateral understandings[27] or secret protocol.[28] In the third category, incremental as distinct from comprehensive approaches essentially seek to focus on particular areas of dispute, in order to make step-by-step progress. Compensation strategies are distinct in that a central assumption is that the distribution of benefits is unequal.

Constraints on mediation

As essentially an exercise in *persuasion*, mediation initiatives force a number of possible constraints. Almost immediately the mediator crosses the threshold from being simply a transmitter of messages, and moves along the continuum of more direct or less passive involvement, then he faces differing degrees of risk.[29] His assets are principally political and diplomatic – negotiating skill, past success, knowledge and perceived track record. Nor should mediation be considered in too mechanistic a manner with a mediator having deployable assets (e.g. trading off unrelated items in the UN), or, threat–reward type models.[30] Rather, in most types of mediation, the mediator must generally rely on diplomatic skills of persuasion, explanation, concept creation and drafting,[31] and not trading economic rewards or coercion. In this context, risk may be encountered relatively quickly on the continuum of involvement. For example decisions on whether the contents of a letter might be usefully transmitted or not can expose the function or office of mediator to possible criticism or loss of confidence. A second area of constraint may occur if a mediator attempts to overcome a sticking point by making proposals which are too far ahead along the route of perceived acceptable outcomes. For example, during the so-called 'proximity talks' to resolve the Cyprus problem, UN Secretary-General Pérez de Cuellar attempted to make progress through a combination of procedural initiatives and narrowing the focus of negotiation:

I told the leaders that I would concentrate in the first instance on the two outstanding issues – territorial issues and displaced persons, and that I would proceed to a discussion of the other issues once I was satisfied that reasonable progress had been made in bringing the parties *within agreement range* on those two issues. [emphasis added]

However, the talks broke down because of opposition by both parties to various aspects of the Secretary-General's proposals.[32] More generally, the Cyprus problem is an example of a 'closed' issue-area, where the prospects for mediation are extremely limited, given the domestic and external structural features of the problem. Lengthy UN peacekeeping operations, with routinely renewed mandates, tend to contribute eventually to the *immobilism.*

A further quite common constraint on mediation can arise from different approaches over how the negotiations should be conducted. Differences may occur over whether to proceed on the basis of establishing general principles or take specific issues. A marked feature of

Henry Kissinger's diplomatic style was to prefer to get agreement on sets of principles,[33] which could be subsequently filled out later. Kissinger's approach was not, for example, to the liking of Sadat, who wanted to reach specific or tangible agreements.[34]

Time pressures affect mediation negotiations in several ways such as the resumption or calling-off of talks, loss of momentum or the threat of deadlines. In crises, mediators and other players often perceive that time is running out for political solutions and feel a loss of control. In the latter sense opponents are 'locked' into a dispute; the costs of halting action are seen as too high. Corresponding benefits of alternative proposals or outcomes cannot be easily quantified, evaluated, or are unknown. Under these conditions, the proposals for successful mediation are generally remote. Thus the mediatory efforts of the Russian Federation prior to the Gulf War culminating in the visit to Baghdad by Foreign Minister Alexander Kozyrev ultimately failed because of the essentially 'closed' positions of Saddam Hussein and the advanced military preparations of the Allied coalition group.[35]

Mediation and force

The relationship between mediation and military force is most clearly evident in protracted civil wars in the interplay between diplomatic efforts to reach political solutions and battlefield developments. The interplay is also particularly highlighted in the immediate follow-up processes to implement cease-fire agreements. In protracted civil war, mediation efforts, based on territorial partition plans, unsupported by sustained cease-fires, are unlikely to make much progress as combatants seek to maximise territorial gain or offset losses by extending enclaves or holding communications routes. Partition plans prepared by international institutions' mediators may become rapidly out of date, or require extensive re-adjustment when matched to actual force disposition on the ground while conference negotiators may be able to suspend time procedurally, this seldom happens on battlefields. Moreover, without the political endorsement of principal external powers with stakes in the conflict, partition plans drawn up by third-party international mediators are unlikely to succeed.[36] In turn, divisions between external powers about mediation proposals in themselves may become assets which civil war disputants use to protract a conflict.

As regards the *implementation* of mediated agreements, poorly monitored cease-fires and weak follow-up arrangements, can undermine the prior mediation, and make subsequent mediators more difficult. For example, in the Ecuador–Peru border conflict, violence flared up again in 1995, following the cease-fire mediated under the Rio Protocol by the United States, Chile, Argentina and Brazil, in part because a permanent observer force had not been established.[37] Again, concern over premature reduction on cost grounds of the UN Verification Force in Angola (UNAVEM II) and the breakdown of the Angolan cease-fire in

1995 prompted the UN Secretary-General Boutros-Ghali to seek approval from the Security Council for the restoration of the size of UNAVEM II to enable it to undertake an adequate level of monitoring, governance and good office functions to implement to Lusaka Protocol.[38]

Loss of credibility and bias

Mediators may lose credibility for one or more of the following reasons: technical deficiencies; loss of secrecy; challenges to status and charges of partiality. Within the technical deficiencies category, factors include appropriateness of the cultural or regional background of a mediator; administrative deficiencies and financial constraints. As regards information, mediation perhaps more than any other form of negotiation requires secret diplomacy. If elements of secret negotiations are leaked, difficulties occur in that possible concessions by one party are exposed, thus weakening its position; the credibility of the mediator may be called into question, or an incorrect or misinterpreted version of the 'contact' discussions or negotiations may be presented by the media, which requires denial or correction, and can reduce freedom of action. Third, the status of mediators may be undermined by personality factors; by divisions within a national or international executive or bureaucracy;[39] or be affected by other political initiatives or mediation efforts. An example of the latter are the multiple and competing initiatives in Tadjikistan from CSCE, US–Russian Federation and UN, since the break-up of the Soviet Union.[40] Fourth, mediators may cease to be effective if they lose the confidence of any of the parties to a significant extent through perceived undue partiality.[41] A difficulty for mediators is that their proposals may not necessarily be biased or intended to favour one or more of the parties but represent 'best possible' solutions.

Rejection of mediation

Mediation efforts may be either implicitly or explicitly rejected. In the first category a mediation mission may be accepted for reasons incidental with wanting a mediated outcome, such as symbolic or propaganda endorsement of a cause or have diversionary aims such as providing a cover for military preparations. Formal rejection of mediation is relatively rare, e.g. Mrs Thatcher's refusal to accept the UN mediation offices of Secretary-General Pérez de Cuellar after the Falklands war in 1982.[42]

Successful mediation

In reviewing some of the main factors influencing the successful outcome of mediation, three in particular should be noted. First, the maintenance of secrecy is a central factor in facilitating the formation of new proposals,[43] continued momentum and avoiding the effects of leaked proposals such as mistrust and possible breakdown of contacts. Second, the use of informal mediators and outside powers with no or limited direct stakes can be a useful means of breaking sterile, standing meetings. For example, the PLO–Israel meetings in 1993–94, brokered by then Norwegian Foreign Minister Johan Jurgen Holst,[44] made substantial progress in laying the basis in the informal Oslo talks for a limited PLO–Israeli agreement in contrast to ritualised ambassadorial exchanges in Washington.[45] In addition, informal mediators may enjoy limited or short-run success as channels of communication or last resort envoys (e.g. Carter missions to North Korea, Haiti, Bosnia) though their agreements may be fragile and subject to renegotiation.

Third, an important element in successful mediation is the role of overarching formulae which are used to construct agreements. Examples of these are definitions of areas of military disengagement; composition and functions of a joint administrative regime for disputed territory; and a formula to leave aside or 'suspend' decisions on sovereignty, while reaching agreement on matters of practical co-operation such as bilateral transport, economic or air services.

References and notes

1. Article 12 of the League of Nations covenant identifies three techniques in the event of a dispute: arbitration, judicial settlement or enquiry by the Council. Chapter 6, Article 33, United Nations Charter requires parties to resolve disputes through 'negotiation, enquiry, mediation, conciliation, arbitration, judicial settlement, resort to regional agencies or arrangements or other peaceful means of their choice'.
2. See Sidney D. Bailey, *The United Nations* (Macmillan, London, 1989) pp 45–6
3. Portugal, Russian Federation and United States are part of the UN mediation group on Angola. See SC/5892, 12 Aug. 1994.
4. See A/C.5/48/26 and Add. 10; A/RES/48/259, 1 Aug. 1994.
5. See Agreement for the Implementation of the Provisions of the United Nations Convention on the Law of the Sea of December 1982 relating to the conservation and management of Straddling Stocks and Highly Migratory Fish Stocks, A/CONF.164/22, 23 Aug. 1994, Article 29.
6. For a realist definition which depicts mediation in terms of self-interest and leverage, rather than a functional or international society perspective, see S. Touval and I.W. Zartman, 'Mediation in International Conflicts', in K. Kressel and D.G. Pruitt, *Mediation Research* (Jossey-Bass Inc., San Francisco, 1989) pp. 115–37; and S. Touval and I.W. Zartman, 'Mediation in Theory', in SAIS Papers in *International Affairs*, No. 6 (Westview Press, Boulder, 1985) pp. 7–17. This definition cannot accommodate multiple reasons for action; nor is it able to satisfactorily explain the reason for the involvement of international organisations ('Born to Mediate', *Mediation,* 1989, p. 120). The third difficulty is that of leverage: macro trade-offs such as 'shifts of position' (i.e. threats to change orientation) are not easily related or relevant to the *conduct* of mediation which is at a *micro* level concerned with textual and conceptual construction in most mediation.
7. Henry Kissinger, *Years of Upheaval* (Little, Brown, Boston, 1982) p. 883.
8. Thomas Princen, 'Mediation by the Vatican', in *Mediation in International Affairs* eds J. Bercovitch and Jeffrey Rubin (St. Martin's Press, 1992) pp. 154–5.
9. See V.D. Volkan, J.V. Montville and D.A. Julius, *The Psychodynamics of International Relationships* (Lexington Books, Massachusetts, 1991) pp. 41–69.

10   See John E. Hoffman Jr on the several competing and self-contained channels during the Iran hostage crisis between Iran and the United States, in Warren Christopher, *American Hostages in Iran* (Little, Brown, 1st edn, Boston, 1982) pp. 251–2. These included an informal envoy channel; banking channel; and German counsel to the Iranian Ministry of Foreign Affairs, via the Iranian embassy in Bonn.

11.   The formal 'grey' area channels between Iran and the US were finally merged in December 1980. See W. Christopher, op. cit., p. 255.

12.   See, for example, M. Delal Baer and Sidney Weintraub (eds), *The NAFTA Debate* (Lynne Rienner, Boulder, 1994) especially Chs 3 (environment) and 5 on US domestic politics of the US–Mexico Free Trade Agreement.

13.   Former British prime minister, Edward Heath was one of a number of senior former heads of government or foreign ministers who visited Iraq in 1992 to secure the release of hostages detained as a 'human shield' by Saddam Hussein.

14.   Former British Foreign Secretary Lord Carrington, who acted as mediator in the Yugoslav conflict, held meetings of respective factions at the head offices of Sotheby's in London.

15.   See James C. Jonah, 'The UN and International Conflict: the Military Talks at Kilometre Marker 101', in Bercovitch and Rubin, op. cit.

16.   Princen, op. cit., p. 162. Princen' notes:

In the Beagle Channel mediation, the location – that is, the Vatican itself – probably made a difference. The negotiators were constantly surrounded by the awesome ambience and when the mediator wanted to contact the decision-makers more directly, he would invite the foreign ministers with their advisors to come to Rome. Of course, the people who really needed to be impressed – namely the hard-line military leaders particularly in Argentina, never came.

17.   Ibid., p. 155.

18.   R.P. Barston, 'The Law of the Sea Convention', *Journal of World Trade Law*, Vol. 17, No. 3 (June 1983) pp. 207–24.

19.   See Ch. 5 and also Chs 10 and 11.

20.   See Henry Kissinger, *Years of Upheaval* (Little, Brown, Boston, 1982) p. 811 on avoiding setting time limits.

21.   In the 1979–80 Iran hostage crisis, President Carter decided on 21 Dec. 1980 to mount one last crash campaign to solve the matter with 30 days left before the end of the presidency. See Roberts B. Owen, in Christopher, op. cit., p. 311.

22.   Kissinger suggests that the term 'shuttle diplomacy' was coined by Joe Sisco as the US negotiating team flew between Aswan and Jerusalem, see op. cit., p. 799.

23.   On incremental methods which break a dispute into particular sub parts, see J.G. Stein, 'Structure, Strategies and Tactics of Mediation: Kissinger and Carter in the Middle East', *Negotiation Journal*, No. 1 (1985) pp. 331–47.

24.   The approach used in a number of mediation negotiations involving Henry Kissinger. See, for example, the Nov. 1993 Aswan talks between Israel and Egypt, in which he mediated. Kissinger wanted to approach the Aswan talks on the basis of principles but Sadat wanted definitive agreement. See Kissinger, op. cit., pp. 799 and 81; Ismail Fahmy, *Negotiating for Peace in the Middle East* (Johns Hopkins, Baltimore, 1983) p. 55.

25.   Establishing agreed timetables for withdrawal is an important method in disengagement negotiations. See James C. Jonah, 'The UN and International Conflict', in Bercovitch and Rubin, op. cit., p. 187.

26.   Roberts B. Owen in Christopher, op. cit., on the role of Algeria in narrowing the differences between the US and Iran. The talks were alternated between Algiers and Washington during Nov.–Dec. 1980.

27.   In the 1973 Israel–Egyptian disengagement negotiations on withdrawal of forces the issue of reopening and rebuilding the Suez Canal was extracted from the main negotiations, and dealt with by a side letter between the United States and Egypt. See Kissinger, op. cit., p. 835.

28.   The precise terms of the 1973 agreement concluded in parallel negotiations to the UN 'Kilometre 101' talks, by the US–Egypt and Israel, were not known to UN

negotiators. See James C. Jonah in Bercovitch and Rubin, op. cit., p. 187. Cf. Kissinger's account, op. cit., p. 802.

29. On the mediator's need to assess whether to transmit proposals, see Haig's reaction to Costa Mendez's proposals on sovereignty, 'I'm afraid we'll have to go home. Your proposals will be utterly unacceptable to the British', in *Caveat* (Weidenfeld and Nicolson, London, 1984) p. 281; p. 289.

30. Bercovitch, op. cit., pp. 19–20, sets out a framework which presents mediation as involving the possession and control of (mediator) resources (e.g. money, status, expertise, and prestige) classified in six categories: reward; coercion; referent; legitimacy; expertise and information. The resource-strategy focus tends to obscure the point that an important feature of most types of mediation is the *process* of creating acceptable negotiating concepts and drafting appropriate language. The role of concept building in negotiation is central to construction, readjustment and innovation. The mediation process is likely to be highly incremental and non-coercive. In multiparty disputes, the process could involve *multiple* and competing mediation, as well as other initiatives, constituting a complex framework in which mediation efforts may be supported or undermined and undertaken by more than one mediator.

31. See for example Haig, op. cit., p. 280.

32. See Report of the Secretary-General, S/24472, 21 Aug. 1992, para. 15.

33. In the Falklands conflict the Peruvian mediation approach of President Fernando Belaunde Terry was to attempt to approach the differences between the five basic points or principles: 'Simplify and we can still do it'. Quoted in Haig, op. cit., p. 293.

34. James C. Jonah notes: '… a significant characteristic of agreements arranged by Dr Kissinger is that they usually required very detailed and careful negotiation at a lower level to put their provisions into practical form', in Bercovitch and Rubin, op. cit., p. 154. See Kissinger, op. cit., pp. 799 and 811. Cf. Christopher, op. cit., for his attempt to establish principles at the meeting with the Iranian secret envoy 'The Traveller' (Sadegh Tabatbai) during the Iran hostage crisis, pp. 251, 302, 306.

35. See Lawrence Freedman and Efrain Karsh, *The Gulf Conflict: Diplomacy and War in the New World Order* (Princeton University Press, Princeton, NJ, 1993).

36. See note 29, p. 100. *Keesing* (Sept. 1993) 39658.

37. *Financial Times,* 24 Feb. 1995.

38. See report of the Secretary-General, 4 Dec. 1994 (S/1994/1376) and his letter dated 7 Dec. 1994 (S/1994/1395) on restoring the strength of UNAVEM II, and the authorising Security Council resolution 996 (1994), 8 Dec. 1994.

39. On the impact of leaks during the Haig shuttle diplomacy in the Falklands conflict, and the dispute with US Ambassador Kirkpatrick, see Haig, op. cit., p. 269, and pp. 285–6.

40. On the Secretary-General's Tadjik/Afghan border initiative, see SG/SM/5393, 23 Aug. 1994.

41. For example, the Vance–Owen plan on the partition of Bosnia–Herzegovina was unacceptable to the Bosnian Serb leadership and United States.

42. On abortive de Cuellar visit see *The Times,* 15 July 1982.

43. The UN-led 'Kilometre 101' talks on Israeli–Egyptian disengagement of forces were ultimately successful in part because of their remote location and absence of the media. In addition, the membership of the talks was confined to Egypt and Israel, plus UN officials. The first phase of the talks actually took place at kilometre 109 on 27 Oct. 1973, and not kilometre 101, because of a map-reading error. See Jonah, 'The UN and International Conflict', in Bercovitch and Rubin, op. cit., p. 181.

44. See James Mayall (ed.) The New Intervention (Cambridge University Press, Cambridge, 1996) on the UN role in Yugoslavia.

45. An interesting feature of both the 'Kilometre 101' and the Oslo talks is that in both instances after the breakthrough, the United States, having been shut out, reasserted its public diplomatic position through final phase talks, and (in the latter case) a signing ceremony in Washington. See Jonah's dry comment on Kissinger's intervention, op. cit., p. 186.

CHAPTER 13

The diplomacy of normalisation

Most states in the course of their political history undergo some periods of extreme hostility or abnormal relations with other states or organisations. In general, while many of these are resolved, a growing number persist or are only imperfectly resolved. There are too some states which choose to adopt a maverick isolationist orientation (e.g. Myanmar), or confrontational role (e.g. Iraq, Libya, Iran, North Korea). In this chapter we are concerned with the development of normalisation in the context of severe tension or sustained periods of abnormal relations, rather than abnormality associated with maverick states. As such the chapter will focus particularly on the factors which lead to abnormal relations, since these fundamentally affect subsequent attempts to re-establish normal relations. The remainder of the chapter will present an outline model of the normalisation process and discuss some of the main features of the normalisation process.

Definition of normalisation

Before defining normalisation three general points should be borne in mind. In the first place, there may not necessarily be a common conception of what is the cause of an abnormal state of affairs. Lack of congruence over the definitional aspects generally means that initiatives to improve relations are often not reciprocated and the conflict becomes punctuated by short-lived normalisation efforts. The foregoing argument also underlines a further issue when considering normalisation, and that is establishing a starting-point at which relations may have begun to become abnormal. It may not necessarily be the case that there is always a clear boundary line, such as the occupation of territory or a rupture in all major relations, to demarcate the transition. Finally, apart from questions over the causes of abnormal relations and transition, differences over how to proceed can create ambiguity over the necessary or essential conditions for the initiation of normalisation or steps towards further improvement.

With the above in mind, abnormal relations in this chapter are defined as follows: 'a change in the existing state of relations between states, or states and other actors, through the introduction or intrusion of issues or events which cause significant levels of disruption, tension or animosity between the parties.' Conversely, normalisation is seen as a process involving the recognition of the need for and the introduction of measures to reduce tension or friction; promote the improvement of relations; and isolate, contain or resolve, wholly or partly, major sources of dispute or tension.

The development of abnormal relations at a political level is often evidenced by lengthy and generally obdurate negotiations which are increasingly seen as unlikely to produce any significant results. While in some instances, the unresolved nature of a problem might be seen as being mutually beneficial (for example the Cyprus problem for Greece and Turkey), increasing dissatisfaction is generally accompanied by moves by one of the parties to escalate the problem or abandon negotiations. Thus, during the 1972 'Cod War' Britain and Iceland progressively widened the issues of dispute, following the introduction of Royal Naval protection vessels within the disputed 50-mile limit, culminating in the Icelandic threat to break off diplomatic relations with Britain on 11 September 1973.[1]

In the 1982 Anglo–Argentine conflict, Argentina terminated bilateral talks with Britain and closed the diplomatic channel.[2] It is worth reiterating here, in terms of the definition of abnormality, that there can be quite different perceptions of how serious a decline has occurred, and about the prospects for future negotiations, as the Anglo–Argentine example further suggests.[3]

Other indications of rising tension between states are formal protests, political attacks, retaliatory political action, and in extreme instances, ultimata. Diplomatic protest, while often used to express disapproval of a particular action, such as to condemn the passage of an aircraft or warship which has not been given appropriate clearance, or the behaviour of a diplomatic mission, can be used for a number of purposes including opposition to a policy. For example, the issue of economic conditions of workers in Hong Kong was made the subject of a protest by the People's Republic of China to the United Kingdom in May 1967, beginning a period of intense conflict and progressive deterioration in Sino-British relations.[4] Attacks on British diplomatic personnel and property in Peking and Shanghai, as relations deteriorated, led to a formal British protest later in May 1967.[5]

Introduction of sudden tension

In contrast to progressive deteriorations of relations, sudden tension can be introduced into and be the focus of bilateral relations by quite specific events. Occasionally, these may result from revision of policy following a change of government. Thus the political attack on the Chilean government of General Pinochet by the new British Labour Prime Minister in the House of Commons, was protested by the

Chilean government as 'offensive and intolerable language'.[6] More commonly, offence at intrusion into the domestic affairs of a state can produce sudden sharp deterioration. For example, the decision to permit the showing in Britain of the television film 'Death of a Princess', despite Saudi objections, led to a sharp deterioration in Saudi–British relations in 1980.[7] Of longer impact was the deterioration in Anglo–Chinese *political* relations following the British government's sanctions after the Tiananmen Square massacre in 1990.[8] The commencement of initial normalisation did not begin until 1991, which was symbolised in the visit of the British foreign secretary in April 1991 to China and Hong Kong though the overall scope of Sino–British normalisation remained limited.[9]

Sudden deterioration in relations of the kind under discussion is often signified by attacks on diplomatic personnel and property overseas as in the Sino–British Hong Kong conflict or against the British embassy in Teheran in the wake of the Iran hostage crisis.[10] Attacks too on symbols of overseas corporate presence such as banks and factories are further indicators of deterioration in conflicts which have a strong commercial element, as with attacks by labour union groups on British banks in Uruguay in support of Argentina to halt commercial links between the Falkland Islands and Uruguay in 1989.[11]

Retaliatory action

Other forms of retaliatory political action might be more symbolic than substantive. In expulsion cases, for example, the response to the initiating state might be deliberately low key through the expulsion of low-grade personnel in order to limit the damage to relations.[12] In some instances, though, a state may feel for reasons of political prestige that it has no choice but to make an *equivalent* expulsion, as did the former Soviet Union following the United Kingdom's expulsion of 105 Soviet diplomats on security grounds in September 1971.[13]

Communicating the state of relations

The extensive range of diplomatic methods gives states great flexibility in communicating the tone or state of actual or intended relations with other actors. These range from decisions about the level of diplomatic relations, the choice of envoy through to unilateral or joint termination of diplomatic relations. The downgrading of relations is a serious act, which may only be partially offset by non-residential accreditation and can lead to a general decline unless there are, for example, well established economic relations.[14]

The reversal of this is relatively rare, as is illustrated by one of the few cases in British foreign policy – the upgrading of relations with Guinea.[15] The level of representation can be altered in other ways, such as progressive reduction in staff until a point is reached where the staffing level is token, making it difficult in effect to carry out diplomatic functions. The progressive reduction of staff can be intended to signal foreign policy displeasure. The retention of even token representation, nevertheless, may be seen as important, as with the maintenance of a British diplomatic presence during the Iran hostage crisis[16] or the Gulf War,[17] as an indication of an unwillingness to move to breaking diplomatic relations, or for symbolic purposes.

The issue of non-appointment of an ambassador may arise in a number of different circumstances, including that following the recognition of a new state or government. Failure to nominate an ambassador or high commissioner is very often a 'wait and see' position linked to future behaviour and may reflect unease at the foreign policy of the receiving government. More usually non-appointment of an ambassador and the maintenance of relations at the level of chargé d'affaires occurs as a result of a recall and deterioration in relations. It is intended to indicate extreme sensitivity and displeasure over bilateral matters or some aspect of the receiving country's foreign policy. Thus the United Kingdom eventually restored diplomatic relations at ambassadorial level with Chile in January 1980, after the British ambassador was withdrawn in December 1975 over the arrest and torture of a British national, Sheila Cassidy. Explaining the decision, the Minister of State said that:[18] 'Britain's best interests were no longer served by the absence of ambassadors and the appointment of ambassadors would allow the government to make its views known at the highest level; and Dr Cassidy's case was not closed.' The decision to recall an ambassador may be used by the receiving government as a means of making it known that the return of the ambassador would be unwelcome. Such a serious step could lead to the reciprocal withdrawal of ambassadors. In, for example, the Dikko case, the United Kingdom, following the attempted abduction from London of Mr Umaru Dikko,[19] a former minister in the deposed Shagari government, expelled two members of the Nigerian High Commission in London. In addition, the Nigerian authorities were informed that the Nigerian High Commissioner, who had already been recalled for consultation, would not be welcome to return to Britain.[20] The Dikko affair provoked a major crisis in Anglo-Nigerian relations, which were already severely strained by international debt, IMF, trade credit and educational issues, as well as the financial debts of the Nigerian High Commission.[21] Despite the Nigerian government's apparent wish to limit the diplomatic damage,[22] a new High Commissioner was not appointed until February 1986.[23]

Breaks in diplomatic relations

Formal breaks in diplomatic relations vary in terms of their duration and effect. Those which have been caused by sensitivity to intrusion in domestic affairs tend to be the shortest in duration, at least in terms of *diplomatic* effects. The Saudi–British dispute over the film 'Death of a

Princess' led to a break of only five months.[24] The economic effects on contracts, however, were much longer lasting.[25] Breaks in diplomatic relations over a foreign policy issue can also be short, where the purpose is a nominal demonstration of opposition, as with some members of the OAU over British handling of Rhodesian UDI in 1965,[26] or Arab states towards Britain at the outbreak of the June 1967 Arab–Israeli War.[27]

More substantial disruptions have occurred where there have been persistently uneasy relations, or deep-seated foreign policy disputes, as between Britain and Iraq (1971–74),[28] or Britain and Guatemala over Belize (1981–86).[29] Lengthy breaks in diplomatic relations have also continued since 1986 between Britain and Libya,[30] as well as with Syria,[31] over abuse of diplomatic privileges and involvement with international terrorism.

Economic indicators of formal relations

As far as economic indicators of abnormal relations are concerned, retaliatory economic action can take several forms. There are first of all those actions which are linked to some form of diplomatic response, such as the reinforcement of a break in diplomatic relations linked to widening the impact of retaliatory action. For example, at the outset of the 1967 Arab–Israeli War, Algeria sealed the offices of three Anglo-Dutch Shell companies in Algeria,[32] while Iraq, in addition to breaking relations, banned British and United States aircraft from landing in Iraq. Economic retaliation may not necessarily be linked initially to diplomatic action but may serve as a precursor to more extensive retaliation as with the initial British restriction on military exports and Rolls Royce spare parts to Chile in 1974.

Where economic and diplomatic retaliation are linked, the question of normalisation can become problematical in terms of attempts to make progress in improving one or both levels of relations. Recognition of this point was made by the Guatemalan foreign minister, Sr Quiñónez Amequita, in commenting on Guatemala's decision to resume consular relations with the United Kingdom in August 1986 when he stressed:[33] '[the decision] had been motivated by the desire to facilitate trade between Guatemala and the United Kingdom. It did not mean that the restoration of full diplomatic relations between the two countries was imminent.'

In those instances where the focus of dispute is largely economic, the intensity of dispute can for all intents and purposes make the diplomatic channel ineffective. Indicators of abnormality include, for example, the continued retention of foreign assets, as in the United Kingdom's dispute with Yemen in 1980 over aircraft leasing payments.[34] In this and other instances where there is retaliatory action such as *restrictions* on the use of the goods and services of certain countries, e.g. the Malaysian 'Buy British last campaign' (1981–83) or the Pergau Dam affair (1994), the issue becomes a *focal point* affecting a wide range of transactions between the two countries. These cases should be distinguished, however, in terms of their implications for normalisation, from those in which economic retaliatory action aims to shut off another country, as over Guatemala's actions against Belize in 1981, including closure of the border, expulsion of Belize students from Guatemalan universities and cutting trade ties.[35] The latter cases would seem to present much greater problems for normalisation.[36]

In the final category under discussion here, we should note the effect of actions by or against nationals in precipitating inter-state tension and/or crisis. With the growth in both transnational activity and post-war civil conflicts, the potential scope for incidents involving nationals such as businessmen, tourists, airline pilots, expatriate technical aid personnel, mercenaries, human rights campaigners, religious mediators, sportsmen and even writers, has increased dramatically. Often these disputes over the conditions and release of detained nationals are a common source of varying tension and instability in bilateral relations. For example, the British pilots of the diverted aircraft involved in the kidnapping of Moise Tshombe were detained in Algiers, adding further tension to Anglo-Algerian relations, broken off earlier over Rhodesian UDI. In other instances, human rights cases, such as those involving the United Kingdom with Chile, Iran, Iraq, Malaysia, and the People's Republic of China, have become almost standard features as one of many issues of friction, which foreign secretaries periodically raise, but are occasionally elevated to become a central issue area. Furthermore, quite unexpected events can dramatically surface, as with the Salman Rushdie publication, illustrating the potential fragility of the process of normalisation.

The normalisation process

An indicative model of the stages or phases of normalisation is set out in Table 13.1. In the model ten stages or phases have been set out to indicate the possible phases through which normalisation might go. The model is indicative in that in some instances parties in a dispute may move quite quickly to direct negotiations, especially if there is a joint sense of urgency or defined issue at stake, omitting informal signalling or preparatory exchanges, e.g. economic pressures influencing the United Kingdom to seek *rapprochement* with Saudi Arabia following the dispute over 'Death of a Princess'.[37] In other instances, initial or intermediate states of normalisation may in fact become areas of impasse or deadlock and the withdrawal of concessions. In other instances, progress towards even limited normalisation may be extremely lengthy, e.g. the UK and Argentina[38] or the US and Vietnam,[39] because of the importance attached to single issues of principle. In both instances, domestic economic pressure however was important in influencing the decisions to resume financial and trade relations, and diplomatic relations.

Table 13.1   Stages of Normalisation

1. Re-establishment of contact using formal or informal channels.

2. Informal exchanges, e.g. in areas of procedural or substance disagreement; cease-fire arrangements, including exchange of prisoners of war.

3. Low-level signalling, e.g. conciliatory statements on dispute; positive public statements on changes of government or key officials; secret informal contacts; resumption of limited diplomatic relations.

4. Partial resumption of trade and financial relations.

5. Initiation or resumption of preparatory negotiations, e.g. via third parties, protecting powers or directly; secret negotiations either directly or at margins of other meetings.

6. Removal of trade or other embargo restrictions.

7. Policy revision; bureaucratic search for new formulae; willingness to make new or significant substantive concessions on a unilateral or reciprocal basis; high-level public signalling.

8. Normalisation negotiations on core issues.

9. Conclusion of normalisation agreements; re-establishment of full diplomatic relations.

10. Normalisation implementation.

Factors influencing the normalisation process

The process of normalisation will be influenced by several factors including the effect of the domestic and external setting; the scope of institutions; the relationship between levels of contact, including 'spill over'; and how far key stumbling-blocks to improved relations are removed or otherwise dealt with.

Carry over effects

As regards possible external influences from the setting, in those instances in which parties to an armed conflict are seeking to take initial steps to terminate hostilities and lay the basis for future normalisation, repercussions from cease-fire agreements or other arrangements to terminate hostilities can significantly affect relations after the end of hostilities. These include the geographic scope of the cease-fire; what weapons are covered and the terms and conditions set for future military operations by a defeated military power. A further 'carry over' factor of importance concerns the significance or weight attached to diplomatic institutions put forward prior to or during hostilities. Negotiators may have in some instances adopted advanced positions or made seemingly large concessions to avert conflict or bring hostilities to an early end. Diplomatic proposals put forward *prior to* hostilities may be subsequently withdrawn so creating a *barrier,* which limits future options. For example, at the end of the 1982 Anglo-Argentine war over repossession of the Falkland Islands, the then British Prime Minister, Mrs Thatcher, moved to a so-called 'Fortress Falklands' policy and refused to negotiate on the issue of sovereignty of the Falkland Islands, reversing earlier positions on diplomatic initiatives to resolve the dispute.[40]

Of the other external setting factors affecting normalisation, the previous track record of dispute settlement is especially important. In instances in which relations have been strained over a number of years, the normalisation process may be particularly vulnerable to renewed incidents, which either prevent *rapprochement* or produce agreements which are short-run.

Approaches to normalisation

In terms of efforts to *initiate* normalisation, a number of features need to be distinguished. In the first place, normalisation may be limited or delayed by differences over whether the normalisation of diplomatic relations should be the first step, or, merely part of other moves to bring about normal relations. The former restrictive view seeks to avoid linkage by defining the first stage as taking place through the establishment or resumption of diplomatic ties before other issues can be dealt with. The question of diplomatic relations, for example, was a feature of the Anglo-Albanian dispute after 1945, in which Britain insisted on the need for the establishment of diplomatic relations, before moving into the resolution of the major issue between the two countries – the return of Albanian gold held by Britain since the Second World War.[41]

Differences in approach to normalisation most frequently recur over the assessments each party makes over what they think are the most important issues to be resolved to enable normalisation to proceed. For example, after the Vietnam War, United States policy towards normalisation with Vietnam was based on a satisfactory resolution of the POW issue, whereas Vietnam considered relaxation of economic restrictions and economic assistance as critical measures. The question of differing 'states' of interests has been usefully addressed by Iklé using the concept of 'residual disagreement' in negotiations. Iklé distinguishes three forms of residual disagreement: *explicit* in the sense that issues are earmarked for future negotiations; *implicit,* in that an agreement may contain equivocal language, or *latent* if differences are ignored, reviewed as unimportant or put to one side, but later turn into serious dispute.[42] For example, British policy in the dispute with Argentina in the Falklands conflict gradually shifted from making the sovereignty question an area of *implicit* residual disagreement via trade to one which put sovereignty 'on hold'. The problems in using this approach, however, were increasingly underlined for Britain through Anglo-Argentine boundary disputes over straddling fish stocks, and more importantly, rights over the exploration and landing of potential oil discovered in Falkland Islands waters. 'Sovereignty' would not go away, despite convenient political fictions, and the vicissitudes of domestic Argentine politics.

The effect of the failure to include an issue on a normalisation agenda is clearly illustrated in the deterioration of Anglo-Nigerian relations because of the continued detention of British nationals despite apparent normalisation after the Dikko affair.[43] In this instance, while detention of British nationals was an important issue for Britain, it was not included within the main group of largely trade and debt issues, which were seen as the main vehicle for normalising Anglo-Nigerian relations. In effect a secondary issue eventually became a primary source of dispute.

Development of normalisation

Two aspects of the development of normalisation will be briefly discussed in this section: the 'transfer effect' of sectors of relations between two or more states, and the issue of the extent to which bureaucratic approaches to problem-solving inhibit the search for policy implementation shifts to break deadlock and further normalisation. At an economic level, normalisation initiatives frequently attempt to separate trade and financial relations from the political aspect of a dispute. A number of questions arise which centre on whether trade and other economic transactions remain discrete sectors of activity, largely without 'transfer effect' (e.g. enhanced political goodwill) or neutral as far as political impact on dispute settlement is concerned. Can international financial relations be resumed without prejudice to the political elements of a dispute? Other questions centre on some of the effects of the development of two-way trade on normalisation. The extent to which governments 'control' trade as an instrument of policy is frequently overstated. What are the implications for normalisation of bilateral relations of measures to reduce trade imbalances? Limitations on the ability to either correct imbalances or use trade for political purposes can lead to increasing domestic pressure to remove all trade restrictions and political conditions on trade normalisation. For example, following the Falklands conflict, the United Kingdom eventually abandoned the principle of trade reciprocity in July 1985, and withdrew unilaterally trade restrictions on Argentine goods and vessels coming into the United Kingdom.[44]

Solutions, shifts of policy and the bureaucracy

Of the stages listed in the normalisation process in Table 13.1, the most crucial is stage 7 – policy revision and the search for new formulae to facilitate solutions. Considerable attention has recently been devoted to foreign policy implementation and the extent to which decisions formulated by the executive are implemented by the bureaucracy.[45] A number of the propositions concerning weak or defective implementation are also supported from the diplomacy of normalisation. Bureaucratic limitations in creating new options are particularly evident at the stage of a major shift or concession to promote normalisation. A number of illustrations suggest that a combination of interdepartmental bureaucratic politics and traditional short-term approaches to problem-solving tends to limit or constrain the creation of new formulae to break the deadlock of inconclusive rounds of negotiations. For example, during the long-running abortive Anglo-Iranian negotiations in 1951–52, following Iranian nationalisation of the Anglo-Iranian Oil Company, the Foreign Office Persian Committee was requested by the British Foreign Secretary Eden to produce new proposals to break the deadlock at the resumed negotiations with Iran in the autumn of 1952. Ironically, pressure on the United Kingdom from the United States (which was presenting the UK position to Iran) to constantly redefine its position and come up with new proposals, caused added resistance within the Foreign Office and other UK Departments. In the event, no substantial new UK proposals to Mossadeq were forthcoming other than low-level incremental concessions, and Eden was reduced to restating his proposals of August 1952.[46]

Normalisation arrangements and agreements

Normalisation arrangements and agreements take a number of different forms. These include informal discussions supplemented by a unilateral statement on relations between the two countries; joint statements; partial normalisation arrangements through to formal normalisation agreements. Normalisation based on informal diplomatic exchanges and a unilateral statement (e.g. apology or statement of revised policy), as in the UK–Chile case, tend to be relatively short-lived and produce only limited results. In recognition of this some normalisation agreements may be deliberately limited in scope. For example the reopening of consulate facilities to promote trade may be seen as more important than resolving a long-standing political dispute (e.g. UK–Guatemala). Finally, we should note the use of *symbolic* normalisation agreements. A symbolic normalisation agreement is generally not related in substance to a dispute but is used to signal the 'new' state of relations (e.g. UK–Yemen Investment Agreement).[47]

Conclusion

In this chapter we have been essentially concerned with looking at the factors leading to the development of abnormal relations between states, as well as discussing some of the features of the initial phases of normalisation. Considerable variability exists in terms of the form in which the normalisation process develops. The *initial* phases of transition can be usefully considered through the concept of 'carry over' (e.g. terms and conditions of a cease-fire, whether or not ostensibly conciliatory proposals are restates or not after the cessation of hostilities). Diplomatic proposals may be withdrawn so creating *barriers* to further progress. Other types may take the form of conditions set by one or more parties which must be met before normalisation can be undertaken (e.g. political or economic reform). Important in this context are mutual perceptions of what constitutes an acceptable range of procedural and substantive concessions, initiatives and undertakings which would facilitate normalisation. In some instances normalisation hinges on one or two focal issues (e.g. return of annexed territory; renunciation of claims or return of persons or assets). The concept of *transfer effect* is useful in focusing attention on the effect of side or sectoral initiatives (e.g. resumed trade) on normalisation attitudes on core issues.

In other cases, reduction of hostility may be based on some form of normalisation agreement. In these instances, the evolution of subsequent normalisation initiatives can be usefully understood by analysing the agreement in terms of areas of *residual disagreement,* which may be explicit, implicit (e.g. equivocal or ambiguous language) or latent (issue side-stepped or postponed). Normalisation is seldom based on clear-cut concessions, but rather is the product of complex and shifting political and diplomatic compromise.

References and notes

1. 'The Anglo-Icelandic Fisheries Dispute', *International Relations*, Vol. 10, No. 6, Nov. 1974, pp. 576–9.
2. *Financial Times*, 3 April 1982; *The Times*, 8 April 1982.
3. For example, see the lack of response to the UN Secretary-General's visit by the United Kingdom, and the rejection of UN Resolution 37/9, 1982. *The Times*, 15 July 1982, and the British position on the link between negotiations and sovereignty, in *Hansard*, 15 Nov. 1982, Vol. 32, col. 31–2.
4. The dispute ostensibly began over wages paid at a plastic flower factory and developed into rioting. See *The Times*, 15 May 1967.
5. The protest was delivered through the acting Chinese chargé d'affaires in London, Mr Shen Ping. The subsequent seizure of the British mission in Shanghai on 14 Sept. 1967 marked a further point of deterioration and was the subject of a further formal protest. See *The Times*, 16 May 1966, and 20 Sept. 1967.
6. See *The Times*, 8 June 1974.
7. See *The Times*, 24 April 1980.
8. See *The Times*, 5 June 1989.
9. The subsequent visit of the British prime minister to China was preceded by that of the Chinese vice-premier to London. See *The Times*, 3 Sept. 1991.
10. Following clashes between police and Iranian demonstrators outside the US embassy in London, subsequent deportation of a number of students, and Iranian demonstrations outside the British embassy in Teheran during Aug. 1980, the British embassy suspended routine operations. Reduced staff continued residual tasks but the embassy was closed the following month as a safeguard against reprisals. See *The Times*, 13 and 18 Aug. 1980; 7 Sept. 1980.
11. British commercial interests in Uruguay were affected as part of demonstrations to prevent shipping services between the Falkland Islands, Uruguay and Chile. See *Times*, Jan. 1989.
12. In an intense period of expulsion from 1982 to 1984 involving the United Kingdom and Czechoslovakia, Britain attempted to indicate its desire to limit the effects of expulsion by expelling a low-grade clerical official from the Czech embassy in London. See *The Times*, 8 Jan. 1982.
13. See *The Times*, 9 Oct. 1971 for the text of the Soviet Note, and 23 Oct. 1971.

14. The withdrawal of the United Kingdom consulate from Taiwan in July 1971 marked a further stage in the decline of political relations, and continued sensitivity to the People's Republic of China. United Kingdom trade and commercial relations were largely unaffected. On the changing state of Anglo-Taiwanese diplomatic relations, see *The Times,* 21 July 1971.

15. The United Kingdom agreed to appoint a chargé d'affaires to Conakry after talks between the then head of government, Colonel Traoré and Mrs Thatcher in July 1984. Prior to this, diplomatic relations had been maintained at consulate level with the British ambassador to Senegal accredited to Guinea.

16. See *The Times,* 15 Aug. 1980.

17. Following the failure of the EC *démarche* to President Bani Sadr, EC governments recalled their envoys in protest and on 22 April imposed non-economic sanctions. EC ambassadors returned to Teheran on 27 April. See *The Times,* 14 and 28 April 1980.

18. See *The Times,* 17 Jan. and 1 Feb. 1980. See also *The Times,* 13 Jan. 1980 for a clarification on the Cassidy case by Mr Ridley (Minister of State, Foreign and Commonwealth Office, London).

19. *The Times,* 13 July 1984.

20. See Foreign Secretary, *Hansard,* 12 July 1984, col. 1366 and col. 1373. *First Report, Foreign Affairs Committee, House of Commons, Session 1984–85* for a review of issues relating to the diplomatic bag and overall government policy, pp. xxiii–xxxi. The British government decided to withdraw its High Commissioner on 15 July 1984. See *The Times,* 16 July 1984.

21. For a review of these, see *The Times,* 10 Jan. 1986.

22. This was apparently put forward following the meeting between the United Kingdom special envoy, Sir Roger du Boulay and the Nigerian Foreign Minister, Ibrahim Gambari. Sir Roger du Boulay, special envoy of Sir Geoffrey Howe, was a retired diplomat who had served in Nigeria from 1948 to 1958. See *The Times,* 12 and 14 Sept. 1984.

23. See *The Times,* 12 and 25 Feb. 1986. At the conclusion of a visit to Britain for talks with the prime minister in January 1986, the Nigerian foreign minister, Professor Akinyemi, indicated: 'that there were no longer any obstacles in the way of normalising diplomatic relations between London and Lagos. We are back on track.' See *The Times,* 10 Jan. 1986. Relations, however, remained tense over the closure of the UK visa office, trade and debt questions.

24. Prince Fahd ordered the British ambassador to leave within 48 hours in April 1980 and diplomatic relations were restored on 26 Aug. 1980. See *The Times,* 24 April 1980.

25. See *The Times,* 4 July 1980.

26. Nine of the 39 members of the OAU broke diplomatic relations with Britain between 15 and 18 Dec. 1965 over Rhodesian UDI: Tanzania, Ghana, Algeria, Congo (Brazzaville), Guinea, Mali, Mauritania, Sudan, UAR. The group resumed relations in 1966, except for the Algiers 'group' of Mali, Mauritania, Congo (Brazzaville) and Algeria which maintained the break until April 1968. Negotiations on the resumption of relations were held with Algeria on behalf of the Algiers group, by Sir Richard Beaumont, Deputy Under Secretary, Foreign and Commonwealth Office, from 17 to 22 March 1968. See *Keesing,* April 1968, p. 21181. Relations were only resumed with Tanzania.

27. The United Arab Republic resumed relations in December 1967 after breaking in 1965 over Rhodesia. See *Keesing,* Dec. 1967, p. 22433A.

28. *The Times,* 11 April 1974.

29. Diplomatic relations had been reduced from ambassadorial to consular level in July 1963, over British policy of increasing Belize's self-government. Guatemala withdrew its consulate in London in July 1981 and severed all remaining diplomatic links by closing the Guatemalan consulate in Belize. El Salvador took over representation of Guatemalan interests in London until 1986.

30. The United Kingdom broke diplomatic relations with the Socialist People's Libyan Arab Jamahiiya on 22 April 1984. An interests section was established by Libya in

the Royal Embassy, Saudi Arabia. For an outline of Anglo-Libyan relations from 1979 until the termination of relations following the shooting of WPC Fletcher outside the Libyan embassy, see *First Report,* Foreign Affairs Committee 1984–85, HMSO, London, 1985, pp. xxiii–xxvi.

31. Relations with the Syrian Arab Republic were broken on 31 Oct. 1986. Syria established an interests section in the Lebanese embassy.

32. *Keesing,* 11 June 1967, p. 22135.

33. *Keesing,* Sept. 1986, p. 34612, *The Times,* 2 Aug. 1986.

34. *The Times,* 17 Jan. 1980.

35. See *The Times,* 14 July and 8 Sept. 1981.

36. See for example Guatemala's reiteration of the rights to Belize; opposition to unilateral independence granted by the United Kingdom; non-recognition of Belize and non-acceptance of its land and maritime boundaries, in General Assembly, A138/PV.24 1983–4, 7 Oct. 1983, 38th Session, p. 67.

37. See note 24.

38. See Foreign Affairs Committee, 1983–84, Falkland Islands, Vol. 1, pp. xxiv–xxxix; and interim agreement of Madrid talks, Joint Statement by British and Argentinian delegations, 19 Oct. 1989.

39. The United States re-established diplomatic links with Vietnam on 11 July 1995. See *Financial Times,* 12 July 1995.

40. The 'Fortress Falklands' policy was symbolised in Mrs Thatcher's visit to the Falkland Islands in January 1983. See *Hansard* (House of Commons), 17 Feb. 1983, col. 218; *The Times,* 10 and 13 Jan. 1983.

41. *Financial Times,* 18 July 1995.

42. F.C. Iklé, *How Nations Negotiate,* p. 14.

43. See note 19.

44. The UK decision to remove trade relations restrictions would appear to have been taken surprisingly quickly. Contrast the reply of the prime minister to Mr Hoyle, rejecting exceptions, *Hansard* (House of Commons) 19 April 1985, col. 293, with Mr Eggar's statement explaining the lifting of restrictions in July 1985, *Hansard* (House of Commons) 18 Nov. 1985, col. 30. Argentina did not lift trade restrictions on direct British goods until 1 Aug. 1989. See *Financial Times,* 3 Aug. 1989.

45. S. Smith, M. Clarke (eds), *Foreign Policy Implementation* (Allen and Unwin, London, 1985).

46. The 20 Aug. United Kingdom proposals were based on an arbitration formula and set of principles for compensation. The small incremental concessions (carrot and stick) announced in Sept. 1952, which characterised the British approach were limited to the delivery of 16 railway locomotives to Iran. See Middleton to FO, Tel750, 27 Sept. 1952.

47 Yemen had been in conflict with the UK after a Yemeni Airways aircraft had been impounded in London on debt grounds. A UK–Yemen investment agreement was subsequently signed during the later visit of the North Yemen Foreign Minister. See *Keesing,* April 1980, p. 30200.

CHAPTER 14

International treaties

Introduction

Treaties can be defined as agreements which establish binding obligations between the parties, usually though not exclusively, states, and whose terms and provisions are governed by international law.[1] While treaties in the main take a written form, oral exchanges or declarations may give rise to commitments binding on the state or parties concerned.[2]

The Vienna Convention on the Law of Treaties defines treaties in terms of states, in the following way: 'An international agreement concluded between states in written form and governed by international law, whether embodied in a single instrument or in two related instruments and whatever its particular designation' (article 2).[3] The wider definition, however, includes agreements between states and international organisations and between international organisations *inter se*,[4] although for example McNair excluded agreements not in a written form.[5]

The term 'treaty' has in fact come to refer to a wide range of instruments. In its advisory opinion concerning the *Customs Regime between Germany and Austria*, the Permanent Court of International Justice noted *inter alia* that: 'from the standpoint of the obligatory character of international engagements, it is well known that such engagements may be taken in the form of treaties, conventions, agreements, protocols or exchanges of notes'.[6] Two points need to be mentioned therefore with respect to the definition of treaties. In the first place, not all instruments of an international nature are intended to have an obligatory character, as in the case of certain forms of declarations, which may set out aspects of policy or principles. Secondly, the requirement that the agreement be governed by international law serves to differentiate a treaty from other agreements between states or other subjects of international law, which are governed not by international law *per se* but by the national law of one of the parties (or mutually agreed national law of a third party). An agreement, for example, between two states for the supply of rice or petroleum products, from one of the parties, drawn up on the basis of a standard form of contract relevant to those commodities, would be governed by the terms of the contract, appropriate national regulations, as well as general principles of law, and not international law.

The criteria for determining whether an undertaking, oral agreement, document or set of documents, including an exchange of notes or correspondence, constitute an international agreement have been outlined in recent Department of State provisions and are worth citing as a clear indication of the considerations involved.[7] The four criteria identified were (1) the identity and intention of the parties, (2) the significance of the arrangements, (3) specificity, including criteria for determining enforceability, and (4) the necessity for two or more parties. As regards the first of these, the provisions stipulate that a party to an international agreement must be a state, state agency or an intergovernmental organisation and that the parties intend the undertaking to be legally binding and not merely for political or moral purposes. Thus the Helsinki Final Act would not, according to this view, be considered legally binding.[8] 'Significance' in the provisions is determined according to political importance, the size of grant made by, or credits payable to, the United States and the scale of continuing or future obligations. Under the third criterion, undertakings couched in vague or very general terms containing no objective criteria for determining enforceability or performance are not normally international agreements. The provisions under discussion also concluded that any oral agreement that meets the above criteria is an international agreement, but must be reduced to words.[9]

Treaties

In international relations treaties are the instruments for many kinds of legal acts ranging from bilateral or multilateral agreements on trade, customs, the creation of international organisations, to the ending of a military conflict and redistribution of territory.[10]

Treaties in the main are concluded in the following forms: (a) heads of state; (b) interstate; (c) intergovernmental; (d) international organisation.

The choice of the type of party may depend on political considerations, such as the degree of symbolic or political importance attached to the matter and constitutional requirements. The choice of form, however, does not affect the binding nature of the obligations. Treaties between states are less formal, and more frequently used than those in heads of state form. Traditionally, treaties were concluded in heads of state form, but in modern practice treaties can be concluded in heads of state, interstate and intergovernmental form. When used in interstate form, the expression 'contracting parties' or 'states parties' is normally used in the text rather than 'high contracting parties', in the heads of state form.[11]

The designation 'treaty' itself has frequently been reserved for international agreements which are considered to be of particular importance, such as a peace treaty, alliance (e.g. North Atlantic Treaty of 4 April 1949, the Southeast Asia Collective Defence Treaty of 8 September 1954) or marking significant changes in relationships (e.g. the Treaty of

Amity and Co-operation in Southeast Asia of 24 February 1976 signed at Bali; the Montevideo Treaty establishing the Latin American Free Trade Area, 18 February 1960; the Treaty of Rome establishing the European Economic Community of 25 March 1957 and the Treaty of Lagos of 27 May 1975).[12] However, state practice indicates that the range of issues regulated by treaty is now very wide, including such matters as extradition, navigation, treaties of friendship and setting up international institutions.[13] Treaties may be concluded bilaterally or multilaterally. The decision to use the designation 'treaty', rather than, for example, 'agreement' depends very much on individual state practice, assessments of the issue and the 'style' of conducting external relations.[14]

Conventions

Multilateral instruments of a law-making or regulative type are generally given the designation 'convention'. Conventions are normally negotiated under the auspices of international or regional organisations or diplomatic conferences involving states and other subjects of international law. Examples of codification conventions include: the Vienna convention on Diplomatic Relations of 18 April 1961;[15] the Vienna Convention on Consular Relations of 24 April 1963;[16] and the Vienna Convention on the Law of Treaties of 23 May 1969. Law-making or regulatory conventions negotiated through conferences include the Convention on the Prohibition, Development, Production and Stockpiling of Bacteriological and Toxin Weapons of 10 April 1972,[17] the several Geneva conventions dealing with international humanitarian law including the rights and status of combatants and civilians, e.g. Geneva Conventions of 12 August 1949;[18] Single Convention on Narcotic Drugs of 30 March 1961.[19] In the field of civil aviation, the Convention on International Civil Aviation (Chicago) 1944[20] sets out general principles of air law, such as exclusive sovereignty over airspace above a state's territory, the nationality and registration of aircraft and provisions for establishing a permanent International Civil Aviation Organisation (ICAO). Since 1947, ICAO itself has produced a number of conventions dealing with civil aviation standards and practices, as well as establishing rules on questions such as damage caused by aircraft to third parties (Rome, 1952)[21] and air 'piracy' through the Convention for the Suppression of Unlawful Seizure of Aircraft, The Hague, 16 December 1970.[22]

Treaties of a law-making or regulatory kind produced by the specialised agencies of the United Nations normally take the designation 'convention'. Examples of these are the various labour conventions produced by the International Labour Organisation (ILO), the Universal Postal Union and the telecommunication conventions.[23] Conventions have also been concluded by regional and other bodies such as the Council of Europe and the UN Economic Commission for Europe across a wide range of subjects such as human rights,[24] refugees[25] and transboundary pollution.[26] Conventions have also emerged from international and regional organisations in other areas such as maritime regulation and pollution control. The Intergovernmental Maritime Consultative Organisation, the main organisation in this field, was restyled International Maritime Organisation (IMO) in May 1982. It has concluded *inter alia* the 1973 International Convention for the Prevention of Pollution from Ships[27] and the International Convention for the Safety of Life at Sea (1974).[28] In order to avoid or reduce delays in entry into force and speed up the process IMO has developed the concept of express or tacit acceptance procedure.[29]

While the above conventions can be classified into a number of general types, such as if the purpose is predominantly codification, institutive or regulative, a great many conventions usually evidence more than one of these features. Modern practice, too, suggests that some of the so-called 'law-making' conventions have developed distinctive legal formats and characteristics which resemble administrative law rather than traditional international public law. For example, the United Nations Convention on the Law of the Sea, opened for signature in Jamaica in December 1982,[30] is not simply a codification instrument, but goes much further than the four 1958 Geneva Law of the Sea Conventions in establishing new types of international regulations, rights and responsibilities, for example for the Exclusive Economic Zone and Deep Sea-bed Area. The Law of the Sea Convention of 1982 resembles administrative law in the way regimes are formulated and in the considerable amount of devolution of power and responsibility to international organisations and diplomatic conferences to continue the process of building and developing maritime law.[31]

Although the above sections have discussed conventions as multilateral instruments produced by international and regional organisations, as well as diplomatic conferences, the designation is also used for many different kinds of bilateral treaties, such as on consular conventions and double-taxation conventions. As with other forms of treaties, conventions can be concluded in heads of state, interstate or in intergovernmental form. They can often be simple single-article instruments such as between France and Madagascar of 4 June 1973,[32] on postal and telecommunication matters, which has one article only *(article unique)* in which it is agreed to establish postal and telecommunication services.

Agreements

Treaties and conventions are the two most formal instruments in the range of various mechanisms available to states and other subjects of international law. Less formal and in more frequent use are agreements and exchanges of notes. Although less formal, the subject-matter covered by agreements need not be routine. Agreements are, in fact, used for a variety of purposes, such as establishing the framework and mechanisms for interstate trade co-operation,[33] land and maritime boundaries,[34] resolving debt questions,[35] fisheries regulations,[36] air services arrangements[37] and many other similar forms of undertaking. However, whatever the subject-matter, for an agreement to be properly considered as a treaty it is necessary to distinguish those agreements which are intended to have an obligatory character from those which do not.

Agreements are distinct from treaties and conventions in a strict sense in that the latter are generally of a more comprehensive kind and have a permanent subject-matter. Agreements normally take the form of a single instrument and tend to be bilateral rather than multilateral. Exceptions to the latter are agreements made by regional groupings or organisations, e.g. ASEAN agreements such as the Agreement on the Establishment of the ASEAN Secretariat,[38] signed at Bali on 24 February 1976, the Agreement on ASEAN Preferential Trading Arrangements, signed at Manila on 24 February 1977,[39] and the ASEAN Cultural Fund.[40]

In general, agreements are usually concluded between governments, rather than in heads of state or interstate form, and take the form of a single instrument.

Finally, it should be noted that agreements can be concluded between respective government departments in different countries. Interdepartmental agreements of this type have become very common, given both the increase in the volume of international business and the growing involvement of departments other than the foreign ministry.

Some examples of the subject-matter of international agreements in British practice are:

South Africa. Agreement for air services between and beyond their respective territories, 11 August 1992.[41]

South Korea. Agreement for co-operation in the peaceful uses of nuclear energy.[42]

Reciprocal Fisheries Agreement between the United Kingdom and United States with respect to the British Virgin and American Virgin Islands, 1983.[43]

Headquarters Agreement International Maritime Satellite Organisations, 25 February 1980.[44]

Russian Federation. Agreement on the establishment of direct secure telephone links between 10 Downing Street in London and the Kremlin in Moscow, 9 November 1992.[45]

Cameroon. Agreement concerning certain commercial debts, 3 November 1993.[46]

Examples of international agreements in Malaysian practice are:

Malaysia–Federal Republic of Germany Loan Agreement, 21 December 1976.[47]

Malaysia–Australia Sugar Supply Contract Agreement, 5 September 1974.[48]

Malaysia–Bahrain Air Services Agreement, 17 October 1994.[49]

Malaysia–Japan 8th Yen Loan Agreement (M$210 Million), 22 March 1982.[50]

Malaysia–Norway Double Taxation Agreement, 9 September 1971.[51]

Malaysia–Bosnia-Herzegovina, Croatia Trade Agreement in Encouragement and Reciprocal Protection of Investments, 26 October 1994.[52]

Malaysia–Saudi Arabia Cultural and Scientific Co-operation Agreement, 19 May 1976.[53]

Malaysia–ADB, 10 December 1981 (Batang Ai Hydropower Project).[54]

Malaysia–IBRD, 7 February 1983 (Kedah Valley's Agricultural Development Project).[55]

Malaysia–Vietnam Cultural Agreement, 30 March 1995.[56]

Exchange of notes

The most common and frequently used treaty instrument for recording agreements between governments is through an exchange of notes or letters. The exchange of notes can be between an ambassador or other appropriate representative and the ministry of foreign affairs of the country to which he is accredited; take the form of a letter between the foreign or other ministers (or their empowered officials) of two respective countries; or be in the third person. The initiating note will set out matters such as definitions, terms and attached schedules, if any, or other provisions. If these are acceptable then the initiating note and the other government's reply accepting these is to constitute an agreement.

In order to avoid the exchange becoming a correspondence through the passing of several notes, the terms of the notes to be exchanged are normally agreed upon through discussion beforehand. If the notes do not bear identical dates then the agreement takes effect from the date of the last note or such other dates as may be specified. Exchanges of notes are not usually bilateral and as a general rule do not require ratification. It should not be concluded, however, that the subject-matter need necessarily be routine in nature.

The following example illustrates the main features of an agreement in this form:[57]

No. 4703 Trade agreement between the Commonwealth of Australia and the Federation of Malaya signed at Kuala Lumpur on 26 August 1958.
Exchanges of notes constituing an agreement amending schedule to the above-mentioned agreement, Kuala Lumpur, 25 July 1968

Authentic Text: English
Registered by Australia on 12 January 1970

I
(EMBLEM)
Kuala Lumpur, 25th July 1968
Your Excellency,
I have the honour to refer to the Trade Agreement between the Federation of Malaysia and Australia, which was concluded at Kuala Lumpur on 26th August, 1958. Paragraph I of Article III of the Agreement provides that the Federation Government undertakes to apply to the Australian goods listed in Schedule A to the agreement, rates of duty no higher than those specified in that Schedule. In this connection, I refer to recent discussions between representatives of Malaysia and Australia regarding the desire of the Federation Government to levy a protective duty on wheat flour entering Malaysia.

Accordingly it is proposed that the item 'wheat flour' be deleted from Schedule A to the Agreement.

If the foregoing proposal is acceptable to the government of the Commonwealth of Australia, I have the honour to propose that this note and your reply in the same sense shall be deemed to constitute an agreement between our two governments to that effect, which agreement shall enter into force on the date of your reply.

Accept, Excellency, the assurances of my highest consideration.

Tan Sri (Dr.) LIM SWEE AUN, P.M.N., J.P.
Minister of Commerce and Industry Malaysia
His Excellency Mr. A.J. Eastman, C.B.E.
High Commissioner for Australia in Malaysia

From this example it can be also be seen that the exchange of notes was registered by Australia with the United Nations Secretariat on 12 January 1970 in accordance with article 102 of the United Nations Charter.

Exchanges of notes or letters constituting agreements do also occur frequently between states and international organisations in connection with a variety of questions, such as headquarters facilities, arrangements for peacekeeping forces and the arrangements and the costs to be borne in respect of an international conference hosted by a member country. In the following example, the exchange of letters concerns the financial and other related matters for the Second General Conference of UNIDO, held in Peru.[58] The exchange of letters between the executive director of UNIDO and the Peruvian Deputy Minister of Industry and Peruvian Permanent Representative to UNIDO, amended section V of the Lima agreement of 12 March 1975, on the financial arrangements for the conference to take into account the additional expenditure incurred by the Peruvian authorities. The agreement came into force on 26 March by the exchange of letters.

Declaration

Since 1945 declarations have increasingly been used by states, reflecting the growing number of new states entering the international scene, diverse political groupings and the perceived need to demonstrate collective co-operation, as well as project national and regional aspirations. Whether in fact a declaration constitutes a treaty *per se* is open to considerable uncertainty. Difficulties of classification arise over declarations which are primarily political documents concerning future policy intentions, such as the Anglo-Irish Declaration of December 1993 on Northern Ireland. In this context it is interesting to note the use of the term 'declaration' in the Anglo-Chinese agreement on the future administrative arrangements for Hong Kong after 1997. The choice of 'declaration' in this case would suggest the provisional and ambiguous nature of the instrument.

Another aspect of the difficulty can be found in declarations which have mixed purposes and language. For example, declarations of this type feature extensively in the diplomatic practice of ASEAN, which frequently seeks to exhort its members but often falls short of creating legally binding obligations. For example, the 1992 ASEAN Singapore Declaration contains a variety of general proposals for greater ASEAN political and security co-operation, including the Zone of Peace Freedom and Neutrality (ZOPFAN), and restructuring ASEAN institutions.[59] One section of the Singapore Declaration, however, on ASEAN functional co-operation, contains a mixture of political statement and more precise obligations of an administrative kind, on for example transfer of technology, the establishment of a student exchange programme in the ASEAN region, and measures to combat drug trafficking.

While certain declarations can be properly regarded as treaty instruments as such in view of their law-making function (e.g. Barcelona Declaration of 1921 recognising the right to a flag of states having no sea-coast),[60] or because of specific undertakings in the agreement (e.g. the declaration on the Neutrality of Laos, signed at Geneva on 23 July 1962),[61] others may not. In these latter instances, declarations published after a heads of government conference may partly contain agreements to do or not do something and partly statements of common policy, causing considerable difficulty in determining whether they may be regarded as a treaty instrument or are more properly regarded as policy documents. In general state practice suggests that declarations to have full treaty effect tend to be reinforced by treaty instruments. The Minsk Declaration on the Establishment of the Commonwealth of Independent States is an example.

Two further forms of declarations can be distinguished, both of which cannot be regarded as treaty instruments. Firstly, unilateral declarations by states, such as declarations of war, declarations by third states on the outbreak of war that they will remain neutral, or declarations during or prior to an armed conflict such as made by the United Kingdom with regard to the total exclusion zone during the Falklands conflict with Argentina in 1982, or the total exclusion zone declared by Iraq in the Iran–Iraq War, do not constitute treaties.[62] Secondly, declarations which take the form of a communication to other states of an explanation and justification of a line of action taken in the past, or explanation of views and policies on an issue such as the Spanish–Argentine Declaration on the Falklands and Gibraltar of 13 June 1984 are not treaties as such.[63]

Other forms of treaties

Treaties exist in a number of other forms apart from those discussed in the last section. Differences in title derive from a number of factors such as the political context in which the instrument was drafted, the type of subject-matter and others such as the institutional 'style' of the instruments produced by the organisation (e.g. international labour conventions).

Among other forms of treaties are charter (e.g. United Nations Charter, San Francisco, 1945),[64] pact, which is used often for an alliance or solemn undertaking (e.g. ANZUS Security Pact;[65] Kellogg–Briand Pact, 1928 on the renunciation of war,[66] properly titled Treaty Providing for Renunciation of War as an Instrument of National Policy, 27 August 1928; or non-aggression, e.g. South Africa–Mozambique Nkomati accord of 1984.[67] 'Pact' is also used as noted above in a journalistic sense to mean a collective agreement, e.g. 'Tin Pact' to refer to the Association of Tin Producing Countries, including Malaysia, Indonesia, Thailand and Bolivia. Other forms of treaties are constitutional, e.g. Constitution of the United Nations Educational, Scientific and Cultural Organisation (UNESCO);[68] statute, used to designate an instrument which regulates an international institution or regime, e.g. Statute of the Council of Europe,[69] Statute of the International Court of Justice.[70]

Miscellaneous treaty forms and other international instruments

The term 'act' has widespread use and is distinguished from 'general act' in that the designation 'act' usually refers to an instrument that is part of a complex of agreements. The act usually contains the main terms and provisions of a treaty and takes the form of a *chapeau*, such as the Act of the International Conference on Vietnam, of 2 March 1973, acknowledging the Paris agreement ending the Vietnam War.[71]

A further form of usage of 'act' is the general act, which need not be a treaty in the strict sense, forming rather part of the overall instrument. As a treaty instrument the general act is often of an administrative nature, e.g. the General Act for the Pacific Settlement of Disputes, of 26 September 1928,[72] prepared under the League of Nations, and the subsequent Revised General Act for the Pacific Settlement of Disputes, prepared under United Nations auspices, of 28 April 1949.[73]

Final act

The term 'final act' (*acte finale*) normally denotes a document which serves as a summary of the proceedings of an international conference. A final act is a form of *procés-verbal* and, accordingly, signature does not serve as an indication of being bound by the treaty or mean acceptance of the obligations contained in the treaty, which requires separate signature and ratification. In some circumstances the final act of a conference may contain not only the treaty or agreement itself but also resolutions connected with the treaty or agreement, including interim arrangements before the latter's entry into force. For example, the Final Act of the Third UN Conference on the Law of the Sea[74] provides in resolution I(2) that:

The commission (for the International Sea Bed Authority) shall consist of the representatives of states and of Namibia, represented by the United Nations Council for Namibia, which have signed the convention or acceded to it. The representatives of signatories of the Final Act may participate fully in the deliberations of the Commission as observers but shall not be entitled to participate in the taking of decisions.

In those cases in which a final act is produced by an international conference, the document records *inter alia,* the organisation of the conference, a survey of the texts and conclusions of the main committees and the texts of any resolutions. In the case of the third UN Conference on the Law of the Sea, the Final Act contained *inter alia*:

1. Record of the prior United Nations' resolutions on the law of the sea;
2. Dates of sessions;
3. Officers and committees;
4. Conference documents and outline of major developments;
5. Resolutions.

Apart from the question of the effect of signature with regard to a final act, a further issue is that of the status of annexes in the main convention.

In the Law of the Sea Convention, for example, article 318 of the Final Provisions of the convention stipulates that, unless otherwise provided, the annexes form an integral part of the convention. In contrast, resolutions contained in the Final Act are not incorporated in the main text of the convention, although there are references in the main convention to certain of the resolutions, e.g. article 308(5). In an effort to link the convention and the resolutions, paragraph 42 of the Final Act refers to the convention and resolutions I–IV 'forming an integral whole'.

Protocol

Of the other available international instruments, the protocol is widely used and extremely versatile. Eight main uses can be distinguished in international practice.

In the first place a protocol can be used to extend an agreement which is due to run out. International commodity agreements have, for example, been extended in this way: the International Olive Oil Agreement, the International Coffee Agreement and the International Wheat Trade Convention.[75] Second, a protocol may be used to amend or modify an agreement. Protocols are particularly used in this way in respect of agreements which are likely to need quite frequent revision, such as fisheries,[76] double-taxation agreements (DTAs), e.g. Protocol amending the Agreement for the Avoidance of Double Taxation between the United Kingdom and Trinidad and Tobago, 10 December 1969.[77] If subsequent amendments proved necessary these would normally be termed 'additional protocols' or 'further supplementary protocols'.[78] Protocols can be used for many other types of amendments, such as procedural amendment altering the membership of a technical commission of an international organisation[79] or the substantive provision of a multilateral law-making convention.[80]

Third, a protocol may be pursuant to the main provisions of an agreement. For example, the Protocol to the Franco-Soviet International Road Transport Agreement[81] is concerned with the application of the agreement and provides details of competent institutions and documentation procedures to facilitate road traffic in the two countries. Often a protocol may in fact be a separate instrument or set of instruments for dealing with questions connected with the running of an international organisation, such as the Fourth Protocol to the General Agreement on Privileges and Immunities of the Council of Europe – Provisions Concerning the European Court of Human Rights.[82]

Fourth, in those instances in which it is necessary to supplement an agreement, a protocol can be used for the additional provisions. For example, a supplementary protocol to an air services agreement may provide for additional fifth freedom landing rights, to allow either or both of the parties to pick up passengers at additional points in order to balance passenger trade between the respective airlines.[83]

Fifth, a protocol may be used to replace or supersede an existing arrangement, e.g. United States–Philippines Protocol[84] on safeguards with regard to the nuclear non-proliferation treaty, which replaced the tripartite agreement with the International Atomic Agency.

Sixth, a protocol may be an optional instrument to a main agreement, concluded with the aim of extending the area of possible substantive agreement, e.g. Optional Protocol to the Vienna Convention on Consular Relations of 24 April 1963.[85]

Seventh, a protocol can be a technical instrument within a general agreement. In this usage, protocols are especially found, though not exclusively, in trade agreements between the EC and third parties. The agreement between the EC and Portugal of 22 July 1972[86] has, for example, eight protocols, covering a wide variety of matters such as tariff quotas, product 'ceilings' and detailed provisions on the term 'originating products'. The treaty on European Union, Maastricht, 7 February 1992, lists 17 protocols, and 33 declarations.

Protocols can also be found within many other types of general agreements, including peace treaties, cease-fire and similar agreements. The short-lived Paris agreement of 27 January 1973, ending the Vietnam War, contained an attached protocol on the return of captured military personnel and captured foreign civilians.[87] Protocols may sometimes be used in a main agreement to indicate some technical exception or interpretation, though this is more normally done through a side memorandum or agreed minute.

Finally, protocols can be found in use as general instruments quite frequently in some treaty practice, being preferred to an agreement or exchange of notes, e.g. Protocol on Financial Co-operation between the Federal Republic of Germany and Brazil.[88] In the style of the European Union, the financial protocol is used to cover a wide range of economic arrangements with third parties.[89]

Memoranda of understanding

Memoranda of understanding are now in widespread use by states for regulating many aspects of their external relations in defence, aviation, commerce, education, science, industrial co-operation and other areas.[90] Whether they constitute international agreements in a strict treaty sense varies according to state practice. Much depends on the intentions of the parties and the terminology adopted.[91] Most are not published in official or other series and are not readily available beyond particular government departments, which tend to use the instrument most frequently. Indeed it may be some time before other departments become aware of an agreement. The latter point illustrates another aspect of the problem of national control over external policy, which was earlier highlighted in the discussion of national financial policy and the debt crisis (see Ch. 7). The main reasons why states use memoranda of understanding instead of treaties are speed, flexibility and confidentiality. Often they are adopted in order to avoid having a formal binding agreement. The delay arising from constitutional procedures is then avoided. Memoranda of understanding are flexible in that they can be brought into force without formal treaty procedures and amended by the respective agencies as appropriate. They are also frequently used by states to protect arrangements they have entered into involving sensitive political, commercial or other economic information.

In addition as a matter of style, certain states and groupings prefer to use informal instruments. For example the Commonwealth practice of using memoranda of understanding is perhaps in keeping with the concept of the Commonwealth as a club, with relations between members being furthered by informal rather than formal agreements.[92] Examples of memoranda of understanding are:

> Memorandum of Understanding between the United States and Soviet Union on the establishment of a Standing Consultative Commission, 21 December 1972.[93]

> Memorandum of Understanding to lay an undersea natural gas pipeline, Oman–India (Ministry of Petroleum), 11 May 1993.[94]

Memorandum of Understanding on Prohibiting Import and Export Trade in Prison Labour Products, China–United States, 7 August 1992.[95]

Memorandum of Understanding to provide Yen 400 million to keep the Straits of Malacca Pollution Free, Malaysia, Indonesia, Singapore, Japan, 13 February 1981.[96]

Memorandum of Understanding Implementing Guidelines for Transfers of Nuclear Related Dual Use Equipment, Material and Related Technology, 3 April 1992.[97]

A number of issues have arisen in the use of memoranda of understanding. In the first place there is the question of the status of the instrument. Reference to the title alone of an instrument can be misleading, since some documents although entitled memoranda use treaty language and establish legal obligations. With regard to the language of an instrument, British practice differs somewhat from that of the United States, in the weight given to the language used in deciding the status of an instrument. The use of 'shall' rather than 'will', an express indication that the exchange 'shall constitute an agreement between our two governments', rather than 'record the understandings' and 'enter into force' and not 'come into operation' or 'come into effect' are considered consistent with treaty language.

Memoranda of understanding are most often used as subsidiary instruments to treaties. That is they supplement the treaty by providing the framework for subsequent implementation. In air services agreements the main agreement is often accompanied by a confidential memorandum of understanding which contains the generally critical details of flight frequencies and capacities. Difficulties over a subsidiary memorandum of understanding can occur on signature, or after the instrument has become effective, over its status and the interpretation of its provisions. For example, such a memorandum subsidiary to a treaty may contain provisions which purport to amend or are in other ways inconsistent with a treaty. In the case of confidential memoranda, a common problem with civil aviation, arms purchase and similar arrangements, is that the agreements, given their informality, may be challenged or even repudiated by one or more of the parties. Equally, too frequent recourse to the modifying subsidiary memoranda of understanding can undermine the purposes of the governing treaty.

Two further issues are worth comment. As noted above, since memoranda of understanding may be considered confidential by a department or agency, the question can arise over the extent, if at all, the general public should be informed of their contents. For example, in a recent British case only the outline contents of the memorandum of understanding concluded with the United States on SDI contracts were released to Parliament.[98] The frequent use of memoranda of understanding undoubtedly creates another grey area in terms of its effect in reducing public knowledge about foreign policy. A related aspect, from a governmental perspective, is what has been called the 'retrieval' problem. A general argument earlier in other chapters has been put in terms of the modern problem of internal control over foreign policy. It can be argued that excessive use of memoranda of understanding can create retrieval problems, in that instruments remain unpublished and within the organisational 'memory', such as it might be, of an individual department or agency. Since memoranda of understanding remain unpublished it could be argued it may contribute to inconsistency, low norm setting and poor co-ordination in foreign policy.

Agreed minutes

An agreed minute is an informal instrument which may or may not be a treaty. Agreements and conventions are often accompanied by an exchange of side letters or an agreed minute,[99] which serve to provide elaboration on an issue[100] or reflect points of interpretation in a negotiation which do not appear in the main body of the text.[101] The use of signed records of minutes alone frequently reflects the provisional or tentative nature of the exchange or the perception of its level of importance.

Interim agreements

In those instances when states are unable to reach complete agreement on a problem, a *modus vivendi* may be reached through an interim agreement or arrangement. In such cases the parties are unable to reach a full or final resolution of the issue and seek accordingly to arrive at interim or temporary measures pending a settlement of a particular problem or certain overall aspects of a dispute. In the strategic arms field, the Interim Agreement, for example, between the United States and Soviet Union of 26 May 1972, which accompanied the Moscow ABM Treaty, ran under article 8 for five years.[102]

The style 'interim agreement' or 'arrangement' is often used as a device for reaching a *modus vivendi* or temporary solution in fisheries disputes: for example, the exchange of notes constituting an Interim Agreement between the United Kingdom and Iceland of 13 November 1973.[103] The agreement, which set out fishing areas, time periods for fishing and size of trawlers, was to run for two years. Article 3, in particular, provided that the termination of the agreement would not affect the legal position of either party with respect to the substantive dispute. The provision of a time limit on the duration of this agreement is generally found in arrangements of this type – although the actual title 'interim agreement' need not necessarily be used. For example, the agreement between the Government of the Gilbert Islands and the Government of Japan of 26 June 1978,[104] concerning the coasts of the Gilbert Islands, entered into force on signature and ran for two years. It is clear that by nature interim agreements, especially of this type, are at best temporary 'holding arrangements' and in consequence the parties face the prospect of almost continuous renegotiation of interim arrangements or arrangements to replace them.

The side-stepping of an issue holding up an *interim* solution is well illustrated by the Soviet–Japanese Interim Fishing Agreement of 24 May 1977. The dispute over the 200-mile exclusive fishing zone extension by Japan was complicated by the long-standing conflict over the disputed northern islands. The Interim Agreement used the manoeuvre of side-stepping the territorial stumbling-block and focused on fisheries only. Article 8 of the agreement provided that no provisions of the agreement could be 'construed so as to prejudice the positions ... of either Government ... in regard to various problems in mutual relations'.[105]

Interim agreements are also frequently used in air-services negotiations. The interim agreement provides a temporary mechanism to enable air services to be revised or new routes and frequencies added. For example, the United States–Federal Republic of Germany Interim Agreement on Aviation Transport Services of 27 April 1993 has been periodically revised.[106]

Interim agreements can be used in circumstances other than those in which the parties are in considerable dispute over an issue. Thus, a state may wish to establish a temporary framework pending more technical negotiation. For instance, a substantial rise in financial investment in a foreign country by a state's corporation may lead it to consider an interim agreement on investment protection with that country, for reasons of political confidence.[107] Again, pending a comprehensive arrangement, states may seek an interim arrangement, as for example with the United States–GDR agreement, in this case termed an agreed minute on consular matters: 'The two governments agreed that pending entry into force of a comprehensive consular agreement their consular relations will be based on the Vienna Convention on Consular Relations, which they regard as the codification in most material respects of customary international law on consular relations.'[108] In the event that international agreement is seen as unlikely or the terms possibly unacceptable, states also sometimes safeguard their interests through an interim agreement, as for example the agreement between the United States, United Kingdom, FRG and France, on interim arrangements[109] of 2 September 1982 relating to the regime for exchanging co-ordinates of deep sea-bed mining operations for polymetallic modules.

Formalities of treaties

The following section examines some of the formal questions concerned with finalising and concluding treaties.

Language

A bilateral treaty drawn up between two countries sharing the same language will be drawn up using that language.[110] A treaty may, however, be drawn up in a language other than that of the parties. In those cases in which the treaty is drawn up in the language of the parties and a third language (e.g. French, Korean and English), the third language normally prevails in the event of any divergence of interpretation.[111] In cases in which more than one language is used,[112] particularly in a bilateral treaty, it is important that the languages used in the texts are harmonised by the appropriate drafting group to minimise excessive divergence of meaning.

The languages of treaties prepared under the auspices of the United Nations are Arabic, Chinese, English, French, Russian and Spanish, the official working languages of the United Nations.

Signature

Bilateral treaties are prepared for signature in duplicate in order that each of the two parties may have precedence in the original it retains, in terms of, if appropriate, language and title. Each country will appear first in the title and preamble of the origin it retains and the order of signature either above or to the left of the document. The country in whose capital the treaty is going to be signed is normally responsible for preparing the treaty for signature. Unless a treaty provides otherwise, it will come into effect from the date of signature. Exceptions to this are those instruments which make the entry into force of the treaty dependent on ratification. Entry into force is then achieved through an exchange of instruments of ratification.[113]

In exceptional circumstances a treaty, subject to ratification, may come into force provisionally, pending the ratification – for example the Malaysia–Indonesia Trade Agreement, 16 October 1973 (article VIII).[114]

Initialling and signature

In some circumstances, particularly if there is likely to be some delay before the conclusion of negotiations and signature, a treaty may be initialled as a means of authenticating the text. Initialling itself can be the equivalent of signature if this is the agreed intention of the parties. This is the case with less formal instruments, such as the memoranda of understanding. In other cases, initialling may really mark a stage in the negotiating process, for example where a text is referred back to their governments by the negotiators. Further contact or negotiation may be required before a text is agreed for signature.

Entry into force

Entry into force may be made conditional on matters other than the number of ratifications. This is especially so in respect of technical international agreements. In international shipping agreements, entry into force may be made conditional on ratification or accession by states possessing a particular percentage of world gross shipping tonnage in order to give the greater effectiveness. Entry into force after signature (e.g. ninety days) is a device which enables the parties to make the appropriate technical adjustments, or administrative changes (e.g. in civil aviation schedules, visa regulations). In international loan agreements entry into force in multiparty instruments of the World Bank, or ADB, is made conditional on the subsidiary loan arrangements being concluded satisfactorily, and the loan becomes effective at a date specified in the agreement, for example ninety days after signature.

Registration

The concept of registering treaties has essentially been aimed at lessening the effect of secret diplomacy. By requiring states to register their treaties and agreements it was hoped to bring greater openness into international relations. The concept of registration was especially associated with US President Woodrow Wilson (open covenants of peace, openly arrived at). The League of Nations provided for registration under article 18 and in particular that 'no such treaty shall be binding until so registered'. The significant change in article 102 of the Charter of the United Nations from article 18 is avoidance of the principle that unregistered treaties would lack binding force for the parties in question. As for the act of registration itself, registration of an instrument does not confer on that instrument the status of a treaty or agreement. In other words, registration cannot validate or make effective instruments which have failed to fulfil the requirements laid down by international law. On the other hand, failure to register a treaty or agreement does not invalidate it, though the position of the parties may be affected before organs of the United Nations. Instruments lodged with the UN Secretariat for registration include treaties and agreements concluded between states, and made by or with the specialised agencies and other organs of the UN, declarations accepting the compulsory jurisdiction of the ICJ and other miscellaneous treaty matters such as termination, ratifications, accessions and details of supplementary treaties. In general, however, most states in practice take a restrictive view of registration out of political preference, for administrative reasons, or the wish to maintain the confidential nature of a transaction. Conversely, there are those high-profile states who selectively use registration – for example of aid or technical assistance agreements – to demonstrate their 'active' involvement in international relations.

Duration

Unless a treaty specifically expresses otherwise, no specific duration is set. In those cases in which it is felt necessary (e.g. visa abolition;

investment protection agreement; commodity supply arrangement; technical assistance agreement on training) to limit the duration, a specific provision is required on the length of the agreement and the procedures to be allowed upon expiry.

A common device used in certain agreements is the so-called 'revolving formula' by which upon the expiry of an agreement provision is made for the continuation of the agreement for further periods of one year, provided that neither of the contracting parties indicates in writing to the contrary by a specified date prior to expiry.

Reservation

A reservation is a unilateral statement in whatever form made by a state when signing, ratifying or acceding to a treaty, issued with the intention of excluding or modifying the legal effects of particular provisions. Reservations in this sense should be distinguished from interpretative statements made during the negotiation process and declarations made by states on signature, ratification or accession. Such statements or declarations could take the form of clarification of provisions which are unclear or ambiguous. In so far as a declaration seeks to modify the intention of a provision or denounce as non-applicable or unacceptable a provision, then the better view is that it should be considered as a reservation.

Implications of reservations

The question as to the effect of reservations becomes acute with regard to multilateral agreements. The issue of reservations can also be relevant in a bilateral treaty context. In a bilateral treaty specific provision can be made through either an accompanying confidential memorandum of understanding or in an attached protocol.

As regards multilateral instruments, the issues which arise include the effect on: (i) the position of a state which accedes to a treaty with reservations *vis-à-vis* the treaty; (ii) states objecting to the reservation *vis-à-vis* the reserving state; (iii) those states who accept the reservations. For example, the issues are illustrated in the case of the separate objections of Hungary, FRG and Belgium, to the individual reservations made by Bahrain, Egypt and Morocco, to article 27(3) of the Vienna Convention on Diplomatic Relations.[115]

In an attempt to overcome those types of difficulties many international conventions adopt a 'no reservations' formula, or a provision to the effect that reservations are not permitted unless otherwise specifically allowed for in the provisions.

The review of the issue by the International Law Commission concluded with recommending that, in those cases where reservations were permitted, it would be a matter for the objecting state as to how it would view its relations with the reserving state. This approach is amplified in articles 20 and 21 of the 1969 Vienna Convention on the Law of Treaties.

Notice of termination

In considering the question of termination it is important to distinguish termination which is permitted or implied within a treaty from unilateral denunciation or withdrawal. A treaty may be considered to remain in force unless it has been brought to an end by provisions in the treaty relating to expiry or lapse, or the parties have consented, in the absence of such provisions, to terminate it. Many treaties contain provisions of this kind which set a specified period for the duration of the treaty.[116]

The right of termination proper is provided for in modern treaty practice through provisions for denunciation or withdrawal from the treaty upon giving a specified period of notice. Provisions may be drafted to allow for a withdrawal or denunciation after an initial period (e.g. three years following entry into force) or withdrawal at any time upon notice, taking effect generally six months after receipt of the notification of denunciation or withdrawal. An exception to the latter is for the withdrawal or denunciation at any time to take immediate effect. An example of this is article XVIII of the articles of agreement of the IMF, 27 December 1945.[117] More difficult is the question of under what circumstances a state may unilaterally withdraw from a treaty which contains no provision for withdrawal or denunciation with or without notice. While in the main unilateral withdrawal under these circumstances is contentious, grounds may exist if there is evidence to indicate the parties intended a right of unilateral termination on notice, or the subject-matter of the treaty implied the existence of such a right.

Article 56(1) of the Vienna Convention on the Law of Treaties provides that:

> A treaty which contains no provision regarding its termination and which does not provide for denunciation or withdrawal is not subject to denunciation or withdrawal unless:
> (a) it is established that the parties intended to admit the possibility of denunciation or withdrawal; or
> (b) a right of denunciation or withdrawal may be implied by nature of the treaty.

The scope for dispute, however, in instances of unilateral withdrawal from a treaty which does not contain provision for withdrawal or denunciation is considerable. At this point it is sufficient to note that the Vienna Convention on the Law of Treaties nevertheless sets out three possible grounds a party may invoke for terminating or withdrawing from a treaty: a material breach of a bilateral treaty by one of the parties (article 60(1)); impossibility of performance (article 61(1)), although this may not be invoked by a party if inability to carry out the obligation is a result of the breach of the obligation by that party of the treaty (article 61(2)); and third, fundamental change of circumstances (article 62). The convention follows a relatively restrictive definition of fundamental change:

1. A fundamental change of circumstances which has occurred at the time of the conclusion of a treaty and which was not foreseen by the parties, may not be invoked as a ground for terminating or withdrawing from a treaty unless:
    (a) The existence of those circumstances constituted an essential basis for the consent of the parties to be bound by the treaty; and
    (b) the effect of the change is radically to transform the extent of obligations still to be performed under the treaty.
2. A fundamental change of circumstances may not be invoked as a ground for terminating or withdrawing from a treaty:
    (a) if the treaty establishes a boundary; or
    (b) if the fundamental change is the result of a breach by the party invoking it either of an obligation under the treaty or of any other international obligation owed to any other party to the treaty.
3. If, under the foregoing paragraphs, a party may invoke a fundamental change of circumstances as a ground for terminating or withdrawing from a treaty it may also invoke the change as a ground for suspending the operation of the treaty.

Procedure for termination

A notice of termination, withdrawal or denunciation is communicated through the diplomatic channel from the relevant authority to the other party or parties, or depository government or authority.

The notice must follow the manner and procedure provided for in the treaty or in the Vienna Convention. Unless the treaty provides otherwise, conditions cannot be attached, and the notice of termination will apply automatically to any other documents integral to the treaty such as protocols, annexes, agreed minutes and declarations.

The notice takes effect from the period set, if any, from the date of deposit of the notice with the other party. It may be withdrawn or revoked before it takes effect.

Summary

In this chapter we have been concerned to examine the range of modern international agreements. Along with the growth in the volume of treaties and agreements a notable trend is in the diversity of instruments. Of the range of instruments in British practice, exchange of notes and agreements are the most frequently used.[118] A more important feature of the diversity of instruments is the increasing use of informal instruments such as memoranda of understanding and gentlemen's agreements. Informal instruments are often used for reasons of administrative ease, speed and political or commercial secrecy. Use of such instruments does give rise to a number of issues including the effect on public accountability and the enhancement of bureaucratic power in diplomacy. There are, too, inevitably problems connected with the interpretation and binding nature of informal instruments, particularly memoranda of understanding, in the event of political and administrative change.

A final important change is in the content of agreements. States and other entities conclude agreements in order to manage better particular aspects of their external relations. Thus, greater governmental involvement in the economic sector has seen the emergence of a number of novel government-directed trade agreements. On the other hand, failure to accommodate conflicting interests has resulted in increasing use in many areas of interim-type agreements which in themselves reflect the fragility and incompleteness of the understandings. Apart from using agreements to promote interests and resolve conflict, states seek to reduce risk. In this respect in particular the content of agreements is rapidly altering to reflect the broader diplomatic agenda with agreements on such matters as investment protection, counter-terrorism and the intergovernmental regulation of securities markets. Above all, the expansion in the subject-matter of agreements underlines the growing fusion of public and private interests in many areas of modern diplomacy.

References and notes

1. Treaty collections vary considerably in terms of availability and coverage. For treaties deposited with the United Nations, see the Multilateral Treaties deposited with the Secretary-General (ST/LEG/SER.E.3) and the *UN Treaty Series* (*UNTS*). The *UNDOC* current index ST/LIB/SER.M.71 (Part II) contains information on texts, reports of conferences and occasionally information on registers of certain treaties, e.g. UNEP. Countries produce information on agreements concluded in gazettes and foreign ministry bulletins while a number have national treaty series. For example, United States treaties are published on a calendar basis in *United States Treaties and other International Agreements* (*UST*) and singly in the *Treaties and Other International Acts Series* (*TIAS*) published by the Department of State. Other relevant sources are *Foreign Relations of the United States*, *Treaties in Force*, the *Federal Register*, *Digest of US Practice in International Law* and *Department of State Bulletin*. United Kingdom treaties appear as Command Papers and on entry into force in the *UK Treaty Series* (*UKTS*), which is indexed annually. For a consolidated index see Clive Parry and Charity Hopkins, *An Index of British Treaties 1901–1968* (HMSO, London, 1970). European Community treaties with third parties can be found, along with internal directives, in the *Official Journal*. The external treaties of the Community are in *Treaties, Agreements and Other Bilateral Commitments Linking the Communities with Non-Member Countries* (I/29/84 EN), and *The European Community, International Organisation and Multilateral Agreements*, 3rd rev. edn (Commission of the European Communities, Luxembourg, 1983). Other sources for agreements and related documents can be found in *International Legal Materials* and the various yearbooks of national and international law associations and similar organisations. For example, the *Italian Yearbook of International Law* has a treaty section and the Japanese *Annual of International Law* has a documents section and a chronological list of bilateral and multilateral treaties concluded by Japan. M.J. Bowman and D.J. Harris, *Multilateral Treaties: Index and Current Status* (University of Nottingham Treaty Centre, Nottingham, 1992) is a useful general though essentially European-based index of agreements, which does not cover other regional agreements, e.g. ASEAN trade law or other functional areas. ASEAN agreements are contained in the ASEAN Documentation Series (ASEAN Secretariat, Jakarta); ILO agreements can be found *inter alia* in the ILO *Legislative Series 3/85*; the ICAO in the index to ICAO publications, and Thomas Buergenthal, *Law Making in the International*

Civil Aviation Organisation (Syracuse University Press, 1969) pp. 231–6 for a note on ICAO documentation; Chia-Jui Cheng (ed.), *Basic Documents on International Trade Law* (Martinus Nijhoff, Dordrecht, 1986); and M.H. Claringbould, *Transport: International Transport Treaties* (Kluwer, Antwerp, 1986). Council of Europe agreements are published in the *European Treaty Series* (*ETS*). For agreements on maritime law see R.R. Churchill and A.V. Lowe, *The Law of the Sea* (Manchester University Press, 1985), and R.R. Churchill and Myron Nordquist (eds), *New Directions in the Law of the Sea*, Vols I–XI (Oceana, Dobbs Ferry, NY, 1973–81). The office of the Special Representative of the Secretary-General for the Law of the Sea has begun to collate data on the history of the Law of the Sea Convention, as well as treaties relevant to it. Among these are *The Law of the Sea: Pollution by Dumping* (United Nations, New York, 1985) and *Multilateral Treaties Relevant to the United Nations Convention on the Law of the Sea* (United Nations, New York, 1985). Charles Rousseau and Michel Virally's *Revue Générale de droit international public* (A. Pedone, Paris) is a very useful survey of a wide range of current international issues, covering, for example, agreements, territorial claims, disputes and breaks or resumptions of diplomatic relations. A valuable collection of treaty provisions for dispute settlement can be found in *A Survey of Treaty Provisions for the Pacific Settlement of International Disputes* (United Nations, New York, 1966).

2. For discussion of the main issues concerning treaties see Lord McNair, *The Law of Treaties* (Clarendon Press, Oxford, 1961) Ch. XV, pp. 272–305. On rules concerning interpretation of treaties see L. Oppenheim, *International Law: A Treatise*, Vol. I, 8th edn, H. Lauterpacht (ed.) (Longman, London, 1967) pp. 950–8. See also Ian Brownlie, *Principles of International Law,* 3rd edn (Oxford University Press, London, 1979); D.P. O'Connell, *International Law*, 2nd edn (Stevens and Sons, London, 1970); T.O. Elias, *The Modern Law of Treaties* (A.W. Sijhoff, Leiden, 1974); Paul Reuter, *Introduction au droit des traités* (Armand Colin, Paris, 1972).

3. UN Doc. A/Conf. 39/27, 23 May 1979, and *UKTS*, No. 58 Cmnd. 7964. The convention entered into force on 27 Jan. 1980. See UN Multilateral Treaties, ST/LEG/SER.G/, 1982, p. 619.

4. See Vienna Convention on the Law of Treaties between States and International Organisations or between International Organisations, which was opened for signature on 21 March 1986. For text see *Revue Générale de droit international public* (1986) pp. 501–44.

5. For further discussion of this point see Lord Gore Booth, *Satow's Guide to Diplomatic Practice* (Longman, London, 1979) p. 236, and McNair, op. cit.

6. Gore Booth, op. cit., p. 238.

7. The provisions are pursuant to 1 USC 1126 (the Case-Zablocki Act) requiring disclosure to Congress of all concluded agreements and consultation by agencies with the secretary of state over proposed agreements. See *Code of Federal Regulations* (*CFR*), Vol. 22 (1985) pp. 448–54.

8. Ibid., p. 448.

9. Ibid., p. 450.

10. See O'Connell, op. cit., pp. 195–205 on the classification of treaties.

11. Gore Booth, op. cit., pp. 240–1.

12. North Atlantic Treaty, 4 April 1949, *UNTS*, Vol. 34, p. 243; South-East Asia Collective Defence Treaty, 8 Sept. 1954, *UNTS*, Vol. 209, p. 23. By a decision of the council of the Southeast Asia Treaty Organisation on 24 Sept. 1975, the organisation ceased to exist as of 30 June 1977. The Collective Defence Treaty, however, remains in force; Treaty of Amity and Co-operation in Southeast Asia, 24 Feb. 1976, *Foreign Affairs*, Malaysia (March 1976) p. 80; the Latin American Free Trade Area, established by the Treaty of Montevideo, 18 Feb. 1960, was replaced by the Latin American Integration Association, concluded at Montevideo on 12 Aug. 1980, *ILM*, Vol. 20, p. 672. Treaty Establishing the European Economic Community (EEC), *UNTS,* Vol. 298, p. 11. The Economic Community of West African States was set up by the Treaty of Lagos, 27 May 1975, *West Africa*, 16

June 1975, p. 679, while the treaty establishing the East African Community came into force on 1 Dec. 1967. The community was dissolved in 1977 and finally wound up on 10 July 1984. See *The Times*, 12 July 1984.

13. See Bowman and Harris, op. cit., pp. 481–90.
14. Hans Blix and Jirina H. Emerson, *The Treaty Maker's Handbook* (Ocean Publications, Dobbs Ferry, NY, 1973). On the effect of international revolution on diplomatic style see Philippe Ardant, '*China's Diplomatic Practice During the Cultural Revolution*', in Jerome A. Cohen, *China's Practice of International Law* (Harvard University Press, Cambridge, Mass., 1972) pp. 86–128.
15. *UNTS*, Vol. 500, p. 95. Entered into force, 24 April 1964.
16. *UNTS*, Vol. 596, p. 261. Entered into force 19 March 1967.
17. *UKTS*, No. 11, 1976, Cmnd. 6397.
18. Conventions for the protection of war victims concerning (i) amelioration of the conditions of the wounded and sick armed forces in the field (238); (ii) amelioration of the condition of wounded sick and shipwrecked members of armed forces at sea (239); (iii) treatment of prisoners of war (240); (iv) protection of civilian persons in time of war (241), *UNTS*, Vol. 75, p. 31.
19. *UNTS*, Vol. 520, p. 151; Vol. 557, p. 280.
20. *UNTS*, Vol. 15, p. 295; Thomas Buergenthal, *Law Making in the International Civil Aviation Organisation* (Syracuse University Press, 1969).
21 *UNTS*, Vol. 310, p. 181.
22 *UNTS*, Vol. 860, p. 105.
23 See Edward W. Plowman, *International Law Governing Communications and Information* (Frances Pinter, London, 1982).
24. European agreement on transfer of responsibility for refugees, 16 Oct. 1980, Misc. No. 3, 1981, Cmnd. 8127.
25. Council of Europe, *Directorate of Human Rights of Aliens in Europe* (Martinus Nijhoff, Dordrecht, 1985).
26. *Convention on Long-Range Trans-Boundary Air Pollution*, 13 Nov. 1979, Misc. No. 10, 1980, Cmnd. 7885.
27. Done at London 2 Nov. 1973; entered into force 2 Oct. 1983; see R.R. Churchill and A.V. Lowe, *The Law of the Sea* (Manchester University Press, Manchester, 1985) pp. 220–1.
28. *UKTS*, No. 46, 1980, Cmnd. 7874.
29. See R.P. Barston and P.W. Birnie, *The Maritime Dimension* (George Allen and Unwin, London, 1980) pp. 116–20.
30. UK Misc. No. 11, 1983, Cmnd. 8941.
31. See Churchill and Nordquist, op. cit.; for further discussion on the evolution of state practice see R.P. Barston, 'The Law of the Sea', *Journal of World Trade Law*, Vol. 17, No. 3 (May–June 1983) pp. 207–23, and 'The Third UN Law of the Sea Conference', in G.R. Berridge and A. Jennings, *Diplomacy at the UN* (Macmillan, London, 1985) pp. 152–71.
32. *UNTS*, Vol. 978, p. 361.
33 Chia Jui Cheng, *Basic Documents on International Trade Law* (Martinus Nijhoff, Dordrecht, 1986).
34. See J.R.V. Prescott, *The Maritime Political Boundaries of the World* (Methuen, London, 1985); Philphot Tansubkul, *Asean and the Law of the Sea* (Institute of Southeast Asia Studies, Singapore, 1982).
35. Lars Kalderen and Qamar S. Siddiqi, *Sovereign Borrowers* (Butterworths, London, 1984).
36. J.E. Carroz and M.J. Savini, 'The New International Law of Fisheries Emerging from Bilateral Agreements', *Marine Policy*, Vol. 3 (1979) pp. 79–98; P. Coper, 'The Impact of UNCLOS III on Management of the World's Fisheries', ibid., Vol. 5 (1981) pp. 217–28; FAO, *Fisheries Technical Paper*, No. 223 (FIPP/T223, 1982); *International Joint Ventures in Fisheries* (FAO, Rome, 1983); Gerald Moore, 'Limits of Territorial Seas, Fishing Zones and Exclusive Economic Zones' (FAO, Rome, 1985). *Coastal State requirements for Foreign Fishing* (FAO, Rome, 1985).

262 *Modern diplomacy*

37. Anthony Sampson, *Empires of the Sky. The Politics, Contests and Cartels of World Airlines* (Hodder and Stoughton, London, 1985).
38. *10 Years Asean* (ASEAN Secretariat, Jakarta, 1977) pp. 125–32; *Foreign Affairs,* Malaysia (March 1976) pp. 21–6.
39. Alison Broinowski (ed.), *Understanding ASEAN* (Macmillan, London, 1982) pp. 283–93; *Foreign Affairs,* Malaysia (March 1977) pp. 41–50.
40. Agreement on the Establishment of the ASEAN Cultural Fund (ASEAN Documents, Jakarta, 1980) pp. 76–80.
41. *UKTS,* No. 78, 1992, Cmnd. 2105.
42. *UKTS,* No. 38, 1992, Cmnd. 1961.
43. *UKTS,* No. 32, 1983, Cmnd. 8932.
44. *UKTS,* No. 44, 1980, Cmnd. 7917.
45. *UKTS,* No. 12, 1993, Cmnd. 2223.
46. *UKTS,* No. 26, 1994, Cmnd. 2543.
47. *Foreign Affairs,* Malaysia (Dec. 1976) p. 57.
48. *Foreign Affairs,* Malaysia (Sept. 1974).
49. *Foreign Affairs,* Malaysia (Dec. 1994) p. 63.
50. *Foreign Affairs,* Malaysia (March 1982) p. 92.
51. *Foreign Affairs,* Malaysia (Sept. 1971) p. 93.
52. *Foreign Affairs,* Malaysia (Dec. 1994) p. 63.
53. *Foreign Affairs,* Malaysia (June 1976) p. 65.
54. *Kertas Statut,* 43 Tahun 1982.
55. *Kertas Statut,* 116 Tahun 1983.
56. *Foreign Affairs,* Malaysia (March 1995) p. 49.
57. *UNTS,* Vol. 325, p. 253.
58. *UNTS,* Vol. 962, p. 399.
59. 31 *ILM,* 498 (1992).
60. *UNTS,* Vol. 7, p. 73.
61. *UNTS,* Vol. 456, p. 301.
62. See R.P. Barston and Patricia Birnie, 'The Falkland Islands/Islas Malvinas Conflict: A question of Zones', *Marine Policy,* Vol. 7, No. 1 (Jan. 1983) p. 20 *passim.*
63. *Financial Times,* 14 June 1984.
64. *UNTS,* Vol. 1, p. xvi.
65. Security treaty between Australia, New Zealand and the United States (ANZUS), 1 Sept. 1951, in J.A.S. Grenville, *The Major International Treaties 1944–73* (Methuen, London, 1974) pp. 337–9.
66. *LNTS,* Vol. 94, p. 57.
67. *The Guardian,* 4 July 1984.
68. *UNTS,* Vol. 4, p. 275.
69. *UNTS,* Vol. 87, p. 103.
70. *UKTS,* Vol. 67, 1946, Cmnd. 7015.
71. *UNTS,* Vol. 935, p. 405.
72. *LNTS,* Vol. 93, p. 343.
73. *UNTS,* Vol. 71, p. 101.
74. UK Misc. No. 11, 1983, Cmnd. 8941.
75. Olive Oil Agreement extended by protocol, 23 March 1973, *UKTS,* No. 58, 1979, Cmnd. 7581; International Coffee Agreement, extended 26 Sept. 1974, *UNTS,* Vol. 982, p. 332, and protocol for the fourth extension of the Wheat Trade Convention, 26 April–17 May 1978, *UKTS,* No. 1, 1980, Cmnd. 7775.
76. Protocol on Procedures and Conditions for Japanese Salmon Fishing in the North East Pacific Ocean, *UNTS,* Vol. 1402, p. 253.
77. *UKTS,* No. 70, 1970, Cmnd. 4444.
78. The Anglo-Swedish Convention for the Avoidance of Double Taxation (as amended) 27 Sept. 1973, *UKTS,* No. 33, 1974, Cmnd. 5607, is a good illustration of this usage, with the protocol being used as the means to bring into effect the several amendments to the convention.

79. See, for example, the modification of Article 56 of the Convention on Civil Aviation of 7 July 1971, extending the membership of the Air Navigation Commission from 12 to 15 members, *UNTS*, Vol. 958, pp. 217–18.
80. See, for example, the protocol amending the Paris Convention on Obscene Publications, 4 May 1949, *UNTS*, Vol. 47, p. 159.
81. *UNTS*, Vol. 951, p. 187.
82. Paris, 16 Dec., 1971, *UKTS*, No. 58, 1971, Cmnd. 4739.
83. Protocol supplementary to the Air Services Agreement, 13 April 1970 between the United Kingdom and Soviet Union, *UKTS*, No. 42, 1970, Cmnd. 4388.
84. 21 Feb. 1973, *UNTS*, Vol. 963, p. 267.
85. Vienna Convention on Consular Relations, 24 April 1963, *UNTS*, Vol. 596, p. 262, p. 470, and Optional Protocol Concerning the Compulsory Settlement of Disputes, p. 488.
86. UK Misc. No. 51, 1972, Cmnd. 5164.
87. Protocol to the agreement on ending the war and restoring peace in Vietnam concerning the return of captured military personnel and foreign civilians, *UNTS*, Vol. 935, 1974, p. 202.
88. 7 March 1974, *UNTS*, Vol. 945, p. 163.
89. See, for example, financial protocol between the EC and Greece 28 Feb. 1977, *UKTS*, No. 91, Cmnd. 7839, and between the EC and Cyprus (with Final Act), 15 Sept. 1977, *UKTS*, No. 31, 1979, Cmnd. 7490.
90. See McNair, op. cit., p. 15.
91. Anthony Aust, 'Memoranda of Understanding: The Theory and practice of Informal International Instruments', *The International and Comparative Law Quarterly*, Vol. 35 (1986) pp. 787–812.
92. A number of institutions in the Commonwealth have been set up by informal instruments. The Commonwealth Secretariat was established by an unsigned and undated 'Agreed Memorandum', Cmnd. 2713.
93. The memorandum was part of the large number of agreements at the height of *détente* signed at or subsequent to the SALT I negotiations, *UNTS*, Vol. 944, p. 28. See also the Protocol relating to Commercial Activities, Pursuant to the Oct. 1972 Trade Agreement, 22 June 1973, *UNTS*, Vol. 938, p. 128.
94. *Financial Times*, 11 May 1993.
95. 31 *ILM*, 1071 (1992).
96. *Foreign Affairs*, Malaysia (March 1981) p. 89.
97. 31 *ILM*, 1094 (1992).
98. *Hansard*, 9 Dec. 1985, cols. 623, 629, 631, 634.
99. The defence leasing arrangements between the United Kingdom and the United States for the Turks and Caicos Islands provide a good illustration of the use of a memorandum of understanding and an agreed minute. The memorandum to the main agreement deals with *inter alia* exemption from taxation and the status of local regulations, while the agreed minute refers to article X of the agreement on civil claims, and clarifies the procedures under which islanders can make claims against the United States Government. See *UKTS*, No. 42, 1980, Cmnd. 7915.
100. United States–German Democratic Republic Agreed Minute on Negotiations Concerning the Establishment of Diplomatic Relations, 4 Sept. 1974, *UNTS*, Vol. 967, p. 336.
101. The agreed minute in this case records the main issues and points of interpretation in the negotiations. See *UNTS*, Vol. 953, p. 293. Cf. United States–Philippines agreement of 30 April 1974 (agreed minute) *UNTS*, Vol. 953, p. 161.
102. *UNTS*, Vol. 944, p. 3.
103. *UKTS*, No. 122, 1973, Cmnd. 5484.
104. *Kiribati Gazette*, No. 5, 29 May 1981.
105. See Horoshi Kimura, 'Soviet and Japanese Negotiating Behaviour', *Orbis*, Vol. 24, No. 1 (Spring 1980) p. 67.
106. United States–Federal Republic of Germany, Interim Agreement on Aviation Transport Services, 27 April 1993. Text Department of State.

107. See the interim agreement between France and the Republic of Korea of 22 Jan. 1975. The agreement entered into force on signature and provided for termination either on the entry into force of the reciprocal convention or within a maximum of three years *UNTS*, Vol. 971, p. 385.
108. *UNTS*, Vol. 967, p. 336.
109. *UKTS*, No. 46, 1982, Cmnd. 8685.
110. Multilateral socialist treaties were either drawn up in Russian or the language of some of the parties. For example, the Charter of Comecon was in Russian; the Russian, Polish, Czech and German versions are authentic. The other language apart from Russian might be that of the depository country. For example, the 5 July 1962 Customs Convention is in Russian and German, since the GDR was the depository of the convention. See György Haraszti, *Some Fundamental Problems of the Law of Treaties* (Akadémiai Kiadó, Budapest, 1973) pp. 174–9. For the agreement establishing the Commonwealth of Independent States (Belarus, Russian Federation and Ukraine) see 31 *ILM*, 138 (1992).
111. The English text of the 25 June 1971 Soviet–Argentinian trade agreement is specifically designated under the provisions of the agreement as the text to be used for interpretation and reference, *UNTS*, Vol. 941, p. 14.
112. See F.A. Mann, *Foreign Affairs in English Courts* (Clarendon Press, Oxford, 1986) pp. 107–9 on foreign texts in British Courts.
113. In some multilateral treaties the date of entry into force is suspended until some contingent circumstances occur, such as a given number of ratifications is achieved for entry into force.
114. Ministry of Trade, Malaysia, 1973, p. 8.
115. *UNTS*, Vol. 798, p. 341; Vol. 973, p. 328.
116. Under Article VI of the Long Term Agreement between the United States and Soviet Union, 29 June 1974, the agreement remained in force for ten years, *UNTS*, Vol. 961, p. 118. A further example is the 1975 United Kingdom–Poland five-year trade agreement, *UKTS*, No. 64, 1976, Cmnd. 6874. When agreements of this type run out they are frequently kept in force, pending a new agreement, by an exchange of notes. An alternative procedure if there is a time limit set to the duration of the agreement is to include a simple provision in the final section to allow for the continuation of the agreement for further periods (e.g. of 12 months) provided that one or more of the contracting parties does not express objection to the continuation.
117. *UKTS*, No. 21, 1946, Cmnd. 6885.
118. A survey of British practice over the period 1972–82 based on the *UK Treaty Series* indicates that exchanges of notes on average account for some 40 per cent of the instruments concluded.

CHAPTER 15

International agreements: case studies

In this chapter we look at five types of international agreements concerning: arrangements for embassies and consulates; trade; financial loans; fisheries; and cultural, educational and technological co-operation.

Arrangements for embassies and consulates

The arrangements regarding the establishment and operation of embassies and consulates are often concluded in the form of informal memoranda of understanding, reflecting their essentially private and sensitive nature, even for states enjoying relatively normal relations. The relevant international agreements concerning the operation and functioning of diplomatic missions include *inter alia* the Vienna Convention on Diplomatic Relations,[1] Vienna Convention on Consular Relations,[2] and that for relations between international organisations.[3]

The issues arising regarding sites are extensive, including such questions as reversion of title to freehold property; dates and payments under lease arrangements; application of planning regulations, including alteration of buildings; interim arrangements and the effect of the revision of any sites agreement or obligations under the existing agreement. In some instances as a mark of political good will, economic expediency, or to facilitate securing an appropriate site in congested high-cost national capitals,[4] reciprocal arrangements are agreed to charge nominal or token rent. The vacation of existing embassy premises and provisions for new premises involve similar, often lengthy negotiations. The following extract from the United Kingdom–Oman Agreement,[5] illustrates a number of these, including vacation of existing property; cost of relocation and title; planning and cessation of use.

AGREEMENT
BETWEEN THE GOVERNMENT OF THE
UNITED KINGDOM OF GREAT BRITAIN AND NORTHERN IRELAND
AND THE GOVERNMENT OF THE SULTANATE OF OMAN
CONCERNING THE VACATION OF THE BRITISH EMBASSY
COMPOUND IN MUSCAT AND THE PROVISION OF NEW BRITISH
EMBASSY PREMISES

The Government of the United Kingdom of Great Britain and Northern Ireland ("The Government of the United Kingdom"), and The Government of The Sultanate of Oman ("The Government of the Sultanate of Oman"),

Wishing to arrange for the vacation of the existing British Embassy premises and the provision of new British Embassy premises with freehold title;

Have agreed as follows:

ARTICLE 1

The Government of the United Kingdom shall:

(a) on or before 31 January 1993 vacate that part of the existing British Embassy premises marked in red as "Site Area A" on the plan attached at Annex A;

(b) on or before 1 January 1995, vacate the remainder of the existing British Embassy premises marked in green as "Site Area B" on the plan attached at Annex A;

(c) on or before 1 January 1995, vacate the additional site at the existing British Embassy premises known as the British Embassy tennis court, marked in yellow as "Site Area C" on the plan attached at Annex A;

(d) on or before 1 January 1995, vacate the additional site at the existing British Embassy premises known as the British Embassy Escort Lines, marked in red as "Site AIea D" on the plan attached at Annex B.

ARTICLE 2

The Government of the Sultanate of Oman shall take sole possession of and responsibility for those parts of the existing British Embassy premises specified in Article 1 of this Agreement on the day following the date of vacation by the Government of the United Kingdom.

ARTICLE 3

The Government of the Sultanate of Oman shall:

(a) in accordance with the schedule set out below, pay to the Government of the United Kingdom the sum of ten million pounds sterling (£10,000,000) by way of contribution towards the cost of relocating the British Embassy:
  (i) two million five hundred thousand pounds sterling (£2,500,000) upon signature of this Agreement by both parties; and
  (ii) two million five hundred thousand pounds sterling (£2,500,000) not later than 31 January 1993; and
  (iii) two million five hundred thousand pounds sterling (£2,500,000) not later than 31 March 1993; and
  (iv) two million five hundred thousand pounds sterling (£2,500,000) not later than 30 September 1993.

(b) upon the date on which this Agreement enters into force, transfer absolutely ownership and title to the Government of the United Kingdom of the site at Al-Khuwair, known as site no. 33, which is marked in red as "Site Area E" on the plan attached at Annex C, for the purposes of construction of a new British Embassy and related accommodation, such site to include additionally the area of land marked in yellow as "Site Area F" on the plan attached at Annex C and the existing vehicle access way and existing sub-station site marked in green as "Site Area G" on the plan attached at Annex C;

(c) provided the proposed buildings at Al-Khuwair (Site Area E) conform to the laws and regulations enforced by the Muscat Municipality and planning authorities, authorise planning consent for the proposed buildings.

ARTICLE 4

The Government of the Sultanate of Oman shall:
(a) transfer absolutely ownership and title to the Government of the United Kingdom of the site at Rawdha marked in red as "Site Area H" on the plan attached at Annex D, for the purpose of constructing the Residence of the Ambassador of the United Kingdom of Great Britain and Northern Ireland;
(b) provided the proposed buildings at Rawdha (Site Area H) conform to the laws and regulations enforced by the Muscat Municipality and planning authorities, authorise planning consent for the proposed bnildings;
(c) in addition to the existing access to Site Area H from the public highway, grant a vehicular right of way to the Government of the United Kingdom over the tracks to the south of Site Area H on to the public highway.

ARTICLE 5

In order to secure freehold title to the sites specified in Articles 3 and 4 above for the Government of the United Kingdom, the Government of the Sultanate of Oman shall take all necessary steps according to the law. Such title shall, however, be subject to the following matters:
(a) such ownership and title are exclusively for the purpose of occupation as the British Embassy with related accommodation and as the Ambassadorial Residence and cannot be assigned or transferred in any way whatsoever to any third party;
(b) in the event that the Government of the United Kingdom has no further need for the sites for the purposes mentioned above they shall notify that fact to the Government of the Sultanate of Oman in writing. Title to the sites shall revert to the Government of the Sultanate of Oman three months after such notification;
(c) the sea shore shall not be part of either property. It may be used by the Embassy and Residence, but may not be fenced or otherwise interfered with.

ARTICLE 6

This Agreement shall enter into force on the date of signature.

In witness whereof the undersigned, duly authorized thereto by their respective Governments, have signed this Agreement.

Done in duplicate at Muscat this fourth day of January, 1993, in the English and Arabic languages, the two texts being equally authoritative. In case of divergence between the two texts the English text shall prevail.

For the Government of the United Kingdom of Great Britain and Northern Ireland,	For the Government of the Sultanate of Oman,
T.J.CLARK	QAIS ZAWAWI

Consulates

The following example of the United Kingdom–People's Republic of China mutual agreement to establish consulates-general[6] illustrates several aspects of consular agreements, including inviolability and special duty of the receiving state to protect the premises against intrusion or danger (article 3); number of officers (article 4); immunity (article 7) and rights of consular officers to communicate with nationals arrested or committed to prison (article 8).

AGREEMENT BETWEEN THE GOVERNMENT OF THE UNITED KINGDOM OF GREAT BRITAIN AND NORTHERN IRELAND AND THE GOVERNMENT OF THE PEOPLE'S REPUBLIC OF CHINA ON THE ESTABLISHMENT OF A BRITISH CONSULTATE-GENERAL AT SHANGHAI AND A CHINESE CONSULATE-GENERAL AT MANCHESTER

The Government of the United Kingdom of Great Britain and Northern Ireland and the Government of the People's Republic of China;

Proceeding from the common desire to develop friendly relations and strengthen consular relations between the two countries;

Have agreed to establish a Consulate-General of each country in the other, as follows:

ARTICLE 1

(1) The Government of the People's Republic of China gives its consent to the Government of the United Kingdom to establish a Consultate-General at Shanghai, with the consular district comprising the Shanghai Municipality directly under the jurisdiction of the Central Government and the Provinces of Jiangsu and Zhejiang.

(2) The Government of the United Kingdom gives its consent to the Government of the People's Republic of China to establish a Consulate-General at Manchester, with the consular district comprising the counties of Greater Manchester, Merseyside, Lancashire, Tyne and Wear, North Yorkshire, South Yorkshire, West Yorkshire, Durham and Derbyshire.

(3) The dates on which the two Governments will establish the above-mentioned Consulates-General shall be determined by mutual agreement.

ARTICLE 2

In accordance with the relevant laws and regulations of their respective countries, and following friendly consultation, the Contracting Governments shall mutually provide necessary assistance for the establishment of the Consulates-General, including assistance in the acquisition of premises for the Consulates-General and accommodation for its members.

ARTICLE 3

(1) The consular premises shall be inviolable. The authorities of the receiving State may not enter the consular premises without the consent of the head of the consular post or the head of the diplomatic mission of the sending State, or a person designated by one of those persons.

(2) The receiving State is under a special duty to take all appropriate steps to protect the consular premises against any intrusion or damage and to prevent any disturbance of the peace of the consular post or impairment of its dignity.

(3) The provisions of paragraph (1) of this Article shall likewise apply to the residences of consular officers.

ARTICLE 4

(1) Unless otherwise agreed by the Contracting Governments, the number of members of the consular post shall not exceed the limit of 30 persons, of which that of consular officers shall not exceed the limit of 10 persons, and that of consular employees and members of the service staff shall not exceed the limit of 20 persons.

(2) Consular officers shall be nationals of the sending State, and not nationals or permanent residents of the receiving State.

ARTICLE 5

(1) The receiving State shall take all steps necessary to provide full facilities for the performance of consular functions by the consular officers of the sending State.

(2) With the consent of the receiving State, consular officers shall be able to exercise consular functions in areas outside their consular district when necessary. The receiving State shall render necessary assistance in this regard.

ARTICLE 6

The receiving State shall treat consular officers with due respect, and shall take all appropriate steps to prevent any attack on their person, freedom or dignity.

ARTICLE 7

(1) Members of the consular post and members of their familiar shall be immune from the criminal jurisdiction of the receiving State and shall not be liable to arrest or detention pending trial.

(2) Members of the consular post shall be immune from the civil and administrative jurisdiction of the receiving State in respect of any act performed by them in the exercise of consular functions.

(3) The provisions of paragraph (2) of this Article shall not apply in respect of a civil action:

(*a*) relating to private immovable property situated in the receiving State, unless the member of the consular post holds it on behalf of the sending State for the purposes of the consular post;

(*b*) relating to succession in which the member of the consular post is involved as executor, administrator, heir or legatee as a private person and not on behalf of the sending State;

(*c*) relating to any professional or commercial activity exercised by the member of the consular post in the receiving State outside his official functions;

(*d*) arising out of a contract concluded by the member of the consular post in which he did not contract, expressly or impliedly, on behalf of the sending State;

(*e*) by a third party for damage arising from an accident in the receiving State caused by a vehicle, vessel or aircraft.

(4) No measures of execution shall be taken against any of the persons mentioned in this Article, except in the cases coming under subparagraphs (*a*), (*b*)

and (*c*) of paragraph (3) of this Article and provided also that the measures concerned can be taken without infringing the inviolability of the person concerned or of his residence.

(5) Members of the consular post and members of their families may be called upon to attend as witnesses in the course of judicial or administrative proceedings. If a consular officer or a member of his family should decline to give evidence, no coercive measure or penalty shall be applied to that person. Consular employees and members of their families, as well as members of the service staff and members of their families, may not decline to give evidence except as provided in paragraph (6) of this Article.

(6) Members of the consular post are under no obligation to give evidence concerning matters relating to the exercise of their official functions or to produce official correspondence or documents. They are also entitled to decline to give evidence as expert witnesses with regard to the law of the sending State.

(7) In taking evidence from members of the consular post, the authorities of the receiving State shall take all appropriate measures to avoid interference with the performance of their consular functions. At the request of the head of the consular post, such evidence may, when possible, be given orally or in writing at the consular premises or at the residence of the person concerned.

(8) Members of the consular post who are nationals or permanent residents of the receiving State and members of their families, as well as those members of the families of the members of the consular post who are themselves nationals or permanent residents of the receiving State, shall not enjoy the rights, facilities and immunities provided for in this Article, except the immunity provided for in paragraph (6) of this Article.

ARTICLE 8

(1) Consular officers shall have the right to communicate with nationals of the sending State and to have access to them in the consular district. The receiving State shall not in any way limit the communication of nationals of the sending State with the consular post or their access to it.

(2) If a national of the sending State is arrested, committed to prison or detained in any other manner in the consular district, the competent authorities of the receiving State shall notify the consular post of the sending State to that effect as soon as possible and at the latest within seven days from the time at which the personal freedom of that national is restricted. A visit to that national as requested by consular officers shall be arranged by the competent authorities of the receiving State two days after the consular post is notified of the restriction of the personal freedom of that national. Subsequent visits shall be permitted at intervals not exceeding one month.

(3) The rights mentioned in this Article shall be exercised within the framework of the laws and regulations of the receiving State, it being understood, however, that those laws and regulations shall enable full effect to be given to the purposes for which the said rights are granted.

ARTICLE 9

Consular matters which are not dealt with in this Agreement shall be settled by the Contracting Governments in accordance with the relevant provisions of the Vienna Convention on Consular Relations of 24 April 1963([1]), through friendly consultation and in a spirit of mutual understanding and co-operation.

ARTICLE 10

Paragraph (2) of Article 4 and Articles 5, 8 and 9 of this Agreement shall also apply to the diplomatic missions of the two States with respect to the exercise of consular functions.

ARTICLE 11

Each Contracting Government shall notify the other in writing of the completion of the procedures required by its respective national laws. This Agreement shall enter into force on the date of the later of those notifications([2]).

Done in duplicate at Beijing this 17th day of April 1984, in the English and Chinese languages, both texts being equally authoritative.

For the Government of the United Kingdom of Great Britain and Northern Ireland:	For the Government of the People's Republic of China:
GEOFFREY HOWE	WU XUEQIAN

([1]) Treaty Series No. 14 (1973), Cmnd. 5219.
([2]) The Agreement entered into force on 14 January 1985.

Trade agreements

States use a variety of means to promote (or regulate) international economic, financial and commercial relations. These include domestic measures, such as taxation and administrative concessions, tariffs, export subsidies, export-free zones, trade financing loans, anti-'dumping' measures, internationally agreed preference schemes and customs and other economic unions. Trade agreements are but one of the many instruments which are available in this broad range of measures.

In some state practice a trade agreement is styled an 'economic co-operation agreement' (e.g. Romania).[7] However, most economic co-operation tends to cover not only trade matters but also a wide range of other items such as industrial co-operation, research and development, scientific exchange with, and the establishment of, economic and scientific working committees and commissions. Occasionally a time limit is put on the duration of the agreement, e.g. the United Kingdom–Poland five-year trade agreement.[8]

In a bilateral context, the decision to conclude a trade agreement will depend partly on the range of other agreements already in existence between the two parties, as well as other considerations such as the level and nature of total trade (e.g. whether it is one-sided, low in overall volume, excessively commodity oriented or limited in the existing range of manufactured or semi-manufactured goods traded).

In other words, a trade agreement is usually designed to serve one or more specific purposes. In a political sense, a trade agreement might be signed to cement better relations which have perhaps been dormant for many years. However, not all economic or commercial relations between states require the conclusion of an agreement of this type. Sometimes trade exchange is at an acceptable level and content without any major structural irregularities.

The general purpose of a trade agreement is to establish a legally binding framework within which to promote and conduct economic relations. Among the matters dealt with by an agreement are: most-favoured nation (MFN) and like product treatment.[9] For example the Malaysian–Indonesian trade agreement of 16 October 1973 is pursuant to article II of the Basic Agreement on Economic and Technical Co-operation (same date) between the two countries.[10]

Article 1(2) contains provision for MFN treatment in issuing import and export licences, and in the following sub-paragraph (2(3)) provides for 'like product' treatment:

Any advantage, favour, privilege or immunity granted or which may be granted by each Contracting Party on import or export of any product, originating or consigned to the territory for a third country, shall be accorded immediately and unconditionally to the like product originating in or consigned to the territory of either Contracting Party.

This type of provision is not always provided for, e.g. the Malaysia–Czechoslovak trade agreement of 20 November 1972.[11] Those parts of the MFN clause itself, which make the exchange of goods subject to relevant import and export laws, and foreign exchange controls, may be drafted in a number of ways to strengthen the MFN, for example, so that: 'such laws and regulations shall not invalidate the most-favoured-nation provisions'[12] or it may be weakened by qualification: 'the contracting parties shall, subject to their respective import, export, foreign exchange or other laws, rules and regulations, provide the maximum facilities possible for the purpose of increasing the volume of trade between the two countries ...' (Malaysia–Czechoslovak Socialist Republic trade agreement, 20 November 1972, article 2).

Scope and application of MFN and related provisions

The scope of a trade agreement with another state is often limited by excluding from the provisions the preferences, advantages or exceptions that have been or may be granted to generally defined groups of states or named countries. In this exception list might be the preferences granted to:

(a) neighbouring countries in order to improve frontier traffic or regional trade;
(b) countries who are members of a customs union or free trade area;
(c) the Commonwealth;
(d) specified countries;
(e) goods and commodities imported under economic or military aid programmes.

In a separate sense the provisions of a trade agreement may be drafted so as not to preclude the states party to the agreement having the right to adopt or execute measures relating to *inter alia*:

(a) public security, national defence;
(b) public health;
(c) agricultural and veterinary regulations;
(d) trade in specified items, e.g. precious metals, weapons, historical artefacts.

The scope of the trade agreement itself will often be set out in the form of two schedules referred to in either the first or second articles which are set out as an annex (though still an integral part of the agreement). The respective schedules list the goods and commodities, e.g. rubber manufactures, timber and timber products, machinery and transport equipment, traded for beans, fresh fruit, fish, plywood, cement and bicycles. The schedules can be relatively simple and based on broad categories, as in the example below to the Singapore–People's Republic of China trade agreement of 1979.[13]

SCHEDULE A
EXPORTS FROM THE REPUBLIC OF SINGAPORE TO THE PEOPLE'S REPUBLIC OF CHINA

Industrial Machinery and Transport Equipment and Parts
Industrial and Domestic Electronic and Electrical Equipments and Components
Rubber, Rubber Products and Processed Wood
Chemicals, Petrochemicals, Pharmaceuticals and Fine Chemicals
Medical and Scientific Instruments
Others

SCHEDULE B
EXPORTS FROM THE PEOPLE'S REPUBLIC OF CHINA TO THE REPUBLIC OF SINGAPORE

Rice and Other Cereals
Foodstuffs and Canned Goods
Tea, Native Produce and Special Products
General Merchandise
Stationery and Sports Articles
Textiles
Machinery and Instruments
Agricultural Implements and Tools
Chemicals and Chemical Products
Steel Products and Non-Ferrous Metals
Animal By-Products
Others

The content of the schedule is a matter for negotiation between the parties. Among the considerations relevant to the content are whether it is considered appropriate to have a detailed list, whether the categories of goods should be broken down according to a classification (e.g.

primary products, manufactures), and whether the subcategories themselves need to be broken down so as to refer to detailed items (e.g. industrial machinery and equipment: offshore oil-rig compressor pumps). In some cases the schedule is open-ended, and after listing certain manufactures concludes the list with a miscellaneous category 'other manufactures'. The schedule clause in the main agreement may, if considered necessary, make provision for the parties to hold consultation on any amendment to the list of goods in the future.

Apart from these provisions it is worth noting that additional provisions may be required for trade agreements involving centrally planned or socialist-type economies and market or quasi-market economies. In such cases trade agreements may need to take into consideration and reflect through specific provisions such matters as the legal status of state trading organisations, principles of non-discriminatory commercial treatment, financial subsidy and forms of currency payment. In addition, the question of the treatment of imports of products for immediate or ultimate consumption in governmental use may be an issue for negotiation between the parties.[14]

Miscellaneous provisions

Apart from the above, other provisions of trade agreements normally cover *inter alia*: (a) means of payment; (b) trade promotion; (c) dispute settlement; (d) merchant shipping; (e) commercial aircraft; (f) transit rights; (g) duration of the agreement; (h) entry into force. While some of these items follow a generally standard form, e.g. means of payment (acceptable convertible currency), others can take a number of widely differing forms depending on what the parties seek to achieve or are able to agree in their negotiations as an acceptable outcome. For example, provisions on the treatment of merchant vessels may be extended to provide an analogous treatment of each of the parties' commercial aircraft at their respective airports (blanket charge). Again, the merchant shipping clause in the MFN section can be based on MFN provisions for port charges and harbour facilities or the cargo status of a ship. If MFN status is granted to vessels without cargoes then this affords wide rights to the MFN party. On the other hand, a state may not wish to see vessels without cargoes frequently using its ports claiming MFN status, on economic and security grounds, and so may seek a more restrictive MFN shipping clause not based on whether vessels had cargo. Article VIII of the Singapore–People's Republic of China trade agreement of 29 December 1979, has, for example, a restrictive clause: 'Merchant vessels of each Contracting Party with cargo thereon shall enjoy: in respect of entry into, stay in, and departure from the ports of the other country most-favoured-nation treatment, granted by the laws, rules and regulations applicable to ships under any third-country flag.'[15]

In some cases, the shipping provisions section of a trade agreement is used as a means of putting mutual shipping and cargo handling on a firmer basis. For example, article II of the Brazilian–Ghanaian trade agreement provides that: 'the contracting parties agree to promote the preferential participation of Brazilian and Ghanaian ships in the transportation of cargo between ports of both countries.[16] Apart from this type of general obligation, agreements may, in particular, seek to limit the amount of trade carried out by third-party shipping. In the Brazilian–Nigerian trade agreement, for example, article VI provides that ships of third countries should not carry more than 20 per cent of trade between the two countries. An exception in this agreement is made for full bulk cargoes (article VI(v)).[17] As relatively new states have sought to build up their small merchant fleets, the frequency of shipping provisions in bilateral trade agreements has tended to increase. In fact, this tendency has been enhanced by the growing number of bilateral agreements exclusively devoted to shipping.[18]

Re-export, barter, and transit trade

Other miscellaneous provisions worth noting are firstly on transit trade. Transit trade provisions,[19] deal *inter alia* with reciprocal measures for the movement of goods from ports and other facilities of each of the contracting parties to those of third states. The growth in popularity of 'export zones' in or nearby the ports of new states has influenced the need for additional provisions to cover the transference of goods to and from export zones and ports.

Secondly, in some trade agreements the form in which the trade is carried out is defined in the general framework. Apart from the questions of schedules and means of payment already referred to, provisions may be included which seek to limit or prohibit certain kinds of trade between the parties, e.g. barter trade. That is, goods directly traded (or involving a third party) between the two parties are prevented from being exchanged on a barter or 'counter-trade' basis, without the prior written consent of appropriate authorities in both countries.[20]

Finally, commonly found in trade agreements concluded between advanced industrial countries and new states are provisions to protect the national identity and 'integrity' of the product exported. Such provisions may take one of a number or forms. For example, an 'origin of goods' clause may be used to facilitate the eradication of origin, or prevention of goods and commodities being given false places of origin, by including provisions on trade marks, packaging and an agreed definition for export purposes of what constitutes a 'locally'-made product. Thus article V, for example, of the trade agreement between Canada and Afghanistan provides:

With respect to trade marks, each of the contracting Parties shall protect the trade marks of the other Party to the extent that the national law of each Party permits. Each Party agrees to protect within its territorial scope the products of the other Party against all forms of dishonest competition particularly with regards to the use of false indications relative to place of origin. The contracting

Parties undertake to assist one another in the prevention of any practice which might be prejudicial to their trade relations.

In a multilateral treaty context, the question of what constitutes 'locally' made is often difficult to reach agreement on in negotiations of a 'certificate of origin' clause, but also particularly difficult to enforce. This is especially so if, for example, component parts are imported from outside the region and re-exported within it; if there is high regional protectionism; or if one or more of the states in the regional grouping is generally involved in low-value-added re-export trade. Another approach in some international trade agreements to the related question of the end use of goods is to include provision on the re-export of goods. The parties may agree, for example, to either allow 're-export only by written mutual consent',[21] or 'take steps to prevent the re-export of commodities and goods imported from the other within the framework of the agreement'.[22]

Trade administration

Apart from the above, trade agreements often contain provisions for the establishment of joint consultative machinery, e.g. that of the Australia–People's Republic of China[23] meets annually or semi-annually at official level to deal with the implementation of the agreement, and to review its scope and effectiveness. The agreement may also include provisions on holding regular trade-promotion conferences. Provisions concerned with the establishment of a trade representative office would not normally be included in a trade agreement.[24] Instead, they would be the subject of a separate diplomatic or consular agreement. Such an agreement need not be negotiated simultaneously with the trade agreement, and indeed negotiations for a trade representation office (or additional consular office) are likely to follow quite some time later against the background of the effectiveness and impact of the trade agreement.

Entry into force and duration

In general, trade agreements enter into force on signature, though in special cases entry is provisional, with full entry into force on an exchange of notes. In those cases in which ratification is required, entry into force takes effect on the date of the exchange of instruments of ratification. In the event of the expiry of an agreement, commercial transactions concluded before the date of expiry but not fully executed are governed by the provisions of the agreement. A common formula for the duration of trade agreements is one which provides for the initial agreement to last for one to three years with automatic continuation of the agreement for further periods of one year unless either party notifies the other in writing of its intent to terminate the agreement, at least 90 days prior to the expiry of each period.

International loan agreements

Finance for projects and capital-related activities can be generated from several sources including domestic organisations, international capital markets and international institutions. The purpose of the remaining part of the chapter is to provide a discussion of the legal framework of loans negotiated through international institutions, and highlight some of the broad issues which arise in terms of the construction of the agreement.

We should note first, though, that apart from fund sourcing from international institutions, such as the IBRD, IMF and regional institutions such as the ADB, states obtain financial resources from a variety of other sources – some are internally generated through bond issues, others by floating notes in a denominated currency, on the domestic capital market of a foreign country, syndicated foreign loans, as well as bilateral loan and grant arrangements with other states.

Financial loans secured through international institutions for project finance under discussion here differ in a number of respects from funds obtained on the international commercial capital market or through bilateral official arrangements. Among the major differences between international institution funding and international capital market funding are the structure and composition of interest rate spread and external supervision. Commercially acquired funding on the international capital market is generally geared to an internationally accepted lending rate, such as the London Interbank rate (Libor). This variable rate is used to form the base point for the loan 'package', the terms of which are then spread at different percentage points above Libor for specific phases or periods of the amortisation. In some arrangements not only a mix of interest levels is used, e.g. $\frac{3}{8}$ per cent above Libor for five years, $\frac{3}{4}$ per cent above for ten years, but agreements too can contain a mix of *base points*, for example a combination of Libor and the US prime rate. The structure then of this type of package is a set of variable interest rates related to one or more base-point systems, which is applied to various tranches or blocks of the loan. The interest rate of the loan, since it is negotiated, provides one of the key differences from the repayment provisions of projects funded by international institutions which tend to be made up of relatively fixed components such as interest rates which are not greatly negotiable. This is not to say that there are *no* areas for negotiation, as we shall point out below. In addition as far as the IBRD is concerned, from 1982 loans themselves have been based on a variable-rate system, calculated by the Bank, rather than the previous fixed-at-commitment system.

The second major difference between international institution sourced loans and commercial capital loans, is in the role of the international institution in the various phases of the project. This involvement includes project evaluation, tender procedures, monitoring project implementation and, in general terms, the acceptability of projects –

reflecting the development philosophy of the institution, expressed in terms of preferences for particular kinds of projects (e.g. ADB agricultural sector development).

Although this chapter, in the loan agreement section, is concerned with project loans since they are commonly used instruments, other types of instruments have developed. Experimentation with differing instruments is particularly noticeable in the IBRD.[25] Included in the range of development finance instruments created in recent years are: sector adjusting lending[26] designed to support specific programmes and institutional development; the more comprehensive structural adjustment loans,[27] and financial intermediary loans for small and medium-sized enterprises. These facilities have been augmented by attempts to create new instruments to increase the flows of commercial capital to developing countries by linking the IBRD more directly through IBRD guarantees of late maturities and direct participation in syndicated loans.[28]

Format and structure of international loan agreements

Loan agreements between a government and an international institution, such as the IBRD or ADB, with respect to project funding can be broadly broken down into six areas:

1. General conditions;
2. Terms of the loan;
3. Execution of the project;
4. Other covenants;
5. Effective date and termination;
6. Schedules.

The overall process from initiation to project completion can be put into the following categories:

1. Project identification;
2. Appraisal mission (international institution);
3. Pre-qualifying tenders (if appropriate);
4. Government report (submission) to international institution;
5. Negotiation (with international institution, co-financing partners (if any) of draft subsidiary loan agreement, e.g. between the government (the borrower) and subsidiary political unit (where applicable); draft relending agreement (e.g. to a public utility by the subsidiary political unit) (where applicable);
6. Implementation (signature of agreement; effective date; tender, subcontracting, progress evaluation).

Loan agreements financed through international institutions are governed by the framework or general conditions of the institution, e.g. the IBRD General Conditions Applicable to Loan and Guarantee Agreements, or Ordinary Operations Loan Regulations of the ADB.[29]

The general conditions set out certain terms and conditions to any loan agreement or guarantee with any member of the Bank, including such matters as the application of the general conditions, the loan account and charges, currency provisions, co-operation and information, cancellation and the effective date of the agreement. The general conditions may be revised from time to time and are supplemented by guidelines, e.g. ADB Guidelines on the Use of Consultants, or IBRD Guidelines for Procurement under World Bank Loans and IDA Credits. In the event of any inconsistency between a loan agreement and the general conditions, the latter prevail. Some aspects of the general conditions may be omitted or amended as a result of negotiation, which is normally reflected in the first article of the agreement. Frameworks of this type are also used by official (governmental) sources of capital, e.g. General Terms and Conditions of the Japanese Overseas Economic Co-operation Fund which,[30] although modelled on the IBRD, differ significantly in a number of respects both procedurally (e.g. payment based on presentation of letter of credit by the borrower) and substantively in respect to terms and conditions.

Some particular considerations on structure

Interest rate and repayment
Following the provisions relating to the general conditions and definitions (first article), the terms of the loan are set out including the amount, interest rate and repayment schedule. As we have indicated the interest rate and related Bank charges are normally considered fixed items and are not negotiable in this type of loan. For example in the loan agreement between Malaysia and the ADB[31] for the Batang Ai hydropower project the interest rate is set at 10.1 per cent per annum on $40,400,000 in Article 11, Section 2.02, and the repayment of the principal amount of the loan is in accordance with the amortisation set out in Schedule 2. Included in this schedule are the premiums on advanced repayment on an increasing percentage scale (1.5–10.1 per cent).

The system employed in this ADB loan example differs from that used by IBRD for project loans in two respects. The Malaysian–IBRD loan agreement for the Kedah Valleys agricultural development project of February 1983[32] can be used to illustrate the differences. In the first place (the question of different interest rates apart) the premiums on prepayment are calculated differently. In this example they are based on the interest rate (expressed as a percentage per annum) applicable to the outstanding balance multiplied by a factor from 0.2 to 1.

Second, the interest rate in the IBRD example is variable and is determined by applying the concept 'cost of qualified borrowings'. Thus, section 2.07(a) of the Kedah loan (IBRD) cited above, reflects the changes in the IBRD's method of setting interest rates for new loans from July 1982. The revised system replaces the fixed-at-commitment method and has been principally influenced by the increasing exposure of the IBRD to interest-rate risk in recent years. In revising the interest-rate formula the Bank took into consideration that to continue to lend or borrow at fixed rates would have increased its exposure to interest-rate risk. A second influence on the change in lending-rate policy was that continuation of the practice of making fixed-rate loans blocked the bank from making use of short-term or variable-rate instruments. The combination of the old fixed-rate lending policy, combined with variable-rate borrowing, would have ultimately caused severe and unacceptable variability in IBRD net income. Under the revised system the interest rate has been based on the cost of all the outstanding *borrowings* paid out to the Bank after 30 June 1982. Those borrowings are called *qualified borrowings* in the agreement. The Bank interest rate is based on the pool of borrowings, made by the Bank ($US9 billion fiscal 1982) to which is added a spread of 0.5 per cent, as in the Kedah Valleys agricultural development project loan agreement, 7 February 1983, or the Jamaica–IBRD second technical assistance project.[33] For interest periods commencing in 1982, the initial rate for the Kedah Valleys project for example was 11.43 per cent (10.93 + 0.50 per cent), paid on a semi-annual basis.

Commitment charge

Apart from the above structure, which affects the nominal cost of capital, the brief but extremely important provision in loan agreements – the commitment charge – is a further major variable in evaluating project cost. As already indicated, loan agreements contain, in addition to the interest-rate structure, a number of fixed components such as Bank fees, and the *commitment charge*. The commitment charge is a percentage rate (in the case under review 0.75 per cent) per annum applied to the principal amount of the loan *not withdrawn* from time to time.[34] In other words, the effect of this provision is to put a premium on meeting deadlines during a project, which are essential to keeping the overall project 'on stream'. A further general difficulty which brings the commitment charge into play results from short-term alterations to the planning framework of the project. This can be caused by many factors such as national budgetary deficits, switch of development emphasis, competing projects and sheer overload within a decision-making unit. These can result in the project either not being taken up for some time or being abandoned, and in consequence, the incurring of high first and second 'phase' commitment charges.

Co-financing

Traditionally, co-financing has involved international institutions such as the World Bank, ADB and certain official sources, such as the Kuwait Fund or the Overseas Economic Co-operation Fund of Japan. However, since the late 1970s, co-financing has been extended to involve commercial sources of capital. The basis of this change lies in two main factors. In the first place international institutions involved in capital and project finance have increasingly come under pressure as their resources became stretched, and correspondingly, access to borrowing became both difficult and costly in a period of high exchange-rate volatility. The involvement of commercial source funding served to stretch resources of regional institutions such as the ADB and the Inter-American Development Bank.[35] Second, apart from increasing calls on the resources of international institutions, the profile of development projects put forward by less developed and newly-industrialised countries altered to include more large-scale, cost-intensive projects such as gas separator plants, chemical complexes and public utility schemes.[36] Therefore, commercial source funding became an increasingly important part of loan packages. By 1982, for example, commercial source funding of ADB projects had increased from 5 per cent in the early 1970s to over 14 per cent.

Within the World Bank co-financing has been further developed with the establishment in 1982 of co-financing instruments which link the Bank more closely with the private commercial banking sector. The loan arrangements were informally termed 'B-loans' to distinguish them from the main long-term World Bank loans.[37] Under the scheme the Bank committed $US500 million in order to mobilise $US2 billion for some twenty selected lending operations.[38] The two main objectives of the B-loan programme were to make additional funds available to developing countries from sources not otherwise available and to achieve a lengthening of maturities more suitably matched to the borrowers capacity to repay. In one unusual case, the Bank guaranteed $US150 million of a commercial co-financing of $US300 million for a Chilean highways project in order to assist the borrower in bringing together a much larger overall package of almost $US6 billion in reschedulings and over $US1 billion in new money.[39]

Some implications of multi-party funding

The introduction of commercial source funding into international loan agreements sourced by international institutions has a number of implications for both the structure and substance of the agreement. An important element in these arrangements, therefore, is the linkage between the parties, expressed in terms of the separate loan agreements which make up the package, which have to be completed to the satisfaction of the international institution, before the commitment (loan amount) and, in consequence, the *overall* loan can become effective. Other issues involved in multi-source funding include *inter alia* the conditions which lead to the suspension, cancellation or acceleration of the maturity of the loan, harmonisation or not of the different interest-rate structures in the loan, and the phase in which an international institution becomes involved in a joint co-financing arrangement.

Finally it can be argued, in terms of B-loans, that the Bank, in providing in effect trigger finance for much larger loans, is taking on a much wider role as a guarantor and through economic monitoring than is reflected in its nominal financial involvement. While this may unlock commercial finance and provide some measure of risk relief, it is not clear what the overall effect would be on the Bank and its co-financing policies in the event of a major default.

Some additional considerations

So far loan agreements through international institutions have been discussed in terms of structure and issues relating to repayment. The bulk of the remainder of the provisions of loan agreements are concerned with obligations or undertakings with respect to the organisation and management of the project (e.g. accounting records, appointment of personnel, access by the institution to information on, and general, progress through inspections of the project). In loan agreements these provisions are styled 'covenants' and, as was suggested earlier, constitute one of the important areas of negotiation. Apart from the issues listed above, other areas of negotiation involve, for example, the details of provisions concerning other external debt which the borrower might incur, and conditions related to the financial capabilities of the party (e.g. a public utility) for whom the loan agreement has been negotiated.

Entry into force

The effective date of international loan agreements is determined by the general conditions, particular modifications to these, and other appropriate conditions in the loan agreement. The procedures for the effective date differ somewhat between types of loan agreements. For IBRD loans, for example, entry into force occurs when the relevant conditions described above have been met, including legal opinions submitted to the Bank, whereupon the Bank despatches to the borrower notice of acceptance. The effective date clause also stipulates a period (e.g. 90 days) by which the agreement should have come into force, otherwise all obligations are terminated unless the IBRD considers the reasons for delay acceptable. Multi-party co-financing loans under the ADB require the subsidiary and relending agreement, and the agreements with lenders other than the ADB, to have been executed and delivered for the effectiveness of the agreement.

Fisheries agreements

Fisheries agreements are an important and in a number of instances critical component of a licensing state's domestic and external economic relations. The form and range of subject-matter will depend on how the agreement is negotiated, whether intergovernmentally or between a national fisheries agency and operator(s), or as an informal arrangement (e.g. between national fisheries agencies and/or associations), and on whether or not global, regional and sub-regional organisations are involved. Types of agreements can vary from simple cash-resource exchange agreements to complex arrangements involving fishing effort, financial, enforcement and other provisions. For example, third-party fisheries agreements negotiated by the EU have taken a number of forms including fisheries–trade access swaps (EC–Iceland); quota access – cash ('compensation') agreements and agreements involving the swap of different species with third parties (e.g. EU–Norway).[40]

Negotiation issues

The major issues for negotiation can include the following categories:

1. *Operator* licence conditions: company, registration, export, import, and/or transhipment
2. *Vessels*: number, type, size, registration, call-sign
3. *Fishing Operations*
   (a) definitions (e.g. fish; operator; closed area; licence; offence; fisheries officer)
   (b) area (closure; conditions; exclusion; limitations – territorial sea; conditions regarding operations within *and* beyond EEZ)
   (c) species covered by the licence
   (d) by-catch
   (e) volume of catch
   (f) landing (ports; catch reporting *at sea*)
   (g) transhipment (if any)
4. *Economic*: amount; schedule; payment procedures; review of financial provisions
5. *Enforcement*
   (a) observers/inspectors (number; access on vessels and obligation to co-operate)
   (b) Board and inspection (at sea)
   (c) Port inspection
   (d) Detention/arrest
   (e) Penalties
6. *Scientific and technical co-operation*
7. *Duration of agreement and revision*

In considering operator conditions, a point of increasing concern is that of the effective registry of foreign fishing vessels, and corresponding flag state enforcement. In this respect international guidelines have been introduced by FAO (FAO 'Flagging Agreement') on vessel registration and inspection[41] and obligations introduced into international conventions, e.g. UN Convention on Highly Migratory and Straddling Fishing Stocks.[42]

Regulations in international fisheries agreements regarding vessels vary considerably. As can be seen from the following EC–Angola example (article 1)[43] the effort formula for the number of allowable vessels was based in part on GRT on a monthly average.

PROTOCOL
ESTABLISHING THE FISHING RIGHTS AND FINANCIAL CONTRIBUTION PROVIDED FOR IN THE AGREEMENT BETWEEN THE EUROPEAN ECONOMIC COMMUNITV AND THE GOVERNMENT OF THE PEOPLE'S REPUBLIC OF ANGOLA ON FISHING OFF ANGOLA

Article I

From 3 May 1987, for a period of two years, the limits referred to in Article 2 of the Agreement shall be as follows:
1. Shrimp vessels: 12,000 GRT per month as a yearly average.
   However, the quantities to be fished by Community vessels may not exceed 10,000 tonnes of shrimps per year, of which 30 per cent shall be prawns and 70 per cent shrimps.
2. Ocean-going tuna freezer boats: 25 vessels.

Article 2

1. The financial compensation provided for in Article 7 of the Agreement for the period referred to in Article I of this Protocol is fixed at 12,050,000 ECU, payable in two annual instalments, the first before 30 September 1987 and the second before 31 July 1988.
2. The use to which this compensation is put shall be the sole responsibility of Angola.
3. The compensation shall be paid into an account opened at a financial institution or any other body designated by Angola.

Article 3

1. The Community shall also contribute during the period referred to in Article I up to 350,000 ECU towards the financing of Angolan scientific and technical programmes (equipment, infrastructure, seminars, studies, etc.) in order to improve information on the fishery resources within Angola's fishing zone.
2. The competent Angolan authorities shall send to the Commission a report on the utilization of the funds.
3. The Community's contribution to the scientific and technical programmes shall be paid in two annual instalments into a specific account determined by the competent Angolan authorities.

Article 4

The Community shall assist Angolan nationals in obtaining places for study and training in establishments in its Member States or in the ACP States and shall provide for that purpose, during the period referred to in Article I, 12 study grants of a maximum duration of five years, equivalent to 60 years of study, in scientific, technical, legal, economic and other subjects connected with fisheries.

Two of these grants, equivalent to a sum of no more than 90,000 ECU, may be used to finance the cost of participation in international conferences aimed at improving knowledge regarding fisheries resources.

Article 5

Should the Community fail to make the payments provided for in Articles 2 and 3 within the time limits laid down, the application of the Agreement may be suspended.

However, difficulties can occur over agreeing monthly GRT figures, combined with a coastal state wish for stricter control over numbers. Other EC instruments have been based on limitations on vessels (e.g. EC–Madagascar, article 1),[44] though the lower limit on 33 vessels fishing simultaneously was removed in the 1990 (EC–Madagascar) protocol, favouring in effect the EC distant-water fleets. See Article 1 below.

AGREEMENT
AMENDING THE AGREEMENT BETWEEN THE EUROPEAN ECONOMIC COMMUNITY AND THE GOVERNMENT OF THE DEMOCRATIC REPUBLIC OF MADAGASCAR ON FISHING OFF THE COAST OF MADAGASCAR, SIGNED AT ANTANANARIVO ON 28 JANUARY 1986

Article I

Protocol I annexed to the Agreement between the European Economic Community and the Government of the Democratic Republic of Madagascar on fishing off the coast of Madagascar[1] is hereby amended as follows:

1. Article I shall be replaced by the following:

"Article I

Pursuant to Article 2 of the Agreement and for the period of application of this Protocol, which is limited to three years, tuna-fishing licences in Madagascar's fishing zone shall be issued for 49 ocean-going freezer tuna boats, although the number of such vessels fishing simultaneously may not exceed 33. The relevant Community authorities shall communicate at regular intervals the list of vessels fishing under these rules."

2. Article 2 shall be replaced by the following:

I   European Communities No. 38 (1986), Cmnd. 9896.

"Article 2

The amount of the contribution referred to in Article 7 of the Agreement shall be fixed at a flat-rate of at least 1,530,000 ECU for the duration of the Protocol, payable in three equal annual instalments. This amount shall cover the fishing referred to in Article 1 up to a catch weight in Madagascar's fishing zone of 10,200 tonnes of tuna fish per year; if the amount of tuna caught by Community vessels in Madagascar's fishing zone exceeds this quantity, the abovementioned amount shall be increased accordingly: however, irrespective of the amount actually caught, the ceiling for financial compensation shall be fixed at 3,000,000 ECU for the duration of the Protocol, and hence at 1,000,000 ECU per year."

Article 2

In the Annex to the Agreement between the European Economic Community and the Government of the Democratic Republic of Madagascar on fishing off the coast of Madagascar, point 2(b) shall be replaced by the following:

"(b) The sum of 555 ECU shall be paid each year by owners for each tuna-boat to the Treasury of Madagascar as an advance on the fees."

Article 3

This Agreement, drawn up in duplicate in the Danish, German, Greek, English, Spanish, French, Italian, Dutch, Portuguese and Malagasy languages, each of these texts being equally authentic, shall enter into force on the date of its signature[2].

It shall apply from 28 November 1986.

ANNEX

Conditions governing fishing activities by Community vessels in Madagascar's fishing zone

1.   FORMALITIES CONCERNING APPLICATION FOR, AND ISSUE OF, LICENCES

After payment of the fees by shipowners, the competent Community authorities shall present to the competent Malagasy authorities an application in respect of each vessel wishing to fish under the Agreement. The application must be made on the form provided by Madagascar for this purpose, according to the attached model.

---

2   For texts in Danish, Dutch, French, German, Greek, Italian, Spanish and Portuguese, see Official Journal of the European Communities No. L 160 of 20 June 1987, available through Agency Section, Her Majesty's Stationery Office, PO Box 276, London SW8 5DT.

The Malagasy authorities shall then send the licence provided for in Article 4 of the Agreement to the Delegation of the Commission of the European Communities in Antananarivo within 15 working days.

Owners of tuna vessels shall be obliged to be represented by an agent in Madagascar.

2. VALIDITY OF LICENCES

The licences shall be valid for one year. They shall be renewable.

Each licence shall be issued for a specific vessel, and shall not be transferable. However, in the event of *force majeure*, a licence for one vessel may be replaced by a licence for another vessel of similar characteristics should the European Economic Community so request. The owner of the vessel being replaced shall return the cancelled licence to the Malagasy Ministry with responsibility for fisheries via the Delegation of the Commission of the European Communities.

The new licence shall indicate:

—the date of issue;

—the fact that it cancels and replaces the licence of the previous vessel.

3. PAYMENT FOR LICENCES

(a) *Freezer tuna vessels*

For ocean-going freezer tuna vessels, the fee provided for by Article 5 of the Agreement shall be set at ECU 20 per tonne of tuna caught in Madagascar's fishing zone.

Licences shall be issued on advance payment to the Malagasy Treasury of a fixed annual sum of ECU 1,000 per freezer tuna vessel.

(b) *Other vessels*

The licence fee for vessels other than tuna vessels shall be set according to gross register tonnage.

4. DECLARATION OF CATCHES

After the end of each calendar year, the Commission of the European Communities shall inform the Malagasy authorities no later than 31 March each year of the provisional catch figures for the preceding calendar year, on the basis of the fishing forms drawn up by the shipowners and referred to in paragraph 6.

5. BREAKDOWN OF FEES DUE

A breakdown of the fees due in respect of a fishing year shall be drawn up by the Commission of the European Communities and the Malagasy authorities, taking account of available scientific opinion and any statistical information gathered in the Indian Ocean by an international fisheries organization.

Shipowners shall be notified by the Commission of the European Communities of this breakdown by the end of April and shall have 30 days in which to meet their financial obligations. The shipowner cannot recover the balance in cases where the amount payable in respect of actual fishing operations is less than the advance payment.

6.   Radio communications and fishing forms

The captain shall notify the coastal radio station at Antsiranana or by telex at least 24 hours in advance of his intention of bringing his vessel into Madagascar's fishing zone.

Vessels shall indicate their position and catches every 3 days, and at the end of each period spent fishing in Madagascar's fishing zone, either by radio to the coastal radio station at Antsiranana or by telex. This information must also be indicated on entering or leaving Madagascar's fishing zone, either by radio to the Antsiranana station or by telex.

The radio frequency to be used and the telex number will be indicated on the licence.

The captain must also fill in a fishing form corresponding to the attached model for each period spent fishing in Madagascar's fishing zone.

The sheet, which must be legible and signed by the captain of the ship, must reach the Malagasy Ministry with responsibility for fisheries via the shipowner's agent as soon as possible and preferably within 30 days of the period spent fishing in Madagascar's fishing zone. A copy must also be sent to the Delegation of the Commission of the European Communities.

In the event of failure to comply with these provisions, the Malagasy authorities reserve the right to suspend the licence of the offending vessel until the formalities have been completed.

7.   Observers

At the request of the Malagasy authorities, tuna vessels shall take an observer on board. The time spent by the observer on board shall be fixed by the Malagasy authorities, but, as a general rule, an observer must not be present for longer than the time required to carry out his duties.

The shipowner shall, via his agent, make a payment of ECU 10 to the Malagasy Government for each day spent by an observer aboard a tuna boat.

Should a tuna boat with a Malagasy observer on board leave Madagascar's fishing zone, every step shall be taken to ensure that the observer returns to Madagascar as soon as possible, at the shipowner's expense.

8.   Employment of seamen

For the ocean-going tuna fleet, two Malagasy seamen shall be signed on permanently for the duration of the fishing season.

Should Madagascar not put forward any candidates, this commitment shall be replaced by a flat-rate sum equivalent to 50 per cent of the seamen's wages, in proportion to the duration of the season; this sum will be used for the training of Malagasy fishermen.

9.   Fishing zones

Community vessels shall have access to all waters under Madagascar's jurisdiction outside the two-mile zone.

Should the Malagasy authorities decide to install experimental fish concentration devices (FCDs), they shall inform the Commission of the European Communities and the agents of the shipowners concerned, indicating the geographical position of the devices.

From the thirtieth day after such notification, it shall be forbidden to approach within 1.5 nautical miles of the devices. The dismantling of any device must be immediately notified to the same parties.

10. USE OF PORT FACILITIES

The authorities of Madagascar and the beneficiaries of the Agreement shall lay down the conditions for using port facilities.

11. INSPECTION AND MONITORING OF FISHING ACTIVITIES

Vessels holding a licence shall permit and assist any Malagasy official responsible for the inspection and monitoring of fishing activities to board the ship and carry out his duties.

12. TRANS-SHIPMENT

When fish are trans-shipped, ocean-going freezer tuna vessels shall hand over the fish which they do not intend to keep to a company or organization nominated by the Malagasy authorities in charge of fisheries.

Application Form for a Fishing Licence

1. Period of validity: from . . . . to . . . .
2. Name and flag of vessel. . . . .
3. Name of shipowner. . . . .
4. Port of registration and registration number. . . . .
5. Type of fishing. . . . .
6. Authorized mesh size . . . .
7. Length of vessel. . . . .
8. Breadth of vessel. . . . .
9. Gross registered tonnage . . . .
10. Hold capacity. . . . .
11. Power of engine . . . .
12. Type of construction. . . . .
13. Number of crew normally carried . . . .
14. Radio equipment. . . . .
15. Radio call sign . . . .
16. Name of captain . . . .

The shipowner, or his representative, is entirely responsible for the accuracy of this information.

Other particular provisions in fisheries licensing found in national legislation and agreements which should be noted are the following:

1. Definitions of fish – provisions to cover species of local concern[45]
2. Conditions of entry into and exit from fishing zone;[46] passage through a zone for non-fisheries purposes; navigation, safety and chart conditions[47]

3. Gear stowage while not fishing[48]
4. Fish on board and catch reporting procedures[49]
5. Transhipment[50]
6. Environmental damage[51]
7. Marine Scientific Research.

Cultural, educational and technical co-operation

Agreements to further cultural and educational co-operation between states are long-standing devices to enhance and promote bilateral and multilateral relations. The arrangements are generally low-cost but have quite high profile value. Technical co-operation agreements have also been used between UN Specialised Agencies to develop new forms and areas of organised co-operation. For example, the United Nations Environment Programme (UNEP) and the International Olympic Committee (IOC) concluded a technical co-operation agreement following the Lillehammer Olympic Games in Norway.[52] The organisations aimed to develop jointly guidelines to cover environmental issues at international sporting events, such as environmental criteria for Olympic host sites, environmental impact assessment and audit systems.

In general intergovernmental agreements will include provisions on language and study visits; mutual science and technology research projects; festivals, conferences and exhibitions; and the establishment of cultural centres. In addition, cultural and technical co-operation agreements generally have provisions for a Joint Commission, or similar body, responsible for implementation and review. For example, the United Kingdom concluded education, science and cultural agreements with a number of the independent states of the former Soviet Union after the break-up of the USSR. The format and scope of these types of agreements is illustrated in the following example concluded between the United Kingdom and Republic of Kazakhstan:

AGREEMENT BETWEEN THE GOVERNMENT OF THE UNITED KINGDOM OF GREAT BRITAIN AND NORTHERN IRELAND AND THE GOVERNMENT OF THE REPUBLIC OF KAZAKHSTAN ON CO-OPERATION IN THE FIELDS OF EDUCATION, SCIENCE AND CULTURE

The Government of the United Kingdom of Great Britain and Northern Ireland and the Government of the Republic of Kazakhstan (hereinafter referred to as "the Contracting Parties");

Desiring to strengthen and develop the friendly relations between the two countries and their peoples;

Being convinced that exchanges and co-operation in the fields of education, science and culture as well as in other fields contribute to a better mutual knowledge and understanding between the British and Kazakh people;

Have agreed as follows:

Article I

The Contracting Parties shall encourage the development of relations between their two countries in the field of education by:
(a) encouraging and facilitating direct co-operation, contacts and exchanges between people, institutions and organisations concerned with education in the two countries;
(b) encouraging and facilitating the study of and instruction in the languages and literature of the other Contracting Party;
(c) encouraging and facilitating co-operation and exchanges in teaching methods and materials, curriculum development and examinations;
(d) providing scholarships and bursaries and promoting other means to facilitate study and research.

Article 2

The Contracting Parties shall encourage and facilitate the development of exchanges and research on problems of mutual interest in the fields of science and technology, including direct co-operation between scientific and research institutions in the two countries.

Article 3

The Contracting Parties shall encourage and facilitate direct contacts in the fields of literature, urban construction and design, the visual arts, the performing arts, film, television and radio, architecture, museums and galleries, libraries and archives and in other cultural areas.

Article 4

The Contracting Parties shall facilitate the exchange of information about measures to protect the historical and cultural heritage.

Article 5

Each Contracting Party shall encourage the establishment in its territory of cultural and information centres of the other Contracting Party to organise and carry out activities in pursuit of the purposes of this Agreement, and shall grant every facility within the limits of its legislation and capabilities to assist such centres. The expression "cultural and information centres" shall include schools, language teaching institutions, libraries, resource centres and other institutions dedicated to the purposes of the present Agreement.

Article 6

The Contracting Parties shall encourage direct co-operation between press and publishing organisations in the two countries.

Article 7

The Contracting Parties shall encourage co-operation between their respective authorities in order to ensure the mutual protection of copyright and, within the terms of their legislation, lending rights.

Article 8

The Contracting Parties shall encourage the development of tourism between the two countries.

Article 9

The Contracting Parties shall encourage co-operation between sporting organisations and participation in sporting events in each other's countries.

Article 10

The Contracting Parties shall encourage contacts between young people and direct co-operation between youth organisations of the two countries.

Article 11

The Contracting Parties shall facilitate in appropriate ways attendance at seminars, festivals, competitions, exhibitions, conferences, symposia and meetings in fields covered by this Agreement and held in either country.

Article 12

The Contracting Parties shall encourage direct co-operation and exchanges between non-governmental organisations in all fields covered by this Agreement.

Article 13

All activities covered by this Agreement shall comply with the laws and regulations in force in the State of the Contracting Party in which they take place.

Article 14

The British Council shall act as principal agent of the Government of the United Kingdom of Great Britain and Northern Ireland in the implementation of this Agreement.

Article 15

Representatives of the Contracting Parties shall, whenever necessary or at the request of either Party, meet as a Mixed Commission to review developments relating to this Agreement.

Article 16

(1)   This Agreement shall enter into force on the day of signature.
(2)   This Agreement shall remain in force for a period of five years and thereafter shall remain in force until the expiry of six months from the date on which either Contracting Party shall have given written notice of termination to the other through the diplomatic channel.

In witness whereof the undersigned, being duly authorised thereto by their respective Governments, have signed this Agreement.

Done at London this Twenty-first day of March 1994 in the English and Kazakh languages, both texts having equal authority.

For the Government of the
United Kingdom of Great
Britain and Northern Ireland:
DOUGLAS HOGG

For the Government of the
Republic of Kazakhstan:

T. SULEIMENOV

An interesting and unusual example of developing state practice in the cultural–technical co-operation field is the treaty concluded in 1993 between the United Kingdom and the Ukraine on Principles of Relations and Co-operation.[53] In addition to undertakings on political and security co-operation, the agreement contained a wide range of other provisions on economic co-operation (article 11); environmental protection (article 12); freedom of contact and travel (article 13); and industrial co-operation (article 17). The treaty is in effect a mixture of political aspiration and legal obligation. Article 23 makes provision for registration of the treaty with the UN Secretariat in accordance with Article 102 of the UN Charter.

TREATY
ON THE PRINCIPLES OF RELATIONS AND
CO-OPERATION BETWEEN THE UNITED KINGDOM OF
GREAT BRITAIN AND NORTHERN IRELAND AND
UKRAINE

The United Kingdom and Ukraine, hereinafter referred to as the Parties;

Reflecting the aspiration of their peoples to develop friendship and co-operation;

Stressing the fundamental significance of the historic changes resulting from the end of the era of ideological and military confrontation in Europe;

Noting that Ukraine is one of the successor states to the former Soviet Union;

Guided by the aims and principles of the UN Charter[1], the provisions of the Helsinki Final Act[2], the Paris Charter for a new Europe[3] and other CSCE documents;

Conscious of their responsibility to help preserve peace and strengthen security in Europe and the whole world;

Convinced of the need to help strengthen the atmosphere of friendship, mutual confidence, understanding and co-operation in international relations and determined to play an active part in this process;

Seeking to create a Europe of peace, democracy, freedom and common human values, and to encourage the deepening of the CSCE process through, *inter alia*, development of security and co-operation mechanisms;

Fully determined to develop their co-operation in political, economic, scientific and technological, environmental, cultural and humanitarian fields on the basis of equality and mutual benefit, and in the spirit of new partnership and co-operation exemplified by the Joint Declaration by the United Kingdom of Great Britain and Northern Ireland and Ukraine signed in London on 15 September 1992;[4]

Have agreed as follows:

Article 1

Peace and friendship are and shall remain the basis of relations between the United Kingdom and Ukraine. These relations shall be built on mutual confidence and understanding, partnership and co-operation.

Article 2

The Parties, reaffirming their obligations under the Charter of the United Nations, undertake to work closely together in upholding the purposes and principles of the United Nations Charter, in strengthening the United Nations Organisation and in ensuring that the United Nations responds effectively to threats to international peace and security.

---

1   Treaty Series No. 67 (1946), Cmd. 7015.
2   Cmnd. 6198.
3   Cm 1464.
4   Not published.

Article 3

The Parties shall collaborate within the framework of other international organisations of which they are members, as well as at international conferences and fora, in order to help consolidate a framework of lasting co-operation between countries of the world.

Article 4

The Parties shall develop their relations in strict observance of the principles of international law and in good faith. They declare their commitment to the peaceful resolution of disputes, to the principles of sovereign equality, territorial integrity and the inviolability of frontiers, to the democratic principles and practices of an open society and to respect for human rights and the rule of law. They affirm that relations between them shall be governed in particular by their commitments under the documents of the Conference on Security and Co-operation in Europe, including the Helsinki Final Act, the Charter of Paris for a new Europe, and the Helsinki Document of 1992[1].

Article 5

The Parties, reaffirming that in international relations it is impermissible for the threat or use of force to be employed as a means of settling disputes, and that all international disputes should be settled exclusively by peaceful means, undertake to work together, bilaterally and within an appropriate multilateral framework, in the search for solutions and for the peaceful settlement of disputes. To this end, the Parties shall hold regular consultations at different levels to develop their bilateral relations and areas of co-operation; and to discuss their positions on international issues of mutual concern. When a situation so requires, the Parties shall be ready to consult each other at short notice.

Article 6

The Parties shall assist in every way international efforts to achieve effective arms control and to enhance military confidence and security. They shall co-operate to support international measures to reduce armed forces and arms to the minimum levels commensurate with legitimate defence needs. They attach importance to the reduction of nuclear armaments and the implementation of nuclear arms control agreements. The Parties shall develop contacts at all levels between their respective armed forces and defence ministries.

---

1   Cm 2092.

Article 7

(1) The Parties shall co-operate in promoting further measures to prevent the proliferation of weapons of mass destruction and the missile technology used to deliver them to the targets, and to pursue responsible policies on the transfer of conventional arms. These measures would not affect legitimate national civil programmes and international co-operation programmes for the peaceful use of nuclear energy and exploration of outer space. The Parties note the continuing importance of the provisions of the 1968 Treaty on the Non-Proliferation of Nuclear Weapons[1]. They agree upon the importance of Ukraine's early accession to the Treaty as a non-nuclear weapon state and, in this connection, of the provision from that time by the United Kingdom, as a Permanent Member of the United Nations Security Council, of relevant and specific security assurances to Ukraine.

(2) The Parties are convinced that the introduction and implementation of effective export controls are essential if these objectives are to be achieved, and agree to co-operate in promoting such controls.

Article 8

The Parties shall co-operate towards strengthening of the 1972 Convention on the Prohibition of the Development, Production and Stockpiling of Bacteriological (Biological) and Toxin Weapons and on their destruction[2]. They shall endeavour to secure the entry into force as soon as possible of the 1993 Convention on the Prohibition of the Development, Production, Stockpiling and use of Chemical Weapons and on their Destruction[3].

Article 9

(1) The Parties shall co-operate within the framework of the Conference on Security and Co-operation in Europe, in particular in the new Forum for Security Co-operation, in order to develop and implement measures to enhance openness, security and stability in military affairs. They shall continue to improve security co-operation through contacts in this and other fora.

(2) The Parties reaffirm their commitment to continue the process of conventional arms control, including through the full implementation of the Treaty on Conventional Armed Forces in Europe[4].

Article 10

(1) The Parties, emphasising the importance of the integration of Ukraine into the international economic and financial system, shall

---

1   Treaty Series No. 88 (1970), Cmnd. 4474.
2   Treaty Series No. 11 (1976), Cmnd. 6397.
3   Miscellaneous No. 21 (1993), Cm 2331.
4   Treaty Series No. 44 (1993), Cm 2294.

co-operate within the International Monetary Fund and other international economic and financial institutions.

(2) The Parties are agreed that the development of relations between the United Kingdom and Ukraine will complement and extend bilateral relations between the European Community and Ukraine. The United Kingdom shall support the further development of relations between Ukraine and the European Community in accordance with the European Community's responsibilities.

Article 11

(1) The Parties shall seek, in accordance with the principles of a market economy and of private enterprise, to promote co-operation between the two countries in different areas of economic activity, including:

—energy, including under the European Energy Charter;
—agriculture, food processing and distribution;
—state finances and taxation;
—banking and other financial services;
—privatisation;
—development of small businesses.

(2) The United Kingdom shall continue to support such activity *inter alia* through bilateral and multilateral programmes to which the United Kingdom may contribute as appropriate.

(3) The Parties shall provide an effective legal framework for private investment. Each Party shall provide legal protection for investment by nationals and legal persons of the other Party.

(4) The Parties shall provide for the creation and maintenance of protection of Intellectual property to the standards generally prevailing in Europe.

Article 12

The Parties, agreeing that environmental protection is a high priority, shall encourage co-operation between relevant authorities in the fields of preservation and improvement of the environment and its protection from damage due to pollution, including exchanges of appropriate information and experts in the event of natural catastrophes, ecological disasters (such as Chernobyl) and major industrial accidents.

Article 13

The Parties shall encourage wide and free contacts between the citizens of the United Kingdom and Ukraine. They welcome the provisions of the Memorandum of Understanding on Unrestricted Freedom to Travel signed in London on 15 September 1992[1]. The Parties shall operate their respective arrangements for the issue of visas with the greatest possible degree of speed and efficiency.

---

1   Not published.

Article 14

The Parties shall extend to each other all appropriate assistance in the operations of diplomatic missions in each other's country.

Article 15

The Parties shall encourage exchanges between members of their respective legislatures. They shall encourage co-operation and exchanges of experience in parliamentary procedures and practice, and in the preparation of legislation. The Parties shall also encourage contacts and exchanges of experience in public administration; in the judiciary and between legal bodies; and between press and media organisations.

Article 16

The Parties shall promote the development of cultural and educational contacts and co-operation and exchanges between organisations and individuals in the two countries. The Parties shall welcome each other's efforts to promote their respective languages in each other's country.

Article 17

The Parties shall encourage co-operation between their respective authorities in other fields, and consider that the following are likely to be particularly appropriate in this respect:
(a) scientific and technological co-operation, including exchanges of appropriate information and specialists and direct links between researchers and research institutes;
(b) civil nuclear energy, in particular safety;
(c) transport, including infrastructure, research and development, science and technology;
(d) construction.

Article 18

The Parties condemn all forms and acts of terrorism regardless of motives and objectives and reaffirm their conviction that terrorism cannot be justified in any circumstances. The Parties shall work closely together in the fight against terrorism, crime, including organised crime, drug trafficking and illegal international dealing in cultural treasures.

Article 19

The Parties envisage that the development of relations between them may lead to the conclusion of separate agreements and arrangements in different areas of co-operation.

Article 20

The Parties declare that this Treaty does not detract from or otherwise displace the Parties' respective rights and obligations either under existing or future bilateral and multilateral agreements to which they are party or arising from their membership of international organisations, and that co-operation under this Treaty shall proceed to the extent that it is compatible with those rights and obligations. They declare that this Treaty is not intended to affect the interests of any other State or groups of States.

Article 21

Each of the Parties shall notify the other of the completion of the procedures required by its law for the entry into force of the Treaty. The Treaty shall enter into force on the date of the later of these notifications.

Article 22

This Treaty shall be of unlimited duration but shall cease to be in force six months after the day upon which one Party notifies the other Party in writing of its intention to terminate its validity.

Article 23

This Treaty shall be registered with the UN Secretariat pursuant to Article 102 of the Charter of the United Nations.

Done in duplicate at London this tenth day of February 1993 in the English and Ukrainian languages, both texts being equally authoritative.

For the United Kingdom of Great   For Ukraine:
Britain and Northern Ireland:

JOHN MAJOR   L. KRAVCHUK

References and notes

1. Vienna Convention on Diplomatic Relations (1961), UN A/CONF. 20/13, 16 April 1961; 55 AJIL 1961, 1062–82.
2. Vienna Convention on Consular Relations, Cmnd. 5219. Treaty series No. 14, Cmnd. 5219.
3. Convention on Relations involving International Institutions.
4. See, for example, United Kingdom–USSR, Cm. 1930, Treaty Series, No. 27, 1992, para. 3.
5. Agreement between the United Kingdom and Oman concerning the Vacation of British Embassy Compound in Muscat and the Provision of New British Embassy Premises, Muscat, 4 Jan. 1993, Treaty Series, No. 45 (1993) Cm. 2298.
6. Agreement between the United Kingdom and People's Republic of China on the Establishment of a British Consulate-General at Shanghai and a Chinese Consulate-General in Manchester, 17 April 1984, Treaty Series, No. 14 (1985) Cmn. 9472.

7. For example, the Romania–Zambia Agreement on Economic and Technical Co-operation (with annex), Bucharest, 14 May 1970, *UNTS*, Vol. 971, 1975, p. 42l.
8. *UKTS*, No. 64, 1977, Cmnd. 6874.
9. For a discussion of the concept of MFN see John H. Jackson, 'Equality and Discrimination in International Economic Law: The General Agreement on Tariffs and Trade', *The Yearbook of World Affairs* (Sweet and Maxwell, London, 1983) pp. 224–39.
10. Ministry of Trade, Malaysia, 1973.
11. Malaysia–Czechoslovak trade agreement, 1972, article 3, pp. 14–16.
12. Federation of Malaya–Republic of Korea trade agreement, 5 Nov. 1962, article II(2).
13. Republic of Singapore, *Government Gazette*, Treaties Supplement, No. 11, 14 March 1980. Trade agreement between the Government of the Republic of Singapore and the Government of the People's Republic of China, 29 Dec. 1979.
14. See trade agreement between the Federation of Malaya and the Republic of Korea, 5 Nov., 1962, article vi(2) and article iv of the trade agreement between Malaysia and Hungary, 2 Feb. 1970; and article iv(2) with Czechoslovakia, 20 Nov. 1972, Ministry of Trade, Malaysia.
15. Singapore–People's Republic of China trade agreement, 29 Dec. 1979.
16. 2 Nov. 1972, *UNTS*, Vol. 975, p. 195.
17. *UNTS*, Vol. 957, p. 174.
18. Malaysia has concluded bilateral shipping agreements with Bangladesh, Turkey and Indonesia and has identified the United States, People's Republic of China, South Korea, Japan and Sri Lanka for future negotiations. *Lloyds List*, 13 June 1984. For the arrangements with Argentina and Turkey see *Lloyds List*, 20 June 1984.
19. See for example article 7 of the Soviet–Zambian trade agreement: 'the two parties shall promote the development of transit trade', *UNTS*, Vol. 958, pp. 18–19.
20. For example, in the Soviet Union–Nigeria trade agreement, 29 Oct. 1971, *UNTS*, Vol. 941, p. 24.
21. See Soviet Union–Costa Rica trade agreement, 16 June 1970, *UNTS*, Vol. 957, p. 342, article 5; Soviet Union–Nigeria trade agreement, op. cit.
22. Brazil–Egypt trade agreement, 31 Jan. 1973, *UNTS*, Vol. 957, p. 219, article III; and see Soviet Union–Bolivia trade agreement, 17 Aug. 1970, article 4, *UNTS*, Vol. 957, p. 36l.
23. Australia–People's Republic of China trade agreement, 24 July 1973. *UNTS*, Vol. 975, p. 59.
24. As an exception see Soviet Union–Bolivia trade agreement, op. cit., and Soviet Union–Costa Rica trade agreement, op. cit.
25. See *The World Bank Annual Report 1985* (The World Bank, Washington, DC) Table 3-1, pp. 50–1.
26. Sector adjusting lending accounted for 14 per cent of total IBRD and IDA commitments during fiscal 1986 ($US2.28 billion up from 1.1 per cent five years previously in 1981 when this technique was first set up). See *The World Bank Annual Report 1986* (The World Bank, Washington, DC) p. 47.
27. See *The World Bank Annual Report 1985*, pp. 52–4. Structural adjustment lending in fiscal 1986, made up of IBRD loans, IDA credits and African facility credits remained small at $US777.2 million. These funds were disbursed to programmes in Burundi, Chile, Côte d'Ivoire, Guinea, Malawi, Niger, Senegal and Togo.
28. *World Bank Report 1986*, p. 29.
29. IBRD Document, March 1982.
30. *Commitment procedure* (Overseas Economic Co-operation Fund, Tokyo, 1983).
31. *Kertas Statut*, 43, 1982, Malaysia.
32. *Kertas Statut*, 116, 1983, Malaysia.
33. *Kertas Statut*, 116, 1983, Article 2(07). See also Article 2(01), of the technical assistance project agreement between Jamaica and the IBRD, 12 April 1985.
34. *Kertas Statut*, 43, 1982, Article 2(03).
35. See *Financial Times*, 29 Jan. 1986.
36. See *Annual Report 1982* (ADB, Manilla, 1985) p. 38.

37. See Harry Sasson, 'World Bank Co-financing with commercial Banks: the new Instruments', *Arab Banker* (Sept. 1983) pp. 15–16; Harry Sasson, 'Co-financing with the World Bank', The World of Banking (March–April 1984) pp. 6–8. *World Bank Annual Report 1986*, p. 29.
38. The countries involved included Thailand, Hungary, Chile, Colombia, Côte d'Ivoire.
39. *World Bank Annual Report 1986*, p. 29.
40. William Holden, *Common Fisheries Policy* (Fishing News Books, Oxford, 1994).
41. FAO Flagging Agreement (Rome, 1993) UK Misc. No. 11, 1995.
42. United Nations Convention on Straddling and Highly Migratory Fish Stocks, Dec. 1995.
43. Protocol Establishing the Fishing Rights and Financial Contribution of the EC provided for in the agreement between EC and Republic of Angola, 3 May 1987.
44. European Communities no. 38 (1988) Cmnd. 9896.
45. See, for example, Turks and Caicos, Ordinance no. 6, 1978, which has specific provisions relating to crayfish and fish products. Cf. Virgin Islands, Fisheries Ordinance, 18 Oct. 1979, article 2.
46. See Falkland Islands, The Fisheries (Conservation and Management) Ordinance (1986) Section 5 (a).
47. Ibid., section 4(2) (4) (d) which identifies that restrictions may be applied by the administration.
48. See e.g. the Fisheries (Conservation and Management Ordinance), British Indian Ocean Territory (1991), section 6, for provisions requiring the stowage of gear by vessels not engaged in fishing.
49. Falkland Islands, Ordinance (1986), section 5(b).
50. See South Georgia and the South Sandwich Islands, Fisheries Conservation and Management Ordinance, no. 3, 1993, South Georgia and South Sandwich Islands *Gazette*, no. 2, 23 July 1993, prohibiting transhipment without a licence. Cf. Falkland Islands Ordinance (1986), section 6: 'Within the fishing waters the transhipment from a fishing boat or the receiving of fish by a fishing boat from another fishing boat or the transport from the territorial sea or internal waters by any fishing boat of fish transshipped from any other fishing boat is prohibited unless authorised by a transhipment licence or export licence granted under this section.'
51. UN DPI, HE/862, 16 Aug. 1994
52. Agreement between the United Kingdom and the Republic of Kazakhstan on Co-operation in the Fields of Education, Science and Culture, 21 Mar. 1994, Treaty Series, No. 66, 1995, Cm. 2954.
53. Treaty Series, No. 16, 1995, Cm. 2769.

Conclusion

In the period under discussion diplomacy has changed substantially. The developments discussed in this book which have affected methods, content and style can be reviewed around four broad themes: the widening content of diplomacy; the decentralisation of the international system; the quest for new diplomatic methods and developments regarding diplomacy and international norms.

As regards the first of these, the content of diplomacy has undoubtedly become more diverse and complex as has the volume of negotiation, mediation and regulation. The major effects have been felt nationally in terms of the engagement of ministries other than those of foreign affairs, defence and trade in international diplomacy. A second implication has been with respect to the ability of states to co-ordinate and manage their foreign policies. Organisationally, states have attempted to deal with the growing complexity of international business in a number of different ways, although a noticeable general development is a shift to an increased concentration of decision-making at the centre, at the expense of traditional embassy–foreign ministry channels, where these exist. Deciding how best to participate effectively is an increasing dilemma for most states, given the increasing volume of international business. The continuous overstretching of resources is reflected in the complaints of many smaller and some larger actors, as we have seen, about their inability to attend multiple meetings of long-standing international conferences. Thus the early post-war principle of dispersing diplomatic centres, particularly of specialised UN agencies, to regions on a geographical basis, has increasingly given way to that of holding meetings at UN headquarters in New York.

Smaller actors too have to increasingly make strategic decisions about whether to attend *ad hoc* global conferences, as they juggle limited budgets, airline schedules and competing domestic expenditure requirements against the possibility of sponsorship, at a diplomatic cost, by a major 'donor' power. The problem of participation can be seen in several other ways, such as its effect on the quality and representativeness in multilateral conference decision-making, resulting from the high turnover of delegates, together with their diverse level and departmental background.

An important aspect of the changing content of diplomacy is demonstrated by the efforts of states, international organisations and others to deal with new types of threats such as those posed by qualitative changes in international terrorism, commercial crime and international narcotics dealings. In some of these areas, international co-operation through concerted collective action remains embryonic. Another feature of the expanded content of diplomacy is the accompanying growth in competitive ideologies manifested, for example, in international trade negotiations, debates on the composition and role of UN operations, through to nationalist and sub-ethnic claims projected on to the international scene.

Just as the agenda of diplomacy has diversified, so a second striking theme stems from the growth in the number of state and non-state actors involved in modern diplomacy. Along with diversification of membership has occurred significant decentralisation in the international system. The post-war international system characterised by the dominant role of the superpowers, confrontational North–South diplomacy and efforts of the Non-Aligned/G-77 to co-ordinate an alternative grouping and redistributive agenda has undergone substantial change since the end of the Cold War. A strong feature of the contemporary decentralised international system is alliance regrouping, the growth of regionalism and associative diplomacy, reflecting new sets of interactions and configurations. Whilst the North–South conflict does, however, remain a structural feature, both the membership of the respective groupings and the form of multilateral negotiations have undergone significant change, particularly, as discussed below, the weakened role of the G-77.

A third theme is the significant development in diplomatic methods which have taken place particularly in the last decade. In part these developments reflect the greater fusion of public and private interests. In this way the state is assuming or incorporating into its public diplomacy an increasing number of private interests. What is meant here is the acquisition by the state of a stake in both private domestic interests and, particularly, in the external operation of its nationals and corporate entities. Acquired states take the form of internationally negotiated joint ventures, financial support, trade promotion and conclusion particularly of bilateral agreements to facilitate and protect foreign investment and other economic interests.

At a multilateral conference level, diplomatic methods have undergone extensive changes. In this theme we argue that the international community is above all in a period of extensive transition as it searches to find workable methods for its expanded membership and increasingly complex agenda. The quest for workable arrangements has seen the emergence of new groupings such as the GCC, within southern Africa, and the South Pacific Forum, whilst others such as the Lomé agreement have been affected by shifts in the focus of attention to re-grouping in central and eastern Europe.

In terms of process, well-defined blocs and group sponsored resolutions have increasingly become a less important feature of the conduct of multilateral conferences. Rather, the complexity of the issues has been metered by the range of short-term groupings and *ad hoc* arrangements among states. Furthermore, the use of consensus has begun to be qualified, for example, through the introduction in some arrangements on majority voting procedures for implementation once an agreement has entered into force. These developments reflect concern over the illusory nature of many so-called 'package' agreements based on consensus.

Finally, the relationship between diplomacy and evolving international norms requires some concluding comment. As argued above, the expansion of the international community has inevitably brought with it greater conflicts of interests, or what James Eayrs referred to as the problem of accommodating unmarketable foreign policies. Reaching overarching solutions has become more difficult for diplomacy for three reasons. In the first place concepts of what should constitute international order have become increasingly elusive with the fragmentation of the international system and demise of primary power bloc policies. Second, norms derived form the processes of the UN and other international institutions have weakened as a result of financial and other constraints on the UN itself. In addition, norms associated with governance and collective responsibility for environmental problems with global effect remain embryonic, and subject to the commands of other competing interests. A final feature of transition in modern diplomacy is the experimental and short-term nature of many of the solutions to problems, especially in areas such as international debt, security and civil conflict. Stability in these and other sectors remains elusive. It is the essence of diplomacy, however, to continue the search for orderly change in the international system.

Index